Marginal Forces / Cultural Centers

MICHAEL BÉRUBÉ

Marginal Forces/ Cultural Centers

Tolson, Pynchon, and the Politics of the Canon

Cornell University Press

Ithaca and London

First published 1992 by Cornell University Press.

International Standard Book Number 0-8014-2620-0 (cloth)
International Standard Book Number 0-8014-9921-6 (paper)
Library of Congress Catalog Card Number 91-55555
Printed in the United States of America

William Carlos Williams, *Paterson*. Copyright © 1951 by William Carlos Williams. Excerpt reprinted by permission of New Directions Publishing Corp. *Gravity's Rainbow* by Thomas Pynchon. Copyright © 1973 by Thomas Pynchon. Excerpts reprinted by permission of the publisher, Viking Penguin, a division of Penguin Books USA Inc. *The Waste Land* by T. S. Eliot, from *The Complete Poems and Plays, 1909–1950*. Copyright © 1971 by Esme Valerie Eliot. Excerpts reprinted by permission of Faber & Faber and Harcourt Brace Jovanovich. Excerpts from the works of Melvin Tolson reprinted by permission of Melvin Tolson, Jr.

Librarians: Library of Congress cataloging information appears
on the last page of the book.
⊗ The paper in this book meets the minimum requirements
of the American National Standard for Information Sciences—
Permanence of Paper for Printed Library Materials, ANSI Z39.48-1984.

For my parents,
Anne Bérubé and Maurice R. Bérubé,
and in memory of Emerilda Ryan

Contents

Acknowledgments

CHARLES ROWELL first introduced me to Melvin Tolson; for
that I owe him my gratitude, and much of this book, as partial re-
payment for the favor. Raymond Nelson also provided some of the
impetus for my work, and I wish him good luck and Godspeed with
his annotated edition of *Harlem Gallery*. Melvin Tolson, Jr., and
Wiley Tolson offered words of friendship and advice, and Robert
Farnsworth's wonderful correspondence prompted me to pursue
Tolson's work as far as I could.

This book was completed with the help of a summer grant from
the National Endowment for the Humanities. The University of Illinois Research Board enabled me to peruse the Tolson Manuscripts
in the Library of Congress and to devote the fall of 1990 to a graduate seminar in reception theory; from that seminar I sharpened my
focus and direction considerably, thanks in part to my sharp students: Keith Appler, Beth Coleman, Jon D'Errico, Bill Gulstad, Mary
Hocks, Robert McRuer, Robert Nowatzki, Barbara Sebek, Anna
Smith, Juan Sola, Tamise Van Pelt, Alan Walworth, and Xueqin
Zheng. James Hurley, David Jacobson, David McIrvine, Paul Trem-
bath, and John Unsworth have talked Pynchon with me over the
years. Jay Dobrutsky and Barbara Green offered decisive counsel at
the outset of the project and a friendship that got me through the
latter half of the eighties.

I especially thank Amanda Anderson, Eric Lott, and Cary Nelson
for extensive and often brilliant critiques of various sections of the

manuscript and for three years of more informal exchanges about the project as a whole. Patrick McGee and Harryette Mullen offered keen readings that guided my revisions; Nina Baym read the entire manuscript with her characteristic vigor and insight; Robert Dale Parker strengthened an early chapter with engaging comments and questions; Alan Howard and Dick Wheeler were steadfast and reassuring. To Michael Levenson I am indebted chiefly for his surefooted guidance and largeness of brain but also for his generosity as a friend and mentor; particularly in the first two years of this project, his assistance was invaluable. Jerry McGann's extraordinary scope of mind and ready wit (in the eighteenth-century sense) have likewise been crucial to my work; and I have benefited as well from Pat Gill's energy, her encouragement, and her rigorous attention to detail.

I have the luck to live under a roof with my closest colleague, my co-conspirator, my best friend, and my wife. Janet Lyon is all of these. Since she is not only one of the wisest but also one of the most multifaceted people I know, this is no longer surprising to me; and the frequency with which her name turns up in the footnotes can convey only some idea of the extent of her contribution. Suffice it to say that I cannot adequately acknowledge her in an acknowledgment.

Finally, a thanks to Nicholas, who has had to accompany his father on tedious photocopying and printing missions from the tender age of three, and whose only recompense for learning to use word processors and large research libraries is that he now possesses enough of my previous manuscript drafts to draw fish, dinosaurs, vehicles, coastal states, and imaginary countries until the year 2007.

Sections of Chapters 2 and 3 have previously appeared as "Masks, Margins, and African American Modernism: Melvin Tolson's *Harlem Gallery*," in *PMLA* 105/1 (1990): 57–69; and as "Avant-Gardes and De-author-izations: *Harlem Gallery* and the Cultural Contradictions of Modernism," in *Callaloo* 12.1 (1989): 193–215. I am grateful to both journals for permission to use the material here.

MICHAEL BÉRUBÉ

Urbana, Illinois

Marginal Forces / Cultural Centers

I admire your collection of poetry *Dark Crepuscule*. It's solidly in the Western tradition and convinces me that you are the foremost bard of your race. It's about time they produced such a bard!

—Hinckle von Vampton to Nathan Brown,
in Ishmael Reed's *Mumbo Jumbo*

They brought down disrepute upon him as upon an infectious person and cast stones at him to make him go away more quickly. And they were right in their ancient instinct: for he was indeed their foe.

But then, when he did not raise his eyes, they began to reflect. They suspected that with all this they had done what he wanted. . . . And now they changed about and, resorting to the final, the extreme, used that other resistance: fame. And at this clamor almost every one has looked up and been distracted.

—Rainer Maria Rilke,
The Notebooks of Malte Laurids Brigge

Since I was unable to dig
the immortality of John Doe,
fears
(not Hamlet's . . . not Simon Legree's),
my fears
of oblivion made me realistic:
with no poems of Hideho's in World Lit—
he'd be a statistic!

—Hideho Heights, in Melvin Tolson's
Harlem Gallery: The Curator, Book I

Introduction

AT NO POINT in its history has it been a simple enterprise to examine the cultural position and practices of academic literary study. Though we speak often and obsessively of the present crisis in the profession (whatever we imagine this crisis to be), we do so in the knowledge that ours is a profession constituted in part by its sense of perpetual crisis; one would think it is one of the functions of criticism to churn out essay after essay, year after year, on the function of criticism at the present time. As one such recent essay has reminded us, "crisis is both the contemporary condition and the founding moment of humanistic study" (Kaufmann 1990, 522). Yet if the discussion about the profession's contemporary status seems especially heated and confused, perhaps it is because we have never discerned so many intersecting, mutually implicating crises at one time. As we question the institutional practices by which literary canons are constructed and maintained, we also question, more broadly, the university's role as producer of knowledge and as reproducer of a social order in which knowledge is power and information is commodity. We question the relation of critical intellectuals to popular culture, as well as the relation between intellectuals and their institutional matrices of power. We question the relation of literary theory to pedagogical practice, as well as the relation of academic, professional criticism to the nonacademic literary culture around it.

Even within our legacy of permanent crisis, then, it seems there have never been so many imperatives to institutional self-scrutiny, on so many fronts, in so many senses of the word "institutional." By reception theory as by Foucauldian history, by feminisms as by academic neo-Marxisms, by the New Right as by the changing student constituencies of American universities—by all these competing forces, the profession of literature has been charged with justifying its social function in the broadest terms possible. And though I do not claim in these pages to be able to speak for or within the profession in the broadest terms possible, still, I could not have conceived or undertaken this work if I were not already located within the various debates that seek to engage the profession's ongoing self-examination, the interminable analysis by which we determine what we do, for whom, with what purposes.

But precisely because I am located within these various debates, I don't believe we can talk very long about the social mission or legitimation practices of criticism without distorting, by totalizing, the very positions and practices we hope to illuminate. The "institution of literary criticism" is no longer (if it ever was) one solid, monolithic thing; its practices and positions are multiple and contradictory; its canons are diachronically, historically variable (like everything else) and synchronically, socially variable as well. It is true that we can discern, even amid these variables, some of the historical tendencies of academic criticism, and we can contest some of its contemporary practices; but I sincerely hope that the moment for describing *"the function of criticism"* has passed forever. Thus, in taking my impetus from the latest round of polemics on the institution of criticism, I have attempted not to address "the institution of criticism" in toto but to explore in detail the relation of institutional criticism to the work and critical reception of two writers who are nearly at the extremes of contemporary academic discourse: Melvin Tolson and Thomas Pynchon.

Tolson and Pynchon are an odd couple indeed. I have chosen them for examination partly because their works are extraordinarily acute, multifarious, and challenging explorations of our culture's various means of cultural transmission, from canons and museums to gossip and graffiti; but their interventions in (and representations of) the means of cultural transmission have taken vastly different forms—and, of course, they have met with vastly different results. When Melvin Tolson died in 1966, he had just received an award and grant from the National Institute of Arts and Letters for his book-length masterwork, *Harlem Gallery: Book I, The Curator*. A quarter century later, however, Tolson has become our era's most neglected and undervalued modernist poet of consequence. Thomas Pynchon, as it happens, was awarded a similar prize by the National Institute of Arts and Letters and the American Academy of Arts and Letters: the William Dean Howells medal, in 1975. But Pynchon's response to the award was a minor notoriety: he refused it—even though, in his words, it was gold and therefore a good hedge against inflation. And the years since then have seen over four hundred articles, some thirty books, and a journal (*Pynchon Notes*) devoted exclusively or substantially to him.

My juxtaposition of Tolson and Pynchon is designed to serve many objectives at once, not least among them the comparative analysis of how canonization works, or fails to work, for writers in the age of institutional criticism. But I have not carried out this project merely to argue that Tolson has been unfairly overlooked; certainly he has, but there are larger issues at stake here as well. On one hand, we are confronted with the nearly complete neglect of the poet who first sought to bring African-American poetry into the academy; on the other, we are faced with the nearly immediate canonization of the novelist who won't appear, give interviews, accept prizes, write about his reception, or allow his publisher to print books about his work. A marginal figure who wanted nothing more than to be central; a newly central figure who apparently would like nothing better than marginality. Yet within this complementarity lies a still deeper symmetry: in the work and in the reception of *both* authors, we find invoked to widely different ends the post-Romantic construction of "marginality" as the source of authorial authority. That is, the idea of "marginality" as empowerment is central both to the procedures by which we deconstruct the very notion of the canon (or the university, the museum, the archive) and to the demands of underrepresented groups that they be admitted *to* the canon. Yet depending on the specific construction of the "margin," the empowerment enabled by marginality consists in access to (for Tolson) or refusal of (for Pynchon) the authority conferred by institutionalization.

Moreover, this idea of marginality is itself always problematic, and especially so when it is delineated by the authorities of a cultural center such as the university. It is easy to claim here, for instance, that the academic delineation of an "avant-garde" constitutes a central culture's absorption and recuperation of the marginal forces that threaten and oppose it. This is precisely the claim made by many prominent Pynchon critics; and although the claim can be rebutted on the points, it cannot be carelessly dismissed by the countercharge that Pynchon always was an "academic" writer (and therefore belongs in the university as he belongs nowhere else). If we confine ourselves to deciding whether Pynchon's institutionalization is repressive or appropriate, we miss the point, for the process whereby cultural products become institutional, or institutionalized, is not always and everywhere the same.

What is the status, for instance, of Ralph Ellison's *Invisible Man* when it is mentioned on *The Bill Cosby Show*? or the oeuvre of Samuel Beckett in a lavish display book on Ireland titled *The Beckett Country*? or, for that matter, the first seventeen lines of Tolson's "Dark Symphony" when they appear on the frontispiece of the 1976 "Famous Black Americans Historical Calendar," produced by the Schlitz Brewing Company?[1] Each one of these cultural reproductions is qualitatively different, and in each case we are talking about various kinds of margins and variously located centers—and, therefore, different possibilities and procedures of cultural reproduction. It is by no means guaranteed, in any or all of these examples, that the means of reproduction work to vitiate or co-opt the texts they reproduce. It *is* guaranteed, however, that in our present stage of capitalist and artistic production, no artifact can exist apart from its consumption and commodification; indeed, because any text's consumption is also its reproduction, we may say that consumption and reproduction *constitute* the existence of texts.[2] These processes of use and commodification apply to the realm of literary criticism as well. But even as a form of textual reproduction, literary canonization is not a "final" form of consumption; canonization is not what happens when the struggle for representation is over and the institutionalized writer is locked safely in his or her cell. Quite the contrary: canons are at once the location, the index, and the record of the struggle for cultural representation; like any other hegemonic

[1] For *The Beckett Country*, see O'Brien 1986; for the calendar, Tolson 1990. The episode of *The Bill Cosby Show* that involved *Invisible Man* first aired in the spring of 1986.

[2] For a Marxist critique of reception theory that is not limited to reasserting the primacy of textual production, see Weimann 1975. Reading Jauss through Marx's *Introduction to the Critique of Political Economy*, Weimann writes: "Once the dialectic between, on the one hand, production oriented to reception and, on the other, a 'productive kind of consumption' is grasped, the unnecessary dilemma involved in the traditional antinomy between the conception of literature as structure (that is, as pure product) and the conception of literature as function (that is, as a pure object of consumption) is exposed" (20). Such a dialectic also withstands the traditional complaint that reception theory is but another consumerism (for a brief, witty version of this complaint, see Eagleton 1982; for a sustained and highly successful negotiation of the competing claims of material production and textual consumption, see Radway 1984, 6–8, 19–45).

formation, they must be continually reproduced anew and are continually contested.

Tolson and Pynchon, between them, thus allow us to examine how canonicity is produced and theorized by writers and critics, and how, accordingly, academic critics regard their roles as agents of the cultural center. Also, Tolson and Pynchon offer us strikingly different examples of what "marginality" might mean, and what purposes it might be made to serve. Their relative positions are not a matter of ironic circumstance, as if the academy just happened to overlook one of its aspirants and to canonize instead the writer who didn't want to be a member of the club in the first place. Similarly, my work is not simply a comparative exposé; I am not dealing here with two artists in the same medium, one who made it and one who didn't, and seeking thereby to disclose hidden and explicit biases in canon formation. What could possibly be gained by trying to paint Tolson and Pynchon as "equals" who failed to get "equal" treatment in the high courts of culture? One is African-American, one is Anglo-American; one is a poet and the other a novelist; one is dead and the other, at last report, very much alive. But these factors are not somehow extrinsic to their reception, as if we could do a "better" sociology of reception by choosing two white novelists or two black poets. My goals, I think, are wider and more varied: I want to examine the rhetoric of cultural marginality and the uses to which it is put by disparately positioned writers and critics. And the purpose of mapping this rhetoric, in turn, is to make visible the microphenomena of reception and neglect in individual case histories.

In Tolson's case, I have attempted to show that neglect constitutes a kind of reception and that certain kinds of reception attempt to provide justification for neglect. In Pynchon's case, I am more concerned to explain the *effects* of academic reception, especially insofar as reception is theorized by Pynchon critics as institutionalization and recuperation. In neither case, however, do I want to reify the categories of "canonization" and "neglect"; rather, I argue that both are local phenomena with historically specific forms. Although general concepts of the canonical and the apocryphal are necessary to my investigation, I do not seek to produce one more general theory hereby. Tolson and Pynchon will provide for us different accounts of reception and neglect, but these different accounts are not necessarily referable to some more general heading of reception theory, under which the "differences" in question can be compared and contrasted in a scheme of one-to-one correspondence. The difference between these writers' cultural positions, for one thing, necessitates certain differences in tone and approach in my treatment of them. Chapter 3, on Tolson's reception, is far more "narrative" in execution than Chapter 5, on Pynchon's reception, because Pynchon's reception has already been narrated on numerous occasions.[3] In fact, Pynchon's reception was made narrative as soon as it was made academic; and since Pynchon's reception history is in this sense always already narratable, I see no need to tell it yet again, from the ground up. Rather, I rely on and recast previous narratives of Pynchon studies, thus making Chapters 4 and 5 part of an ongoing conversation with other Pynchon critics as well as part of an exposition to more general readers. Over Tolson, however, I am joining a very small conversation, and for this reason my discussions in Chapters 2 and 3 assume that my readers will be unfamiliar with details relevant to Tolson's work and neglect.

My accounts of Tolson and Pynchon differ in other material ways as well. For one thing, when we are examining gatekeepers in Tolson's career, we are examining gatekeepers who (whatever their specific intentions) eventually worked to keep Tolson *out*, whereas Pynchon's reviews in major nonacademic journals were "gatekeeping" reviews solely insofar as they helped to set the terms for his more prolonged and voluminous academic reception. Also, I spend a portion of Chapter 3 examining Tolson's anthologization history, but I have not inquired how Pynchon's anthologization has structured *his* reception, precisely because the dissemination of Pynchon's work is not nearly so dependent on anthologies as is Tolson's.[4] Needless to say, the relative dependence of each writer on

---

[3]Brief reception histories can be found in Levine and Leverenz 1976, 4–9, and Clerc 1983, 3–6; but alongside these explicit narratives there are also less overt narrativizations of Pynchon criticism: namely, determinations by Pynchon critics of what constitutes "major" Pynchon criticism. Collections of essays edited by Mendelson (1978) and Bloom (1986) both "narrate" Pynchon's reception in this way, since they include not only "important" academic articles, but "important" contemporary reviews of *Gravity's Rainbow* as well. Mendelson reprints five reviews and a reply: Poirier 1973, G. Levine 1973, Morrison 1973, Tanner 1974, Schwarzbach 1976, Rosenbaum 1976. Bloom reprints two: Mendelson 1973 and Hendin 1975, the latter also reprinted in Pearce 1981. (Eight of Bloom's fourteen essays had appeared in previous collections: three in Levine and Leverenz 1976, one in Mendelson 1978, and four in Pearce 1981. Pearce's 1981 collection contains an annotated bibliography titled "A Review of Major Pynchon Criticism" (Clark and Fuoroli 1981, 230–54), which also works toward narrating a separation of wheat from chaff.

[4]As this work goes to press, in fact, Tolson is entirely dependent on anthologies for the dissemination of the work he published during his lifetime. *Harlem Gallery* is not to be confused with his one current title in print, *A Gallery of Harlem Portraits* (Tolson 1979), which consists of manuscripts from the 1930s edited by Robert Farnsworth and published posthumously. See Appendix A.

anthologization is a function of the genre in which he principally works; and to say this is to call attention to practices of genre distribution that are not strictly specific to any one poet or novelist but are, more tellingly, indicative of material generic hierarchies in contemporary American writing and criticism. Finally, just as Tolson's dissemination in classrooms is largely dependent on the anthology, his dissemination in future research is dependent on *biography*, in a way that could not contrast more sharply with Pynchon's career. I will come back to this point, but I want to spell out a few of its implications at the outset.

It is one thing to note the spectacular "recoveries" of literary history, the retrievals and recanonizations that make academic headlines: John Donne in T. S. Eliot's hands; William Blake in Yeats's; Zora Neale Hurston in Alice Walker's, Mary Helen Washington's, and Robert Hemenway's. Likewise, it is relatively easy to see canonical advocacy in action: F. R. Leavis for D. H. Lawrence; Harold Bloom for John Ashbery; or even James T. Fields, in another context, for Nathaniel Hawthorne.[5] It is quite another thing, however, to specify in any useful detail the historical conditions and institutional procedures for each of these recoveries and advocacies, including the one I undertake for Tolson. The Hemenway-Hurston relation—posthumous biographer to elusive subject—is perhaps the closest analogue for Tolson studies, which, for now and the foreseeable future, rest heavily on Robert Farnsworth's 1984 biography, *Plain Talk and Poetic Practice: Melvin Tolson, 1898–1966*. (Even Farnsworth's subtitle is significant, for Tolson's birthdate, like Hurston's, was a matter of some confusion throughout his life.) And Farnsworth's work itself rests on a series of institutional practices: Joy Flasch had written a biography of Tolson for Twayne Publishers in 1972, but because Flasch did not have access to the range of materials used by Farnsworth, she unwittingly wound up perpetuating some of the myths Tolson spun around himself, chief among which was the

[5]See Tompkins 1985, 24–25, 28–31. Tompkins's account of Nathaniel Hawthorne's reputation is an admirable historicization of Hawthorne's reception: "All of the historical evidence suggests that what Hawthorne's contemporaries saw when they read his work is not what we see now" (13). However, Tompkins also writes that "modern commentators have tended to ignore the context within which nineteenth-century authors and critics worked" and therefore have "failed to take account of the cultural circumstances that shaped Hawthorne's novel for his contemporaries" (20–21). The difficulty here is that professional academic criticism has not always had one stable understanding of what "context" and "cultural circumstances" mean; one might say that historical evidence suggests that what Matthiessen's contemporaries saw when they read Hawthorne's reception is not what Tompkins sees now.

story of his correspondence with Allen Tate, which I examine in Chapter 3. Farnsworth's biography, however, was begun after Ruth Tolson donated the Tolson papers to the Library of Congress, at former chief librarian Roy Basler's request, and is therefore quite visibly dependent on Tolson's access to one of our country's "central" archives.

The general point at issue here has to do with the challenge of describing canons as the result of literary gatekeeping. As we can see from the careers of one African-American poet and one Anglo-American novelist, there is not, after all, one and only one set of protocols, one determinate series of gates, in the machinery of canonization. It is therefore impossible to determine any necessary sequence to the process of reviewing, anthologizing, teaching, and researching that makes up criticism's procedures of canon making. Although we can often describe the sequence necessary to any one writer's, or group of writers', reception history, we cannot generalize at once about *the* canonization process, *the* locus of neglect and attention. The most we can say, I think, is that academic criticism is both the practice and the consequence of gatekeeping, however many disparately located gatekeepers there be. This is not to say that there is a liberal pluralist canon for everybody. An African proverb, which Tolson was fond of quoting, holds that "an open gate sees both inside and out"; still, we know also that no gate would work in the absence of fences, and gatekeeping inevitably involves exclusion as the necessary corollary of inclusion. The implications of this position should be clear: canonicity, even for "opened" canons, will always involve the expropriation, resemanticization, selective empowerment, and exclusion of cultural products. It is possible to make academic canons less exclusive, more polymorphic—even, to some extent, more "democratic"; but it is not possible for academic critics to forgo their roles as gatekeepers.

I have adapted the methodology of the case history in the hope that it will prove productive for future reception studies. And in order to deal with each case history in depth, I have focused almost entirely on the major works of each writer, Tolson's *Harlem Gallery* and Pynchon's *Gravity's Rainbow*, not only because it is on these texts that their authors' reputations will chiefly stand, but also, and more interestingly, because these texts themselves treat their authors' cultural positions and attendant possibilities for reception and dissemination, meditating on their own and their respective oeuvre's future reception history and, in Tolson's case, self-consciously culminating the oeuvre in the process.

Reader-response criticism has described, among other things, how writers structure forms of address and reader positions to implied, mock, ideal, and "super" readers; reception theory has sought to uncover the historical, political, and theoretical conditions for the actualization of texts in their myriad contexts.[6] But neither reader-response criticism nor reception theory has paid sufficient attention to the means by which writers structure and emplot their institutional readers and receptions, how interpretive communities and their cultural norms and values are located both *within* and *by* textual, rhetorical, and professional strategies specific to "authorship" as practice and as sign.[7] What I have attempted is a way of reconstructing the passages between cultural products and their appropriations by cultural centers, a way of reading texts and their receptions against each other in an interplay that shuttles between textual representation and sociohistorical reception—reception that in turn takes the form of critical (that is, cultural) representation (in journals, reviews, canons, and classrooms).

This methodology implies a series of negotiations between interpretation and evaluation which will perhaps seem unfamiliar to some American critics. For though Barbara Herrnstein Smith is surely right to charge that "the entire problematic of value and evaluation has been evaded and explicitly exiled by the literary academy" (1983, 5), Jan Mukarovsky (1936) might reply that we nevertheless confer "value" on works every time we assign them the aesthetic function; and American criticism, in Frank Kermode's words, assigns the aesthetic function to literary works mainly by designating them "licensed for exegesis" (1979, 83). It follows, then, that even the most apolitically formalist interpretations of literary works constitute an assignation of "value," and that the kinds of exegesis licensed by Kermode's "licensed practitioners" (73) will produce determinate, even if implicit, evaluations in academic criti-

---

[6]For examples of these strategies in practice, see, for reader-response, Iser 1974, Rabinowitz 1977, Fish 1980, Lotman 1982; essays collected in Tompkins 1980b, especially Gibson (1950), Prince (1973), and Riffaterre (1966); see also Suleiman and Crosman 1980. For reception theory, see Hohendahl 1977, Jauss 1982b, Mailloux 1982, Tompkins 1985, Fish 1986, Klancher 1987. And for a thorough, lucid introduction to and distinction between the two, see Holub 1982 and 1984.

[7]One notable exception is Klancher 1987; however, Klancher's discussion deals less with individual writers' strategies or careers than with the location and construction of reading audiences by English periodicals of the Romantic period: "It is this connection between reader and audience that so-called reception theory has never deduced—the vital but by no means simple relation between an act of reading and a location with a collective realm, an audience (social, ideological, historical)" (11).

cism.[8] As Herrnstein Smith herself concludes, "the value of a literary work is continually produced and re-produced by the very acts of implicit and explicit evaluation that are frequently invoked as 'reflecting' its value" (1983, 34). In Tolson's case especially, "close reading" is therefore absolutely crucial to my project, both because it marks our institution's conferral of "value" and, more immediately, because his neglect is due in part to the fact that almost no one has read closely his major work. Mine is, one might say, a case study in which individual cases still need to be made.

My readings thus attempt to describe how the major works of Melvin Tolson and Thomas Pynchon inform and deform the historical conversations that constitute their reception. And if my focus on *Harlem Gallery* and *Gravity's Rainbow* leaves intact the idea of "major work" even as it contests the notion of the "major author," it does so because I agree with John Rodden's recent observation that "conferral of the status of 'major' (sometimes awarded for a single 'masterpiece' or withheld for absurd reasons like the old notion that a major poet must have succeeded in epic) may ensure attention to an author's lesser works or even keep his entire *oeuvre* in print" (1989, 61). My agreement with Rodden, however, tends in two directions. First, I want to suggest that it may be possible for academic criticism to shift more of its attention to a range of major *works* that are partially detached from the currently parallel category of major *authors*, thus giving more play to important works by writers we currently consider irretrievably "minor."[9] Second, even though this partial detachment is possible, it is not likely: it is hard, in the present case, to imagine a revival of interest in *Harlem Gallery* which could operate independently of more general interest in Tolson's life and career. And since all the work Tolson published in his lifetime is out of print as of this writing, it is probably undesirable as well as difficult to make a case for his importance based exclusively on the achievement of *Harlem Gallery*.

---

[8]Against the position once espoused by Jonathan Culler—namely, that our attention to "literary competence" could move institutional criticism past mere interpretation to specification of the codes of interpretive "grammar" that generate all interpretations (see Culler 1975 and 1980)—compare Mary Louise Pratt's response that specifying rules for "literary competence" makes no sense without attention to specific interpretive "performances" of critical rules (1982, 219); see also Rodden 1989 on reputation as "a concealed link between evaluation and interpretation" (65).

[9]Robert Dale Parker (n.d.) has pursued this line of thought far enough to suggest an American novels course made up of excerpts—and a syllabus, therefore, that decidedly detaches works from "authorship," major or minor. The suggestion is provocative, though complicating the major work–minor author distinction should not necessarily be a task assumed only by individual professors and courses.

Still, for now I will argue simply that of all Tolson's work, *Harlem Gallery* should be the one hardest for us to ignore, the one future academic critics should, at the very least, be expected to have heard about. *Libretto for the Republic of Liberia* is doubtless worthy of similar attention; but one can more easily, even if cynically, understand the American academy's inattention to this bewilderingly dense, 770-line poem to an African nation founded by American ex-slaves, if only because most Americans tend not to think about tiny African nations founded by American ex-slaves, should they want to think about American ex-slaves at all.[10] It requires some work, on the other hand, to pass over *Harlem Gallery* once one has been apprised of its existence, if for no other reason than its sheer size, scope, and staggering discursive range; white Americans might easily ignore the appointment and the official work of a Liberian poet laureate, but one generally has some explaining to do when one "ignores" an anvil dropped on one's feet. It might be, conversely, that allusive, 170-page narrative-dramatic poems do not fare well in contemporary market conditions unless they are written by Ezra Pound or William Carlos Williams.[11] But then surely there is bitter irony in the fact that *Gravity's Rainbow*'s reputation, like that of *Paterson* and the *Cantos*, was *enhanced* by its size—which, as contemporary reviewers were quick to note, invited comparisons with *Ulysses*. Certainly, at any rate, there is little justification for the kind of treatment *Harlem Gallery* receives in synoptic literary histories such as David Perkins's 1,200-page, two-volume sweep of modern poetry, which accords Tolson two pages in a thirteen-page chapter titled "Black Poets" and mentions only the name of Tolson's final poem.

Then again, there are innumerable problems in speaking of "justification," as if we could find the level at which justice would be done Tolson or anyone else. This seems to me the overriding problem with Rodden's characterization of "the 'problem' of literary repute" as "essentially the problem of justice in literary terms" (54): it tends to suggest that if bias and prejudice were finally weeded out of institutional reading practices, writers would naturally rise or sink

---

[10] I am leaving *Rendezvous with America* (Tolson 1944) out of the account for now, since I argue in Chapter 3 that part of Tolson's neglect lies in critics' refusal to read, or read sympathetically, most of his work after *Rendezvous*—that is, most of his mature (and deliberately modernist) work.

[11] One study of the modernist long poem, written in the midst of a canon-revising decade, begins with the proposition that "the history of Modernism from the Imagist platform of 1913 to the publication of *Drafts and Fragments of Cantos CX–CXVII* in 1969 remains to be written, but its bare outlines may be detected in the compositions of the long poems that span almost this full period" (Dickie 1986, 3). That study, however, discusses only four long poems: *The Waste Land, The Bridge, Paterson, The Cantos.*

to their proper measure of response. But even though we cannot specify (or inhabit) the ideal realm in which there would be no overvaluation or undue neglect of literary reputations—and Rodden's work itself, despite its invocation of "justice," demonstrates that we cannot—we *can* convincingly show that literary study as it is now conducted suffers from a radically impoverished sense of its own historical materials for study. As Cary Nelson, for one, has forcefully argued, our contemporary understanding of the history of modern American poetry—a history in which Tolson can ("justifiably") claim a significant place—is "already in part a result of what we no longer know we have forgotten," for "we no longer know the history of the poetry of the first half of this century; most of us, moreover, do not know that the knowledge is gone" (1989, 3–4).

Nelson's recent *Repression and Recovery* plays productively with the political and psychoanalytic senses of "repression," elaborating, as no reception theory has yet been able to do, on how the process of canon formation entails also procedures of exclusion that are both motivated and unconscious, active and passive, repressive and neglectful. Most crucial for Nelson, however, are instances of outright, active, political repression, for their effects have been so widespread and durable as to ensure the continual reproduction of the academic view of poetry as "a form of discourse generically guaranteed luminous transcendence" (243). And the suppression of political literary texts, as Pynchon would surely agree, is not merely an academic affair; rather, writes Nelson, it is a standard feature of American history: "Forgetting much and white-washing what it remembers, the profession of English studies behaves in this regard rather like the general culture" (244). For Nelson argues also that "there are no innocent, undetermined lapses of cultural memory" (52), and alleges that much of modern poetry's transmission worked deliberately in the service of repression:

> During the McCarthy era of the 1950s, many people destroyed their copies of political books and magazines from the 1930s. The institution of literary studies cooperated and eliminated the names of political poets from the ongoing conversation of the discipline. Like the leveling movement of the sea, the weight of our cultural memory closed over this part of our heritage, turning it into a shadowed place where nothing could be seen. Only a few books worked against this tendency. Literary studies as a whole devoted itself to establishing the limited canon of modernism. (9–10)

Nelson's work is an exemplary negotiation of literary history and literary theory, a kind of antihistory of modern poetry which argues that literary history and canon formation need not and should not reinforce each other but may work, instead, as "competitive discursive traditions engaged in a dialectical relation of conscious critique" (54). As Nelson has it, literary history is a potentially infinite subject, and literary histories can be potentially centrifugal forces, in deliberate opposition to the inevitable centripetality of individual reading lists. Nelson's own antihistory therefore seeks to exploit the genre's capacity for centrifugality. Because my own work is engaged more in reception history than general literary history, however, I want to suggest that Nelson's study and my own can themselves be viewed as competitive discursive traditions engaged in a dialectical relation of conscious critique.

Nelson argues that we have swept dozens of writers from the map of modern poetry, and I agree, for Tolson is prominent among them. Neither Nelson nor I can endorse the academic practices that currently generate, on the average, more than ninety annual Modern Language Association (MLA) bibliography entries on Ezra Pound and one annual entry on Tolson. But by the same token, Nelson's invocation of "repression" foregrounds a key problem for critics attempting to theorize the noncanonical. To put a complex question simply, can we account for the noncanonical more satisfactorily in latitudinal literary histories or in individual reception histories? On one hand, I cannot agree that each of the writers Nelson discusses was neglected—or repressed—in the same way. Each has a specific reception history, which intersects in various ways with the general repression of political poetry by humanism, McCarthyism, and New Criticism. On the other hand, I cannot coherently counterargue that neglect operates only at the level of individual writers, whether these be Tolson, Blake, and Donne or (among Nelson's many examples) Amy Lowell, Edwin Rolfe, and H. H. Lewis. For if we persist in the belief that repression and neglect always come, so to speak, in individually wrapped slices, directed at individually "neglected" writers, then we also hypothesize "neglecters" for each of these writers, eventually conflating neglect and repression. Neglect is never benign, but though it is always motivated, it may not always be conscious. We cannot, in other words, indict all but a handful of the world's five billion citizens with the charge of neglecting Tolson.

I readily acknowledge, therefore, that Tolson is by no means an isolated case, even though the shape of his critical response is at some salient points unique to him alone. But aside from complementing Nelson's broad social treatment of literary history, my work seeks also to make a specific case for case studies. Though Nelson

rightly calls for a literary history in which "the history of . . . reception would be part of any evaluation" (53), Marilyn Butler has
claimed that such a Jaussian method would issue in "an endlessly
proliferating series of case studies showing how the same work has
been received by different readers over time," and that these kinds
of projects would be notable only for their "impracticality and almost certain tedium" (1985, 36). I could respond that Butler is partly
misconstruing the task at hand, for reception history should challenge the very notion that we can talk about readers receiving "the
same work" over time in any but the most trivial, orthographic
senses. But I want to respond otherwise, by pointing out that the
reception history of *marginal* works cannot possibly be relegated to
the realm of the impractical and tedious. For texts on canonicity's
cusp, I would claim instead that case-study reception history should
be the primary means of discovering why these works were (or are)
marginal or marginalized, and marginal to whom, and in relation to
what possible centers—over time. Perhaps, indeed, it is for lack of
theoretically elaborated case studies that "reception theory" has no
theory of neglect—or repression—worth the name.

John Rodden's case study of Orwell's reputation is in some ways
an analogue of my own work, but here too there are important differences in method. First, Rodden does not need to explicate Orwell's work to a world in which "Orwell" is, as Rodden notes, a
saint, a legend, a household word. Second, the study of Orwell
breaks new ground in the study of literary reputations in general but
cannot illuminate the politics of race in the formation of American
canons, as do Tolson and Pynchon (since the politics of race is, of
course, beyond Rodden's purview). Third and most important, Rodden's work attempts a much wider sociological sweep than mine,
partially because Orwell's very fame was produced by so many different media of cultural reproduction as his name was sounded
throughout the Cold War and in the countdown to 1984 in serious
journalism, the popular press, film adaptations of his work, and so
on. I might conceivably be able to reproduce this method for
Pynchon, whose name and influence do tend to turn up in popular
culture media, from *People* magazine to songs by Devo ("Whip It").
But for Tolson, who was something of a local hero in the black
Southwest, such a "reputation history" will carry us only so far: for
the public sphere in which Tolson was justly famous in his lifetime
was a sphere bounded by segregation, which ensured that although he was a renowned teacher and public speaker in his limited
public sphere, he would not be given license to speak on New York

television or to write reviews for the Herald-Tribune *Book Week* until the mid-1960s—just as segregation was being slowly dismantled, but just as Tolson was succumbing to stomach cancer.[12]

Moreover, I am less interested in the myriad ways authors are "put into discourse" in the culture at large than I am in the institutional practices by which they become available for canonicity. Thus, although I join Rodden in calling for "a 'rhetorical' approach toward literary reception, a *rhetoric of reception*" (70), my interest lies largely in the academic arenas of textual production—that is, in the institutions that grant writers their continued cultural reproduction and the continued reproduction of "value" that such high-cultural dissemination entails. This reproduction of value is the result of specific reading practices but is perceived by means of the semiotics of institutional endorsement in general. The number of Americans familiar with Marxist approaches to *The Waste Land* is exceeded by the number of Americans who have read *The Waste Land*, and this number is exceeded by the number of Americans who know, in a general way, that *The Waste Land* is considered Great Literature and that some knowledge of the poem is an index of one's cultural capital. And academic institutions, as Pierre Bourdieu (1984) has shown in considerable detail, carry the authority of dispensers of such cultural capital.[13]

Rodden himself concedes as much in his final pages, when he notes that Orwell's reputation in the academy "demonstrates that

[12]I am not, of course, suggesting that New York television and *Book Week* were themselves segregrationist; but then again, segregation does not have to operate equally forcefully everywhere in order to operate effectively. Nor, for most of Tolson's career, did segregation always require force; no editor needed to stand with the National Guard outside the doors of publishing houses in order to keep African-American poets out of American anthologies and journals in the 1950s, though Langston Hughes's lifelong encounters with Red-baiting demonstrated that active repression of African-American poets remained an option throughout the period. The point is simply that Tolson had, until the 1960s, comparatively few channels of access to mainstream centers of reproduction; the sphere in which he made his substantial reputation is accordingly difficult to relate, theoretically and socially, to more widely recognized "public spheres."

[13]Bourdieu's analyses of the social processes by which "cultural capital" is acquired and disseminated are, as many commentators have pointed out by now, not easily transferable to the United States, where the educational system is not so stratified as in France. I am merely borrowing the general concept, along with Bourdieu's general caveat against construing this "dispensation" in the rhetoric of equal access: "It is no doubt in the area of education and culture that the members of the dominated classes have least chance of discovering their objective interest and of producing and imposing the problematic most consistent with their interests. Awareness of the economic and social determinants of cultural dispossession in fact varies in almost inverse ratio to cultural dispossession" (1984, 387, 390).

levels of canonization can and do conflict." Because Orwell is reproduced in college classrooms usually for his essays, and thus usually
in classrooms of rhetoric and composition, Rodden finds that "entry
into a 'lower' canon often constrains, rather than facilitates, admit-
tance into 'higher' canons—usually according to some variant of the
notion that an accessible, popular author cannot be 'serious' too." It
follows, then, that academic criticism, for all its insecurities about its
social functions, is a particularly strong form of gatekeeping, for "literary academics—though admittedly influenced greatly by literary-
political intellectuals, publishers, and others—ultimately 'make' the
university canon. Literary-political intellectuals do not. They may
shape cultural opinion through their journals and books, 'leading
the way' for institutional acceptance, but they do not directly establish curricula" (396–97).

If I appear uninterested, therefore, in reproducing in my account
of Tolson's reception the contents of such newspaper items as "A
'Great Poet' Unknown in Our Own Mid-West'" (*Kansas City Star*, 25
July 1965), it is not because my area of inquiry is provincially professionalist. Rather, because I believe that our professional practices are
open to contestation in ways uniquely available now, my interest
lies in those specific features of "reputation" that propel authors into
university curricula and professional research, and I accordingly
confine myself to academic centers of reproduction and their relation
to nonacademic literary gatekeepers. Very little in this study will
reach beyond the pages of, say, the *New York Review of Books* and its
literate nonspecialist audiences; I am not intervening in anything so
widely public as the James Bond phenomenon, "reading the romance," or the making and claiming of "St. George" Orwell.[14] I do
hope, nonetheless, to shed some light on how reception history may
proceed, and how the profession of literature can think its relation
to its immediate neighbors in the spheres of textual production—
and to writers, as disparate as Melvin Tolson and Thomas Pynchon,
who claim to speak from the margins of reading institutions.

For it is by now axiomatic to post-Romantic thought that the rhetoric of marginality can be a powerful enabling device, even though
marginality itself is synonymous with disempowerment: to claim to
speak from the margin is paradoxically to claim to speak from the

[14]Tony Bennett and Janet Wollacott's *Bond and Beyond* (1987) reaches to mass paperbacks, films, comics, and "biographies" of Bond; Janice Radway's *Reading the Romance*
(1984) extends to the promotional techniques of B. Dalton and the "amateur" readers
of "Smithton"; John Rodden's *Politics of Literary Reputation* (1989) includes newspaper
headlines, films, cartoons, and O-level exam questions.

position of authority, and to describe a margin is to describe an authoritative challenge to hegemony. My challenge to this rhetoric of marginality takes two forms: demystification, whereby I argue that Pynchon's putative "margin" is not always as marginal as it appears; and negotiation, whereby I seek to demonstrate Tolson's importance without making the knee-jerk argument that he is important solely *because* he has been marginalized. Margins are real, but they are always relational. To narrate the exchanges between cultural margins and centers, therefore, and the divergent forms of such exchanges in the work and reception of Thomas Pynchon and Melvin Tolson, I will claim to speak from the ambiguous position of a cultural center whose centrality is itself marginal to larger social formations, whether these be Hollywood studios or the military-industrial complex. And from my contested and conflicted cultural position as an academic critic, I hope henceforth to describe a productive series of conflicts: between "American" and "African-American" canons, between academic and journalistic institutions, between the conditions of literary production and the responsibilities of academic reception—between, in as many senses as possible, recent American literature's marginal forces and cultural centers.

CHAPTER 1

Institutional
Authorizations

THIS BOOK is predicated on the professionalization of literary criticism not only in the obvious sense that academic criticism is
my inquiry's condition of possibility, but also insofar as I assume
throughout that academic reception is both the determinant and
measure of canonicity and the single most salient characteristic of
the literary climate in which Tolson and Pynchon have produced
their work. In both senses, academic criticism constitutes the "cultural center" invoked by my title. Neither of these assumptions is
out of the ordinary, but they imply as their corollary that in exploring the relation of academic criticism to these two writers, we will
confront opposing accounts of the forms of institutionalization involved in the practices of academic criticism.

Critics, Clients, and Endorsements

Put most bluntly, the question that faces us here is whether academicization is the life or death of "culture." Is institutional literary
study a means to the preservation of culture(s), or does it mark the
death-by-assimilation of vibrant, challenging writers, movements,
and modes of thought? Of course, to put the question in this way is
to muddy and falsify it, since "life" and "death" can be construed as
variously as a Rorschach blot—even so as to be equivalent states.
On the side of "life," for instance, we have the argument that the
function of the university is "transmission of the cultural heritage,"

an argument that has come in the last decade to involve an entire battery of keywords such as "excellence," "legacy," and "value."[1] Such "transmission" turns out to be a profoundly passive enterprise whereby universities teach a central core of classical texts in the Western tradition, texts whose "classic" and "central" status has been enhanced in this century by their very presence in "central" university curricula. Thus, if we mean by "preservation of culture" an intellectual and patriarchal embalming process for passing on to our students what our fathers passed on to us, then institutional "life," in my question above, is as ideologically suspect a code word for critical intellectuals as it is for advocates of women's reproductive rights.

No progressive literary professional will accede to "life" on these terms; yet even those who reject the easy equation of university with conservatory are capable of imagining institutionalization as death. Take for example the opening sentence of Barbara Johnson's "Nothing Fails Like Success": "As soon as any radically innovative thought becomes an *ism*, its specific groundbreaking force diminishes, its historical notoriety increases, and its disciples tend to become more simplistic, more dogmatic, and ultimately more conservative, at which time its power becomes institutional rather than analytical" (1987, 11). Along similar lines, Michele Wallace, writing in the *Voice Literary Supplement* a few years ago, registered the academy's recovery of Zora Neale Hurston with ambivalence and suspicion: "Not only may we be canonizing a Hurston who never existed, or the wrong corpse, but it may simply be intrinsic to the process of canonization (think mummification) to lay waste to the symbolic and intellectual urgency of this or any other cultural object of our affections" (1988, 18). Johnson's line is but a recent restatement of a flexible and often used springboard for antiprofessional arguments; Wallace's makes vivid the issues of "life and death" at stake in the image of academic criticism as a form of graverobbing. Johnson would leave professional critics and theorists in the uncomfortable position of ruining everything they touch, recuperating and com-

---

[1] John Guillory asks conservatives and revisionists alike, "Why should the coming-into-writing of the formerly excluded be experienced as the degeneration of value?" (1987, 487). The answer, I think, lies in the ideological force of the keywords, especially "excellence." The category of the "excluded" has, in the language that empowers these keywords, supposedly been determined by a Darwinian natural selection of reception: "culture" has spontaneously "chosen" certain texts as repositories of its "values," and any active intervention in the process of natural cultural selection is therefore a violation of value as well.

modifying everything they see, carrying one artifact after another
into the furthest reaches of the museum where their only hope for
life is that they may someday be seen by a critical "ignorance" capable of reading them against the grain, against their institutional context: "If the deconstructive impulse is to retain its vital, subversive
power, we must therefore become ignorant of it again and again"
(16). But Wallace, I think, would leave us in a still more impossible
position, a position in which even our successful attempts at canon
revision are doomed to failure in their success: we might think not
just of "mummification" but also of our industry going on with business as usual, having merely opened a branch office to handle Hurston et al. Or, more insidiously, we might think of Hurston's institutionalization as the process by which we seal her off forever in
canons and classrooms, so that we can prevent her from doing damage to herself or to others in the outside world.

Our most formidable accounts of critical negativity, in other
words, often take the form of antiprofessionalism; and it is hardly
possible to rebut such accounts by construing antiprofessionalism as
a mystified version of professionalism, as though anything were
solved by the argument that "anti-professionalism is professionalism
itself in its purest form" (Fish 1985, 106). Critical intellectuals such as
Barbara Johnson and Michele Wallace may have good reason to fear
and question institutionalization; for Stanley Fish, ordinary professional language may be all right, but as a growing number of commentators have shown, "'professionalization' and 'academicization'
are not neutral principles of organization, but agents that transform
the cultural and literary-critical 'isms' fed into them, often to the
point of subverting their original purpose" (Graff 1987, 5).

Indeed, the fact that those words were written by Gerald Graff
lends them all the greater force, since they testify to the conversion
of an academic intellectual whose previous work attacked the man-
darinism and rarefaction of "theory" but who has since come to believe that the enemy of critical thought is not Francophile innovation
but the American university's passive absorption of any kind of innovation. In the bureaucratic "field-coverage" model of academic
study, writes Graff,

> innovation even of a threatening kind could be welcomed by simply
> *adding* another unit to the aggregate of fields to be covered. Fierce resis-
> tance to innovation arose frequently, of course, but since all instructors
> were on their own, the absorption of innovation did not oblige pre-
> established habits to change, so that in the long run—and increasingly

it was not a very long run—resistance tended to give way. It is only the field-coverage principle that explains how the literature department has managed to avoid incurring paralyzing clashes of ideology during a period when it has preserved much of its earlier traditional orientation while incorporating disruptive novelties such as contemporary literature, black studies, feminism, Marxism, and deconstruction. (1987, 7)

Here Graff depends and expands upon the work of Burton Bledstein, whose study of professionalism maintains that "the university not only segregated ideas from the public, intellectual segregation occurred with the development of each new department in the university" (1976, 327). If we take Graff to be amending Bledstein's "with the development of each new department" to "with*in* the development of each new department," then their conclusions appear much the same: "Departments grew by accretion," writes Bledstein, because the structure of the American university "allowed for an infinite expansion in size" (300).

I bring up Bledstein partly because Fish cites his work as a classic statement of the "anti-professionalist perspective" (1985, 89) even as he skirts some of Bledstein's charges, thus misconstruing the specific idiolect of literary antiprofessionalism. According to Bledstein, professionalism is not only the material instance of a mid-Victorian ideology that sought to reconcile the vertical advancement of the middle class with the ideal of social service (1976, 80); it is also a powerful means of mystification by which a new and specifically American class consolidates its hegemony over the production and dissemination of knowledge. In the creation of the new social relation of professional and client, in what advertisers call a "primary appeal" (the marketing of an unprecedented class of commodities, which seeks to create new areas of "demand"), "symbols of professional authority emphasized the complexity of a subject, its forbidding nature to the layman, the uninitiated, and even the inexperienced practitioner. . . . The more elaborate the rituals of a profession, the more esoteric its theoretical knowledge, the more imposing its symbols of authority, the more respectable its demeanor, the more vivid its service to society—the more prestige and status the public was willing to bestow upon its representatives" (98, 94).

This is perhaps a familiar equation, but what Fish misses in this argument—what cannot be gainsaid by deconstructing the binary opposition between antiprofessionalism and professionalism—is that the problem with applying these mystification procedures to the profession of literature has always been the vagueness of the professional "service" rendered by literary intellectuals. For reasons that have little to do with our own failings, we have usually been unable to articulate convincingly the relation of our "culture" to "society," unable to locate and rationalize the client class that justifies the creation of the profession we inhabit. As Barbara Herrnstein Smith has recently said:

> This is one reason, perhaps, why research in other fields—economics, genetics, physics, and so forth—can be, without complaint or criticism, difficult for members of the general public to understand or indeed totally incomprehensible to them, but not research in literary studies. (I mentioned the sciences, of course, but the contrast holds as well for other humanities disciplines: archaeology, classics, philosophy, etc.) The difference is that literary studies, and especially English, is, for many people—including, it seems, many journalists—not a discipline at all. English is simply their own native language, which is understood by anyone who speaks, reads, and writes it; and the only thing that makes English professors *special* is that—being, perhaps, unable to do anything else—they have chosen to get paid full-time for doing what everybody else does part-time and *could* do full-time if they were not so busy holding down real jobs. (1989, 292)

The professionalization of literature is therefore experienced by nonprofessionals as a disenfranchisement of their rights as readers of English, a means of professorial self-aggrandizement whereby, as one extraordinary argument has put it, "literature ceases to be the commons of all speakers and readers of the common tongue, and becomes only the occasion of a deafening clatter *about* literature" (Berry 1985, 208–9).[2] In the realm of literature, apparently, there should be no "client class" at all, and consequently no profession.

Yet, as Fish rightly notes (1983, 349), this complaint of "disenfranchisement" is not confined to irate nonprofessionals; nor is it solely the province of cultural conservatism, as if it could be one and the same thing to be against professionalization and against theory. Instead, we are as likely to find fear and self-loathing on the profession's left wing as on its right, as in this example from Jim Merod,

---

[2]I call Berry's argument "extraordinary" because of the extremity of its humanist rhetoric, in which literature becomes a discourse of ideal equal access, a democratic idyll shattered only by bumptious and shamanistic professionals. But as I argue below, it may not be in the least extraordinary when it comes from a novelist/essayist such as Berry, for it may very well be part of a historical, interprofessional squabble over critics' reproductive rights. Indeed, the argument is all the more extraordinary when it is advanced by professional critics: cf. Fish 1983, Cain 1988.

which I cite because of its interesting deployment of the term "academic":

> As it stands now, criticism is a grossly academic enterprise that has no real vision of its relationship to and responsibilities within the corporate structure of North American (for that matter, international) life. It is simply a way of doing business with texts. It is in fact a series of ways, a multiplicity of methods that vie for attention and prestige within the semipublic, semiprivate professional critical domain. Thus, academic critics reproduce teachers and scholars and critics, reproduce a humanist but not a fully critical education. (1987, 9)

Merod's "academic" enterprise is "gross" because it obfuscates the relation between culture and society—and because it is a kind of living death, insofar as the institution serves (as it most certainly does) to perpetuate its own legitimation practices, which ensure highly replicable relations of production and make "change" a matter of merely incremental reform. It is also an "academic" enterprise in that it is unsure of the services it provides, as Merod notes, and unsure of the clients to whom it provides them, as Merod does not note.[3]

But antiprofessionalism does not always confine itself to the equation of institutionalization with death. Antiprofessionalism may actually be almost a standard, permanent feature of our discipline: not only because professionalism is considered "a threat to individual freedom, true merit, genuine authority" (Fish 1985, 106) but also because literary professionals inhabit an institution formed in the culture of professionalism but unsure that its machinery for professional self-advancement is sufficiently balanced and justified by the

---

[3]Merod's argument relies on the assumption that we are training "a professional class striving for prestige and privilege, . . . people who pass through colleges and universities and on into the corporate structure of the professional marketplace. The way these people are educated . . . has everything to do with rejuvenating respect for individuals over profit, with creating a society that includes systematically outcast people (the poor, the sick, the elderly, the uneducated), and with promoting the dignity and even the safety of victimized people (women, children, minorities, and laborers of every kind). Or not" (1987, 7). But as Richard Ohmann writes, we cannot simply claim tomorrow's managers as our clients: "By helping to sort out those who will succeed in school from those who will not, we have generally confirmed the class origins of our students, while making it possible for a few to rise (and others to sink). The effect—unintended of course—is to sustain the *illusion* of equal opportunity and convince the majority that their failure to play a significant and rewarding role in society is a personal failure rather than a systemic one" (1987, 8–9).

services it provides to its clients, whoever these may be.[4] One of the many issues at stake in the politics of professional self-justification is the relation of criticism to the "literary public sphere."[5] According to Peter Uwe Hohendahl, the eighteenth-century model of the "liberal public sphere," in which all citizens participate as discursive equals, "was an ideal that social reality never fully achieved. Nevertheless, its effect is evident even today" (1982, 53). That ideal for literary criticism now appears untenable for either of two reasons. It may be that the literary public sphere is now "fragmented" by the "separation of elite and mass culture" (73), or it may be, as Jon Klancher has argued (drawing on Hohendahl), that the public sphere had already by 1790 "become an image to be consumed by readers who did not frequent it," a "representation instead of a practice" (1987, 23, 24). Still, for contemporary criticism the "public sphere" remains a potent mirage, regardless of whether it has been irremediably shattered (Hohendahl) or exposed as almost-always-already textual (Klancher); and either way, the relation between academic criticism and the public sphere is one of *contradiction*, in the Marxist sense.

Hence, one of the paradoxical conditions under which academic criticism now operates is that its discipline was formed, one hundred years ago, in contradistinction to the public sphere it is nevertheless presumed to serve. It is therefore dismaying but not surprising that Russell Jacoby, who laments the decline of public intellectuals and the concomitant "fattening of the universities" (1987, 237) in the postwar era, considers *academic* and *public* to be mutually exclusive terms. According to Jacoby, it is possible— though appalling—that "the entire transmission belt of culture" may be "no longer public in the way it once was but now takes place invisibly in university classrooms and reading assignments" (234). Hard as it is to imagine classrooms as "invisible," it is harder still to agree that the little magazines of the 1920s and 1930s, in contrast to universities in the 1980s and 1990s, constituted a true literary public sphere; for Jacoby, however, such a mirage is real, for "these journals participated, if only through hope, in the larger community" (7).

---

[4]For brief accounts of how difficult it is for the profession to speak of "clients" without reaching for the palliating rhetoric of our Arnoldian mission as guardians of culture, see Ohmann 1987, 3–17; Graff 1987, 81–97; and Kaufmann 1990, 521–24.

[5]The idea of the "public sphere" as a deliberative social mechanism whose origins lie in eighteenth-century bourgeois civil society was first formulated by Jürgen Habermas (1962; for the English translation, see Habermas 1989), from whom Hohendahl derives his treatment of the "literary public sphere."

Bruce Robbins characterizes Jacoby's *The Last Intellectuals* as a "jeremiad, a denunication of decline or demise that, however, leaves open the possibility of moral resuscitation, and indeed finds its justification in moral revivalism" (1990, xvi). Robbins overlooks Jacoby's desire that the intellectual spaces of "public culture" not be ceded by default to cultural reactionaries, but he is surely right to remark that "it requires no paranoia to see attacks on the inadequate 'publicness' of the contemporary academy from left and right as a covert means of undermining the specific (though still fragile) gains scored by feminism there" (1990, xviii). However, since literary anti-professionalism is not always coextensive with antifeminism, inside or outside the academy, I suggest also that the terms of the current debate at once exemplify and rely on the general lack of consensus about the professional services that academic criticism has been his-torically supposed to render—as an institution and as an ideological state apparatus.

This general confusion is ours as well, for academic professionals will lack such a consensus so long as the profession of criticism con-tinues to reproduce the contradiction between its ideals of post-Kantian, Romantic autonomy and its ideals of professional social service. Hohendahl calls this a conflict between "the social institu-tion of criticism and its immanent concept" (1982, 60); in a similar vein, David Kaufmann argues that "literary study in the United States has been forced to justify itself through an antiscientific ideol-ogy that both underscores and denies the very professionalism that sustains its institutional existence" (1990, 522). The result of this con-flict, as Kaufmann concludes (1990, 528), is that we shuttle con-stantly between images of ourselves as highly trained specialists (our "immanent concept") and as publicly accountable generalists (in social institutions).

Jonathan Culler has recently taken up this question in a partic-ularly enlightening and troubling way. Starting not from Bledstein but from Christopher Jencks and David Riesman, who construe pro-fessionalism as "colleague-oriented rather than client-oriented" (1968, 201; quoted in Culler 1988, 29), Culler argues that the profes-sion's increasing reliance on the system of peer review may work to "generate a more specialized yet more innovative criticism than would some other arrangement" and thus to liberate English pro-fessors from a "vertical" review conducted primarily by university administrators (30). The dependence of one's career on one's critical writing is salutory to Culler, for if the profession can avoid having its interests dictated by pressures external to research, its criticism is free to grow in Topsy fashion, heedless of clientele: "Aside from elementary courses, what gets taught and what research is conducted will depend more on professors' sense of the important problems in their specialties, or the availability of grants and their success in obtaining them, than on departmental decisions about what should be transmitted to the young. This structure can be conducive to the production of knowledge, because it encourages individual faculty members to pursue, in their teaching and writing, whatever sort of enterprise seems most likely to bring them recognition" (34).

Culler is right to critique the habit of mind whereby we demand that research justify itself pedagogically—"few would seriously suggest that physicists or historians should restrict their work to what can be communicated to 19-year-olds" (37–38)—but surely the problems of professionalism are not to be waved away by Culler's invisible hand, the invisible hand that orders the free market of jobs, grants, and research so as to maximize the full potential of "individual faculty members" for self-advancement. As Paul Lauter wrote, some years before Culler, "It is no defense to assert that as a literary form criticism has the right to define its own subjects, including the language it uses" (1984, 421). Though Lauter's objection may be a resistance to theory, it is also a resistance to libertarianism in theory; for whereas Culler dismisses over 60 percent of the profession with the phrase "aside from elementary courses," Lauter reminds us that theory and research are still the province of a professional elite (420), that "elementary courses" still make up the bulk of our discipline.[6] For the majority of the profession engaged in teaching "literacy," writes Lauter, "the task . . . contrasts starkly with the vision of the literary life to which most of us in the profession, and particularly those of us who join the Modern Language Association, were bred" (419). From Lauter's perspective, then, Culler's portrait of a self-regulating profession works precisely to obscure the relation between criticism and its institutions, for in emphasizing the individual's freedom of research, Culler has simply restated and glamorized the professional fantasy that professional "recognition" (in teaching *or* writing) transcends any determinate institutional context.

Yet I think Culler's seemingly dispassionate reassertion of the pri-

---

[6]According to Ohmann, the declining enrollments in English courses are counterbalanced only by an increasing emphasis on remedial literacy: "The students still in our classrooms are mostly studying composition, which accounted for 40 percent of English enrollments in the late sixties; it accounted for 60 percent in 1985 and for twice the number of literature enrollments" (1987, 10).

macy of research is due less to any conscious commitment to professional meritocracy than to his characterization of the profession, which relies on a powerful and misleading version of the life/death dichotomy I seek to dismantle. Culler distinguishes two models "by which universities operate and how they may affect critical writing," a bad model and a good model:

> The first makes the university the transmitter of a cultural heritage, gives it the ideological function of reproducing culture and the social order. The second model makes the university a site for the production of knowledge. . . .
> The first model gives criticism the function of elucidating the masterpieces of the cultural heritage that is taught. The second model gives criticism no specific educational function but makes critical progress or innovation the goals of teachers of literature. Critical investigation, in this second model, is simply what professors do: to write criticism is to generate knowledge, and though a canonical body of texts may serve as a starting point, the only prescribed goal is to advance one's understanding of cultural phenomena. (1988, 33, 35)

Given these polarities, between passive transmission of a dead "culture" and active creation of living "knowledge," critical intellectuals should have no trouble deciding which side to choose; but the basis for "choice" is illusory, for both sides of Culler's dichotomy collapse under scrutiny. To critique the "good" model first, we might note that this positivist "production of knowledge" takes place within an institutional context of carefully and rigidly articulated professional hierarchy. As Richard Ohmann has written:

> It is not quite true that we do criticism outside of the system of exploitation. The university and college managements that employ us make indirect use of criticism and all other research they sponsor, though they do not strictly appropriate these products or sell them for profit. Management demands research in order to keep up the "quality" of the faculty and of the institution. That's to say that the university claims its rank among institutions mainly by citing the research that its faculty carries out, even otherwise useless research like criticism. Research supports its official ranking, and all the more informal measures of repute, such as the flow of promising graduate students, the marketability of those students when they gain Ph.D.'s, and the university's position in the bidding for those same students later on when some of them gain distinction as researchers. This rating system and its values permeate higher education, operating with diminished force "down" through the prestigious colleges, the lesser universities, and the state and municipal

colleges. Community colleges and some others may neither reward nor demand research; that fact both reflects and establishes their position at the bottom of the hierarchy. (1987, 23–24)

So much, then, for the freedom of investigation implied in Culler's "second model." Yet the first option created by his dichotomy is equally inadequate. For if the university functions as the transmitter of a cultural heritage, it is not the case that it must do so only to reproduce culture and the social order. The equation of "transmission" with "replication" is an easy one, and Culler does not resist it: insofar as his first model "gives criticism the function of elucidating the masterpieces of the cultural heritage that is taught," it serves as a straw man against which he can profitably oppose the benefits of unfettered research. But in setting up his straw man, Culler has mischaracterized the opportunities and responsibilities of literary study; not everyone envisions the "cultural heritage" as a constant among the variables of criticism and interpretation. Indeed, one of the present—and most important—functions of the literary academy is its *revision* of its cultural heritage, through professional programs for canon revision unprecedented in their scope and in their re-formation not only of canons but of the bases of canonicity. By means of this revision, one might argue, the academy seeks both to "transmit" and "produce" knowledge, to be a cultural archive that takes an active role in the creation of its exhibits.

Canon revision is by no means reducible to affirmative action. It is a new mode of textual production; it instigates new relations of production among literary gatekeepers; and, most interestingly, it reformulates a class of "clients": namely, *authors*, whom academic critics, like attorneys, may advocate and represent in their various professional "agencies."[7] To emphasize canon revision, then, is to topple Culler's dichotomy between "transmission of the cultural heritage" and "production of knowledge"; to emphasize canon revision is also to undo Culler's glamorization of research, which makes the advancement of the discipline dependent on a handful of scholars at well-funded institutions, scholars whose freedom to write is a function of their freedom from teaching. On some counts, Culler does well to contest the notion that classrooms are the primary site of progressive intellectual work, insofar as he reminds us that the idealization

---

[7]This is not to say that such representation must take only its most transparent possible forms, such as reader's guides and critical biographies. Reinterpretations of Foucault, revisionist anthologies, and critical editions of Gaskell's *Mary Barton* are all representations of "authors" in my sense of "representation."

of pedagogy can also be "a conservative, even reactionary gesture": when pedagogical "practice" is invoked by opponents of "theory," Culler suggests that the invocation is "usually an attempt to dismiss new lines of investigation or abstruse critical writings without confronting them directly" (1988, 37). His suggestion is helpful, however, only if pedagogical practice is counterposed to, rather than the result of, innovative research, for in principle, canon revision can be practiced anywhere at all—even or especially in "elementary courses." The availability of canon revision to community college teachers and chaired Ivy League professors alike does not make revisionism good or desirable in itself, but it does break Culler's polemical link between classroom contexts and cultural conservatism.

Canon revision is in this sense the excluded middle term of Culler's argument. But because canon revision always has immediate pedagogical implications, from the redesigning of an individual survey course to the restructuring of an entire department, our discussions of canons have focused almost exclusively on the "canonical" as a category of value production.[8] As John Guillory has memorably put it, "The controversy over the canon is being fought in the enchanted wood of values" (1987, 487). I grant that we cannot possibly disentangle debates over canonicity from debates about value. Since canons are both institutions and the results of institutional practices of legitimation, and since canons are perhaps the most salient productions by which we represent ourselves as a profession to other areas of culture and society, canon revision always carries some undecidable but potent sign value. In the midst of Guillory's enchanted wood, however, we have often forgotten to argue that canons are also the means by which academic criticism operates as an economic force, as a guarantor of last resort, as one of the most stable means of keeping texts on publishers' ever dwindling backlists.

Academic critics are in no sense economic powerhouses in the world of publishing, but the economic functions of our reading lists are all the more urgent precisely because our economic power is precarious and fragile. Moreover, it does not take an epochal social movement to keep works in print (annual sales in the hundreds or low thousands may suffice), though it *has* taken an epochal social movement, such as second-wave feminism, to bring about the con-

---

[8]Demonstrating the bipartisan agreement to equate canons with values, Henry Louis Gates has recently written that "we've got to borrow a leaf from the right, which is exemplarily aware of the role of education in the reproduction of values. We must engage in this sort of canon reformation precisely because Mr. Bennett is correct: the teaching of literature *is* the teaching of values" (1989, 45).

tinued (institutional) reproduction of many works long out of print. In other words, the category of texts in print will always exceed any specific category of canonical texts, but the latter category is dependent on the former in such obvious, material ways that the relation between these two areas of production has gone woefully undertheorized.[9] And in describing academic criticism as a "guarantor of last resort," I do not mean to reinstate academic professionals as the guardians of culture; I mean simply that insofar as canon revision serves as a corrective to the biases and blindnesses of nonacademic gatekeepers, it reclaims authors such as Zora Neale Hurston and Aphra Behn from the "free market" cultural forces that had allowed them to fall silent, and reestablishes (re-presents) authors whose works had been bypassed by other, more "traditional," means of cultural reproduction.

This last point warrants some elaboration, for it marks academic revisionists as both different from and paradoxically in competition with the gatekeepers of nonacademic literary culture. *Different from*, because no reliable nonacademic forum exists for the recovery of the noncanonical; the *New York Times Book Review* and *Esquire* are not in the business of rediscovering "lost" and "forgotten" writers, and contemporary reviews such as Gordon Lish's *Quarterly* are understandably devoted more to finding previously unpublished writers than to paying reprint permissions for recent works now out of print. And yet *in competition with*, because as academic criticism constitutes a new, revisionary form of gatekeeping, it necessarily conflicts with the interests of nonacademic reviewers.

We can instructively compare this account of academic gatekeeping to Richard Ohmann's. In an influential study nearly ten years ago, Ohmann argued that "precanonical" works, "meaning those that are active candidates for inclusion, not those that will in fact be canonical at some later time" (1983, 398 n.2), are made available for canonicity "only if they [have] attained both large sales . . . and the

---

[9]In 1985 Charles Newman reported that "backlist income has fallen from 70% to 30% as a percentage of net income" (164); in 1986, revisions to the U.S. tax code prohibited publishers from counting backlists as depreciation costs. It is still too early to tally the outcome of this tax code revision and the further consolidation of the publishing industry, but if in fact it has recently become more difficult to keep texts in print once they have been reprinted, then the institutionalization of such texts is therefore all the more essential to their survival. As Richard Yarborough has recently pointed out, "only twenty years since the end of the sixties, it is already necessary to salvage the work of important writers of that era. . . . Not to place the recovery of such texts high on our scholarly agenda is to participate in canonization by default: If the texts are not in print, they will not be bought or taught" (1989, 108).

right kind of critical attention" (384). Ohmann's schema places academic criticism at the end of a chain of consumption and selection which begins with publishing and marketing and continues by means of reviews in influential nonspecialist journals. In stressing criticism's dependency on the entire network of textual production, Ohmann thus steers between two monolithic alternatives for construing textual longevity: "On the one side, this hypothesis conflicts with the one most vigorously advanced by Leslie A. Fiedler—that intellectuals are, in the long run, outvoted by the sorts of readers who keep liking *Gone with the Wind*. On the other side, it collides with the hopes or expectations of critics such as [Richard] Kostelanetz or Jerome Klinkowitz, who promote an avant-garde fiction called post-modernist, post-contemporary, antinovel, or whatever" (384).

Because almost all of Tolson's and Pynchon's work had been published by 1975, Ohmann's analysis remains useful for my purposes, but I want to situate the current position of academic criticism elsewhere than at the end of Ohmann's food chain; the academic activities of the past fifteen years positively require modification of Ohmann's thesis, for two reasons. First, we are witnessing the creation of newly "precanonical" works that were never represented in influential journals; for a notable example, Paule Marshall's 1959 novel *Brown Girl, Brownstones*, which has now become the subject of some critical attention, was cited by Richard Kostelanetz almost twenty years ago as one of the "neglected" works of "comparable quality" to the novels of Philip Roth and John Updike, and its neglect was adduced as evidence of the conspiratorial quality of American "literary establishments" (1973, xii). Second, we are witnessing a new kind of competition between academic criticism and professional book reviewing as criticism continues to diversify its holdings in all areas of literary production. Academic critics still rely on publishers' decisions about what to print and what to keep in print, and we do relatively little book reviewing in nonacademic venues; in the *New York Times Book Review*, for instance, academics are more likely to review other academics, while "writers" review other "writers." All the same, we are no longer confronting Ohmann's mid-1970s landscape, in which an academic critic such as Jerome Klinkowitz champions writers generally unknown to nonacademic critics. Instead, we now represent contemporary writers to different audiences from those of the nonspecialist press, and in vastly different ways: critics such as Deborah McDowell, Margaret Homans, and Frank Lentricchia publish articles on writers (Toni Morrison, Gloria

Naylor, Don DeLillo) who are being simultaneously discussed by journalists and reviewers.

This newly formed competition between academic and non-academic critics for the right to represent contemporary and noncanonical authors is perhaps one reason for the vehemence of recent journalistic attacks on the profession of literature. The *New Criterion*'s Roger Kimball, one of the fiercest of the profession's attackers, has gone so far as to argue that the university has no right whatsoever to determine its curriculum: "Liberal-arts education," writes Kimball in his postscript to *Tenured Radicals*, "should concentrate as rigorously as possible on works that have proved to be of permanent value; in practice, that means that few if any contemporary works should be part of the undergraduate curriculum" (1990, 202). Similarly, invective such as Jonathan Yardley's strikingly ill-informed and widely reprinted 1988 diatribe against the "young fascists" responsible for canon revision is understandable, not only as part of another salvo from a professional reviewer who has sniped at the academy before, but also as the result of competition among variously positioned gatekeepers for control over the means of cultural reproduction.[10]

When Yardley sneers at Zora Neale Hurston, his animus may very well have some basis in race, gender, or class; but it may also be fueled by the conviction that Hurston is being whisked into the academy without the imprimatur of professional, nonacademic arbiters of taste. It follows from this conviction, apparently, that Hurston's canonization is merely "political," whereas D. H. Lawrence's was the result of natural forces. And what is true of Hurston criticism holds for all academic retrieval of lost writers: it is both different from and in competition with the work of journalistic reviewers. For Yardley did not review the reprinted *Their Eyes Were Watching God*, and his conviction that writers such as Hurston "previously had been properly regarded as of minor stature and therefore of minor scholarly interest" (1988, B2) is apparently grounded only in his opposition to academic "effluvia," whether these be major works by minor writers or (as in his earlier column on Virginia Woolf) minor works by major writers—effluvia that are periodically "exhumed by literary scholarship" (1982, C6). In the eyes of both Jon-

---

[10]Yardley's first antiprofessional article appeared in the *Washington Post* (1982); see Fish 1983 for further discussion. Yardley's *Washington Post* article on canons (1988) is strongly derivative from one published the previous week in the *New York Times* (Berger 1988).

athan Yardley and Michele Wallace, it seems, lecturing or writing on Hurston is a ghoulish affair, a (re)mummification of decaying corpses by legions of the academic undead.

I am not assuming that canon revision tends all in one ideological direction, or that it is necessarily institutionally "progressive," however institutional "progress" may be understood. But I do think it is finally inadequate to generate "new ways of reading" without also expanding our range of historical reading materials, and on these grounds I dissent sharply from Ross Chambers's argument that "the traditional humanism whose ideology the canon encapsulates cannot be opposed by our merely changing the content of the canon without challenging the structures of thinking that produce the system" (1990, 20). I don't want to argue the contrary position that "merely changing the content" is enough; rather, my point is that the contrary position is not even available, that the dichotomy between changing texts and changing "structures of thinking" is not comprehensible as a dichotomy. For where did our newly canonical works *come from* if not from revised structures of thinking or, to use the term I prefer, revised reading practices? Unless we suspend everything we know about reception theory and argue that new texts always spontaneously appear on humanism's horizon (and, thus, that humanism contains the seeds of its own revolution-which-changes-nothing), we cannot portray canon revision as a choice between changing texts and changing readings, as opposed objects and subjects.

Of course, a text or an author recovered by feminism may be eventually rearticulated to humanism, and this is precisely the danger against which such "recoveries" must struggle, but there is nothing surprising about this. What *is* surprising is to hear that "changing the canon" is useless because it "is what the canon has always been about" (Chambers 1990, 20), for this suggests that "the" canon (whatever that is) operates like a self-shuffling deck of cards, impervious to the social forces impinging upon canonicity. I contend, rather, that if a reading practice is truly "new," it simultaneously generates new objects of reading; even though it may eventually lose this critical edge, it does not automatically do so as a result of its "institutionalization." Still, I do not deny that the American academy has managed for much of its existence to apply "new" reading practices to the same old texts, as new skins for old wine; as Russell Reising has persuasively shown, even in the work of critics of American literature whose political and theoretical differences are acute, "the same authors, the same books, and often the same passages are summoned time after time to support a tautological reading which proves what it assumed in advance, that is, that the writers under investigation are truly our 'major' figures" (1986, 17–18).

One of the reasons I construe canon revision in relation to gate-keeping and publishing economics, therefore, is to de-emphasize the specific content of revised canons, in order to hold at arm's length the question of whether revised canons are necessarily the transparent *vehicles* of (though they are undoubtedly the *products* of) revised reading practices and revised values. Alongside John Guillory's skepticism about the equation of canonical and social "exclusion," I place my own skepticism as to whether our students or our colleagues arrive in our classrooms or departments as blank slates ready to receive whatever revolutionary or reactionary pedagogy we practice. And I want finally to link both skepticisms, Guillory's and mine, to Gerald Graff's caveat concerning textual transmission in general: "In order to specify the ideological effects of the canon," Graff writes, "it should be necessary to do more than make inferences from the canonized texts and interpretations. Though recent reader-centered criticism has taught us that readers appropriate texts in heterogeneous ways, this lesson tends to be forgotten when the ideology of the canon is at stake" (1987, 13).

All the same, despite Graff's caveat, one does not embark on canon revision by first depriving it of the possibility of professional and political change. My sense, instead, is that our work is not over when we have finally made our reading lists more radically democratic, nor is our work over when everyone can read Shakespeare by means of a critique of phallogocentrism. In the interim, between our present confusion and the utopian reading practices of the future, I suggest that we conceive of our canons and values in terms of "endorsement," in the sense that "endorsement" is used by professional politicians. In this account, the profession may endorse specific texts, authors, and canons just as other social institutions, from organized labor to newspaper editorial staffs, may endorse political candidates and platforms; but our endorsements do not guarantee that our canons will be received in a manner that is "ideologically of a piece" (Graff 1987, 13) with their intended transmission, any more than powerful political endorsements guarantee electoral victories. When it comes to how the public receives and appropriates the endorsements of empowering institutions, we cannot project the results of canon revision without lapsing into behaviorism—although we do know that incumbents are not easily defeated.

My reluctance to theorize value stems also from my sense that neither Tolson nor Pynchon can be universally and univocally "valuable," and that even if they somehow were, their "value" would not prevent their being deployed for purposes we cannot now imagine. For even the prospect of Melvin Tolson's canonicity does not challenge all our professional and cultural assumptions at once; I am making on his behalf a comparatively conservative argument for canon revision, the kind of argument that slightly jostles specific works, authors, and periods but leaves intact most of our assumptions about the necessity to literary study of complex, information-rich, high-cultural artifacts of serious intent and execution.[11] We might eventually (though I hope we do not) simply add Tolson to our list of the best that has been known and thought in the world, or quote Lionel Trilling to the effect that Tolson is one of those artists "who contain a large part of the dialectic [of culture] within themselves, their meaning and power lying in their contradictions; they contain within themselves, it may be said, the very essence of the culture" (1950, 20). My placement of the work of Melvin Tolson and Thomas Pynchon in the cultural context of institutional criticism, therefore, cannot serve as a strategy whereby we forge better institutions or more equitable relations of production merely by introducing formerly marginal writers to the centers from which they are excluded.

Just the same, an American academic criticism that takes even minimally sufficient account of Tolson will need to confront its continued willingness to consider "American" and "African-American" literature as mutually exclusive categories. Likewise, a profession that takes seriously Tolson's claims to be a high modernist poet will have to reconsider American modernism and its various legacies, just as it will have to expand its list of significant African-American modernists, a list that since the publication of *Invisible Man* has contained only one name. Certainly, even if we are concerned only with the representation of race in recent American culture, Tolson re-

[11]See Herrnstein Smith 1983, 33–34: "The works that are differentially re-produced . . . will often be . . . works that are structurally complex and, in the technical sense, information-rich." From this it follows that if the canonical work is to be ideologically "challenging" or "subversive," it must have offered challenge or subversion within carefully patrolled parameters: "However much canonical works may be seen to 'question' secular vanities such as wealth, social position, and political power, 're-mind' their readers of more elevated values and virtues, and oblige them to 'confront' such hard truths and harsh realities as their own mortality or the hidden griefs of obscure people, they would not be found to please long and well if they were seen to undercut establishment interests *radically* or to subvert the ideologies that support them *effectively*."

mains an important corrective to Pynchon, whose representations of blackness (American and African) too often rely on a liberal senti-mentalism indistinguishable from exoticization, and whose denun-ciations of racists and racism are welcome but sometimes cartoonish, as the character of Major Marvy (in *Gravity's Rainbow*) demonstrates.

My primary reason for emphasizing the structural position of aca-demic canons, however, is that we need to critique the institutional life/death dichotomy wherein the academy is either the passive re-cipient of cultural products endorsed by nonacademic gatekeepers and previous academic generations, or the central-cultural means of defusing marginal forces by absorbing them into the bureaucracy of institutionalism. I imply a number of ethical imperatives here—from the demand that cultural institutions account for their material prac-tices, to the requirement that academic criticism theorize its audi-ences, to the suggestion that American literature be conceived as broadly as possible—but enfolded into each of these imperatives is my conviction that these kinds of institutional self-examination can-not be solely the province of literary theory. Thus, by representing two of our institution's possible clients in the area of production now known as creative writing, and by reading texts alongside and against their receptions, I therefore hope both to practice a theory and to theorize a practice of academic criticism.[12]

In the disparity between these "clients," we can see by example how individual authors and their reception histories illumine and refract the functions of academic criticism, and how different ideas of the function of academic criticism illumine and refract the work of individual authors. For the few who have attempted to undertake Tolson studies, academic criticism appears to perform the function of the archive, the institutional means of cultural memory; for the many who have already undertaken Pynchon studies, academic crit-icism has appeared to perform the function of co-opting and de-stroying the avant-garde. *Harlem Gallery's* faith in the eventual cen-

---

[12]I am deeply indebted to various kinds of recent theoretical work, but if we are to enact our belief that theories are themselves determinate practices and that all our practices are in turn always already theoretical, then it is incumbent upon us to devise practices explicitly informed by theory, and theories that are always already articu-lated to and through practices. In developing my own negotiation of theory and prac-tice, I want to make it clear, however, that even my use of the phrase "province of literary theory," above, is not meant to invoke "theory" in the totalizing sense em-ployed by Stephen Knapp and Walter Benn Michaels (1985; 11–12, 30): I am not claiming that theory is quackery because it promises transcendental grounds it cannot provide, and I believe it is simply infinite pragmatist regress to claim that "no one can reach a position outside practice."

trality of the avant-garde is contradicted by Tolson's reception; *Gravity's Rainbow*'s critique of the Western will-to-institution is contradicted by Pynchon's reception. When the two are read against each other, each becomes the other's foil: Tolson's academic aspirations are mocked by Pynchon, but Pynchon's ignorance or dismissal of his academic reception is mocked by Tolson; Pynchon's reception demonstrates that canons are made, not born, that reception is less a matter of "time" than of serious reviews in influential intellectual journals; Tolson's reception responds that Pynchon's vaunted "marginality" is a highly privileged affair, the stance of a writer who can well afford not to cooperate in his commodification and canonization.

These various complementary contrasts, however, describe these writers' contemporary cultural positions, positions to which it is irrelevant that one is dead and one alive (though not irrelevant that one is Anglo-American and one is African-American). But these writers did not become available for critical attention or neglect at the same time, and their respective reception histories accordingly take different historical forms. As I argued in my introduction, it would thus be a mistake—albeit a common mistake—for us to reify "canonicity" and "institutionality," as if academic criticism were so monolithic in structure or purpose as to have performed one identical function in one identical fashion for fifty years or more. The first step in mapping the Tolson-Pynchon terrain, then, is to acknowledge their different historical positions relative to the critical industries of their times, for as their reception conditions vary, so too do their receptions.

The "Second Revolution" and After: Adjusting the Reception

The following chapters assume and argue that Tolson is a "modernist" poet and Pynchon a "postmodernist" novelist. I offer no exhaustive theory of modernism and postmodernism here, but I do note that these terms are often taken to be period concepts, and I recognize that an author's affiliation with one or another period has material consequences for his or her reception (since "periodicity" is at least as powerful an organizational tool as "authorship"). I note also that the transition from modernism to postmodernism marks a significant growth in the volume and importance of academic criticism to a writer's reception; after all, it is this very growth that makes possible my professionalist assumption that "canonicity" and "neglect" signify only in an academic context, rather than in some hypothetical public forum for criticism.[13]

Echoing a number of recent critics, Jonathan Culler has written that "our century has witnessed the displacement of public criticism by academic literary criticism" (1988, 3). "Displacement" may be too strong a word; we have not, or not yet, swept all the field of criticism before us. Still, our century has seen the formation of a new critical apparatus, and this apparatus has undergone extraordinary changes over some fifty years. More specifically, this "displacement" begins with the rise, in the 1940s and 1950s, of a series of related phenomena: the maturity of the New Criticism, the assumption that the business of criticism is interpretation, and the transmission of modern literature and modernist ideologies into university curricula—a transmission effected in part by major academic critics who were also practicing poets and novelists, critics such as Robert Penn Warren, John Crowe Ransom, Yvor Winters, Allen Tate, Randall Jarrell, Karl Shapiro. "It comes as no surprise," writes Bruce Robbins, "to learn that the New Criticism was a wing of the modernist vanguard. The point that deserves attention is the extent to which the procedures that the New Criticism helped install, in order to transmit and interpret the modernist canon, have remained intact—the extent to which, in other words, English has remained a modernist discipline" (1983, 238).

Charles Newman has called the institutionalization of modernism, via the New Criticism, a "second revolution" in twentieth-century letters, a "revolution in pedagogy and criticism which interpreted, canonized and capitalized the Modernist industry" (1985, 27). Yet we would err to suppose that this "revolution" was solely the doing of poet-professors, as if modernism became central to our culture because John Crowe Ransom suggested to Allen Tate that "we could really found criticism if we got together on it" (quoted in Culler 1988, 11). The phenomenon is considerably more widespread than any movement within English departments or, for that matter, within universities generally: even modernism's antagonism to mass culture is now a part of our mass culture, and one need only inspect the hair-care aisle of any supermarket to find the influence (or citation?) of Piet Mondrian on a certain line of mousse and hair spray.

[13]A corollary of this postulate is that Tolson's nonacademic reception does not "count" except insofar as it sets out the terms for his academic (non)reception; one cannot rebut my argument by assuming that Tolson's awards or newspaper acclaim somehow offset his neglect by professional critics (see the opening of Chapter 3).

As Fred Pfeil, among others, has noted, modernism's institutionaliz-ation can be said to be synonymous with the development of the American culture industry at its widest reaches: "Schönberg's revo-lution in musical language . . . creeps into the scores of countless TV programs and Hollywood films without announcing its name; surre-alism is swallowed up and surpassed by each day's crop of smugly self-mocking ads; and the hermetic self-inspection of abstract expres-sionism is converted into familiarity, even affability, on the walls of corporate lobbies" (1988, 382).

Still, whereas modernism's absorption into American business has made it standard business practice to lay bare the device, modern-ism's absorption into American departments of English and compar-ative literature has had the somewhat different effect of making modernism *classic*. Most crucial for my present purpose is that liter-ary modernism, having established itself in the academy in the 1950s, was at once retrospectively theorized as an avant-garde whose force lay in its resistance to institutionalization and whose success, to paraphrase Barbara Johnson, was therefore its failure. Richard Chase's "The Fate of the Avant-Garde," published in 1957 and reprinted often since, puts the matter succinctly: "The insurgent movement in this country which defended 'modernism'—that is, the aesthetic experimentalism and social protest of the period be-tween 1912 and 1950—has expired of its own success" (367).

At the very moment of Tolson's "conversion" to modernism, then, modernism's academic critics—themselves both agents and products of modernism's "success"—are writing the epitaphs for what modernism was. Tolson was engaging an already academic modernism, and his "modernism" is an accordingly problematic matter—as we shall see in more detail in the next two chapters. It has been argued that Tolson is nothing more than a belated modern-ist and that his belatedness is a function of his blackness.[14] Plausible as this may be, it is but half the story, for Tolson's "belatedness" gives him a unique and paradoxical vantage point on modernism's institutionalization, a vantage point from which his own modernism attempts to position itself as simultaneously academic and avant-garde.

In the next chapter I take up the question of Tolson's belatedness in order to argue that *Harlem Gallery* is not so much "in" modernism

[14]For more detailed discussion, see Sarah Webster Fabio's response to Karl Shapiro in Chapter 3; my closing argument in that chapter ("A Game of Chess on Lenox Avenue"), and the opening pages of Chapter 2.

as "about" modernism, and thereby to translate the question from the language of influence and chronology (in which Tolson becomes a modernist manqué) to a language of self-defense and self-critique (in which Tolson negotiates his relation to modernism). Here, however, I oppose Tolson's alleged belatedness to the conditions of possibility for his reception in the 1950s in order to suggest that if we insist on construing his relation to modernism as a straightforward matter of belatedness, then we are effectively recapitulating the exclusion of African-American writers from the history of modernism. Tolson missed the filing deadline for modernist poetry; he mistook for "avant-garde" what were by his time institutional means of cultural reproduction; he aspired to the wrong kind of reception: each of these arguments bypasses the question of Tolson's relation to high modernism and, in so doing, evinces the insufficiency of mere chronology to problems in literary history. To put matters starkly, we cannot ask how modernism has been transmitted in our century without also asking how we have determined who *owns* modernism in the first place.

The question is especially urgent because Tolson was, as he knew, engaging not the primary phenomena of literary modernism but a modernism on the cusp between insurgency and classicity; his sense of "modernism," consequently, may appear today to be impoverished, too heavily dependent on the importance to modern poetry of Eliot and Pound. Certainly, from the perspective of revisionists as disparate as Bonnie Kime Scott, Cary Nelson, and Houston Baker, Tolson seems simply unaware of modernisms that were not symbiotic with the development of literary study in the United States.[15] However, Tolson was far from alone in this respect: the "modernism" of Lionel Trilling, Philip Rahv, Theodor Adorno, or F. O. Matthiessen is also a modernism grounded in the subversiveness of experimentation, and a modernism whose status as an oppositional literature is derived almost wholly from the negativity of its experimentalism. In the passage quoted above, for instance, Richard Chase's canonical "modernism" allows him to conflate aesthetic experimentalism and social protest under one sign, that of an "insurgent movement" which "defended 'modernism'"—which is to say that Chase's account leaves no room for avant-garde social protest that attacked (or was at best ambivalent about) modernism, no room for Joseph Freeman, Michael Gold, *New Masses*, or, for that matter,

---

[15]For varying accounts of apocryphal modernisms (and different forms of their representation), see Baker 1987b; Nelson 1989; Scott 1990. See also Klein 1981 for the social context of modernism—and its opponents—in the United States.

writers of the Harlem Renaissance. More generally, Chase has no record of what happened to the insurgent movement in this country which defended the strikers at Passaic, New Jersey, in 1926, or the insurgent movement that made up the Abraham Lincoln Brigades a decade later; for him, these "insurgent movements" have dropped out of sight, their oppositionality subsumed under the rubric of the Euro-American avant-garde. Likewise, though Tolson's equation of the modernist avant-garde with the poetry of T. S. Eliot may seem mistaken, reductive, or, by 1950, ahistorical, it is actually the same equation as that of so central a figure as Philip Rahv, for whom even the *Four Quartets* are to be ascribed to the "venturesome spirit" of an "avant-garde which must be given credit for the production of most of the literary masterpieces of the past hundred years" (quoted in Chase 1957, 365).

Poetry magazine, in which Tolson published almost all his modernist verse in the 1950s, is a prime example both of modernism's consolidation and of Tolson's ambi-valent relation to the modernist canon (modernism's canonization). By the time Tolson first sent his work to *Poetry*, the magazine still remembered as the locus of "Chicago," "Prufrock," and "A Few Don'ts by an Imagiste" had become, in Eliot's felicitous phrase, "not a little magazine but an INSTITU-TION" (1950, 88); in fact, the phrase occurred in the pages of *Poetry* itself, in a letter to then-editor Karl Shapiro. But for whom does Eliot speak in declaring the centrality of *Poetry*? and for whom is this centrality operative, and in what way? By midcentury, African-American poets who were published in the pages of *Poetry* may have had very good reason to feel they were doing the disruptive work of an avant-garde—because by the time Tolson's modernist work appeared, *Poetry* magazine, however "institutional" its status for Europeans and Americans, had published only three African-American poets since 1940, only five since 1930.[16]

Poetry, of course, was not merely a prestigious place of publication, within whose pages the young Hugh Kenner and the aging T. S. Eliot met. By midcentury, *Poetry* was itself engaged in something of a struggle of signs, and the immediate agent thereof was none other than Karl Shapiro. One of these signs was, literally, the maga-

[16]Those three poets were Langston Hughes (fourteen poems between 1940 and 1947, in four different issues), Gwendolyn Brooks (four poems in two issues between 1944 and 1949), and Robert Hayden (one poem in 1943). The two others published in the 1930s were Sterling Brown (one poem in 1938) and Margaret Walker (three poems in three issues from 1937 to 1939). Hughes was also published once in the mid-1920s and once in the early 1930s; Countee Cullen was published five times for five poems between 1924 and 1927.

zine's motto: Shapiro, upon taking the editorial helm in 1950, moved to remove Walt Whitman's "to have great poets, there must be great audiences too," which had been reproduced each month on its back cover. The motto finally disappeared, as history would have it, in September 1951, the month Tolson's "E. & O.E." appeared. But almost forty years earlier—in a dissenting editorial in *Poetry*—Ezra Pound had likewise demanded the motto's removal on the grounds that "the artist is not dependent upon the multitude of his listeners"; though there may be a "great audience" in the sense that "the Lord of the universe sends into this world in each generation a few intelligent spirits, and these ultimately manage the rest," still, wrote Pound, "this rest—this rabble, this multitude—does *not* create the great artist" (1914a, 29–30).

Shapiro's renewal of Pound's attack on the Whitmanian "audience" is something of a historical irony, since Shapiro had almost singlehandedly created the Bollingen Prize controversy in 1948, a mere two years earlier, by opposing the Bollingen Committee's decision to award the prize to Pound for his *Pisan Cantos*. But behind this local irony lies a general consensus, a ground on which Shapiro and Pound are agreed: the necessarily antagonistic relation between great poets and "great audiences." In the March issue of 1950, in his very first month as *Poetry*'s editor, Shapiro published an essay titled "What Is Anti-Criticism?" in which he laid out his "considered statement" on modern literature and the culture industry (351). Notably, his argument relies as much on Pound as on fear and loathing of Madison Avenue:

> A great poet may indeed be popular, as may a great poem like *The Waste Land*. But its popularity is suspect; it is probably popular because it is "famous." . . . Furthermore, the popularity of a poem like *The Waste Land* is somewhat damaging to its reputation. "The thought of what America would be like / If the Classics had a wide circulation / Troubles my sleep," Pound wrote. The thought of a really popular *The Waste Land* makes us shudder. For example, parts of it would be used in advertisements. (349)

The "great audience," Shapiro concludes, is an audience interpellated by Hollywood and the Book-of-the-Month Club (although these forces are not explicitly named), and the function of the critical editor-intellectual is apparently to combine a Fugitive hatred of technocracy with a Mallarméan disdain for the language of the tribe:

> What the great audience comes to we know very well; a million people watching the same film at the same time; a million best-sellers being loaded onto freight cars.

The conception of a great audience for poetry . . . is encouraged by the decline of humanist and literary studies in the schools and universities and the substitution of technological studies. It is supported by semi-literary magazines and book reviews that work in collusion with publishers and employ the merchandising methods of tooth-paste dealers. It appeals ultimately to the base leveling instinct of the mob. (350)

This kind of rhetoric, in 1950, was hardly unique to Karl Shapiro; but that is precisely my point. Beneath the surface (though often serious) "political" differences among Tolson's various advocates, from Allen Tate to Karl Shapiro to John Ciardi, lies the common assurance that literature is important in inverse proportion to its popularity, and that magazines such as *Poetry*, far from disseminating poetry to the public, are to be distinguished from "semi-literary magazines" whose means of dissemination are tainted by their association with filthy lucre, publishers, and toothpaste.

As African-American writers stood in relation to *Poetry*, so, *mutatis mutandis*, did they stand in relation to the Modern Language Association. When Tolson published his first modernist poems in the early 1950s, he hoped to be received by a professional class of poets, critics, and professors—and to have his status ultimately secured thereby. But by 1950 the annual MLA bibliographies had accumulated only three listings of work on individual African-American writers—two books on Paul Laurence Dunbar, and a reprinted letter written over 150 years earlier by Phillis Wheatley—and the MLA had yet to hold a session on African-American writing at its annual convention. The 1950s, by contrast, were the breakthrough decade for recognition of African-American writing in the MLA bibliography, and the crucial year was 1953, which alone saw eight entries under African-American writers; by 1960, there were thirty-eight entries.[17] Since some of these notices refer to journals such as *Phylon* and *The Crisis*, which were publishing work on African-American writers well before 1952, the bibliography figures should not be taken to suggest that there was no critical writing on African-Ameri-

[17]The three listings before 1950 are Benjamin Brawley, *Paul Laurence Dunbar: Poet of his People* (Chapel Hill: University of North Carolina Press, 1937); Virginia Cunningham, *Paul Dunbar and his Song* (New York: n.p. 1947); and Benjamin Quarles, "A Phillis Wheatley Letter," *Journal of Negro History* 34 (1949):462–64. From 1952 through 1960 the MLA bibliographies list eight items under Richard Wright, six under Langston Hughes, and four under Ralph Ellison; three each under Charles Chesnutt, Zora Neale Hurston, and William Wells Brown (one of which accounts for the reprinting of his novel *Clotelle*); two each under Paul Laurence Dunbar, Lorraine Hansberry, and W. E. B. Du Bois; and one each for Claude McKay, Phillis Wheatley, Frank Yerby, James Weldon Johnson, and James Baldwin.

cans at all; rather, the figures suggest that until 1952 the MLA bibliography did not recognize articles in *Phylon* or *The Crisis* as recordable events.

MLA sessions display a similar pattern. Through 1950 there were six papers delivered specifically on "Negro folk-songs" (just as there were some notices in the bibliographies of the 1920s of work songs, ballads, and folk tales—none by specific authors). All six were presented between 1924 and 1934, and the last is surely the most remarkable: a lecture on folk songs by John Lomax, listed as "'Comments on Negro Folksongs' (illustrated with voice and guitar by *Negro convict Leadbelly of Louisiana*)" ("Proceedings" 1934, 1325; my emphasis—the program does not indicate whether Leadbelly was required to perform in handcuffs). Not until 1953 did an MLA paper discuss African-American writing as if it were an art: Blyden Jackson's "The 'Ghetto' of the Negro Novelist." Unlike the papers on folk songs, which were classed under "Comparative Literature II: Popular Literature," Jackson's paper was delivered to the discussion group on American literature. Another decade passed before African-American writing was recognized again by the MLA convention. In 1963 David Levin offered "James Baldwin: The Problem of Negro Identity" under a heading called "General Topics 6: Literature and Society," a heading that did not exist before 1938. In 1964, Jack Ludwig's paper "Bellow, Mailer, and Ellison" was also part of General Topics 6, and in 1965 the American Studies Association meeting presented "The Modern American Writer and the Cultural Experience," comprising talks by John Cheever, Norman Mailer, and Ralph Ellison. It would seem, then, that 1963 was the watershed year for official acknowledgment of African-American writing by the MLA convention.

The "institutions" to which Tolson aspired in the 1950s, therefore, need to be historicized in order to be adequately visible. Truly, *Poetry* may have lost by that time all claim to be a wing of the modernist or New Critical vanguard, and the Modern Language Association could never have been considered the locus of an avant-garde; but it does not follow from the "centrality" of these institutions that Tolson himself aspired to institutionality in the hope that his reception would be business as usual in the cultural center. Rather, both his work and his career show that he acted on the assumption that the engagement of academic modernism with the work of an African-American writer would necessarily entail modification in the cultural center, reconception of what constitutes "business as usual" in the profession of criticism.

From Tolson's position, then, there are three salient features of the institutional study of literature in the 1950s: first, the "death" of modernism, a corollary of which is the retroactive equation of modernism with oppositional writing; second, the centrality of important material witnesses to this "death"—namely, influential academic poet-critics such as Allen Tate, whose approval seemed to Tolson a prerequisite for membership in the academy; and third, the racial and social homogeneity of the decade's leading academic critics and canons. If I were concerned only with laying blame for Tolson's neglect, the third of these features would suffice for my discussion, and I could propose a version of what Michel Foucault called "the repressive hypothesis," in which powerful male, Anglo-American critics banded together to conspire against all writers unlike themselves. But as I will insist throughout this study, neglect is not always a matter of conscious, active *exclusion*; and because my interest lies more in examining the way Tolson became (un)available for academic reception than in leveling charges of racism against all Tolson's nonreaders, the racial homo- or heterogeneity of Tolson's academic audience is for me but one important factor among several.

For an accurate picture of Pynchon's relation to the profession of criticism, we have to adjust the reception in two key areas, for academic criticism since 1950 has described two seemingly contradictory motions, both of which are germane to Pynchon's position. First, though the size of the academy in the 1990s beggars comparison with that of the 1950s, the growth of academic criticism is not just a matter of increasing numbers of enrollments, appointments, course offerings, and critical journals. With growth in size has come, notoriously, a corresponding explosion in the number of functions the academy performs, an explosion in which "theory" is but a fragment. The contemporary English department not only teaches literature and literacy but is home as well to various forms of philosophy, sociology, history, anthropology, linguistics, rhetoric and communications, film, pedagogy, bibliographic and textual studies, psychoanalysis, cultural studies, women's studies, ethnic studies, and (not least) creative writing. Concomitant with this growth, however, and opposed to it, is the profession's increasing segregation from other areas of literary production, a segregation that gives rise to professional and amateur complaints that contemporary criticism is "academic" in the sense we use when we speak of an "academic" question, a question that does not matter; thus academic criticism is a criticism that serves no audience but itself, and least of all an audience of contemporary writers and readers.

In their neoconservative manifestations, such complaints take the form of nostalgia for the days of generalists, "men of letters" who

purportedly wrote for all educated persons; in their radical professionalist manifestations, such complaints amount to professional self-
aggrandisement, whereby academic criticism is seen to have taken
over the functions once performed by the field of "creative writing,"
which is currently moribund or naive, the preserve of mere fiction-
ists. This struggle, too, I ascribe to the current competition among
writers, journalists, and academic critics, which, as I have argued
above, is in part a struggle for the right to represent contemporary
and noncanonical authors. And this struggle is not what it was in
the 1940s or even the 1970s, because the recent proliferation of academic criticism has made it increasingly difficult (though not impossible, as Michele Wallace reminds us) to imagine the university as
somehow a falsification of our literary culture, as though the real
arenas of production and reception lie elsewhere, and the university's role is to discover and ossify them.

Nevertheless, the role of the university remains one of the contested issues in the relation between writers, critics, and theorists,
and the terms of the current competition are clear. Writers as variously positioned as Patrick Parrinder, Gene Bell-Villada, Reginald
Gibbons, Jonathan Culler, Sandra Gilbert, and Gerald Graff have all
remarked, to various ends, on contemporary criticism's "lack of connection to a recognized literary avant-garde" (Culler 1988, 38), its
"total and often willful separation . . . from the basic production
practices, the reasons for being, and the uses and emotions of literature" (Bell-Villada 1985, 125), its tendency to "relegate new imaginative writing to a mere sub-category of information" (Gibbons 1985,
29). I cite these polemics not in order to argue that contemporary
literature and theory should necessarily work hand in hand toward
some common goal, or to claim that professional specialization has
destroyed a once unified field of literary production and reception;
my point is simply that the present relation of criticism to "creative
writing" is thoroughly—and often needlessly—polarized.

If Sandra Gilbert charges that criticism written by contemporary
poets "seem[s] to me to be largely technical and confessional, as
though most of these writers fear that they're ill equipped to make
large judgments of either tradition or the individual talent" (1985a,
121), Patrick Parrinder countercharges that "the major critical theorists of the present day would rather reinterpret the established classics, from Plato to Virginia Woolf, than discuss contemporary poetry
or fiction" (1987, 13).[18] If Culler dares to claim that "the history of

[18]The most notorious example to date must be that of J. Hillis Miller, for whom
even Woolf is a walk on the wild side: "'Deconstruction,'" he has said, "is the current

literature in our day depends on what happens in the critical communities in the universities. . . . today the literary avant-garde simply *is* literary theory and criticism" (1988, 40), Bell-Villada is quick to
retort that the current critical culture is one of a precious "Alex-
andrianism" in which "the brisk traffic in theory-transplants is
mostly a mark of decline, its savorless fruits spawned by a subcul-
ture that has lost its larger sense of purpose and turned inward, and
whose civilized, erudite laborers toil and produce almost exclusively
for one another" (1985, 143). And if Rosalind Krauss once declared
that "Barthes and Derrida are the *writers*, not the critics, that students now read" (1980, 40), the editors of *Esquire* magazine respond
by drawing up a "guide to the literary universe" in the United States
in which academic criticism is relegated to the left-hand margin, under the dismissive heading "Lost in Space" (Hills 1987, 56).

The *Esquire* universe of 1987, in fact, almost tells the story in itself—when it is taken together with the universe mapped by the
magazine in 1963, "The Structure of the American Literary Establishment" (Hills 1963). From *Esquire*'s perspective, the primary difference between the two star charts is that "the youthful 'Cool World'
that existed . . . two dozen years ago—with its beat saints, its intellectual hipsters, and its off-Broadway playwrights—is literally missing from today's horizon" (1987, 53). To academic critics, however,
what must seem most striking is that they have dropped off the
chart entirely—and this after a twenty-four-year period in which the
growth of academic criticism (both in volume and scope) has to be
reckoned among the prominent facts of American literature.

The 1963 chart listed twenty-one influential "academic critics" as
well as nineteen additional "working critics" (who "frequently ele-
vate book reviewing to the level of criticism"), and gave to thirteen
"theoreticians" a privileged place in the scheme (if not in the "red-
hot center"): "Their conception of the nature of literary value *ultimately shapes the structure of the literary establishment*" (1963, 43; my
emphasis).

---

name for the multiple and heterogeneous strategies of overturning and displacement
that will liberate your own enterprise from what disables it" (1987, 291). But Miller's
omniliberational deconstruction does not need to challenge the canon, for as he has
stated in what Sandra Gilbert calls an "almost liturgical academic credo" (1985b, 38),
"I believe in the established canon of English and American literature and in the
validity of the concept of privileged texts. I think it is more important to read Spenser,
Shakespeare, or Milton than to read Borges in translation, or even, to say the truth, to
read Virginia Woolf" (1979, 12).

The Academic Critics. Shifting from their usual work on the classic texts for the learned journals, they frequently apply their techniques to contemporary writing. [List:] John Crowe Ransom, Harry Levin, Walter Bate, Cleanth Brooks, Robert Penn Warren, Henri Peyre, Martin Price, Louis Martz, Leslie Fiedler, Mark Schorer, Richard Ellmann, Leon Edel, Lionel Trilling, Jacques Barzun, F. W. Dupee, Eric Bentley, Albert Guerard, Carlos Baker, Warren Beck, Allen Tate, Hugh Kenner.

The Theoreticians. William K. Wimsatt, Austin Warren, René Wellek, Northrop Frye, Ronald Crane, I. A. Richards, Philip Wheelwright, R. P. Blackmur, Mike Abrams, Yvor Winters, Kenneth Burke, Richard McKeon, Wayne C. Booth.

The Working Critics. Alfred Kazin, Granville Hicks, Robert Gorham Davis, Malcolm Cowley, Edmund Wilson, Anthony West, Paul Pickrel, Arthur Mizener, John Aldridge, Mary McCarthy, Elizabeth Hardwick, Steven Marcus, Norman Podhoretz, Ted Solotaroff, Dwight Mac-Donald, George Steiner, Ihab Hassan, Stanley Edgar Hyman, John Simon. (1963, 43)

In the introduction to the chart, we read that although "the Ivory Tower is without direct commercial influence," still, "the estimates of the central Ivory Tower group—the aestheticians—do filter down; and as they do, values change and reputations change" (1963, 41).

No such trickle-down theory can be found in the 1987 list, which takes account of not a single academic critic, and declares Michiko Kakutani of the *New York Times* the only critic "who [*sic*] serious people take at all seriously" (1987, 53). By 1987, the category of "working critics" has vanished, its place taken simply by "The Critics," a list that includes professional reviewers only: Kakutani, John Gross, and Christopher Lehmann-Haupt of the *Times*; Mike Levitas, editor of the *New York Times Book Review*; Richard Eder, *Los Angeles Times*; Barbara Epstein and Robert Silvers, *New York Review of Books*; Stefan Kanfer, *Time*; Peter Prescott, *Newsweek*; Jonathan Yardley, *Washington Post*; and Robert Wilson, *USA Today*.

I do not intend the juxtaposition of these lists to suggest that *Esquire* is a reliable measure of academic criticism's loss of audience; its 1987 literary universe is impoverished by any standard, including the magazine's own 1963 standard. Academic criticism actually fares no worse in this latest "universe" than does nonfiction or poetry (the latter of which is also "lost in space"), for "literature" in *Esquire*'s language means only "fiction."[19] Whereas the 1963 list re-

---

[19]The 1987 list includes a category given over to "Heavenly Bodies" ("*Gliterati, nonfiction division*") and peopled by writers such as Joan Didion, Jules Feiffer, David Halb-

minded itself that it was a description only of the *American* literary establishment, the 1987 version adopts no such national qualifier, apparently because a description of American fiction *is* a description of the literary universe: we are the world. Finally, academic criticism cannot feel too severely indicted by a map that places the following six writers in its "red-hot center": Saul Bellow, Raymond Carver, Elmore Leonard, Gordon Lish, Norman Mailer, and John Updike. This, declares *Esquire*, is "by absolutely no definition a unified group" (1987, 53), which leads one to surmise that the center is composed simply of (white) man at his best.

Yet even if we say of *Esquire* what Culler says of the *New York Review*—that in joining the "middle-brow opposition" to academic criticism it succeeds "only in depriving itself of influence in the domain of contemporary criticism and revealing to what extent criticism [has] become a university enterprise" (1988, 24)—then we are only arguing with *Esquire* point by counterpoint over whose red-hot center is more central, and what the center is central to. For all my confidence about the centrality of academic critics to the production of canonicity, I myself have to acknowledge that *Esquire* is neither alone nor simply philistine in thinking that the state of American letters can be described without reference to contemporary criticism and theory. For the fields of creative writing and criticism, as I have been arguing, are currently segregated and often in rhetorical and even institutional conflict—a phenomenon of which the division of graduate study in English into Ph.D. and M.F.A. programs is both sign and symptom (Gibbons 1985, 28; Gilbert 1985a, 121).

The result, for now, is that this separation of fields has created two distinct arenas of literary criticism, two distinct prestige systems, neither of which is professionally relevant to the other. The recent debates in creative writing—over the "new minimalism," the function of M.F.A. programs, and Tom Wolfe's call for a new social realism, to take some notable examples—have proceeded, for the

---

erstam, Renata Adler, Ken Auletta, Susan Sontag, Calvin Trillin, and Tom Wolfe (to name half). But then again, readers are warned in Rust Hills's introduction: "You'll find few poets. No playwrights. . . . no reprints at all. . . . no editors or agents specializing in nonfiction, however literary. For reasons of space and sanity, you'll also find few non–North American authors here" (1987, 55). Reasons of space, however, did not prevent the magazine from devoting more pages of its August issue to photos of writers in fashion sweaters than to pages describing the (North American) literary universe. Simply put, *Esquire*'s is an extreme-bourgeois confinement of the word "literature"—and insofar as the magazine opposes the term "*literary*" to the term "*commercial*" in a spread meant to record and enhance the commercial status of "central" writers, its "confinement" is marked by familiar haut-bourgeois contradictions as well.

most part, in different loci, different vocabularies, and different pub-
lications from the recent debates over agency, affirmation, history,
representation, and the subject in "criticism." The problem is not
that there are so few poet-critics; the problem is that there are so few
poet-critics who are read and cited in both kinds of contemporary
criticism, the kind published in *Antaeus* and the kind published in
Diacritics. Adrienne Rich is perhaps the most notable exception here,
as a major contemporary poet whose essays (and poems) are also
acknowledged to be foundational works of feminist theory; but if so,
she is the exception who proves the rule.

Thus it is that many of the claims made for Pynchon's "marginality" rest on his refusal to cooperate in, protest against, or even
acknowledge his academic reception. Pynchon's difficult and apparently resolute obliviousness to the academy is clearest in his introduction to *Slow Learner*, the 1984 collection of his early short stories.
About his reception, academic or nonacademic, he is utterly silent,
preferring instead to retell the story of the impact of Beat anti-aca-
demicism in the 1950s (1984b, xv–xviii); and the piece closes with an
inexplicable potshot at his most often reprinted (and most often
taught) novel, *The Crying of Lot 49*, "in which I seem to have forgotten most of what I thought I'd learned up till then" (xxxiv). Moreover, the introduction explicitly names its intended audience, and
that audience does not include professors: "My best hope is that,
pretentious, goofy and ill-considered as they get now and then,
these stories will still be of use with all their flaws intact, as illustra-
tive of typical problems in entry-level fiction, and cautionary about
some practices which younger writers might prefer to avoid" (xii).

Critics have generally found the introduction puzzling, not least
because Pynchon claims that "it is simply wrong to begin with a
theme, symbol, or other abstract unifying agent, and then try to
force characters and events to conform to it" (xxi) and "simply, as
we say in the profession, ass backwards" to "go about writing a
story . . . without some grounding in human reality" (xxviii), lest
you "get too conceptual, too cute and remote, and your characters
die on the page" (xxiii). But equally startling, surely, is Pynchon's
insistence that he really doesn't know very much about entropy,
that only because his short story "Entropy"

> has been anthologized a couple–three times [do] people think I know
> more about the subject of entropy than I really do. Even the normally
> unhoodwinkable Donald Barthelme has suggested in a magazine inter-
> view that I had some kind of proprietary handle on it. . . . I've been
> able to follow the *OED* definitions, and the way Isaac Asimov explains

it, and even some of the math. But the qualities and quantities will not come together to form a unified notion in my head. . . . When I think about the property nowadays, it is more and more in connection with time, that human, one-way time we're all stuck with locally here, and which terminates, it is said, in death. (xxii, xxiv–xxv)

As far as Pynchon is concerned, that is, he has been linked to such concepts not because of their extended treatment in *The Crying of Lot 49* or *Gravity's Rainbow*, not because dozens upon dozens of articles have been written about Pynchon and the metaphors of science, but simply because anthologists and Donald Barthelme have insinuated that Pynchon and entropy go hand in hand—when in reality he knows little more than any of us who have checked the *Oxford English Dictionary* and Isaac Asimov.

It is possible to read against that introduction, as Richard Poirier has done, to show that Pynchon is a flawed reader of his own work (1985, 18–19); it is possible too to suppose, as Thomas Moore has done, that *Slow Learner* "is partly intended to prepare the ground for . . . a new novel" (1987, 18 n.27), and that academic critics will indeed find ways to read *Vineland* according to the "ground" and direction Pynchon has supposedly given us in *Slow Learner*. But can it really be possible that Pynchon has no idea of, nothing to say about, his status as one of the most written-about postwar writers in English?[20] Does he know or care that Harold Bloom calls him "the crucial American writer of prose fiction at the present time" and defines the present time as "the Age of John Ashbery and of Thomas Pynchon"? (1986, 1). Perhaps the introduction is merely passively hostile to Pynchon's academic reception, for perhaps he is ignorant of his academic reception. Or perhaps Pynchon is more or less aware of his status in academia, and the introduction is *actively* hostile in its refusal to mention *V.* or *Gravity's Rainbow*, in its condescension toward *The Crying of Lot 49*, and in its exclusive address to other creative writers. Are these two possibilities very different from each other? Whether Pynchon is writing to spite or in spite of academic Pynchon, the polarization between literary production and institutional consumption is the same: it is as if Pynchon the M.F.A. instructor were conducting an impromptu workshop on his early stories, blithely unaware of the gathering, down the hall, of graduate seminars and professional symposia on his major work. For all that his novels have done to bridge C. P. Snow's "two cultures," Pynchon himself has nevertheless remained caught between the cul-

[20]For a quantitative measure of Pynchon's reception in relation to that of other postmodern and canonical writers, see Appendix B.

ture of "writing" and the culture of "criticism," as though *these* two cultures spoke in languages each incomprehensible to the other.[21]

Canonicity, Representation, Author Function

The work of Tolson and Pynchon is informed by their respective academic conditions of reception, and these conditions of reception are also, by necessity, the conditions for their reproduction. So much could be said for almost any American writer in the past fifty years, but in *Harlem Gallery* and *Gravity's Rainbow* we can find explicit treatments of the agents and institutions of cultural reproduction. In each work we could be said to find representations of canonicity and canon making; and since canonicity is itself a mode of cultural representation, we will need to distinguish among the levels and meanings of "representation" that this kind of reception study entails. I want to deploy three associated senses of canonicity as "representation": first, the standard democratic-republican sense, in that texts and authors are represented in canons; second, the sense in which the canonical text is taken synecdochically to be representative *of* something, under any and all critical paradigms; third and most important, the legal sense, wherein "representation" denotes the function performed by academic critics for author-clients.

That canonicity is a form of representation has been eloquently stated by Robert Weimann:

> As a cultural institution, a literary canon may be defined as a publicly circulating, usable body of writing which, by definition, is held to be as much representative of certain national or social interests and traditions as it is unrepresentative and exclusive of others. In fact, the very representativity of this privileged body of writing appears as a sine qua non for its function as a tradition or heritage, for receiving and projecting patterns of social, cultural, and national identity. (1988, 68)

This idea of representativity, underwritten as it is by an entire discursive practice of "representation" in which words represent things, critics represent the true (universal) meanings of texts, and texts represent life, human nature, or the fullest flowering of a national spirit—this idea persists, according to Weimann, through the era of modernism and New Criticism:

> The modernist poet-critic [specifically, but not limited to, Eliot] only reaffirmed, through his revisions, the function of poetry and the role of the poet as traditionally conceived in nineteenth-century society. The

---

[21]For Pynchon's argument that "the two-cultures quarrel can no longer be sustained," see Pynchon 1984a, 1.

poet's major creation, like Goethe's *Faust*, was to be representative of the highest aspirations of mankind; the poet himself was, as Emerson put it, a "representative man." There was a connection, I suggest, between the culturally representative role of literary discourse in society and the similar function which a canon, as an institution of cultural identity and regeneration, was designed to serve. (73)

We will see these "modernist" assumptions of authorship and representation at work more fully in the following chapter, but before I discuss *Harlem Gallery* in detail, let me stress once more that Tolson's gallery is a museum, his protagonist is a curator, and the curator's task concerns the representation of great African-American art in a gallery run by commercial interests (though, significantly, it is a *Harlem* gallery, and not a special wing of the Metropolitan Museum of Art). Tolson himself tried for much of his professional life to earn representation in a color-blind canon of modernist poetry, and his major work is not only, in Weimann's words, "representative of the highest aspirations of mankind" but intended also as a re-presentation of the history of African-American poetry in the twentieth century, from blues lyrics and toasts to pre-1960s experimentalism. For Tolson, in other words, representation via institutionalization is not merely "access"; rather, (my construction of) Tolson mobilizes all three of the definitions of "representation" sketched out above—democratic representation, representation *of* (in this case, of the challenges and difficulties of an African-American modernism similar to and simultaneously different from Anglo-American modernism), and legal representation. Tolson's aspiration to canonicity is in all these ways a multivalent faith in the representativity of canonicity, insofar as canonicity would both re-present him and his work and make him available for further cultural representation.

Tolson's faith, as we know, is no longer professed by much of the profession. And as Weimann construes them, our recent crises of canonicity and representation are part of a more general postmodern condition, part of a "larger response to the radical unrepresentativeness of cultural discourse in a society in which the appropriation of a usable part in relation to some common pursuit of social purpose in the present has become an almost impossible undertaking" (1988, 73). Yet it is in the midst of these crises of representation, paradoxically, that Pynchon has achieved canonical status; if Tolson pledged himself to an ideal of canonicity which he never achieved and which academic criticism can no longer sustain, then Pynchon might be said to have attacked representation and representationalism in ways that have made him one of our period's representative authors. Thus, as we might expect, a postmodern Pynchon critiques representation *in* his texts, from the representationalism of narrative realism to the construction of "reasonable facsimiles" of any kind: "no difference between a boxtop and its image," thinks Slothrop, "all right, their whole economy's based on *that*" (Pynchon 1973, *GR* 472). But more sweepingly, this postmodern Pynchon also makes impossible, for many reasons, a traditional conception of his canonicity. For if the canonical author and text are representative cultural artifacts, Pynchon has brought academic criticism face to face with its burden of representation, because he has left it entirely up to his critics to determine what he and his work represent; and even as he eschews the function of the Emersonian representative man, critics hasten to place him safely in the tradition of Emerson (Poirier 1976, 29; Bloom 1986, 9).

This is an issue to which I return in my final chapter, but that discussion of Pynchon's "plurality" is based on the dilemma I present here: whereas a Tolsonian ideal of representation demands that critics take up Tolson's case in order to re-present Tolson as representative "of," a Pynchonian interrogation of representation implicitly indicts all kinds of canon formation. From a Pynchonian perspective, one might ask:

> What else is the projection of a canon, if not—in the language of poststructuralism—the attempt to homogenize discursive space, to suppress discontinuity in favor of some stabilizing hierarchy, to assert some transcendental signified, some unexamined authority such as "order" or, as obvious alternatives, "experience," or "human nature"? And is not, then, this type of authority easily used as some universalizing tool of obliteration, expropriation, and exclusion? (Weimann 1988, 69–70)

In other words, the "authority" constructed by academic criticism yields an amalgamative canon that suppresses both Pynchon's "difference" and his objections to canonicity. Such an understanding of canonicity, however, leaves academic criticism back in the familiar position of co-opting and assimilating oppositions and challenges to it. If on the other hand we agree that "canonicity is not a property of the work itself but of its transmission" (Guillory 1987, 494), then we should recall that even the most monolithic canons have to be continually transmitted in some way and therefore cannot serve one eternal, fixed function. For in the processes of cultural transmission, all representation, even canonical representation, is also misrepresentation. This is not just a fashionable academic slogan; it applies to canonicity, to republican electoral politics, and to the courtroom as well.[22] In every transmission there is interference and noise, and every representation is a construction; or, as Edmund Spenser might have put it, even a work so canonical as *The Faerie Queene* is eternal only in its mutability.

Moreover, it is not the case that we must treat either Tolson or Pynchon in accordance with their assumptions or indictments of canonicity and representation, as if we were constrained to do each author "justice" by alternately representing or declining to represent him, or as if we were representing not authors but their estates and were compelled accordingly to abide by their wills. Reception is not the servant of author-ity, and authority itself is not necessarily traceable to writers as biological/biographical entities who wield "power" and "influence." These are tenets to which even practiced canon revisionists do not always adhere, and to clarify them, I will detour once more through the thickets of reception theory, this time to discover the status of our putative client, the "author."

Jan Mukarovsky's student and explicator, Felix Vodicka (1941) has spoken of the reader's "concretization" of a work, borrowing the neologism from Roman Ingarden but detaching it from Ingarden's theory of ideal readers filling in "gaps" or "places of indeterminacy."[23] For Vodicka, no concretization exists apart from its relation to the aesthetic norm, which, as Mukarovsky had argued, is historically and socially variable; thus, there can be no final, comprehensive concretization of any work. Indeed, in a strict sense there can be no concretization of a "work" at all, for, as Mukarovsky writes, "the direct object of everyday aesthetic evaluation is not a 'material' artifact, but an 'aesthetic object' which is its expression and correlate in the viewer's awareness" (1936, 90). It follows that even "when a certain work in two chronologically separate periods is evaluated affirmatively and equally, the aesthetic object being evaluated is a different one in each case, and hence, in some sense, is a different work" (61), and that the same work gives rise to different aesthetic objects in various social strata, which have various relations to the dominant stratum's aesthetic norm. According to Mukarovsky:

[22]The most severe elaboration of this principle I have come across, one that critiques political representation as a "falsification of democracy" and advocates instead "people's congresses," is Muammar al-Qaddafi's *Green Book*, Part 1: "The Solution of the Problem of Democracy" (1976, esp. 7–12, 23–30).

[23]For an account of the relation between Ingarden's theory and Wolfgang Iser's (and trenchant criticism of the idealism of both), see Holub 1984, 22–29, 83–85, 92–95.

The aesthetic function can also become a socially differentiating factor; cp. the greater sensitivity toward the aesthetic function, and its more intensive utilization, in the higher levels of society which attempt to distinguish themselves from the other social levels (the aesthetic function as a factor in "prestige"), or the deliberate use of the aesthetic function to stress the importance of people in power, as well as to separate them from the rest of the collective (e.g., the clothing of the actual people in power or of their subordinates, their residences, etc.). (21–22)

Contemporary readers may be familiar with these formulations, if only because they sketchily anticipate by a generation the more extensive work of Stanley Fish and Pierre Bourdieu. What is valuable, for my purposes, in Vodicka's extension of Mukarovsky is his use of Mukarovskian structuralism to account for the position of the critic (as the arbiter—and arbitrator—of specific aesthetic norms) and, most of all, his understanding of authorship as sign. As Vodicka phrases it, his concern is not with the author "as a psychophysical being but, in a metonymical sense, as the unity comprised of the works of a particular author in their entirety" (1941, 123). Authorship itself is thereby subject to social processes of concretization, which, in dialogue with specific works and amalgams of works, produces "a generalized concretization of the author coming from within the work but existing without it" (124).

A reception theory conversant with the competing claims of Prague structuralism, cultural studies, and Fish's "interpretive communities"—cf. Mukarovsky's "concrete collectives" (1936, 18–23)— thus has some warrant to suggest the term "authorization," since the concretization specific to canonization is the result of a complex series of readings, some of which simultaneously create and depend on the creation of the concretization of authors.[24] Canonicity is therefore partly a matter of mapping out major works and, as Alastair Fowler has written, partly a matter of positioning works within the canonical hierarchy of genres (1982, 226–34). But it is also, crucially, a matter of assigning author *functions*, of determining what—and *who*—the representative / writer will be representative of. For we may have done away with the Romantic idea of the "author" as the source and plenum of meaning, but we have not begun, nor could we begin, to dismantle authorship *as metonymic sign* (relational and differential), both because of the semiotic importance of authorship as an element structuring the expectations we bring to any determinate reading and, more obviously, because of our industry's prag-

[24]See Vodicka 1941 and Striedter 1989, 121–54, for an introduction to authors, critics, and concretizations in the Czech structuralist sense.

matic, pedagogical reliance on "authorship" as a heuristic tool in everything from course proposals to conference organization.

Hence, "authorization" is not an attribute of authors so much as a result of authors' complex interactions with readers, agents, publishers, reviewers, award committees, and other institutions—which is to say that the study of authorization, like Rodden's sociological study of literary reputation (1989), attends to the ways authors are put into discourse in the widest possible sense. "Put into discourse" is Foucault's phrase, and on a number of points Foucault, Mukarovsky, and Vodicka are agreed: authors, as subjects and as signs, are produced differentially by complex signifying systems. Tony Bennett, following Foucault's "discursive formations," has thus described "reading formations," "a set of intersecting discourses that productively activate a given body of texts and the relations between them in a specific way" (1983b, 5); and, of course, the author function (unlike its pedagogical cousins the genre function and the period function) has long worked both to activate and stabilize a body of texts as the *corpus* of the individual. Nevertheless, in Foucault's words, the sign of the *author* "does not refer purely and simply to a real individual, since it can give rise simultaneously to several selves, to several subjects—positions that can be occupied by different classes of individuals" (1984, 113). Foucault's author is thus a decentered author: if we are to answer the question that gives his essay its title—"what is an author?"—Foucault suggests that doing so "is a matter of depriving the subject (or its substitute) of its role as originator, and of analyzing the subject as a variable and complex function of discourse" (118).

In more general language, we can say that the cultural work authors are allowed to perform hinges in part on the kinds of authors they are understood to be, but we must add the proviso that Foucault's "variable and complex function[s] of discourse" operate even when, as in this book, we are dealing with authors who are both considered to be authors of "literature." For although Tolson and Pynchon may be similar kinds of authors in Foucault's sense— they are neither scientists nor "founders of discursivity" like Marx and Freud (114)—their similarity should not be taken to imply that we have exhaustively described their "functions" when we have determined that their proper names function in broadly similar ways in relation to their works. As Foucault notes, "In a civilization like our own there are a certain number of discourses that are endowed with the 'author function,' while others are deprived of it" (107); but this distinction holds not only for the distinction between writers of novels and writers of laundry lists (as Foucault has it) but, in a more mundane fashion, for the distinction between canonical and noncanonical "literary" authors as well.

The multivalence of my appropriation of "author function"—in which I elide the term with the Marxist notion of the author as cultural producer and the Czech structuralist conception of author as metonymic sign[25]—is exacerbated by Foucault's essay itself, which concludes by discussing the term in two dissimilar ways. First, he employs "author function" as a means of examining "a typology of discourse" that seeks to unravel a discourse's "relationship (or non-relationship) with an author, and the different forms this relationship takes." Such a study Foucault calls "an introduction to the historical analysis of discourse," which examines discourses "not only in terms of their expressive value or formal transformations, but according to their modes of existence," and which attends above all to their "modes of circulation, valorization, attribution, and appropriation" (117). Two paragraphs later, however, in reviewing "the 'ideological' status of the author," he describes a "functional principle" in which the "author" becomes "the ideological figure by which one marks the manner in which we fear the proliferation of meaning." Under this second definition, the author is an apparatus for Foucauldian "confinement," "the regulator of the fictive, a role quite characteristic of our era of industrial and bourgeois society, of individualism and private property." (118–19). The first of these definitions mandates, on my reading, the kind of interactive reception study I have undertaken here; the second marks the author as an "ideological product" (119) secured in law by the copyright and in criticism by theorists of intentionality (cf. Barthes 1977, 160–61).

Nothing necessarily excludes this second definition from consideration here; in fact, the succeeding chapters recall it on two occasions. But it is not as germane to reception study as is the first, and—more to the immediate point—it needs to be distinguished from the first in any case. The definitions are not diametrically opposed; one can create for an author a reliable and replicable author function by invoking a restrictive "author function," as I argue in Chapter 3 with reference to my reading of T. S. Eliot's *The Waste Land*. But I have serious reservations about construing the author

[25]See Striedter 1989, 83–119, on Czech structuralism's unique negotiations of formalism and Marxism: "In this context it should be remarked that Czech Marxism in the thirties, unlike Russian Marxism in the twenties (in its altercations with Formalism) and unlike Czech Marxism after 1948, was not yet the binding political philosophy. This facilitated open discussion and made it possible to accept or reject critical arguments by reason of their systematic validity rather than to make an outward show of conformity or in self-defense" (86).

function as an authoritative limit on anything other than permissions rights, for I am not calling for the death of the author in order to liberate the proliferation of meaning. Nor do I have to; my sense is that despite Foucault's remark about our fear of meaning, "meaning-proliferation" like nuclear proliferation takes place on a daily basis whether or not we think we have secure, international (industrial, bourgeois) limits on its spread. If the "author function" is supposed to set boundaries on "legitimate" interpretations of Milton or Joyce (or Orwell), it must be a very weak function after all.

Then again, this can be said only of our most canonical texts, which, as every professional critic knows, now generate a truly staggering number of exegeses every year. Let me make clear, then, that canonical representation is a highly privileged, wholly institutional form of authorization, which involves the creation and maintenance of major and minor authors who are authorized to speak from and through cultural centers—sometimes in their own defense, but more usually through critics as their legal-but-contested representatives. But just as canonical "representation" may be alternately a means of making texts publically available and a strategy for eliminating difference, so too the term "authorization" holds forth no guarantees. It does not ground in advance what texts may be authorized to do, because, for one thing, no one can secure in advance what functions academic critics will themselves be authorized to perform.

Authorization, then, is not synonymous with canonization. It is constituted only by the most minimal perception requisite to reception, which means that it is simultaneously less coercive and more precarious than canonicity. It remains a threshold term: all texts in print are in that sense (and that sense only) authorized for further use in that they are "given" an author who remains current (and who remains an item of currency, in the temporal and economic senses). A small number of texts assigned author functions are also assigned the "aesthetic function," which, if I may borrow again from Mukarovsky, means that they are authorized to be read "as literature" (and not as diet books). A still smaller number of literary texts qualify as Ohmann's "precanonical" works; and very, very few of these—the "critical canon" (Fowler 1982, 215) that has survived even the challenges of the past twenty years—are licensed for exegesis by the entire profession of literary study.

To arrange these Chinese boxes another way, I might say that any work must be somehow concretized, therefore somehow *interpreted*, to be "authorized"; but only a small handful of texts so authorized are authorized for the kind of interpretation practiced by contemporary criticism. Ludwig Wittgenstein writes: "'Seeing-as . . .' is not part of perception. And for that reason it is like seeing and again not like" (1945, II.xi, 197e). That is, the object first has to be *seen* to be *seen as*; or, to move closer to home, the text has to be granted the status of "text" (and not, say, "fly swatter") in order to be inserted into the various structures of "reading as" that make up any reading practice whatsoever. When confronted with *Harlem Gallery*, for instance, we first understand (or, when all else fails, argue) that the object "is" a text and is, furthermore, the kind of text to which we normally attribute the author function. These are matters of interpretation, of "seeing as," just as one could say that the "initial" act of perception was itself interpretive. But in the sense we more commonly apply whenever we speak of a particular critic's *interpretation* of Tolson, "interpretation" is a culturally specific, culturally learned form of reading that proposes to establish a work's "meaning." Interpretation in this sense, of course, takes place well above the threshold of authorization.

As a threshold term, therefore, "authorization" in my sense recognizes that many authorized texts go largely uninterpreted. Tolson's neglect, in particular, shows us that for a text or an author to problematize interpretation, canonicity, and representation at all, it/he/she must be somehow authorized to do so in the first place. Thus it is that recognition (in this case, professional authorization) of Tolson's work by the academic cultural center can be effected not primarily by a glorious paradigm-shift but by the quotidian cultural work of an ongoing research program, which, given my methodological assumptions, would take the form of an academic conversation registered institutionally as a reliable number of Tolson entries in each year's MLA bibliography.[26] For authorization at the academic level means the creation of author functions that generate interpretations, and such author functions are not a simple matter of fixing this or that discrete representation, this or that specific interpretation of a work; they are the very devices by which representativity is determined.[27]

[26]The phrase "reliable number" may seem to be a waffle, but my point is that unless reception reaches some quantifiable critical mass, the number of bibliography entries cannot be reliable, for in the absence of broadly understood research programs on critical problems, critical conversations simply become too irregular and sporadic to carry on. I suggest, therefore, that a given number of annual entries (in Pynchon's case, the number is usually in the high twenties, and in 1983 leaped into the fifties) indicates that research is being undertaken on what researchers consider salient objects of inquiry in authors and texts—and that, conversely, underneath threshold numbers there are no research programs because there is no baseline agreement as to what constitutes important problems in the field.

[27]To quote Weimann one final time: "The representing and the represented may

Allow me, in closing this chapter, to leave this level of abstraction for a moment and descend to an elementary and pervasive example. Tolson, like all African-American writers, was expected throughout his career, by both white and black critics and readers, to "represent" his race and to be somehow authorized to "speak for the Negro." No one to my knowledge has ever asked that Pynchon speak for white Americans, or for New York suburbanites, or for descendants from the Puritans; Anglo-American writers are not commonly asked to shoulder the representation of Anglo-Americans in toto. As long as Anglo-Americans are not generally considered by other Anglo-Americans to possess the attribute of *race*, there will simply be nothing for Anglo-Americans to represent on this score, whereas there has been no treatment of Tolson—from outright dismissal to high praise—which has not made an issue of the extent to which Tolson represents African-American poets. If authorization—and, finally, canonization—is accordingly a different affair for writers of different races, it is precisely because American writers of different races have historically been assigned radically different author functions.

This much will be clear, though somewhat newly phrased, to any student (or practitioner) of American literature, and I will not belabor the obvious. Instead, I will move directly to my own authors, whom I will attempt to represent, as clients, in good faith. The following four chapters, divided between analyses of texts and analyses of receptions, will necessarily project author functions for Tolson and Pynchon, and thereby authorize Tolson and Pynchon, as they simultaneously report on and critique the ways these authors have been made to function. Though I do not claim to be able to see Tolson and Pynchon steadily and see them whole, I do believe I have set out the tools for a composite sketch of their major works and their cultural positions. For the more difficult fragment of this sketch, I turn first to the unauthorized, the marginal, the noncanonical—to Melvin Tolson, and the exhibits of the Harlem Gallery.

---

incongruously clash, but they may also engage in areas of concurrence," and thus "representation [i.e., authorization] becomes a site of sociolinguistic contradiction, a site of social and cultural struggle, where authority itself is dramatized" (1988, 79).

CHAPTER 2

Tolson's Negativity:
Harlem Gallery and the
Idea of an Avant-Garde

IN LATE May 1955, a small black college in Oklahoma put on what was only the second American college production of Jean-Paul Sartre's *No Exit* (Princeton had staged the first). The college was Langston University; the locus was the Dust Bowl Theatre; and the director, a Langston University professor, was both the founder of the Dust Bowl and the mayor of the town of Langston—Melvin Tolson. As poet laureate of Liberia, Tolson dedicated *No Exit*'s premiere to the Liberian ambassador to the United States, Clarence L. Simpson. In November of the same year, the Dust Bowl Theatre staged Langston Hughes's *Simply Heavenly*, a play about the further adventures of Jessie B. Simple (Hughes's alternative title: "Simple Takes a Wife"), also under Tolson's direction. Sartre, Hughes, Ambassador Simpson, Dust Bowl: such, in brief, is one cross-section of the breadth of Tolson's cultural purview; such is the extent of Tolson's claims on disparate cultural realms. How remarkable it is, then, that even what little attention Tolson has so far received has tended to discuss his neglect, unilaterally, by casting his modernism as a historical anomaly. It has been said that *Harlem Gallery* rolled off the presses "just as Eliot and the New Criticism began to wane as dominant forces in literary fashion," leaving Tolson "momentarily out of step" (Farnsworth 1979, 255); that "while Tolson busied himself out-pounding Pound, his fellow poets forgot to send him the message that Pound was out" (Fabio 1966, 57); and simply, that "the timing was bad for such a complex piece" (Dove 1985, 109).

Whatever the relative merits of these claims (and they are not without merit), the result so far—a quarter-century and more after Tolson's death—has been that, in Raymond Nelson's words, Tolson "may be the most elusive, most endangered of important American poets" (1986, 271). Yet Tolson is not merely another example of the visionary artist overlooked by his contemporaries: we confront here a situation both more complex and more poignant. More poignant because of the manifold ironies of Tolson's position—not least among them the irony that he has been disdained by the academy even as he has been disdained by African-American critics precisely for having written academic verse. More complex because in an important sense most of the accounts cited above are doubly mistaken: first, in that Tolson's neglect does not hinge entirely on his poetic practice, and second, in that modernism did not just go "out of style."

On the latter count, to be sure, some of the confusion was created by Tolson himself: he spoke repeatedly of modern poetry as if it were somehow historically inevitable, as if its "revolution" were at once totalizing and irreversible. He writes, for instance, in his review of Jacques and Raissa Maritain's *The Situation of Poetry*, that "when T. S. Eliot published *The Waste Land* in 1922, it sounded the death knell of Victorianism, Romanticism, and Didacticism. When Eliot was awarded the Nobel Prize in Literature, the victory of the moderns was complete. . . . The modern idiom is here to stay—like modern physics" (1955, 113–14). The curious terms of Tolson's certainty—he participates in the professionalist desire to link the humanities to the prestige of the sciences on the basis of their new-found "difficulty"—are worth remarking, but even more curious is the focus on Eliot's Nobel Prize as the sign of modernism's "victory." It is small wonder, therefore, that *Harlem Gallery*'s more hostile critics read Tolson as if he were simply out of touch, a late modernist writing in the midst of the Black Aesthetic of the 1960s. Only after the Nobel Prize was awarded to Eliot, apparently, did Tolson decide that modernism would leave behind the poets who did not confront and assimilate it; accordingly, his reaction, self-consciously belated, seems something of an overcompensation. Witness his declaration, in a 1948 address at Kentucky State College:

Now the time has come for a New Negro Poetry for the New Negro. The most difficult thing to do today is to write modern poetry. Why? It is the acme of the intellectual. Longfellow, Whittier, Milton, Tennyson, and Poe are no longer the poets held in high repute. The standard of poetry has changed completely. Negroes must become aware of this.

This is the age of T. S. Eliot who has just won the Nobel Prize in Literature. If you know Shakespeare from A to Z, it does not mean you can
read one line of T. S. Eliot! *But Negro poets and professors must master
T. S. Eliot!* (TM; my emphasis)

This speech seems to me at least as striking as his Maritain review
of seven years later—for its ambiguous commitment to the politics
and poetics of assimilation (who is to master whom here?) and for
the thoroughness of its adoption of modernist polemics; his dismissal of Milton and Tennyson is an especially accurate touch. And
sure enough, in his "New Negro Poetry"—"E. & O.E." in 1951 and
Libretto for the Republic of Liberia in 1953—he deliberately and pedan-
tically suggests his affiliation with *The Waste Land* by appending to
each poem pages of footnotes, like Eliot's both explanatory and obscure. But despite such testimony, and despite even the grain of
truth in the characterization of Tolson as a modernist poet out of
date, I intend to show that *Harlem Gallery* is neither explained nor
contained by descriptions of literary fashion and its author's belatedness, that Tolson's reception is not just a regrettable accident of
literary history.

To begin with, *Harlem Gallery* is not so much an artifact, a fossil, of
modernist poetry as it is an enactment of the contradictory poetic
and cultural claims of that poetry. On one hand, this amounts to
saying that Tolson's "embrace" of modernism in *Harlem Gallery* goes
far beyond the mere imitation of Eliot's and Pound's difficult techniques of allusion, compression, and ellipsis—that Tolson embraced
not merely a technique but an entire ideology. On the other hand, it
also suggests that, oddly enough, Tolson was right to think that
"the modern idiom is here to stay"—but that it is here to stay in a
way none of Tolson's critics have realized. The influence of Eliot and
the New Critics has unquestionably waned as a force in the production of literature, giving way to, among other things, Beats and
Black Aesthetics; nevertheless, the legacy of modernism—namely,
an academy that fulfills the modernist impulse to create a literature
to be studied rather than read[1]—has changed irrevocably the practices of criticism, annotation, and explication on which Tolson's life-
work self-consciously depends. And as I argued in Chapter 1, the

[1] I am thinking not only of Joseph Frank's famous line that Joyce (and, by extension,
modernists generally) "cannot be read—[they] can only be re-read" (1948, 385) but
also of Roland Barthes's opening remark in *S/Z* that rereading is "an operation contrary to the commercial and ideological habits of our society, which would have us
'throw away' the story once it has been consumed ('devoured'), so that we can then
move on to another story, buy another book, and which is tolerated only in certain
marginal categories of readers (children, old people, and professors)" (1974, 15–16).

institutionalization of criticism means that it can be described in terms of legitimation practices, demographics, and economics—and that neglect is therefore not a matter of anomaly or accident.

I will save for Chapter 3 a full discussion of how we might most productively read Tolson's reception; here I limit myself to the question of how we might productively read *Harlem Gallery*, and how the poem can be seen as an enactment of conflicting modernist assumptions about poetry and the poet's function. In keeping with the first principle of my discussion—namely, that the poem is generally unread or unheard of—and in order to keep this chapter as accessible as possible, I will sketch out a brief synopsis of the poem and its dramatis personae.[2]

The primary function of *Harlem Gallery*, like that of any art gallery, is to put art on display; in Tolson's gallery, however, it is the artists themselves who get displayed. From painter John Laugart to poet Hideho Heights to composer Mister Starks, they span not only different media but vastly different possibilities of author function and audience relation for the African-American artist of the mid-twentieth century. Laugart, whom we meet first, is our representative of the marginal artist, the neglected, avant-garde visionary whose masterpiece, *Black Bourgeoisie*, "a synthesis / (savage-sanative) / of Daumier and Gropper and Picasso," will wring from the "babbitted souls" of the Gallery's Regents "a Jeremian cry" (Tolson 1965, *HG* 38). Heights, to whom almost a third of the poem is devoted, is a self-proclaimed people's poet and singer of ex tempore blues and jazz ballads about figures such as Louis Armstrong and John Henry. Mister Starks, who has written a series of verse sketches of the poem's characters (transcribed in full in an eighteen-page metapoem, *Harlem Vignettes*, two-thirds of the way through), is the composer both of a serious piece, *Black Orchid Suite*, and a best-selling boogie-woogie record, "Pot Belly Papa."

The poem is narrated by none of these, however, but by an "exprofessor of Art /. . . / not gilded . . . / with the gift of tongues" (*HG* 24–25) who claims, "In the drama *Art*, / with eye and tongue, / I play a minor vocative part" (*HG* 23)—the Curator himself. Closest to the Curator, and serving simultaneously as his complement and foil, is the Bantu expatriate professor Dr. Obi Nkomo, "the alter ego / of

---

[2]For a more detailed synopsis and running paraphrase of *Harlem Gallery*, see Farnsworth 1984, 227–70. His discussion is primarily a careful walk through and explication of the poem, an almost indispensable aid for any reader sufficiently baffled by Tolson to think the port not worth the cruise.

the Harlem Gallery," who believes, with Picasso and the Curator, that "The lie of the artist is the only lie / for which a mortal or a god should die" (*HG* 43). Finally, and furthest from the Curator, we have his antagonist, Mr. Guy Delaporte III, one of the Gallery's patrons and president of Bola Boa Enterprises Inc.—that is, a member of the Black Bourgeoisie, whose babbitted "soul of gold" is "the symbol / of Churchianity" (*HG* 64).

The poem is divided into twenty-four sections, each of which is headed by a letter of the Greek alphabet. The first five sections, from "Alpha" through "Epsilon," are given over entirely to the Curator as he muses more or less sequentially on his relation to the Gallery, his own history, the inhabitants and workings of the "mecca Art" (*HG* 26), the artist's cultural role, and art's enemies (about whom more below): critics, patrons, "idols of the tribe" (*HG* 34), and "the Lord of the House of Flies" (*HG* 19), Beelzebub, who would presumably would have us worship these false idols. These five sections are among the poem's most difficult, partly because of their extraordinary density and range of allusion ("Under the Lesbian rule of the seeress Nix / . . . / Élan, / the artist's undivorceable spouse / becomes / a Delilah of Délice / or / a Xanthippe bereft / of sonnets from the Portuguese" [*HG* 31]) but also because of their refusal to specify the nature of the monologue they transcribe. It remains unclear, that is, throughout the five sections, whether the Curator is addressing a silent interlocutor and whether his monologue might therefore be termed "dramatic"; similarly, it is unclear, even to the poem's most careful readers, when the poem takes place or whether these five sections can be said to "take place" at all, for they seem to be entirely lyric. Not until the sixth section, "Zeta," in which the Curator visits John Laugart, do we get any idea that the poem is narrative ("I entered, under the Bear, a catacomb Harlem flat" [*HG* 37]); and even that section closes with a postscript informing us that Laugart was later "robbed and murdered in his flat, / and the only witness was a Hamletian rat" (*HG* 42)—thus rendering ambiguous, once again, the episode's (and the poem's) temporal status.

"Eta," like "Zeta," seems to recount a specific incident, an encounter with Nkomo in Aunt Grindle's Elite Chitterling Shop; less than twenty lines into the section, "a news-waif hallooed, 'The Desert Fox is dead!'" (*HG* 43)—thus placing this section, at least, in 1944.[3] But its primary purpose is to introduce us to Nkomo, and

---

[3]Farnsworth takes this reference to imply that the action of the *poem* can be dated to 1944 (1984, 238), but as I discuss more fully below, such an assertion cannot possibly

when "Theta" follows with yet another of the Curator's meditations on art, we are left to wonder once again whether, in rhetorical terms, *principium* has ended and *initium* begun. "Iota," however, unambiguously begins the "action" of the poem proper: "The hour with the red letter stumbles in" (*HG* 57), and the Harlem Gallery opens to its first visitors—which is to say that *Harlem Gallery* opens its text to its first textual "audience." "Iota," "Kappa," and "Lambda," then, recount the Gallery's opening; "Mu," "Nu," and "Xi" move us into the world of the Zulu Club and the "rich and complex polyrhythms" (*HG* 73) of Frog Legs Lux and his Indigo Combo; "Omicron" and "Pi" return us to the Curator's meditations, in which he quotes a good deal of Dr. Nkomo. "Rho," "Sigma," and "Tau" tell the story of Mister Starks, and in "Upsilon" we are given the entire manuscript of his *Harlem Vignettes*. In "Phi" we are back in the Zulu Club, presumably on another night; and "Chi," "Psi," and "Omega" not only close the poem structurally but resolve its major ideological and poetic conflict as well.

That conflict is played out not between any two of the artists in the poem but rather (for the most part) between the Curator and Hideho Heights, and the drama of their conflict is precisely what *Harlem Gallery* enacts—precisely what, in one sense, the poem is "about." The opposition between the two figures, although rooted and embedded in specifically modernist conflicts, is fundamental and can thus be cast in any number of ways. In one sense, the struggle is waged between the Curator's conception of the artist as lone-voice-in-the-wilderness—a conception illustrated and seemingly underwritten by the figure of Laugart—and Hideho Heights's claims for the artist as *vox populi*, which inform his declaration that the Gallery's function is to regulate the flow of cultural capital. In poetic practice, the struggle takes place between the Curator's arcane and ambiguous interior monologues and Hideho's accessible, declamatory, narrative performance poems—the ballads to John Henry and Louis Armstrong, and a verse parable in "Phi" on the "sea-turtle and the shark" (*HG* 140–41) (although in this context, as we shall see, Mister Starks's poetry comes into play as well); and I cast this opposition as a struggle between competing conceptions of poetry as either written or oral discourse. Finally, because each conception of the poet and his practice entails a commitment to a specific kind of audience relation and author function, we might see the struggle,

---

be maintained for the poem as a whole. The relevant question, instead, is why "Eta" should be set so explicitly in 1944.

at its greatest reach, as a conflict between cultural language games in which *Harlem Gallery* debates with itself the artist's obligation to join the avant-garde of his time. In all these respects, however, the struggle is fueled by Heights's and the Curator's competing visions of the role of the African-American artist in the United States—just as, in all respects, the struggle is latent in the history of modernist poetics and polemics. But whatever the terms employed to describe the opposition between the Curator and Hideho Heights, their struggle is, in its most primary sense, a struggle for control of the poem itself.

One final prolegomenon before we enter the Harlem Gallery, for I want to make clear what I take to be "modernist conflicts" if I am going to chart their enactment in Tolson's poem. I deal first with the question of modernist poetic practice and then come back to modernist polemics—that is, the modernist's and the modernist critic's theory of modernism's cultural position. First things first: my discussion of modernist "practice" throughout this chapter turns primarily on the question of poetic diction and secondarily on the issue of poetic allusion. When, therefore, I claim to discern a conflict in the "history of modernist poetic practice," I am making three claims simultaneously: that the conflict can be seen diachronically, in an about-face performed by Pound between 1913 and 1916 and consolidated by Pound and Eliot thereafter;[4] that it can be seen synchronically from about 1916 onward, as Pound jettisons "Amygism" and skirmishes with a speech-model poetry growing in America (more or less) out of Imagism, exempla of which we might take to be William Carlos Williams's "Tract" (1917) and Marianne Moore's "Poetry" (1921); and finally, that the literary history of modernism, as promulgated by critics such as Hugh Kenner, has unintentionally suppressed these first two conflicts in the process—paradoxically enough—of creating something called "the Pound Era." The first of these conflicts takes place during Pound's formative and re-formative years in London, as he adopts and then abandons what he called "a practice of speech common to good prose and to good verse alike" (1913, 662); the second takes place across the Atlantic (or, simultaneously, in the pages of Harriet Monroe's *Poetry*) between poets expatriate and poets at home over the nature of the poetic revolution at hand.

For my purposes, however, the third of my implicit claims proves

---

[4]For a detailed discussion of this "about-face," see Levenson 1984, 103–64.

most fertile, since Tolson himself, when he sought to modernize his poetry, thought not of synchronic or diachronic struggles but simply of the kind of poetry Kenner invokes when he writes, in an essay on Faulkner, that "every twentieth-century avant-garde movement one can think of was dedicated to canons not oral but literary. . . . In this sense the entire thrust of twentieth-century modernism . . . was toward a consolidation of all that printed paper implies: the well-wrought artifact, the tireless revision, the skilled reader, the habitual rereader" (1983a, 65). Of course, Kenner's claim is true enough in one sense, since we are talking about a movement that has left us such irreducibly literary artifacts as *The Waste Land*, *Ulysses*, and *A Draft of XVI Cantos*; but even the author of those *Cantos* wrote to Harriet Monroe, as late as 1915, that poetry should be conceived as the image of the spoken word, that it must be "a fine language, departing in no way from speech save by a heightened intensity (i.e. simplicity). There must be no book words, no periphrases, no inversions . . . nothing—nothing you couldn't, in some circumstance, in the stress of some emotion, actually say. Every literaryism, every book word, fritters away a scrap of the reader's patience, a scrap of his sense of your sincerity" (Pound 1950, 48–49).

If Tolson allowed us to make such easy equations, we might want at this point to take the Curator as representative of post-Imagist modernism and Heights as representative of Pound's earlier phases; but the Curator's foil with regard to the historical development of modernism is not Heights but Mister Starks, who, we are told, "had published / a volume of imagistic verse" (*HG* 111). The Curator does not think much of Starks's work, and Robert Farnsworth suggests that "the Curator's judgment on *Harlem Vignettes* probably is infused with Tolson's own stern judgment of his own *A Gallery of Harlem Portraits*. It belongs to a pre-modern style of writing doomed to extinction" (1984, 259).

Tolson himself apparently considered Imagism to be premodern:

The first finished manuscript of the *Harlem Gallery* was written in free verse. That was the fashion introduced by the Imagists. It contained 340 pages. The *Spoon River Anthology* of Edgar Lee Masters was my model. . . . Then I stashed the manuscript in my trunk for twenty years. At the end of that time I had read and absorbed the techniques of Eliot, Pound, Yeats, Baudelaire, Pasternak and, I believe, all the great Moderns. God only knows how many "little magazines" I studied, and how much textual analysis of the New Critics. To make a long story short, the new *Harlem Gallery* was completed. (1966, 194–95)

And although Heights's oral poetry links him more with Starks than with the Curator, the nature of Heights's conflict with the Curator is nevertheless more general, and more important, than is the conflict between, say, Williams and Eliot. For the Curator-Heights struggle is a disagreement not so much over poetic diction but, in the terms I have employed above, over conceptions of the artist and the function of cultural institutions: that is, not over this or that poetic language as more or less "literary" but over literary languages and ideologies, in their entirety, as forms of cultural life.

In order to address this struggle, I turn to the second of my modernist conflicts, the contradictions of modernism's cultural position. This conflict is a little more difficult to unpack, for it is not only visible in modernist poetry's simultaneously symbiotic and antagonistic relation to the institutionalization of literary criticism (and is thus bound up with the history of the English department in the United States) but visible as well in the modernist's dual role as polemicist for the avant-garde revolutionary who creates art which (as Pound put it) "the public will do well to resent" (1914b, 68) and as publicist for the cultural revolution he or she launches. To tie Pound's predicament to the fate of Anglo-American romanticism, I might say instead that he acted on a Mallarméan contempt for the masses alongside a Wordsworthian imperative to create the taste by which his revolution was to be enjoyed; "but this attitude," notes Michael Levenson,

> stands in uneasy relation to his relentless propagandizing. On the one hand his inclination is to publicize and legitimize new aesthetic doctrine; on the other, the aim is to avoid the democratization of art, since once democratized it loses the force of a cultural vanguard. In order to "keep alive" the movement Pound exploits the particular character of mass culture—its susceptibility to publicity, celebrity and fashion—but at the same time he defines himself against the logic of mass appeal, the dissemination of high cultural values. (1984, 148)

At the same time, he also appropriates the genres of the contemporary anthology and the "little magazine," and in adapting to his ends new means of production and reception, he ensures his movement the exposure necessary to its survival and consolidation. For this reason, as Levenson concludes, "if we look for a mark of modernism's coming of age, the founding of the *Criterion* in 1922 may prove a better instance than *The Waste Land*, better even than *Ulysses*, because it exemplifies the institutionalization of the movement, its accession to cultural legitimacy" (213).

The rhetoric of English modernism, then, ranges from Ezra Pound's and Wyndham Lewis's cannon firing in *Blast* to T. S. Eliot's and F. R. Leavis's canon defining in the *Criterion and Scrutiny*. And because the history of English modernism leads us eventually to the history of the English department, part of modernism's convoluted cultural legacy has been a kind of cultural schizophrenia over the aims and achievements of modernism, for we ourselves are part of its legacy, and part of its schizophrenia is ours. The academy thus gets pictured, and pictures itself, as both the destruction and the fruition of the modernist revolution: as conservative antagonist of the margin and as institutional guarantor of its existence and survival. And in Melvin Tolson's magnum opus we find this cultural schizophrenia at its most acute: for not only does Tolson take up, at their extremes, both sides of the Pound/Wordsworth positions, whereby he valorizes the avant-garde over against the "kitsch" of mass culture even as he renews the Romantic revolutionary's faith in the power of the avant-garde to transform the masses; he also takes up modernism's institutional imperatives and conceives of poetic success, finally, as acceptance by the academy. Melvin Tolson winds up, in short, a poet divided profoundly against himself; *Harlem Gallery*, a poem divided against itself. To examine these divisions is my task for the remainder of this chapter, and I will set out by casting Hideho Heights's cultural position against that of the Curator.

Scripture and Gossip: The Art of God and the Voice of the People

It is central to what Jerome McGann calls the Romantic Ideology that art is above ideology, "that only a poet and his works can transcend a corrupting appropriation by 'the world' of politics and money" (1983, 13). As Jane Tompkins charges, we have been trapped for roughly two hundred years by the chimera that aesthetic production and reception is by its nature free from "interest" (and principal, and capital): from Kant's third critique to New Criticism's irony and ambiguity to Adorno's aesthetic theory, art's power has resided in its autonomy, "*because,* unlike other forms of discourse, it has no particular uses, no loyalties, no causes to plead" (1980a, 219). Even for avant-gardes bent on fundamental social critique, such critique is to be located in and launched from art's refusals, its negativity, its resistance to any immediate utilitarian purpose. Thus it is that so revisionary a Marxist as Louis Althusser, who redefined "ideology" so thoroughly, still found it possible to write that true art, as opposed to the products of mass culture, "is not among the ideologies" (1971, 203). If, then, there has been a paradigm shift in recent criticism and theory, surely it can be located partially in the status of "ideology," which once signified "all that which great art transcends" and now is taken to mean "the complex production of 'common sense' which constructs the field of meaning in which all human activity—especially art—takes place." And if the ideological forces at work in *Harlem Gallery* are visible only now, perhaps this is because it is only when we find ourselves self-consciously undergoing (or debating) such a paradigm shift that we are enabled to glimpse the forces suppressed or marginalized by previous paradigms.

This point is worth making in some detail, since the Curator seems precisely to subscribe to (and expound) the belief that art exceeds any determinate purpose or institution. In "Delta," for instance, we are asked not to ask whether the artist worked for the church, the public market, or even for art itself:

> Ye weeping monkeys of the Critics' Circus
> (colorless as malic acid in a Black Hamburg grape),
>   what profit it to argue at the wake
>   (a hurrah's nest of food and wine
>   with Auld Lang Syne
>   to cheer the dead),
>   if the artist wrought
>   (contrary to what the black sanders said)
>   for Ars',
>   the Cathedra's, or the Agora's sake?
>   (*HG* 29)

The Curator then goes on to claim that whatever the ills of an age or a nation, "the pain is only the ghost of the pain / the artist endures, / *endures*, / —like Everyman— / alone" (*HG* 30). The duality of the claim is instructive: the artist is at once *Übermensch* and Everyman, a superhuman "ape of God" (*HG* 21) and all-too-human "paltry thing with varicose veins" (*HG* 30); indeed, the Curator writes a few lines later of "The St. John's agony / of the artist / in his gethsemane" (*HG* 31). Writ large, as a paradox not merely in the presentation of an artist but in the idea of art's function in toto, it is the paradox inherent in what Sacvan Bercovitch calls the "Romantic-democratic concept of art," which demands a "dual commitment both to 'high' literature (as the expression of transcendent personal genius) and to a literature that represents 'the people' at large" (1986, 650).

Thus it is, in the Curator's scheme of things, that we go to art— even the most experimental art of the early century—for the most ancient of reasons, to see the mirror held up to nature:

> But if one seeks the nth verisimilar,
> go to Ars by the way of Pisgah:
> as the telescope of Galileo
> deserted the clod to read the engirdling idioms of the star,
> to the ape of God,
> go!
>
> (HG 21)

The relation of an ideal art to an ideal audience, then, becomes at once antagonistic and transformative: the artwork must disturb and instruct; the audience must resist and then gradually capitulate. *Harlem Gallery* opens, in fact, with an image of the first half of this relation, as "The Lord of the House of Flies, / jaundice-eyed, synapses purled, / wries before the tumultuous canvas" (HG 19); forty pages later, when the Harlem Gallery opens, we see another rendition of this tableau, its antitype and fulfillment, as Guy Delaporte confronts Laugart's *Black Bourgeoisie*. And although the Curator takes a grim outlook on the painting's effect, Dr. Nkomo responds with a sanguine assessment of its antagonistic/transformative potential: "This work of art is the dry compound / fruit of the sand-box tree, / which bursts with a loud report / *but* scatters its seeds quietly" (HG 66).

Surely there is nothing especially insidious about either the Curator's or Nkomo's claims; after all, they are only telling us, on one level, things we have heard many times before—that art may, and often does, effect its purpose by shocking or startling us, by defamiliarizing the familiar, or by holding the object at a cognitive distance that allows for its aesthetic apprehension, "As the Utrillo of the Holy Hill *trans*figured / a *dis*figured Montmartre street / into a thing of beauty" (HG 27). In so doing, art thereby offers us possibilites for order, self-knowledge, and insight which we cannot otherwise discern in the surface noise of life; or, as the Curator puts it elsewhere, life is so Other that only its aesthetic representation is fathomable:

> We who are we
> discover *altérité* in the actors on
> the boards of the Théâtre Vie.

> No catharsis homes:
> no empathy calls:
> synapses of the thinking reed snap
> from too little reality
> when the heavy dark curtain falls.
> (*HG* 26–27)

We are very close here to the idea of "tragic gaiety" that Yeats expresses most movingly in "Lapis Lazuli"—right down to the echo of the earlier poem's "great stage curtain about to drop." As in the Yeatsian vision, art is a profound affirmation and consolation, a basso continuo in the threnody of human history: just as "All things fall and are built again, / And those that build them again are gay" (Yeats 1983, "Lapis Lazuli," lines 35–36), so too does the Curator, in difficult moments, console himself with stories of the authentic artist's resistance, if not immunity, to history.

Nkomo's forecast of *Black Bourgeoisie*'s effect on Guy Delaporte, for example, fails to persuade the Curator. He is moved not to hope but to anxious self-scrutiny as his reflection on his conflicted relations— to the Gallery's artists and to its Regents—reminds him of the ex-Fauvist André Derain's decision to visit Germany in 1941, which led, understandably, to accusations that Derain was a collaborationist:

> *Give voice to a bill*
> *of faith at another hour.*
> *My humor is ill.*
> *A night like this, O Watchman,*
> *sends a Derain to Weimar*
> *to lick the Brissac jack boots*
> *of Das Kapital that hawks things-as-they-are.*
> (*HG* 67)

In 1941 Derain was still considered one of the most important and innovative of modern artists; since then his reputation has so plummeted that Derain has been pointed out—as he is here—as the exemplum of the modern artist gone bad.[5] His growing conservatism

---

[5]Tolson's citation of Derain as a failed modern artist is so apposite—and Derain is apparently so little known today—that the reference has tripped up its only two commentators: Huot writes of the Weimar Republic's conversion of Wilhelm's palace into an art museum (1971, 162), and Farnsworth supposes that Derain abandoned "his compatriot Fauves to organize a famous collection of modern French masters for Crown Prince Wilhelm's palace" (1984, 242). Tolson appears to be alluding either to the Weimar Republic or to the geographical Weimar located so close to Buchenwald

after World War I; his estrangement from his former colleagues, capped by his willingness to associate with the Nazi regime; in short, his immersion in the nightmare of human history—all this makes Derain the precisely appropriate figure for the Curator's vision of despair. It follows just as appropriately that where Nkomo's words could not soothe his humor, the Curator turns instead to his version of tragic gaiety:

> Then O then, O ruins,
> I remember
> the alien hobnails
> of that cross-nailing Second of September
> did not crush like a mollusk's shell,
> in café and studio,
> the *élan* of Courbet, Cézanne, and Monet,
> nor did the self-deadfall of the Maginot
> palsy the hand of Chagall,
> Matisse,
> and Picasso.
>
> (HG 67)

Again, just as there is nothing sinister about the notion that the artist is at once genius and Everyman, so too is there nothing terribly suspicious about this version of art history: the Great War did not end the careers of Chagall, Matisse, and Picasso, and certainly the work of the great Realists, Impressionists, and Postimpressionists has found its way to notecards and calendars despite the century of devastation between the Franco-Prussian War and the present day.

But the difficulty with the Curator's vision is not that it is somehow "false," that it does not "fit the facts"; the difficulty is that it is selective, and that the principle of selection serves a specific and, as we shall see, problematic ideological function. For although many artists' careers survived "the self-deadfall of the Maginot," those of

---

(which the Curator calls a "melismatic song / whose single syllable is sung to blues notes" [HG 164] at the end of "Psi"). The question here, as with Matisse (below), is which Weimar, and therefore which Derain, Tolson means to evoke: is he suggesting that Derain's decline was already latent in the 1920s (Derain had in fact begun to appear in German galleries by 1930), or is he, as I argue, linking Derain to the Holocaust? For evidence of Derain's prewar reputation, see Malcolm Vaughan (1941, 13): "Of all the painters alive today, André Derain is perhaps the ablest. . . . The estimate is conditional, of course, for final judgment of an artist's work is not to be reached in his lifetime. Yet when we measure Derain by the standards by which we measure the masters . . . he seems to stand the tallest among contemporary painters."

Henri Gaudier-Brzeska and Wilfred Owen, among others, did not. Furthermore, even a cursory comparison of *Blast*'s first two issues (June 1914 and July 1915) will reveal a remarkable reversal in the position of the self-proclaimed vanguard, as Wyndham Lewis, unable to cash his military metaphors (of which "avant-garde" itself is one) in the face of a *real* military attack on the complacent British middle class, switches his strategy and casts the Great War as a conflict between artistic schools: "Germany has stood for the old Poetry, for Romance, more stedfastly [*sic*] and profoundly than any other people in Europe. . . . Under these circumstances, apart from national partisanship, it appears to us humanly desirable that Germany should win no war against France or England" (Lewis 1915, 5).[6] During a world war, that is, even revolutionaries may find themselves forced to contrive national allegiances.

In suppressing historical and cultural conflicts such as these, however, the Curator clears the way for a simpler, less ambivalent vision of the oppositional functions of art—especially in regard to art's relation to history, audience, politics, and the material base. Although the Curator purports to believe that "Art / is not barrel copper easily separated / from the matrix" (*HG* 33), he does a thorough job of casting its relation to the "matrix" in largely antagonistic terms. My point is simply that the Curator's claims both serve and reinforce the ideal of art's radical autonomy, wherein arise two parallel and mutually supporting critical tenets. First, cultural transmission is detached from the moorings of milieu, from conditions of aesthetic production and reception; second and more important for *Harlem Gallery*, all "contingent" forms of art, from outright propaganda to the most innocuous forms of mass culture, are indiscriminately vilified—or, in the more genial manner of a Northrop Frye, distinguished from the "autonomous verbal structure" of literature on the grounds that their "final direction is outward" (1957, 74).

The first of these tenets is secured by the introduction of the "castaway talent" Laugart (*HG* 39), who advances the Curator's assertions to the point at which he would have us believe that a work of art survives, and manifests its worth, irrespective of its audience:

John Laugart,
alive beyond the bull of brass,

---

[6]Cf. Levenson 1984, 140–45; for a parallel account of the competing polemics of militant British suffragettes and the English avant-garde; and their parallel co-optation into the war effort, see Lyon 1992.

measured my interior—and said:
"A work of art
is an everlasting flower
in kind or unkind hands;
dried out,
it does not lose its form and color
in native or in alien lands."
(HG 39)

Laugart is in this sense at the center of the poem, the poem's apotheosis; he is the demonstration of the argument that, as one of
Tolson's undated journal notes has it, "the size of an audience that
understands a work of art at the time of its first appearance is no
argument against the merit of the work of art" (TM). If we take the
seemingly neutral term "size" here in its intended sense—that is,
"smallness"—then this note could reasonably stand as the Curator's
motto, with a crucial proviso: although it is no argument *against* the
work of art that its immediate audience is small or uncomprehending, to the Curator's mind the reverse is very nearly true—that an
audience's failure to understand the artwork is an indication of its
timeless worth.

Here is where our problems begin, for although we could not reasonably take exception to the first half of this argument, we too often find ourselves willing to assume the second half as well, as if it
followed necessarily from the first. This is the signal limitation of
Hans Robert Jauss's first formulation of "reception aesthetics"; it
was immediately critiqued, in the 1970s, by East German Marxists
and acknowledged to be ahistorical by Jauss himself as early as 1972,[7]
but it is so forceful and common an equation as to warrant citation:

The distance between the horizon of expectations and the work, between the familiarity of previous aesthetic experience and the "horizontal change" demanded by the reception of the new work, *determines
the artistic character of a literary work*, according to an aesthetics of reception: to the degree that this distance decreases . . . the closer the work
comes to the sphere of "culinary" or entertainment art [*Unterhaltungs-
kunst*]. This latter work can be characterized by an aesthetics of reception as not demanding any horizonal change, but rather as precisely
fulfilling the expectations prescribed by a ruling standard of taste, in
that it satisfies the desire for the reproduction of the familiarly beautiful;
confirms familiar sentiments; sanctions wishful notions; makes unusual

[7]See Weimann 1975, 24–28; Holub 1984, 57–68. Holub (69–73) summarizes Jauss's
early reversals of field and belated reaction against Adorno.

experiences enjoyable as "sensations"; or even raises moral problems, but only to "solve" them in an edifying manner as predecided questions. (1982b, 25; my emphasis)

The longer the lag between production and reception, therefore, the greater the value of the work, and vice versa. And as Jauss writes in the same essay, "the resistance that the new work poses to the expectations of its first audience can be so great that it requires a long process of reception to gather in that which was unexpected and unusable within the first horizon," until we finally "find access to the understanding of the misunderstood older form" (35). Reception therefore gradually "uses up" a work's initial value, to the point at which the society has somehow caught up with the work, many years later. At such a point the revolutionary work becomes canonical, and, as Jauss would have it, canonical works become so like *kitsch* that "it requires a special effort to read them 'against the grain' of the accustomed experience to catch sight of their artistic character once again" (26).

Thus is Tolson's note oddly contradicted, for like the Curator, Nkomo, and the early Hans Robert Jauss, we find ourselves believing that no work of art (or, to cite Barbara Johnson again, no "radically innovative" school of thought) can be authentically powerful unless it is sufficiently misunderstood by its immediate popular and critical audience, and that the size of one's audience *is* an argument against the merit of one's work—if, that is, its audience becomes too large. To paraphrase *Poetry* and Walt Whitman with a critical difference, to have great poets, you must have disdain for great audiences too.

Given the force of this version of the rhetoric of marginality, it is fitting that the Curator's version of art history is selective—and that in some instances the lives of the Curator's favorite unappreciated Heroes of Art have been selectively edited. For in the list of Impressionists and Postimpressionists the Curator rehearses time and again in *Harlem Gallery*, he includes, as we have seen, even such figures as Cézanne, Monet, Matisse, Chagall, and Picasso, who were anything but perennially "unappreciated" and who did not die, as does Laugart, alone and unmourned in an inner-city garret. Instead, each of these painters, regardless of whether he achieved either critical or popular success at any point in his lifetime, is characterized as that familiar Bohemian figure, the neglected visionary unknown to all but a few fellow artists. As Nkomo puts it in a remarkable passage, "Remember / Paul Cézanne, / the father of modern Art, / a Toussaint L'Ouverture of Esthetics":

"... Remember, yes, remember ...
Zola, Renoir, Degas, Gauguin, Van Gogh, and Rodin
hailed Cézanne;
but *vox populi* and red-tapedom
remained as silent as spectators in a court
when the crier repeats three times, 'Oyez!'"

(*HG* 101)[8]

Not only in its disparagement of the masses but also in the manner in which it chooses to disparage them, Nkomo's version of Cézanne's reception is uncannily similar to Pound's aspersion of "homo canis" in his version of *Blast*'s reception (note too, here, the Curatorian deployment of the "mirror to nature" argument):

OYEZ. OYEZ. OYEZ.
Throughout the length and breadth of England and through three continents BLAST has been REVILED by all save the intelligent.
WHY?
Because BLAST alone has dared to show modernity its face in an honest glass. (1915, 85)

But this is only half the matter: let us unpack Nkomo's claim more slowly. First, the father of modern art is a Toussaint L'Ouverture of aesthetics, freeing his people from oppression despite his eventual martyrdom at the hands of the oppressors. Yet whereas the father of Haitian independence was betrayed by Napoleon, Cézanne is betrayed instead by *vox populi* and red-tapedom. Cézanne's oppressors become, in this tangled analogy, the public he seeks somehow to liberate. It is not merely that the artist leads a popular revolution to which nobody comes; the artist *must* be unpopular in order to be revolutionary. Thus even as Tolson appeals, like Wordsworth, to the figure of Toussaint, he does so in the name of what Allon White has called the "ideology of rarity which endeavours to value the art object by placing it beyond the reach of the multitude" (1981, 52); and for the Curator, the rarity-value equation is constitutive of great art: "Even when / his world is ours and ours is his— / . . . / the artist, like a messiah, is egoistic / and the work of art, like the art of God, / is a rhyme in the Mikado's tongue to all save the hedonistic" (*HG* 98).

Even on its face, this is a troubling assertion. But if it troubles us to hear Joyce demand an insomniac reader, it should trouble us all

---

[8]I have reproduced Tolson's suspension points without spaces (...); my own deletions from Tolson's text are signified by the usual points of ellipsis.

the more to hear something similar from Tolson, combined as it is with a Poundian distrust of *vox populi*. And it will trouble us especially if we recall here that *vox populi* in *Harlem Gallery* is Hideho Heights, and that the "ideology of rarity," therefore, will determine the outcome of the agonistic encounter between "high" and "low" cultures with which the poem will climax. Still, this ideology, and its concomitant equation of social marginality and artistic power, are by now so familiar to us that it may be hard to imagine them as "troubling." In Bercovitch's post-Althusserian definition, however, this kind of familiarization is any ideology's constitutive function: "an ideology . . . arises out of historical circumstances, and then re-presents these, symbolically and conceptually, as though they were natural, universal, and right" (1986, 636). More to our specific purposes, Bercovitch goes on to address the second extremity of the Curator's claims, the vilification of mass culture; what he describes as "the old [critical] consensus" might be taken, in an institutional genealogy of modernism, as the academic version of the ideology of rarity:

> The traditional dichotomy between art and ideology—a pillar of the old consensus—is problematic and has increasingly become a subject of debate for this generation. For though in some sense, certainly, a work of art transcends its time—though it may be transhistorical or transcultural or even transcanonical—it can no more transcend ideology than an artist's mind can transcend psychology; and . . . obviously any defense of literature (as art) which requires a pejorative view of popular culture (as ideology) is itself ideological, part of a strategy designed to enforce the separation of "spheres of influence": business from family, government from religion, politics from art. Like other apologias for literature, as handmaid to theology or as servant of the state, this one has its origins neither in the laws of nature nor in the will of God but in history and culture. (639)

The Curator, to be sure, does not deny the existence of these "other apologias"; actually, he suggests at one point that they are endemic to art:

> Doubt not
> the artist and his age
> (though bald as the pilled head of garlic),
> married or divorced
> and even vying downstage,
> are both aware
> that God or Caesar is the handle
> to the camel's hair.
> (*HG* 29)

But the matter of art's origin has never been the issue for the Curator; nowhere has his defense of art's autonomy degenerated into a defense of art for art's sake. In fact, the passage immediately following this one, which I have already quoted above, proceeds to toss out the question entirely ("what profit it to argue at the wake . . . if the artist wrought . . . for Ars', the Cathedra's, or the Agora's sake?"). The relevant argument, instead, pivots on the question of how a work of art is so transmitted as to become transhistorical— how, since "No critic" can be "a Gran Galeoto" ("spiteful gossip," from an 1881 play by José Echegaray),

> between the Art-lover and the work of art,
> the world-self of the make-
> believe becomes the swimming pool of a class,
> the balsam apple
> of the soul and by the soul and for the soul,
> or silvered Scarahaeus glass
> in which Necessity's *figuranti* of innocence and guilt
> mirror themselves as they pass.
>
> (HG 29)

And the answer, according to the Curator, demands a kind of definition by negation, a sealing-off of art from the inimical forces that would bend it to serve supposedly non- or anti-aesthetic ends. Hence his antagonism to the material means of cultural reproduction, for in his view, true art is beset on all sides: by the Critics' Circus, by profiteering patrons—also known as "bulls of Bashan" (HG 35) and represented here by Guy Delaporte III and the rest of the Gallery's Regents, who "exhaust summer and winter / in grinding / the spirit of The Curator" (HG 171)—and, most insidiously, by "the idols of the tribe," who, "in voices as puissant as the rutting calls / of a bull crocodile, bellow: / 'We / have heroes! Celebrate them upon our walls!'" (HG 34). Mallarmé himself could have put it no better; and when we hear the refrain again in "Iota," we realize that we are in the Gallery's South Wing, the Curator's concession to vulgar popular taste. Here we see paintings of the tribe's heroes, "dusky Lion Hearts" (HG 61)—paintings which, although "authentic as a people's autography" (HG 62), are described as "bizarres and homespuns / in a cacophony of colors" (HG 61), "unsynchronized opposites, / gentlemen and galoots / from Afroamerica" (HG 62)—of which the Curator's final judgment is severe:

> However, this immaturity,
> like the stag tick's,

will disappear
like its wings,
when it settles upon a red red deer.
(*HG* 62)

Juxtaposed to the rest of the Gallery's "rigors and vigors" (*HG* 58), the South Wing is no less than a profanation of art's temple. In the Curator's canonical hierarchy, "autography" is apparently among the most debased of genres.

The idea here, then, is that once we have bracketed off the *kitsch* and the chaff, high art, like the "Attic salt" of man in the Curator's "afroirishjewish" grandpa's account, "*somehow* / . . . survives the blow / of Attila, Croesus, Iscariot, / and the Witches' Sabbath in the Catacombs of Bosio" (*HG* 27–28). No accident is it that Laugart's *Black Bourgeoisie* is hung in the Gallery's distinguished North Wing, "Harlem's Aganippe" of "Attic wit and nerve" (*HG* 60). For it is thanks to this Attic wit/salt that art like Laugart's proves itself timeless, the motive force of a history it nevertheless always transcends:

In Chronos Park
the Ars-powered Ferris wheel revolves
through golden age and dark
as historied isms rise and fall
and the purple of the doctor's robe
(ephemeral as the flesh color of the fame flower)
is translated into the coffin's pall.
(*HG* 31)

Despite the thoroughly un-Yeatsian diction of "Ars-powered Ferris wheel," we are back, here, to the idea of tragic gaiety—only this time, art is valued for its resistance not merely to history but to the passing parade of Ph.D.s. More important, though, the means of art's survival are, once again, apparently intrinsic and natural, the workings of the disinterested movements of art history, a "great god Biosis" who "begets / the taste that sets apart / the pearls and olivets" (*HG* 22). Great art, like the cream the Curator drinks in an episode from Mister Starks's *Harlem Vignettes*, will simply rise to the top, sooner or later, of its own accord.

The process is, needless to say, not always quite that simple. Even Laugart's work requires the mediation of the Curator if it is to be shown before a public at all, as "curator and creator / meet— / friend yoked to friend at the candle end" (*HG* 170). But this mediation, significantly, does not compromise the artwork's merit—"friend" here does not imply partiality—because the Curator operates as a kind of ideally disinterested Fryean critic, canonizing only those works which, tautologically, have earned canonicity because of their greatness, "in exhibitions, / when a genius gets through / with a nonpareil of art whose exegesis / exacts patience" (*HG* 165). And it is crucial to Laugart's cultural position that he dies before the public exhibition of his work, for his death ensures the purity of his motives. Eduardo Sanguineti has described the ideology of the avant-garde at stake here in precisely apposite terms: Laugart's negativity, as an example of avant-gardism generally, "expresses a heroic and pathetic straining for an immaculate product, which would be free of the immediate interplay of demand and supply" (1973, 390). But such a product is also, in its very rarity, "commercially enviable" (390). Thus, its lack of exchange value is the guarantee of its aesthetic value, which becomes in turn the basis of its market value:

> Avant garde work carries with it an artistic guarantee, at the outset, of complete (or virtually complete) freedom from any formal connection with the familiar contemporary market product. . . . It is as if the absence of demand for it or or its refusal to comply with any current demand (which is then interpreted as a guarantee of the work's purity and honesty) could free it, now and for ever, from its nature as merchandise.
>
> Thus the heroic and pathetic impulse implies that one should be heroically and pathetically blind. (391)

Laugart may be only half-blind, but for the Curator he remains fully heroic and pathetic.

When Hideho Heights bursts into the Harlem Gallery in "Lambda," however (simultaneously bursting in on *Harlem Gallery*, intruding violently on the poem as on the scene), we get a different view of art altogether: playfully signifying on both the Curator and the Gallery's opening night, Hideho speaks "From the mouth of the Harlem Gallery":

> "Hey, man, when you gonna close this dump?
> Fetch highbrow stuff for the middlebrows who
> don't give a damn and the lowbrows who ain't hip!
> Think you're a little high-yellow Jesus?"
> (*HG* 68)

Hideho violates not only the decorum of the opening but the decorum of galleries everywhere by announcing what Bourdieu would call his "refusal of the refusal which is the starting point of the high aesthetic, i.e., the clear-cut separation of ordinary dispositions from the specifically aesthetic disposition" (1984, 32). Sure enough, Heights goes on in his next few lines to mock one of the paintings, to declare the priority of writing to painting, and to feign an apology for his tardiness: "Sorry, Curator, I got here late; / my black ma birthed me in the Whites' bottom drawer, / and the Reds forgot to fish me out!" (*HG* 68).

But in more formal terms, Hideho's disruption of the Gallery's opening is also a disruption of *Gallery*'s development: after his entrance, the poem alters significantly, and the sections dominated by the Curator are similarly "altared"—set apart as an artifact of the sacred and also as merely one mode of expression among many. The poem thus becomes "dialogic" in Bakhtin's sense—not simply because another voice has entered it (we have already heard Laugart's and Nkomo's) but because the speaker behind that voice is, as Mikhail Bakhtin writes in "Discourse in the Novel," "not the image of a man in his own right, but a man who is precisely the *image of a language*" (1981, 336). The Bakhtinian conception of an "image of a language" may be construed as a more explicitly social form of Wittgenstein's "language-games," in that for Bakhtin "the dialogic nature of language" is "a struggle among socio-linguistic points of view" (273). But though Bakhtin and Wittgenstein both depict a world filled with competing idiolects and dialects, the difference between Bakhtinian "socio-linguistic points of view" and Wittgenstein's "to imagine a language means to imagine a form of life" (1945, § 19, 8e) is that the former must be *heard* directly in order to be imagined: "It is impossible to represent an alien ideological world adequately without first permitting it to sound" (Bakhtin 1981, 335).

And sound it does through the Harlem Gallery, in "a voice like a / ferry horn in a river of fog" (*HG* 68). For Hideho does not stop at translating artistic value into its cultural "brow" differentiations, as above, but goes on to "rhetorize in the grand style" and juxtapose to the Curator's mode of poetic expression his own "pure inspiration" (*HG* 69): a four-stanza ballad to the glory of Louis Armstrong, complete with alternate-line rhyme and a very loose iambic tetrameter jog:

> *King Oliver of New Orleans*
> *has kicked the bucket, but he left behind*
> *old Satchmo with his red-hot horn*
> *to syncopate the heart and mind.*

> The honky-tonks in Storyville
> have turned to ashes, have turned to dust,
> but old Satchmo is still around
> like Uncle Sam's IN GOD WE TRUST.
> (HG 69)

Not only is the ballad a metrical rupture of *Harlem Gallery's* texture; its "allusions" to artists, too, serve a different function than do the Curator's. In invoking, in the second stanza's *ubi sunt* roll call, the names of Bessie Smith, Jelly Roll Morton, W. C. Handy, and Leadbelly, Heights does so not as Nkomo and the Curator invoke their favorite painters—to appeal to the idea of an avant-garde—but to place Louis Armstrong among legendary African-American musicians who are figures in an indigenous, biracial, oral American popular culture: *"Wyatt Earp's legend, John Henry's, too, / is a dare and a bet to old Satchmo"* (HG 70).

Heights's verse-form, casual as it is, holds for only three of the four stanzas; the fourth, interestingly enough, conforms more closely to *Harlem Gallery's* irregular ode form: "Old Satchmo's / gravelly voice and tapping foot and crazy notes / set my soul on fire" (*HG* 70). Metrically, it is the only stanza Hideho speaks which sounds even vaguely like one of the Curator's or Nkomo's. Yet although the Curator's metrics may be said to "leak" into Hideho's at this point, Hideho's entrance has on the whole a far more telling immediate effect on the poem than the poem has on him. For the Harlem Gallery's response to the ballad goes unrecorded, as the ballad closes the section "Lambda," but *Harlem Gallery's* response is dramatic: the scene shifts at once, in "Mu," from the "ebony doors of the Harlem Gallery," where Nkomo and the Curator had stood like "Hrothgarian hosts" (*HG* 57), to the Zulu Club, where Hideho and the Curator "like the brims of old hats, / slouched at a sepulchered table" (*HG* 71).

The Zulu Club scene, which runs from "Mu" through "Xi," marks the transition in *Harlem Gallery* from a written model of poetry to an oral model. Simultaneously, the poem moves, we might say, out of a vacuum and out before an audience. As I noted earlier, it is not clear whom the Curator was addressing, if he was "speaking" at all, and even though the text of the poem admitted its first "image of an audience" in "Kappa," it did so simply to dramatize the confrontation between Delaporte and Laugart's masterpiece. In the Zulu Club, however, we find an audience of a different order; and once the Zulu Club Wits are congregated, once the Indigo Combo of Frog

Legs Lux begins to play, and once (as Hideho chants) "the Zulu Club is in the groove . . . / and the cats, the black cats, are *gone*" (*HG* 74), the poem no longer transcribes the Curator's obscure internal monologue but instead re-presents the patois and gossip of the Wits. To borrow a dichotomy from Karen Chase Levenson (1986), this transition represents, in *Harlem Gallery*'s dialogics, the substitution of a kind of poetry as "gossip" for the Curator's model of poetry as "Scripture," and the concomitant substitution of the image of the *vox populi* for the image of the castaway talent—of the balladeer for the messianic ape of God.[9] Scripture and gossip are, then, the dipolar images-of-languages between which *Harlem Gallery* vibrates, and it is Hideho Heights who induces the vibration.

In characterizing the Curator's poetics as "scriptural," I have two things in mind. First, I want to suggest Scripture in Chase Levenson's (1986) sense—as unassailable Text, as the epitome of writing in that it seeks to veil its origins in speech and to embed its authority in itself by referring to itself in the formula "it is written."[10] Scripture, in this sense, is monologic, univocal, and thus Author-itative.[11] Second, I want to suggest that whatever the wider ramifications of the author function specific to "Scripture," this model for poetry, as the Curator conceives it, is specifically modernist; and I invoke "modernist poetry" here not only in a general, Kennerian sense as poetry "dedicated to canons not oral but literary" but also, and more specifically, in the sense applicable to English modernism after Eliot's arrival in London, when modernist poetry first began to think of itself as antithetical to speech. Of this period Pound wrote fifteen years later, in 1932, that he and Eliot "decided that the dilutation of *vers libre*, Amygism, Lee Masterism, general floppiness had gone too

---

[9]Chase Levenson's characterization of the oral/written opposition in terms of "gossip" and "Scripture" was first articulated in a lecture (1986) on *Mansfield Park* and *Wuthering Heights*. As Chase Levenson notes, the duality speech/writing has been hierarchized in favor of the *right*-hand term when it comes to the discourse of women ("gossip"). And in keeping with the polarity of the opposition, I insist throughout that the Curator *writes*, whereas Hideho Heights *speaks*.

[10]The Old Testament's first reference to itself in the formula "it is written" occurs, coincidentally, in Daniel 9:13, not long after Daniel reads the writing on the wall at the feast of Belshazzar.

[11]That is, poetry-as-Scripture, as I apply the term to *Harlem Gallery*, has the characteristics Bakhtin ascribes to *all* poetry (see 1981, 285–88, 296–99). His castigation of poetry, however, seems primarily a rhetorical strategy of definition-by-negation, wherein "poetry" becomes a discursive Other, a projection of "all the novel is not." Without pronouncing on the adequacy of Bakhtin's genre theory here, I do want to acknowledge my appropriation of his terminology for use in a genre he would find either inappropriate or, tautologically, "novelistic" to the extent that it is "dialogic."

far and that some counter-current must be set going" (1932, 590). The result, as we now know, was a decisive reversal in modernist strategy: Pound disowned the aesthetics he had elaborated with Ford Madox Ford, that poetry "must be a fine language, departing in no way from speech," in favor of inversions, periphrases, and book words of various languages (compare the first seven lines of 1917's Ur-Canto II with 1925's draft). And Eliot, in the midst of his quatrains, declared that "*Vers libre* does not exist. . . . it is a battle-cry of freedom, and there is no freedom in art" (1917, 31–32).

Once again, however, a disclaimer: it does not necessarily follow from my assertion that the Curator's poetics are "scriptural," in the narrow sense of "post-Imagist," that Heights is therefore a pre-modern Imagist; that role, I reiterate, is reserved for Mister Starks. We might nevertheless align the Curator with the technique of Eliot's preconversion poetry and restate the claim thus: in defending the cultural position of the high modernist poet, the Curator is able to wage two poetic struggles at once—a local skirmish with Starks which replays a conflict in modernist technique, and a major series of battles with Heights over what I am calling "forms of cultural life," over the means of cultural reproduction in two opposed conceptions of the poet's function.

Over against Scripture, therefore, I take Chase Levenson's idea of "gossip" as the medium and milieu of the ballad singer, the populist poet: it is transient, revisable, always spoken, rarely authoritative; and it operates on a model of direct, dialogic, multivocal communication such as that which takes place among the Zulu Club Wits, or between Hideho Heights and his audience in his recitation of the ballad/toast on John Henry. And gossip's characteristic references to itself, by which it seeks to disclose the speaker as speaker, rather than to refer to the author-ity of a Text, consist generally of such phrases as "and then what did *you* say?" "and do you know who told me that?" No doubt *Harlem Gallery*'s models of speech and writing are themselves two forms of writing; certainly, it would be a bizarre form of logocentrism to pretend that "speech" is present, or present-to-itself, in this written text. But what Chase Levenson shows, oddly enough, is that speech *as gossip* is actually more attentive to (and dependent on) its means of transmission than is the Text that no mortal writes. For Hideho Heights, speech is not a self-identical *presence*; speech in the mouth and the milieu of the people's poet is always dialogic, requoted and requotable, intertextual and intersubjective.

Only in the Zulu Club scene, then, could Black Diamond, ex-student of the Curator and "heir presumptive to the Lenox Policy Racket" (*HG* 86), defy the Regents of the Gallery in public, swearing on "his Grandma's family Bible / that the sons-of-bitches / had better not fire his beloved teacher, / because his stool pigeons / have dedicated to him / a dossier on *each* and *every one* of the bastards!" (*HG* 88). In fact, the only time the poem transcribes speech in this way— that is, the only time it deploys narrative diegesis mimetically, without the framing of quotation marks—is in the gossip world of the Zulu Club, in the speech of Black Diamond, as he explains to the Curator that he's holding on to the dirt on the Regents because

> if an ace boss squeals
> in the blackjack game of his free enterprise,
> it sets a bad example—*bad* for the little guys!
>
> His Grandma used to dingdong a scripture,
> "By their tails ye shall know 'em."
> That's the reason he planks down his church dues,
> at Mt. Sinai, a year in advance.
> You see,
> if a fluke flunks in his free enterprise
> and the Sweet Chariot swings low, the preacher can't blab
> and St. Peter can't gab
> to the Lord God A'mighty
> that Black Diamond's record was in the red—like
> a Red editor's among gnawing bellies in Greenwich Village.
> ... Then, too ...
> it's a good example for the little guys.
>
> (*HG* 88–89)

Numerous features of Black Diamond's discourse seem especially pertinent. First, it is only in the Zulu Club that the Gallery's ultimate authorities, the Regents, can be challenged in this way—by a hustler's gossiping that he has collected damaging documents on them. Moreover, in delivering himself of such a boast, Black Diamond refers twice to his Grandma's Scripture, and strange things happen to scripture when it is invoked by gossipers. Either the Text itself (Matthew 7:16) is garbled in transmission, so that it comes out, dingdonged, as "By their tails ye shall know 'em," or—more tellingly— the transmitters of Scripture are themselves cast as gossipers, preachers who "blab" in a world whose theology holds that God Himself depends on the "gab" of St. Peter in order to ascertain the status of His worshippers. Reference to Scripture in the Zulu Club is

parodic, subversive; the gossip world here is something like Bakhtin's "carnival," in which "the common people's creative culture of
laughter . . . destroys any hierarchical (distancing and valorized)
distance" (1981, 20, 23). It is a world in which Hideho's ballad pictures the discourse of prayer as a version of signifying on the oppression of the Master, by equating prayer with pretended complai-
sance before whites, as two genres of discursive obliquity directed at
Great White Fathers:

> Ma taught me to pray. Pa taught me to grin.
> It pays, Black Boy; oh, it pays!
> So I pray to God and grin at the Whites
> in seventy-seven different ways!
>   (HG 84)

Finally, it is only in the Zulu Club that we can hear such lines as
"I felt Hideho's breath against my ear" (*HG* 73); "The yanking fish-
ing rod / of Hideho's voice / jerked me out of my bird's-foot violet
romanticism" (*HG* 76); "Hideho's voice was the Laughing Philoso-
pher's" (*HG* 79); "In a faraway funereal voice, / Hideho continued"
(*HG* 80)—for the simple reason that it is only in the Zulu Club that
the poem emphasizes such speech attributes as "breath" and
"voice." Hideho's performance in the Zulu Club strikingly fulfills
the idiom of his entrance into the Gallery in "Lambda": he speaks
"from the mouth of the Harlem Gallery," indeed.[12] In one of the best
treatments of *Harlem Gallery* to date, Rita Dove (as poet-critic) has
written that the sections dominated by Heights "display a virtuoso
rendering of narrative layers—a tribute, perhaps, to Heights's own
extravagant linguistic paeans. . . . The dialogues in the Zulu Club
scenes show how close Tolson's baroque surface mirrors typical
black street speech. . . . Hideho Heights's John Henry poem . . . is
right in the tradition of great black ballads, as well as incorporating
the bawdiness . . . of a toast" (1985, 112). My only qualification of
this is to suggest in return that the Hideho Heights sections mirror
"typical black street speech" not because Tolson is "paying tribute"
to Hideho but because Heights himself has seized control of the
poem's diction, its locale, and its image of author function; in the

[12]Earlier drafts of the poem read "from the *front* of the Harlem Gallery"; in what
appears to be the earliest, handwritten version of the line, Hideho enters "from the
front of the empty Harlem Gallery" (TM). The Tolson Manuscripts in the Library of
Congress contain a complete typescript of *Harlem Gallery*, galley proofs, undated
notes, a working draft dated 1956, a number of drafts dated 1959, and folders of
undated snippets.

Zulu Club, as Rufino Laughlin, M.C., declares, Heights is "the poet laureate of Lenox Avenue / . . . / a great big poet and a great big man" (*HG* 77). Here is the milieu in which Heights is at home, and in which we can discover that he is the author of *Skid Row Ballads* (*HG* 84) and *Flophouse Blues* (*HG* 86); here the poem counters its own opening couplet ("The Harlem Gallery, an Afric pepper bird, / awakes me at a people's dusk of dawn" [*HG* 19]) with "a poet's feast in a people's dusk of dawn *counterpoint*" (*HG* 83; my emphasis); and here, best of all, is the triumph of Heights's form of cultural life, as "The Zulu Club patrons whoop and stomp, / clap thighs and backs and knees: / the poet and the audience one, / each gears itself to please" (*HG* 81). Fittingly enough, the Heightsian climax is rendered in a jaunty, Heightsian approximation to ballad meter, and Heightsian alternate-line rhyme to boot.

Dove is right on target, however, about the "virtuoso rendering of narrative layers" in "Xi." For not only is the John Henry ballad/toast itself partly the product of a kind of antiphonal call-and-response as a character named Wafer Waite "leaps to his feet and shouts, / 'Didn't John Henry's Ma and Pa / get no warning?'" (*HG* 81), but the ballad gets more strident as Heights takes from his hip flask a swig which, as Rufino Laughlin appreciatively laughs, "would make / a squirrel spit in the eye of a bulldog!" (*HG* 82). The ballad itself is the result of a dialogic process in which performer and audience work synergistically; as the Club inspires Heights's performance, so Heights inspires the atmosphere of the Club, and vice versa. And just as "the creative impulse in the Zulu Club / leaps from Hideho's lips to Frog Legs' fingers" (*HG* 83), so too does it leap into the audience and spark a battle of first-rate Wits: thus, yet another narrative "layer" is inspired as Heights's toast initiates another form of oral African-American discourse, and the Zulu Club Wits embark on a round of something like a benign version of "the dozens": a chain of signifying from Joshua Nitze, ex-professor of philosophy, to Vincent Aveline, to Shadrach Martial Kilroy, president of "Afroamerican Freedom, Inc.," to Lionel Matheus, the "Sea-Wolf of Harlem," to Dr. Nkomo. The topic is race and the difference it makes, and the keynote is Nitze's wry anecdote of a black stevedore trying to order chitterlings from a white waitress in a newly integrated Bible Belt restaurant. Appropriately, the punch line depends on a carnivalesque reversal of a standard racist maxim:

> The ofay waitress smiled a blond dolichocephalic smile,
> "That's not on the menu, Mister."

> Then the stevedore sneered:
> "Night and day, Ma'am,
> I've been telling Black Folks
> *you* White Folks ain't ready for integration!"
>
> (*HG* 85)

Moreover, although the Curator does not take part in the discussion, Heights, who had earlier asked, "Do I hear The Curator rattle Eliotic bones?" (*HG* 72), apparently moves him to acknowledge the social utility—and necessity—of the characteristic indirectness of African-American oral performance: "Metaphors and symbols in Spirituals and Blues / have been the Negro's manna in the Great White World" (*HG* 91).

Despite all this, Hideho Heights's zenith is evanescent, and a disturbing, discordant minor key runs throughout the scene as well. At the end of "Nu," for example, after Hideho's presence has first been announced to the Zulu Club, he is propositioned by "a tipsy Lena / who peddled Edenic joys / from Harlem to the Bronx," and responds curiously: "the soul seemed to pass out of the body as he announced, / 'Sister, you and I belong to the people'" (*HG* 78). The line sounds merely odd in its immediate context but will become trenchant by poem's end—when the Curator recounts his discovery in Heights's apartment of a modernist poem entitled, of all things, "E. & O.E." It should perhaps cast resonances backward as well, to the ominous preface the Curator provided to Heights's first performance, the delivery of the ballad on Satchmo Armstrong: then, as Heights swigged from his ever ready whiskey bottle, the Curator wrote, "I heard a gurgle, a gurgle—a death rattle" (*HG* 69). The Curator may rattle Eliotic bones, but Heights's rattle is apparently more self-destructive yet.

As if this "framing" of Heights's performances weren't enough, the Curator goes on, as Heights takes the stage to deliver his John Henry ballad, to cast a murky, sinister light on the proceedings:

> In spite of the mocker's mask,
> I saw Hideho
> as a charcoal Piute Messiah
> at a ghetto
> ghost dance.
> Does a Yeats or a beast or a Wovoka
> see and hear
> when our own faculties fail?
>
> (*HG* 79)

The stylistic self-reflexivity of these lines bears attention, as the Curator couches a reference to Yeats in a particularly Yeatsian rhetorical question; but more noteworthy, and more unsettling, is the association the Curator draws between Heights and Wovoka. Wovoka, a Paiute Indian of the late nineteenth century, claimed to have had a vision in which he foresaw the end of European progress westward and promised his fellow Native Americans that white Americans would disappear from the continent in an apocalyptic flood—if his followers would faithfully perform the Ghost Dance and peacefully wait for the next spring. The religion was immediately popular among plains Indians from the moment of its inception in 1889, and it contributed to the massacre of the Sioux at Wounded Knee in 1890—when Wovoka's "ghost shirts," in which the Sioux placed their faith, proved not to be bulletproof after all.[13] The implied answer to the Curator's question, then, is that the poetry of a Yeats may be the poetry of a seer, whereas the poetry of the false prophet Wovoka Heights will prove to be no less than the self-destruction of nonwhite America.

The Curator's momentary apocalyptic vision notwithstanding, he is nevertheless moved both by Heights's performance and by the response of the Wits—until, that is, the very end of "Xi," when, as the Wits get progressively drunker, the Lenox Avenue poet laureate's poetic triumph is given the lie:

> Hideho Heights,
> slumped in the shoal of a stupor,
> slobbers and sobs,
> "My *people*,
> *my* people—
> they know not what they do."
> (HG 92)

Heights, no longer a Paiute Messiah, now echoes Christ—and as he falls, Scripture citation in the poem loses its subversive force, though the nature of Hideho's "betrayal" is as yet far from clear. One thing, however, is clear: the scene's conclusion demolishes what had seemed to be the crowning moment of oral narrative, "the poet and the audience one."

[13]For a more thorough account of Wovoka and the Ghost Dance, see Brown 1970, 406–18, and 391 for a text of Wovoka's speech.

Narrative "Translations" and Narrative Time

"The graven image topples, / breaks in pieces" (*HG* 94); so we hear in the following section, "Omicron." The line is not a specific reference to Heights, but it is the apposite image for the conclusion of "Xi"; the idol of the tribe has fallen, and the poem will not resurrect him again until "Phi." In the meantime, in "Omicron" and "Pi" we are returned to the world of the Curator and Nkomo and to their vision of art; the lines I cited some pages earlier as exempla of the "ideology of rarity," casting the work of art, "like the art of God, [as] a rhyme in the Mikado's tongue," and celebrating Cézanne against the philistines, "*vox populi* and red-tapedom" (*HG* 98, 101), are both from "Pi." "Omicron," though it contains complexities we will return to, contributes yet another image of art-under-seige:

> The school of the artist
> *is*
> the circle of wild horses,
> heads centered,
> as they present to the wolves
> a battery of heels.
> (*HG* 96)

If these two sections reverse the direction of the poem so dramatically, then, I have some critical business to conduct before we move on to the final sections. In the course of doing so, I want to reopen the question of when the poem takes place. But the first question I address, appropriately, has to do with why the narrative of the poem undergoes the transitions it does—why Hideho Heights's entrance into the Gallery should have led the poem into the Zulu Club, and why his collapse should have ushered it back out.

Karl Shapiro, in his introduction to the poem, called it "a narrative work so fantastically stylized that the mind balks at comparisons" (1965b, 14), and so far, apparently, *Harlem Gallery*'s few critics have been sufficiently daunted by the poem's embarrassment of stylistic riches to take the claim at face value. I, for one, remain unsure what Shapiro means by "stylized," for although the poem is certainly as difficult as any text produced by the throes of modernism (save *Finnegans Wake*), and although the poem's movement from "Alpha" to "Omega" implies the kind of comprehensive structural unity we associate with secondary epics from the *Divina Commedia* to *Paradise*

Lost, I do not find (frankly, to my relief) any architechtonic structural principle underlying the whole of Tolson's work. Of course, it is one of the legacies of modernist critical practice that readers even look for such architechtonics, as if all narrative aspired finally to spatial form, as if all poetry grew organically into verbal icons. And perhaps it is the case with *Harlem Gallery,* too, that the text contains calculated intricacies of pattern and form so staggeringly coherent that they can be done justice only by the kind of thoroughgoing, minute, institutional study we have lavished on our "central" modernist texts.

But my claims for the structural principle behind *Harlem Gallery* are a good deal more modest. I discover here no parallel to the fearful symmetry of Joyce's Telemachy and Nostos, no Viconian or Yeatsian cycles of history, no retelling of the Grail quest. I suggest instead that we see *Harlem Gallery*'s narrative "progession" as a series of transactions—or "translations," in the literal sense of "carryings-across"—between the Curator and the Other, usually Heights. On this view, the first five sections form the poem's "preface," and its first trans-action is the encounter with Laugart in "Zeta." Laugart's section brings on Nkomo in "Eta," since Nkomo, as the Curator's closest ally in the mecca Art, mirrors the Curator's thoughts on the cultural position of the Laugarts of the world. Thus, in "Theta" we can be returned to the Curator solo, because although the poem has conducted some narrative exchange, it has not quite become dialogic: the Curator has not had to *confront* either figure; he has only danced a pair of *pas de deux.* In "Lambda," however, Heights's entrance is, as I have said, a genuine disruption; the Curator might write, upon first hearing his voice, "I welcomed Hideho Heights" (*HG* 68), but Heights's usurpation of the poem gives birth to a force it will take most of the remainder of the poem for the Curator to quell.

The principle of narrative "translation," then, holds that the outcome of one series of sections creates the narrative frame or locale of the following sections, as the poem is "carried across" into varying "sociolinguistic points of view" and their corresponding images of aesthetic production and reception. We might say, in shorthand, that the poem's major transitions are trans-lations between the language games of the Curator and Hideho Heights. Thus, for our purposes, the "major" translations occur at "Lambda"/"Mu," "Xi"/"Omicron," "Pi"/"Rho," and, in rapid sequence, "Upsilon"/"Phi"/"Chi"/"Psi." In the first of these, the sounding of Heights's poetic

voice (his contestation of the Gallery and his reading of the Armstrong ballad) shifts the poem firmly into the gossip world of the
Zulu Club; and his ambiguous "betrayal" and drunken lament at the
end of "Xi" transmits the narrative back to the Curator. The "Pi"/
"Rho" transition is problematic, but the poem's remaining fissures
are fairly clear: the Curator's stunned response to Starks's meta-
poems ("my conscience, / when it has a tittle to do, / feels pricks of
Harlem Vignettes" [HG 134]) leads him, and us, back into the Zulu
Club; Heights's final poetic triumph in that section, "Phi," is immediately deflated by his confession to the Curator that he has a "private gallery" (HG 143); "Chi" completes Heights's deflation by revealing him to be a modernist in disguise; and finally, Heights's
unmasking turns the poem back to the Curator, in whose hands it
will conclude.

The poem, in other words, reverses and re-cants itself (also in the
literal sense, "sings itself again") as it goes. Its movement between
the dipoles of "Scripture" and "gossip" is thus a dynamic one: the
outcome of the Curator-Heights struggle is ambiguous until "Chi,"
three-quarters of the way through the poem, which suggests (since,
roughly speaking, Heights enters after the first quarter of the poem)
that the poem's middle sections enact its "central" drama. In this
light, then, it would be Hideho, and not Laugart, who is central to
the poem's ideological figurations, and if we make such a substitution of "central figures," we arrive at a poem that is not demonstrative but dramatic, not logically argued but dialogically enacted.

I call the "Pi"/"Rho" trans-lation problematic, however, because it
is not clear why "Pi," which for the most part sounds so much like
the Curator's and Nkomo's earlier pronouncements on art, should
lead us to the story of the quasi-Heightsian figure of Mister Starks.
In "Pi," it would seem, we are in the world of Scripture, where
artists are messiahs and texts are sacred; where, as the Curator
writes, the artist is iconic, though he may appear an iconoclast:

> Image-breaking?
> Perhaps,
> to the euclidian; but,
> to the perspectivist
> —in the curved space of aeons of cultures—
> the mixed chalice and wafer bread
> may become as dead
> as the dead spindles of lathes.
>   (HG 98)

This, I think, is a wonderful stanza—not only for the *logopoeia* by which Tolson makes visible the analogy between the relativism of historical horizons and the space-time of general relativity but also for the suggestion (again Yeatsian) that all images, even the images of consecrated bread and wine, may be turned by the artist into a machinery for the creation of more images. Lest we believe, however, that the "perspectivist" view de-glorifies art by denying art's iconoclastic force, the Curator reassures us a few stanzas later that, on the contrary, the "perspectivist" view allows us to see that the artist spindles (and folds and mutilates) icons only to create the *verbal* icon:

> Therefore,
> let us beg
> in the court of error
> no ape of God for a fool,
> although
> the scriptures of Art
> (schools within school)
> be
> as esoteric, pluralistic, contradictory
> as texts of the *Koran*,
> the *Book of the Dead*,
> the *Bhagavad-Gita*,
> the *Vulgate*,
> whose disciples
> (tempers fermented to a head
> like yeasted malt)
> babble in the babel of debate
> for eternity and a day.
> (*HG* 100)

Though great art may be as "canonical" here as anywhere else in the Curator's language, still, "Omicron" and "Pi" are not, as it were, untouched by Hideho Heights's passing and may therefore provide some basis for smoothing over the transition between "Pi" and "Rho." For one thing, even though "Omicron" returns us to the Curator's musings on art, those musings sound nothing like his earlier opacities, such as "Art / leaves her lover as a Komitas / deciphering intricate Armenian neums, / with a wild surmise" (*HG* 33). Instead, the section closes with a nine-stanza peroration, a series of proverb-like rhetorical bursts structured around the heavily accented second line, "*is*." At their best, the stanzas are reminiscent of the brilliant fifth section of *Libretto*, in which are transcribed proverbs of African griots, such as "Fear makes a gnarl a cobra's head. / One finger cannot kill a louse. / The seed waits for the lily" (Tolson 1953, *L*, lines 179–81). And one of "Omicron"'s nine closing stanzas dispatches a freight train, as if the proverbs of griots met the image of the blues:

> The temperament of the artist
> *is*
> the buffer bar of a Diesel engine
> that receives the impact
> of a horizontal of alpine and savanna
> freight cars drawn along in the rear.
> (*HG* 97)

Just as the Curator's poetic diction here is a good deal more "oral" than is his overture in "Alpha" to "Epsilon," so too does "Pi" represent a slight modification, a re-cantation, of the poem in that it offers the Curator's first explicitly conciliatory word to critics: "Sometimes / a critic switches the dice and gambles on / his second sight, / since the artist's credo is / ... *now* a riding light ... / *then* a whistling buoy in / a Styx' night" (*HG* 101). Moreover, perhaps one of the quatrains that follows this, in which the Curator describes in the abstract his own critical process, stands also as a description of his relation to Starks's *Harlem Vignettes*: "I visit a work of art: in the garden How / I pluck the pansy; blink the weed; / fish in the dark tarn Auber for the Why; / seek out the What and trace its breed" (*HG* 102). It may be, then, that "Pi" prepares us for the introduction of a metatext that will challenge the Curator and demand his own critical response.

But it is not simply for the sake of structural nicety that I seek to "smooth" the transition between these sections: the opening of "Rho" introduces yet another problem, the problem of the poem's temporal sequence. Its first two lines, "New Year's Day / Hedda Starks telephoned me" (*HG* 103), begin the narrative of Starks's (alleged) suicide; but just as the postscript to "Zeta" retrospectively placed the visit to Laugart's flat in the pluperfect tense, at an unspecified time before his death, so too does "Phi" render ambiguous the temporal status of "New Year's Day," since Hedda Starks gives the manuscript of *Vignettes* to the Curator *after* her phone call, and in "Phi" we find that the Curator has read it. In both cases (Starks's and Laugart's), the "present tense" of the poem's time of narration remains unclear. This is more than a matter for critical pedantry, for two reasons. First, it begs the questions I have attempted to answer above: namely, if the twenty-four episodes of the poem are not narrated in chronological sequence, what sequence do they follow, if any? and if they follow no sequence, then why do the "narrative" sections of the poem appear where they do? Second, and far more important, it complicates our efforts to determine the Curator's cultural position, for the simple reason that it renders impossible the determination of his *historical* position; and in a poem whose central issues concern the ultimate place of the marginal artist, "historical position" is necessarily a central issue.

The first question, then, leads us to seek some principle of atemporal causality in the poem, even if that principle operates on the presumption of a *post hoc ergo propter hoc* logic of narrative "translations," and even if such a principle cannot account exhaustively for each and every one of the poem's transitions. But the second question here is much more basic: does the poem take place in the 1920s, the 1940s, the 1960s, or an amalgam of temporal loci scattered over this span? If the last possibility is the case, as it appears to be, what are the ramifications of this temporal "dispersion" for the poem's invocation of great artists? When the Curator deploys an allusion to Matisse, for example, is he invoking the turn-of-the-century Fauvist Matisse, or the mid-century Matisse of paper cutouts who claimed to want to create art the tired businessman could come home to? And to what end in either case? To put the question another way, if the poem wants to narrate, in its allusive subtext, the story of how the Impressionists of the 1874 Paris show (which really was reviled by critics) became the Impressionists we see in coffee-table tomes, then is the poem celebrating the process by which revolutions in aesthetics eventually make their way into the cultural lingua franca, or is it alerting us to the historical process by which the avant-garde is transmuted into *kitsch*, and thus calling us to carry on the revolutions of the avant-garde?

We cannot answer these questions—not because we do not have enough textual evidence, but because the textual evidence itself will not allow the questions to be answered. In the matter of narrative time, indeterminacy is inscribed in the poem at every turn; it is as if the poem itself, like the electron in Heisenberg's Principle, cannot say where it is; its position can be specified only in terms of probability and range. And Tolson has apparently been careful to cover his tracks: in "Beta" the Curator writes of "Young Men labeled by their decades / The Lost, The Bright, The Angry, The Beat" (*HG* 25); but in "Eta" we hear that Rommel has just died. One of the more crucial perfect-tense flashbacks in *Harlem Vignettes* concerns an "ex-

Freedom Rider," and CORE's Freedom Rides began in May 1961; but the final vignette, also narrated in the perfect, narrates Mister Starks's encounter with famous bootlegger Dutch Schultz in the midst of Prohibition.[14] Dr. Nkomo likewise brings the poem into the 1960s when he urges

> the artists
> of the Market Place Gallery in Harlem:
> "Remember
> the Venerable Yankee Poet
> on the unfamiliar red carpet of the Capitol
> as he visaed the gospel of the Founding Fathers
> ... Novus Ordo Seclorum ...
> spieled by every dollar bill."
>   (HG 100–101)

We may find this temporal ambiguity even in the poem's opening quatrain:

> The Harlem Gallery, an Afric pepper bird,
> awakes me at a people's dusk of dawn.
> The age altars its image, a dog's hind leg,
> and hazards the moment of truth in pawn.
>   (HG 19)

For even given the oblique allusion, in line 2, to W. E. B. Du Bois's 1940 Dusk of Dawn, it is unclear when this dusk of dawn takes place. It may be, as Gordon Thompson has it, that "Harlem Gallery" refers metonymically "to the artists who contribute to the gallery; in which case, this may also be a topical allusion to a cultural revolution brought about by the Harlem Renaissance" (1986, 170). It may as well be, on a similar principle, that the "people's dusk of dawn" occurs not in the 1920s but in the early 1940s, amid the dawn of hipsters, zoot suits, and the riot of 1943[15]—or, for that matter, during the 1960s dawn of the northern wing of the civil rights movement. Lines 3 and 4 compound the uncertainty: the appositive noun

---

[14]Even Tolson's reference to CORE's Freedom Rides is encased in a series of pluperfects, thus further blurring the poem's "present" tense. When we meet the ex–Freedom Rider, he is working as the Zulu Club's janitor; formerly a chaplain at Alabama Christian College, he has apparently been fired for his activism (HG 122, 124). He appears in the milk/cream debate (see n. 20 below), which is itself a narrative flashback within the Vignettes; and still more (unspecified) time intervenes between Starks's literary recreation of the scene and the Curator's eventual reading of it.

[15]This was suggested to me by Eric Lott's fascinating "Double V, Double Time: Bebop's Politics of Style" (1988).

phrases in line 3 parallel those in line 1, and line 4 closes the quatrain on a rhyme; pattern is evoked by repetition and completion,
yet the metrical pattern of the first line's symmetrical trochees and
dactyls (*Harlem Gallery, Afric pepper bird*) is broken, in line 3, on "altars," just as the fourth line, constructed of two anapests flanked by
iambs, disrupts the iambic pentameter of the second.[16]

Leaving aside for the moment the nearly sprung rhythm of "a
dog's hind leg," we find that the most emphatic stresses of lines 3–4
work to highlight a curious concatenation of words. *Altars, image,
hazards, moment, truth*: the collision of noumena with phenomena,
essence with appearance, extends the tension of the dusk of dawn;
and the pun on "altars" suggests the extraordinary lability of the
moment of consecration, a lability the poem will continue to exploit.
The opening quatrain employs the present tense even as it undoes
the present tense: it does not signify a present, it throws a present
tens-ion over a tenseless moment of flux.

This systematic temporal confusion helps the poem to dodge the
most important cultural questions it raises: namely, if the dissemination of high culture to the masses is an end devoutly to be wished,
how can dissemination avoid trivialization, dissolution, and
"kitschification"? If the Tolsonian avant-garde is driven by the desire
to create the taste by which it is to be enjoyed, how—to borrow a
phrase from Lillian Robinson (1984)—do we know when we've
won, and how do we go about "winning"? What, then, is the cultural position of the avant-garde artist who finally *has* transformed
the masses, or been transformed by them?

On these issues the poem is silent, content to affirm in the abstract the transformative power of art, content to let stand the contradictory demands of the "Romantic/democratic" concept of art,
wherein, we recall, the artist is both solitary genius and representative of the masses. It is in the face of serious cultural conflicts such
as this that ideology does its most useful work; and Tolson was for-
tunate, in this respect, to have as a professional friend and sup-
porter John Ciardi, for it was Ciardi's defense of high culture which
provided Tolson with the means for smoothing over and denying
the conflict. In 1958, as poet and poetry editor of the *Saturday Review
of Literature*, Ciardi wrote his own version of Karl Shapiro's "consid-

---

[16]It is possible also to scan the first line as iambic hexameter; however, even if we
do so, we have not diminished the disruptive force of "altars," nor have we upset the
symmetry of the first line, wherein the half-lines on either side of the caesura mirror
each other.

ered statement" on the relation between modern poetry and modern audiences. The piece, published first in Ciardi's weekly column and reprinted often, is entitled simply "Dialogue with the Audience," and it stages a lecture-dialogue in which a Poet answers the question put to him by a Citizen: "Who *are* you modern poets for? Is there no such thing as an audience?" Ciardi's Poet responds by distinguishing between two kinds of audience, which he calls "horizontal" and "vertical." I quote the column at some length, not only because Tolson himself cited it so often but also because it displays almost every one of the assumptions I have been addressing in this chapter, from its defense of the "ideology of rarity" right down to its faith in a version of the "great god Biosis."

> "The horizontal audience consists of everybody who is alive at this moment [explains the Poet]. The vertical audience consists of everyone, vertically through time, who will ever read a given poem. . . .
> "Isn't it immediately obvious that [Wallace] Stevens can only 'be for' a tiny percentage of the horizontal audience? . . .
> "The point is that the horizontal audience always outnumbers the vertical at any one moment, but that the vertical audience for good poetry always outnumbers the horizontal in time-enough. And not only for the greatest poets. Andrew Marvell is certainly a minor poet, but given time enough, more people certainly will have read 'To His Coy Mistress' than will ever have subscribed to *Time*, *Life*, and *Fortune*. Compared to what a good poem can do, Luce is a piker at getting circulation."
> "Impressive, if true," says the Citizen, "but how does any given poet get his divine sense of this vertical audience?"
> "By his own ideal projection of his own best sense of himself. It's as simple as that," says the Poet. "He may be wrong, but he has nothing else to go by. And there is one thing more—all good poets are difficult when their work is new. And their work always becomes less difficult as their total shape becomes more and more visible. As that shape impresses itself upon time, one begins to know how to relate the parts to their total." (1958, 12, 42)

Notable here are at least three features: the useful confusion as to who outnumbers whom; the implicit claim that "vertical" audiences always form and that worthy marginal poets therefore always eventually become central; and, not least, the deft elimination of specificity and agency in the last two sentences, which leave us ultimately with the incomprehensible image of a "shape" that "impresses itself upon time."

No doubt part of this argument's attractiveness lies in the very fact that it was published not in a professional journal by an academic critic seeking to justify his institution to himself and his colleagues but in a nonspecialist weekly by a generalist poet-critic seeking only to give modern poetry a fair hearing. For part of what Ciardi is doing in his "Dialogue" is echoing and translating the modernist credo for the average citizen, as that credo had been set forth in the mid-1940s by Eliot himself: in "The Social Function of Poetry," Eliot warned that "if a poet gets a large audience very quickly, that is a rather suspicious circumstance: for it leads us to fear that he is not really doing anything new, that he is only giving people what they are already used to" (1945, 11). However, adds Eliot, there must nevertheless be some market for new production, a market properly "independent" of the market:

> That a poet should have the right, small audience in his own time *is* important. There should always be a small vanguard of people, appreciative of poetry, who are independent and somewhat in advance of their time or ready to assimilate novelty more quickly. The development of culture does not mean bringing everybody up to the front, which amounts to no more than making everyone keep step: it means the maintenance of such an *élite*, with the main, and more passive body of readers not lagging more than a generation or so behind. The changes and developments of sensibility which appear first in a few will work themselves into the language gradually, through their influence on other, and more readily popular authors; and by the time they have become well established, a new advance will be called for. (11)

One notices here, too, that there are no agents-with-active-verbs in the crucial last two sentences, except for "changes and developments"—that is, those special cultural productions that "work themselves." It should be clear, in any case, why such an argument would appeal to Tolson, and it should be clear why such an argument would be more appealing to Tolson when supported by a more "readily popular" writer such as Ciardi.

But despite Ciardi's (and Eliot's) confident implication that the avant-garde always eventually becomes the cultural "center" over time, Tolson's poem, by confining itself to the image of an avant-garde already nearly a century old, has left ambiguous the nature of that avant-garde's contemporary cultural position. And this ambiguity, like the poem's deliberate confusion of times, is woven into its very fabric: Nkomo's citation of Robert Frost at Kennedy's inauguration, for example, is immediately followed by his reference to Cézanne as a "Toussaint L'Ouverture of Esthetics" hailed only by his fellow artists. What, then, is the relation of the two allusions—oppositional or appositional? If the former, then Frost is an example of the kind of popular recognition and acclaim Cézanne never achieved; if the latter, Frost becomes an image of how the state can defuse the power of a Toussaint L'Ouverture by falsely embracing him, by giving him an "official" role. The Curator actually does entertain the latter possibility, not in "Pi" but in "Omega":

> Now and then a State,
> when iron fists and hobnails
> explode alarms at the citadel's gate,
> dons the ill-fitting robes of the Medici
> and initiates Project CX,
> to propagandize a rubber-stamped pyramid of Art
> and to glorify the Cheops at the apex.
> (*HG* 169)

Is this the light in which to read the Frost tableau, as a modern version of the hostile silence of *vox populi* and red-tapedom with which Cézanne was supposedly received—a version wherein "hostile silence" has now become "repressive tolerance"? The question should trouble some of our earlier readings of the poem as well: for we may not be sure, after all, what the Curator means by writing that the "world-self of the make- / believe becomes the swimming pool of a class" (*HG* 29). Does "swimming pool" here potentiate or subvert the image of art as a "balsam apple / of the soul"? is this swimming pool a comfort and refreshment for the sweltering multitudes, or has the work of art been transformed into sheer commodity, as suburban status symbol?

Even some of the poem's allusions, which seem on the surface unproblematic, recapitulate this ambiguity. Take, for instance, this fairly straightforward stanza from "Epsilon":

> Again
> by the waters of Babylon we sit down and weep,
> for the pomp and power
> of the bulls of Bashan
> serve Belshazzarian tables to artists and poets who
> serve the hour,
> torn between two masters,
> God and Caesar—
> this (for Conscience),
> the Chomolungma of disasters.
> (*HG* 36)

Clearly enough, this passage laments the power of various market forces, cast here as Psalm 22's bulls of Bashan, to lure artists into lucrative positions that compromise or adulterate their artistic commitments; the sentiment is closely akin to Clement Greenberg's when he writes, "Kitsch's enormous profits are a source of temptation to the avant-garde itself, and its members have not always resisted this temptation. Ambitious artists and writers will modify their work under the pressure of kitsch, if they do not succumb to it entirely" (1939, 41). But then the Curator's allusion to "Belshazzarian tables" is troubling, for Belshazzar's feast in Daniel 5:1–4 is immediately followed by the appearance of the writing on the wall in 5:5. In that case, we may be weeping because the bulls of Bashan have bought off the artists, or we may be weeping because we are as yet unaware that a Daniel is about to arrive, to signify on the oppressors. But perhaps (to carry the ambiguity further yet) there is no Daniel here at all. Will, then, the prophet-in-exile arrive to refuse riches and rewards, speak the truth, overthrow the king and usher in the new, benevolent administration of Darius the Mede? Or are the artists and poets, their mouths stuffed full of Belshazzar's food, unable to speak?

I suggest that the poem deliberately invites and ignores such questions, chiefly, I think, in order to keep alive and plausible its primary myth: the myth of an avant-garde which, despite the opposition of critics, capitalists, and philistines, has survived to become part of "the heritage of Art" which, as "Omicron" has it, "nurtures everywhere / the wingless and the winged man" (*HG* 93) and which allows the Curator to write, near poem's end, "I envision the Harlem Gallery of my people" (*HG* 171). The myth's power, in *Harlem Gallery*, is a function of the power with which the poem itself defends its complexity as a privileged (God-like) practice of mimesis:

> White Boy,
> Black Boy,
> freedom is the oxygen
> of the studio and gallery.
> What if a *chef-d'oeuvre* is esoteric? . . .
> Is it amiss or odd
> if the apes of God
> take a cue from their Master?
> (*HG* 169)

The poem thus needs to assert a kind of supreme cultural fiction, a fiction in which it does not seal itself off forever from all but an intellectual or artistic margin, or, worse, from any audience whatsoever. To this end, the poem maintains its contradictions as sedulously as it refrains from any reference to post-Depression marginal artists; and both strategies, mutually supporting, help the poem avoid confronting directly its relation to the audience, and the avant-garde, of its own time.

For where, in a poem that refers repeatedly to jazz greats Louis Armstrong and King Oliver, are Charlie Parker, Thelonious Monk, John Coltrane? Where, in a poem whose temporal range extends to the Kennedy administration, are Jackson Pollock, Robert Motherwell, Willem de Kooning? The youngest artist in the poem, William Gropper, was born in 1897; Louis Armstrong, its youngest musician, in 1900. Thus, of all the figures in the Curator's anthology, only Satchmo is younger than Tolson himself. On one level, the omission of more recent experimental artists may be a part of Tolson's reaction to his own self-conscious belatedness, an attempt to conjure the image of the avant-garde as it appeared in the heyday of the Harlem Renaissance;[17] but more significantly, it points to *Harlem Gallery*'s profound refusal to contemplate its own conflicted and ambiguous position—not only in relation to the mass audience it seeks to disturb and instruct but also in relation to its fellow-travelers on the margins of cultural production.

I return in Chapter 3 to these questions, in different form, when I discuss *Harlem Gallery*'s reception history. In the meantime, let us return to the poem where we left it, at the beginning of "Rho," to examine its remaining "translations"—Mister Starks's *Vignettes* in "Upsilon," and Heights's last hurrah in "Phi." For although the poem is deliberately vague about its idea of a contemporary avant-garde, in the closing sections the power of the idea is a corollary of its vagueness: whatever else the avant-garde may be in *Harlem Gallery*, and whoever may be its denizens, it is, as the Curator writes of

[17]The Harlem Renaissance had special significance for Tolson, not only in that it was the central African-American cultural configuration of the first half of the century but, more specifically, in that Tolson lived briefly in New York during 1931–32, on a fellowship at Columbia, writing an M.A. thesis titled "The Harlem Group of Negro Writers." At no other point in his life, certainly, was he as near the epicenter of a movement as he was during his year at Columbia. In fact, the mustard seed from which *Harlem Gallery* eventually sprouted was apparently a sonnet composed during that year. The sonnet grew into *A Gallery of Harlem Portraits*, completed in 1935 (and published posthumously in 1979). In a sense, then, the poem we have now was gestating for thirty years, and some of its temporal confusion is undoubtedly the result of a kind of "time-capsule" effect. For Tolson's life in New York, see Farnsworth 1984, 30–61.

art in "Pi," "a domain . . . with an Al Sirat of its own" (*HG* 99). That Al Sirat, that true path, will prove to be the difficulty of modernist technique, and the poem's penalties for refusal to accommodate one's cultural position to the forces of modernism will be very severe indeed. For in *Harlem Gallery*, it is not enough for an artist to be "politically correct"; political protest that takes too recognizable a form turns out to be self-defeating insofar as it "confirms familiar sentiments," as Jauss put it. Only negativity, as the violation of aesthetic horizons of expectation, is *critical* in the political sense: thus will we discover what it means, in the Curator's formulation, to be caught in "the Afroamerican dilemma in the Arts— / the dialectic of / to be or not to be / a Negro" (*HG* 146).

The "Afroamerican Dilemma" and the Imperatives of Modernism

If, after Hideho's collapse in "Xi," we entertained any dark suspicions about the nature of his "betrayal" or the reason he likened himself to a prostitute in "Nu," the next few sections of the poem appear not only to exonerate him from the charge of racial ambivalence but to establish him as an unmistakably powerful voice in the Harlem community. Hideho, as we are told in one of the character sketches that make up Starks's *Vignettes*, is every bit as much an antagonist of the status quo as is Laugart: "To the black bourgeoisie, / Hideho was a crab louse / in the pubic region of Afroamerica" (*HG* 114). To Starks, Hideho's political stance is precisely what the moment requires:

> Plato's bias will not banish,
> from his Republic,
> the poet laureate of Lenox Avenue—
> for he is a man square as the *x* in Dixie,
> in just the right place,
> at just the right time,
> with just the right thing.
> (*HG* 113)

In Starks's manuscript, we are clearly back in the gossip world— Heights's laurels are undisputed here—but the vignettes are more equi-vocal a gossip text. On the one hand, they do tend to dialogize the poem they inhabit, for they yield us images of Heights, Laugart, and the Curator himself which at times differ significantly from those we have received from the Curator; likewise, they contribute to the poem's "reality effect," in a manner similar to the Zulu Club scenes, by giving us the inside scoop on minor characters whom the Curator either doesn't mention or doesn't know of. On the other hand, although these poems are not nearly so "literary" as are the early sections of *Harlem Gallery*, they do constitute, and are "read" in the poem as a written text. They are Scripture and gossip at once; more important, they are "framed" in the same ominous way as was Hideho's discourse in "Lambda"—not only by the wistful epigraph Starks has scribbled on the manuscript's title page ("I should have followed—perhaps—*Des Imagistes* / down the Macadam Road" [*HG* 111]) but also, and more tellingly, by the news that Mister Starks has apparently committed suicide.

In other words, it is clear from the outset that *Harlem Vignettes* is a posthumous text; the "death rattle" that preceded Heights's ballad to Louis Armstrong becomes here a death knell as Starks's last will and testament arrives at the Angelus Funeral Home in "Sigma." In fact, Hedda Starks called the Curator on that New Year's Day, back in "Rho" (whatever year it may have been), in order to capitulate at last to her dead husband's request to turn over the manuscript to the Curator. *Harlem Vignettes* is therefore prefaced both by Starks's admission that his poetry is premodern "Lee Masterism" and by the even more damning text of his own will. Starks's death, in *Harlem Gallery*'s version of twentieth-century literary history, represents also the death of his poetics. Moreover, just as Heights's triumph in "Xi" is punctured by his collapse, so too is Starks's work followed by the Curator's dismissive judgment that the *Vignettes* "will doubtless fetch / no white laurel of joys, / no black crepe of regrets" (*HG* 134). But despite the "framing" of the quasi-oral poetry in "Upsilon" by the written documents of "Sigma" and "Tau" (Starks's will and epigram, respectively), Starks's poems do translate *Harlem Gallery*, even if ambiguously, back into the gossip world of subversion and signifying. For the *Vignettes* is a narrative realm in which Starks, in the poem's penultimate stanza, can come across a vice squad cop trying to entrap a prostitute, and expose him by seeming to acknowledge his authority: "I felt sorry for the unsuspecting woman. / About to pass, I said, 'Hello, Officer!'" (*HG* 132). A minor gesture, but one of which any trickster figure could be proud.

In terms of the ambivalence of Starks's text as scriptural gossip, the Janus-faced icon under which we enter the *Vignettes* is the minor figure of Ester Bostic, who, as we hear in "Sigma," has a "hobby [of] making checkerwork / with her fingers or with her lips" (*HG* 106).

Bostic seems to be mentioned only because she is the bookkeeper to Ma'am Shears, the owner of the Angelus Funeral Home; she inhabits only four stanzas, yet the Curator feels compelled to devote a stanza to the fact that she is a gossiper. The reference is somewhat self-reflexive, for the Curator himself seems to be gossiping here: the mention of Bostic leads him into a pointless tangent about Ma'am Shears's annual trips to Trinidad, a tangent from which he has to recall himself in a highly uncharacteristic parenthesis: "(But let / us get on with the classic version of the Zulu Club Wits)" (*HG* 107). The passage is uncharacteristic for at least three reasons: first, it is the only time the Curator implies an interlocutor through the use of the first-person plural pronoun; second, it is the only time the Curator catches himself in a digression; and third, it is the only time the Curator acknowledges the origin of his tale in oral discourse—here, the story of Starks's suicide as told (communally?) by the Wits.

Ester Bostic, then, despite her inconsequentiality to *Harlem Gallery*, is in a way the perfect figure of transition into Starks's oral/written verse, for her gossip will eventually become an "archetype for newsmongers" (*HG* 106)—the printed, newspaper version of Starks's tale—and her oral/written gossip is itself "checkerwork," like the text of the *Vignettes*. And the vignettes draw from Rita Dove the same kind of praise she bestowed on Hideho Heights: "Can I get a Witness? Because what Tolson has been doing all along is testifying, which is nothing more than to 'tell the truth through story.' The *Vignettes* are important not only as an advancement of the plot, but for their function as narrative history—in designing them, Tolson is a sort of literary counterpart to the African griot, the elder assigned the task of memorizing tribal history" (1985, 114). Although I would not assign the *Vignettes* directly to Tolson, I do like the notion of Starks as "a literary counterpart to the African griot," for I think the phrase expresses concisely the half-written, half-oral nature of the work.

For my own purposes, the vignettes themselves are useful for three reasons, the first two of which, like Starks's premodernism and his unqualified praise of Hideho Heights, help indicate their author's position in *Harlem Gallery*. One lies in the opening line of Starks's self-portrait, in which he makes himself out to be more or less the opposite of John Laugart: "My talent was an Uptown whore; my wit a Downtown pimp" (*HG* 112). He has prostituted his gifts by writing a million-selling boogie-woogie record, even though his Stravinskian masterpiece, *Black Orchid Suite*, was premiered by the Harlem Symphony Orchestra with Starks himself as conductor. He has, in his own words, "tried to poise that seesaw between *want* and *have*"; he has equated *vox populi* with *vox Dei* (*HG* 112)—which is to say, in the terms of *Harlem Gallery*'s Romantic ideology, that he committed suicide long before he took his own life.

My second interest in the vignettes lies in the possibility that, curiously enough, Starks may not have taken his own life at all; "Sigma" told us that he'd been shot in the heart but that a .38 was found hidden in the toilet of a character named Crazy Cain. Cain's portrait in the *Vignettes* fleshes out the tale, telling us not only that Cain was the bastard son of Guy Delaporte III and Starks's wife Hedda (an ex-stripper with the stage name of Black Orchid—hence the title of Starks's symphonic suite) but that he might conceivably have had a motive for the killing: Starks had fired Cain from the Harlem Symphony Orchestra. Whatever the cause of Starks's death, therefore, it is the direct result of his personal and artistic compromises: if he did *not* take his own life in despairing acknowledgment of his prostitution, then he was killed, even more allegorically, by the issue of the illicit union of the Black Bourgeoisie and his own capitulation to temptation, in the form of Hedda Starks.[18]

In these two respects, Starks demonstrates the fatality of his artistic choices; he has been inspired by a tainted muse, he has eaten at the table of Belshazzar, and he has failed to follow the posthumous history of Imagism down the winding Macadam Road to the destinations of *Hugh Selwyn Mauberly*, *The Waste Land*, and *Harlem Gallery*. Surely, Farnsworth's characterization of Starks's poetic style as "doomed to extinction" is morbidly apt. And it may be helpful to recall here not only Farnsworth's judgment but Tolson's own claim to have stashed in his trunk for twenty years a 340-page manuscript version of *Harlem Gallery* inspired by Edgar Lee Masters.[19] For Starks

[18]The status of women in all this is highly suspect. Whether as prostitutes (and as figures for the prostitution of art as commodity) or as bearers of the illegitimate (as in Hideho's confession, below), women are precisely that against which Art must struggle. Like yet unlike the polar opposition of writing and speech in poetic diction, woman as a figure of adultery, illegitimacy, and commodity is an aspect of Tolson's modernism open to our contemporary challenge and revision. Women were so figured *before* the twentieth century, of course, but the association of women with mass culture is specifically modernist; see Huyssen 1986, 44–62.

[19]This, apparently, is *A Gallery of Harlem Portraits*. See Farnsworth 1979, 273–75: "Biographical and Bibliographical Notes." Starks's epigraph is slightly puzzling, for *Des Imagistes* was practically stillborn: by the time the anthology hit the press, Pound had moved on to Vorticism, leaving Richard Aldington and H.D. to fend for themselves—which they have not done entirely successfully. But whether the confusion here over Imagism's "history" is Tolson's or Starks's, the point remains: in bracketing off Starks as somehow premodern, Tolson is also bracketing off *A Gallery of Harlem Portraits*, and yet evoking its shadow, in the *Vignettes*.

is not only the reverse image of Laugart; he is also, in one way, a projection and rejection of the early Tolson.

But one of Starks's poems startles the Curator and provides my third point of interest: the portrait of the Curator himself. Although the vignette is on the whole highly sympathetic, it retells the story (in best gossip fashion) of the night when the Curator and Nkomo engaged (in best signifying fashion) in a dispute over the relative values of milk and cream. The episode makes evident what, for Starks as well as for the reader, had previously been invisible: "the differences between / The Curator and Doctor Nkomo" (*HG* 121). Nkomo opens the debate by asking the Curator why he drinks cream instead of milk, and the dialogue runs as follows, as the Curator responds:

> "I remain a lactoscopist
> fascinated by
> the opacity of cream,
> the dusk of human nature,
> 'the light-between' of the modernistic."

> Doctor Nkomo's snort
> was a Cape buffalo's.
> "You brainwashed, whitewashed son
> of bastard Afroamerica!"
> The Curator grinned
> his Solomonic grin,
> for the nettle words were stingless like
> a mosquito bee.
> As a Bach fugue piles up rhythms,
> the Africanist heaped his epithets:
> "Garbed in the purple of metaphors,
> the Nordic's theory of the cream separator
> is still a stinking skeleton!"

> "Since cream rises to the top," said the Curator,
> "blame Omniscience—
> not me."
>
> (*HG* 123)

We should recognize here, garbed in the purple of metaphors, the reception theory the Curator advanced in the poem's first five sections, wherein "The great god Biosis begets the taste that sets apart

the pearls and olivets" (*HG* 22); and we should be somewhat sur-
prised, at first, to find the implicit elitism of the theory challenged
by none other than Nkomo.

But the Curator also suggests that historical exigencies may demand an elitist praxis—that is, that times are tough and we may not
be able to drink deeply of the cultures of milk:

> "Between the ass and the womb of two eras,"
> said The Curator, gloomily,
> "*taste* the milk of the skimmed
> and *sip* the cream of the skimmers."
>
> (125)

Yet Nkomo's response to what Starks calls the Curator's "eclipse of
faith" (*HG* 125), it turns out, is not so much a challenge to the Curator's idea of canonicity in toto as it is an insistence that the canon be
opened to the best works of all cultures and taught to all classes;[20] he
concludes his mock attack by simultaneously quoting Virgil,[21] echoing Eliot, and demanding (in my translation) that the syllabus include and assimilate all cultural literacies:

> "*Mens sibi conscia recti*,"
> said Doctor Nkomo
> —definitively—
> "is not a hollow man who dares not peddle
> the homogenized milk of multiculture,
> in dead ends and on boulevards,
> in green pastures and across valleys of dry bones."
>
> (*HG* 126)

The Curator's reaction is invisible to Starks—"it was hidden behind The Curator's mask" (*HG* 126)—but is visible to us in "Phi,"
when the Curator writes, self-reproachfully, that Starks "had seen in

[20]This reading would see Nkomo as the kind of canon reviser who, according to
Lillian Robinson, attempts an "uneasy compromise" in arguing for the inclusion, in
curricula and anthologies, of literature that "conforms as closely as possible to the
traditional canons of taste and judgment" (1985, 111). I admit, however, that this
reading misses one of the crucial complications of the Curator-Nkomo debate; the
chaplain–Freedom Rider–janitor's contribution, which signifies on the fact that neither the Curator nor Nkomo has considered how "perhaps there is a symbolism / —a
manna for the darker peoples— / in the rich opacity of cream / and the poor whiteness of skim milk" (*HG* 125).

[21]"A mind conscious of the right" (*Aeneid* 1.604). The allusion does not seem to have
any specific purpose, as the phrase is taken from Aeneas's speech of thanks to Dido
(1.595–610).

me / the failure of nerve / Harlem would never see— / the charact in the African / that made / him the better man" (*HG* 133). Although the argument between himself and Nkomo is ultimately a friendly exchange, conducted, as it were, between two tenured professors with similar interests and outlooks (Nkomo's nettle words are "stingless," and Starks's tableau closes with an image of the two "staring into space, / united like the siphons of a Dosinia" [*HG* 126]), the Curator apparently feels himself outflanked for the first time in the poem. And thus the text of the *Vignettes* translates us back into the world of the Zulu Club for the last time, as the Curator strikes a pose more sympathetic to Hideho Heights than any he has yet adopted:

> *Harlem Vignettes* read,
> I felt I should make
> (like Hideho)
> a second Harlem marriage bed—
> take
> (like Hideho)
> the Daughter of the Wine to Spouse.
>
> (*HG* 133)

And in "Phi" ensues the penultimate confrontation between the Curator and Heights, a confrontation that Hideho clearly wins.

For "Phi" is doubly the Curator's low point—not only because he has been chastened by Starks's portrait but also because Starks's poems have problematized racial politics more explicitly, and more cynically, than any other section of *Harlem Gallery*. "Like all 100-p.c. Negroes," writes Starks in his final portrait,

> I knew a white skin was the open
> sesame to SUCCESS—
> the touchstone of
> Freedom, Justice, Equality.
> Hadn't a white poet said when they cut off his leg,
> "I am the master of my fate ..."?
>
> (*HG* 129)

Such talk is troubling to the Curator, as is Nkomo's description of him as a "whitewashed son of bastard Afroamerica," because, as he himself will confess in "Psi," the Curator is an octoroon with blond hair and blue eyes. That confession explains a temporarily veiled line in Starks's portrait of the Curator, a reference to "the Afroamerican's features of *A Man called White*" (*HG* 125): it becomes clear to us eventually (though the Curator would catch the allusion at once) that Starks is likening the Curator to Walter White, who was physically indistinguishable from white folk, by alluding to the title of White's autobiography.[22]

On another front altogether, Crazy Cain, bastard and possible homicide, is cast by Starks as the offspring of "hybrid chattel": "His Negro tradition bitched the night / an Irish field hand raped a Mandingo woman in / an Alabama cottonfield" (*HG* 115). With Cain's portrait we are undoubtedly in the land of the tragic mulatto, where the racially liminal and marginal man is dangerous, disturbing, and deadly. Thus the Curator is in a dubious position when Nkomo, in the Zulu Club scene of "Phi," gainsaying Shadrach Martial Kilroy's "a specter haunts the Great White World— / the specter of *Homo Aethiopicus*, the pigmented Banquo's ghost" (*HG* 136), casts the African-American's polyglot heritage as a handicap: "you / are a people in whose veins / poly-breeds / and / plural strains / mingle and run— / an Albert Ryder of many schools, and *none*" (*HG* 136).

In short, it is small wonder that in "Phi" we see the Curator at his most defensive. Also, if we take into account his ambiguous racial status, it might be possible for us to read his chagrin, at "Phi'"s opening, as a form of displacement, a substitution of professional for racial and cultural anxieties. For in a sense, Nkomo has not "outflanked" the Curator at all; Nkomo is a good pluralist, peddling the "homogenized milk of multiculture," but still a pluralist who believes in the concept of the "masterpiece" as "the *vis viva* of an ape of God" (*HG* 46), as he puts it in "Eta." And if this is the case, then Nkomo is arguing from a position of utter security, for it's all very well to speak of homogenization when one is oneself sure of one's own racial identity. Perhaps, for that matter, Nkomo's nettle words "whitewashed" and "bastard" are as stinging as words can be.

The Curator may not have good reason to feel chastened by Nkomo's injunction, but he may very well have reason to feel *unheimlich*—in a Heideggerian sense, not-at-home—at Starks's and Nkomo's critique of the African-American's polyglot genealogy. Surely, the Curator's mixed ancestry links him with the outcast Crazy Cain—and perhaps, too, if the Curator is as well versed in African-American literary history as he is in modern French paint-

---

[22]Walter White is also the author of *Fire in the Flint* (1924), which Tolson adapted to the stage and directed, at the Dust Bowl Theatre, in 1952. See Farnsworth 1984, 128–31.

ing, he may wince at the thought that Cain is an allusion to Jean Toomer's *Cane*, and at the reminder that he himself looks even less Negroid than Toomer—looks as white, in fact, as Walter White. Be that as it may, "Phi" certainly presents us with an embattled Curator, the Curator Agonistes, a Curator unprepared to deal with Heights at his most successful—and his most militant.

Immediately after the Nkomo-Kilroy exchange, Hideho nods the Curator to the bar, confides to him that the "bunkum session on the Negro / . . . / has sparked an inspiration" (*HG* 138), and proceeds to announce, in Heightsian idiolect,

> "The Centennial of the Emancipation Proclamation,
> Ye Muses!
> As the People's Poet,
> I shall Homerize a theme that will rock the Nation!
> And every damned Un-American will know it!"
> (*HG* 139)

The Curator is positively bitter in return: "You poets come too soon or too late, / Hideho Heights, / with too little, / to save the Old Ship of State" (*HG* 139). At this point the stage, down to the last prop, is set for the Curator's nadir, for the Curator himself follows his retort with a realization of its inadequacy:

> To Hideho Heights,
> at that moment in the throe
> of creation,
> I was a half-white egghead with maggots on the brain.
> I ate my crow,
> for the unconscious of the artist
> cannot say to itself *No.*
> (*HG* 139)

And as though it were not sufficiently humiliating for the Curator to see himself reflected by Heights as a "half-white egghead," Heights's parable of the sea-turtle and shark, a tale of "the instinctive drive of the weak to survive" (*HG* 140), in which black America is pictured first as the shark's dinner and then as triumphantly eating its way out from inside the shark, forces the Curator to admit, "I knew his helm was in line with his keel / as an artist's helm should be" (*HG* 141). This, finally, from the Curator, is an unconditional surrender.

Yet even more telling is the powerful reaction of the Zulu Club's bartender, a Jamaican veteran of the Second World War:

> "God knows, Hideho, you got the low-down
>   on the black turtle and the white shark
>   in the Deep South."
>   Then,
>   describing a pectoral girdle,
>   his lower lip curled,
>   and he blurted—like an orgasm:
> "And perhaps in many a South of the Great White World!"
> He fumed, he sweated, he paced behind the bar.
> "I too hate Peeler's pig in the boa's coils!
> I was in the bomb-hell at Dunkirk. I was a British tar.
> In Parliament, *white* Churchill quoted one day,
>   'If we must die, let us not die like hogs....'
> The words of a poet, my compatriot—*black* Claude McKay."
>   (*HG* 142)

Colonialism as a labor resource in world war: the British swallow the bartender. Quotation as radical recontextualization: Churchill swallows, regurgitates, and fails to acknowledge McKay's sonnet on the American race riots of 1919. Hideho's tale is brought to climax ("blurted—like an orgasm") by the bartender's foregrounding of global racial conflict against the backdrop of two world wars. And Heights's stance of resolute opposition, of the turtle gnawing its way to freedom, appears in this light as the only resistance possible in the face of (to use the terms of the Curator-Nkomo debate) cultural homogenization. Here, then, is a racial politics and a vision of cultural reproduction diametrically opposed to the formation of a "homogenized milk of multiculture"—a vision in which the spectacle of Claude McKay's words in Churchill's mouth carries with it none of the ambiguous hope or promise of the spectacle of Robert Frost on the steps of the Capitol. For here the instinctive drive of the weak to survive speaks to the politics of separatism in the language of the parable; here all amalgamation-and-assimilation is repressive tolerance and therefore cultural genocide. Hideho Heights and the Jamaican bartender, between them, have dared to suggest an answer to the question *Harlem Gallery* has so scrupulously sought to avoid, and though that answer be couched in a parable, the suggestion is clear: in the melting pot we will be eaten.

Unless, that is, we eat our way out "in a way that appalls"—and perhaps it appalls the Curator himself. For it is surely a measure of the threat Hideho poses to *Harlem Gallery* at this point that only one stanza intervenes before his triumph is framed, once again, by a crushing defeat. "Never before," writes the Curator, "in the tavern of the Zulu Club, / nor in the cabaret downstairs, / had Hideho left the cellar door / of his art ajar" (*HG* 143). And just as Hideho's performance in "Xi" was fraught with minor overtones of the prostitution of his talents, so too does "Phi" end on a false note, for out from Heights's "cellar door" come his cryptic remarks about the secret status of the People's Poet—remarks which, not incidentally, echo the opening line of Starks's *Vignettes*:

> "Everybody has a private gallery.
> In mine is a whore giving birth
> to a pimp's son, Curator, on a filthy quilt . . . .
> Then, too,
> consider the abortions
> of the *howl-howl-with-the-combo* quacks;
> the little Eddie Jests and Shortfellows who use no rubbers
> when copulating with muses on the wrong side of the tracks."
>
> (*HG* 143–44)

The passage should be, at the very least, disturbing, for Heights here snipes—by way of a derisive allusion to the "poetry" of Longfellow and Edward Guest—not only at his own performance earlier in the poem but also, conceivably, at both Allen Ginsberg's 1956 howl and at Langston Hughes's jazz readings as well. More than disturbing, because now the man who had entered the Gallery claiming that its art was merely "highbrow stuff" for "middlebrows who don't give a damn and the lowbrows that ain't hip" (*HG* 68) turns his own parodic socioeconomics on himself—to devastating effect. Muses, apparently, now come from all walks of life, and in Hideho's present formulation it is the poet's duty not to sleep with those beneath his station. The wrong side of the tracks, indeed: is it that to seek inspiration from muses on welfare, muses who may be turning tricks to pay the rent, is literally to prostitute one's talents?—is it, in *Harlem Gallery*'s terms, that commerce with such muses induces a kind of paternity anxiety similar to that of Mister Starks, wherein one never knows the real father of the artwork? Perhaps you are the Author absolutely; perhaps, on the other hand, authorship can at best be attributed to a collective of the great unwashed. If you—like tipsy Lena—belong to the people, or if tipsy Lena or Hedda Starks or your own private whore be your muse, you will never be quite certain.

Still Heights's fall is not yet complete. Congruent with the poem's principle of narrative translations, Hideho's self-immolating remarks recall to the Curator the night he found in Heights's apartment "in the modern idiom, / a poem called *E. & O.E.*," and discovered that the bard of Lenox Avenue had once lived and worked in Paris— "That he had been / a bistro habitué, / an expatriate poet of the Black Venus / in the Age of Whoopee" (*HG* 146). As "Omicron" followed Heights's brief poetic victory in "Xi," so then does "Chi" follow his fable-and-confession in "Phi," this time interring his poetics for good.

This, then, is the ideological climax of *Harlem Gallery*, the final, simultaneous defeat both of Hideho's claims to be a People's Poet, and of Starks's glowing depiction of him in *Harlem Vignettes*. Appropriately, the Curator is the only figure in the poem who knows of Heights's double poetic personality:

> He [Heights] didn't know
> I knew
> about the split identity
> of the People's Poet—
> the bifacial nature of his poetry:
> the racial ballad in the public domain
> and the private poem in the modern vein.
> (*HG* 145)

Farnsworth's reading of the Curator's discovery makes out "E. & O.E." to be "an oblique advertisement for Tolson's own critically neglected poem by the same name" (1979, 262)—in fact, the poem with which Tolson launched his "New Negro poetry"—but Farnsworth is circumspect about the implications of such an "advertisement." For in the context in which it appears, the attribution of "E. & O.E."'s authorship to Heights suggests that Heights's popular poetry—and, by implication, the African-American oral tradition in which it runs—is an untenable and historically inappropriate poetic stance. Simultaneously, it marks off and condemns Heights as the poet Tolson deliberately chose not to become—just as, unlike Starks, he *had* followed Des Imagistes down the Macadam Road. Furthermore, the revelation of Hideho Heights's professional schizophrenia, in a final reversal of the two Zulu Club scenes, demonstrates that Heights's audience controls *him*. As Tolson once wrote of J. Saunders Redding's skeptical review of *Libretto*, "Away with the simple Negro!" (TM). Heights is unmasked as a modernist in populist clothing and thereby unwittingly bears out the Curator's theses: he has capitulated to his own version of the bulls of Bashan, the Zulu Club milieu, and has been content to make himself out "the *Coeur de Lion* of the Negro mass" (*HG* 147)—that is, a Lion Heart of the South Wing, an idol of the tribe. He becomes, thereby, another version of Mister Starks–style accommodation and fatal artistic compromise.

The outcome of the struggle for poetic and ideological control of *Harlem Gallery*, then, is that the Curator's socio-linguistic point of view—his poetic language game—is ultimately valorized *at the expense of* Hideho Heights. In the narrative terms I have been employing, the poem's Scripture paradigm supersedes its gossip paradigm once the impossibility of sustaining the gossip paradigm (of forever remaining a Zulu Club Wit, a People's Poet) is illustrated by Heights's example. The Curator, of course, does not put his discovery in such terms; rather, he attributes Heights's duplicity to his conflicted position as an African-American artist:

> Poor Boy Blue,
> the Great White World
> and the Black Bourgeoisie
> have shoved the Negro artist into
> the white and non-white dichotomy,
> the Afroamerican dilemma in the Arts—
> the dialectic of
> to be or not to be
> a Negro.
>
> . . . .
> here was the eyesight proof
> that the Color Line, as well as the Party Line,
> splits an artist's identity.
> (*HG* 146–47)

There is no mistaking the Curator's tone: however antagonistic he may be to Heights's "bifacial nature," he is genuinely saddened at the fate of the black poet who aspires to little magazines and contemporary anthologies, to an ultimately academic context of reception. Nevertheless, the Curator does take his discovery to be a betrayal: as he reads over Hideho's hidden poem, he refers to himself as "conscious of my Judas role" (*HG* 148). Hideho, in other words, is not what we might take him to be on a more benevolent interpretation—a man who knows his various audiences and his most productive relation to them, who saves the difficult, hypertextual poem for the printed page while resorting to more accessible and politically productive language in the street. No, Hideho's unmasking is a deauthorization: both Heights and his self-destructing practice of art are held at ironic distance from Tolson as the false semblance of Tolson, and the agent of the deauthorization likens himself to Iscariot. The Curator's "My Judas role" tends even to undo a straightforward reading of Hideho's lament in the first Zulu Club scene—a reading wherein Heights, crying "*my* people—they know not what they do" (*HG* 92), suggests that his audience has betrayed him by acceding to a performance that did not sufficiently challenge them— for here, instead, Judas turns out to be the Curator. Curiouser and curiouser, as Alice might say: perhaps the Hideho of "Xi" has already read the end of *Harlem Gallery* and, like Christ, tells his brethren at the "poet's feast" (*HG* 83) that one of them will betray him before the poem's end—or perhaps, even more fancifully, the passage in "Xi" is Heights's premonition of a "Chi" in which he is betrayed not by being sold but by being exposed.

Whatever the case—and I want only to suggest that the two literal readings of Heights's "betrayal" undercut each other here—the Attic salt in man may survive "the blow of Attila, Croesus, Iscariot" (*HG* 28), but Heights's "bifacial nature" does not survive the Iscariotic Curator's perusal of his "serious" work. For as the Curator knows, the nature of Heights's poetry is induced by his secret desire to be canonized (for "E. & O.E."), to make the syllabus: "I had overheard the poet say: /. . . / 'my fears / of oblivion / made me realistic: / with no poems of Hideho's in World Lit— / he'd be a statistic!'" (*HG* 145). And only in *Harlem Gallery*, it appears, does the desire to be taught in World Lit somehow invalidate the desire to be the bard of Lenox Avenue as well; only here does a canonical principle of mutual exclusivity apply.

As if this weren't enough to smash the graven image, there is worse: the Curator applies to Tolson's "E. & O.E." the same kind of ideologically pointed selective editing he applied to the lives of his pantheon of artists. Here, however, the editing casts Hideho's position in the dimmest possible light: the version in *Harlem Gallery* opens with the bleakest moment of "E. & O.E.," in which the poet is confronted by a casino's "Tartufean shill,"[23] who taunts him with the idea of the possible futility of his task:

---

[23]In the original poem, it is not clear that Tolson stands in the lyric relation to his speaker that obtains, in the Curator's reading (and mine), between Hideho Heights and *his* "speaker." Tolson goes out of his way to embed the New Critical byword in the text of "E. & O.E.," opening his notes to the poem with the awkward locution

> "Why place an empty pail
> before a well
> of dry bones?
> Why go to Nineveh to tell
> the ailing that they ail?
> Why lose a golden fleece
> to gain a holy grail?"
>
> (*HG* 147)

If we take this passage, as we are most likely intended to do, to be Hideho's comment on his return from Paris to Harlem, then we have here a plaintive and self-tormented figure indeed. And if Hideho casts himself as Jonah on his way to Nineveh (lest we think the reference incidental, the notes to the original "E. & O.E." direct us twice to Father Mapple's sermon in *Moby-Dick*), then the passage gives the lie to Hideho's turtle-and-shark parable as well: for a Jonah who tells such stories is narrating mere fantasies of his own gastric rebellion even while he refuses to believe that his audience is worth salvation.

But then again, just as this reference to the Book of Jonah omits to mention that the people of Nineveh *did* hearken to the Word of God and repent, so does the Curator's re-presentation of Heights's poem omit the ambiguous moment at the end of "E. & O.E.," section XI, when the speaker either has been found inadequate to his divinely ordained mission or has discovered a new and less grandiose task to perform: "I sought / in a Tarshish nook / neither the Golden Fleece / nor the Holy Grail / but a pruning-hook."[24] Instead, the Curator

---

"the man in the poem takes the title from the phrase 'errors and omissions excepted'" (1951, 369). Here, we have not only a "speaker" but a "man in the poem" who titles his own lyric; even a title, according to Tolson's notes, may be subject to the intentional fallacy.

[24] Farnsworth reads the conclusion to section XI as a "modest, but assured, claim" that "indicates that the poet-protagonist may well accept the burden of living in a far from favorable moment of history with purposeful modesty and dignity" (1984, 184, 262). Maybe, but then what is he doing in Tarshish? It is also possible, I think, that the speaker has reneged on his commitment, as did Jonah—with this difference: the speaker of "E. & O.E." has been allowed by God to sail on to Tarshish; no storms have arisen against his vessel. It is as if the speaker here disclaims even the possibility of being a prophet (and therefore worthy of God's wrath); as if he had written, after Prufrock, "No! I am not Jonah, nor was meant to be." Although I agree with Farnsworth generally that the Curator's reading of "E. & O.E." makes Heights's position seem "even more dramatically pathetic than . . . the original poem" (1984, 184), I find the citation of Tarshish—and the function of the pruning-hook—so thoroughly uncertain as to forestall determination of its position in either "E. & O.E." or *Harlem*

jump-cuts from section VIII to XII, and the closing seventeen lines of "E. & O.E." close "Chi" as well; thus, the defeat of Heights as the poem's champion of oral, narrative poetry is sealed with his own written words—words to the effect that, well, poetry makes nothing happen:

> "I do not shake
> the Wailing Wall
> of Earth—
> nor quake
> the Gethsemane
> of Sea—
> nor tear
> the Big Top
> of Sky
> with Lear's prayer,
> or Barabas' curse,
> or Job's cry!"
> (*HG* 151)

Hence, the last two sections, "Psi" and "Omega," bring the poem back full circle and serve as monologic epilogue to its action. This time, however, the Heights-to-Curator translation is occasioned not by a "frame" around Heights's ballads or his public performance but by his own *written* work, and *Harlem Gallery* thereby effects the narrative and structural closure both of Heights's poetics and the principle of narrative translation itself. The bow on the package is the second stanza of "Psi," which ironically echoes the opening to section II of "E. & O.E." even as the Curator seems to be admitting he's left loose ends untied: "Many a *t* in the ms. / I've left without a cross, / many an *i* without a dot" (*HG* 152) refers, obliquely, to the all but opaque lines from the earlier poem:

> Though
> I dot my *i* in this
> and rend the horns
> of tribal ecbasis,
> the Great White World's
> uncrossed *t*
> pockets the skeleton key

Gallery. Tolson's notes to "E. & O.E." suggest comparing the Tarshish passage with Isaiah 2:4 on swords and plowshares, but I leave this comparison to better sleuths than myself.

>   to doors beyond
>   black chrysalis.
>
>   (20–29)

The section then proceeds from the "Chi" rendering of Heights to a one-stanza conclusion on the place of the African-American artist: "Black Boy, / in this race, at this time, in this place, / to be a Negro artist is to be / a flower of the gods, whose growth / is dwarfed at an early stage" (*HG* 153).

The remainder of "Psi" is devoted to apostrophes to Black Boy and White Boy as the poem asks and then jettisons the question of racial identity. The section is driven by a series of change-the-joke-and-slip-the-yoke routines, the first of which is the association of anthropologists Johann Friedrich Blumenbach and Franz Boas with Mississippi's white supremacist senator, Theodore Bilbo:

>   Black Boy,
>   summon Boas and Dephino,
>   Blumenbach and Koelreuter,
>   from their posts
>   around the gravestone of Bilbo . . .
>   summon the ghosts
>   of scholars with rams' horns from Jericho
>   and facies in letters from Jerusalem,
>   so
>   we may ask them:
>   "What is a Negro?"
>
>   (*HG* 154)

Joseph Koelreuter was an eighteenth-century botanist who experimented with hybridization; "Dephino" I take to be the Curator's wry comment on the project of articulating clear distinctions between races, for "Just as the Chinese lack / an ideogram for 'to be,' / our lexicon has no definition / for an ethnic amalgam like Black Boy and me" (*HG* 163).

Turning the tables, then, on white supremacists, the Curator mocks "the Nordic's thin lips, his aquiline nose, / his straight hair, / orangutanish on legs and chest and head," recalling that "the Black Belt White / . . . / rabbit-punched old Darrow" (*HG* 155) for the crime of suggesting that *homo sapiens* descended from the ape—the creature so successfully associated with African-Americans by a racist imagination that found its apotheosis in Edgar Rice Burroughs's *Tarzan*. And in unmasking himself as an octoroon, the Curator slips yet another yoke, the one imposed by Starks and Nkomo earlier in the poem: he takes his "mongrelization," his position on the margins of "race" and his ability to pass for white, as a strength rather than as a source of self-loathing, and presents himself as the man ideally suited to expose the absurdity of "race." In so doing, he tosses out the question raised in "Alpha"—"the *What* in Socrates' '*Tò tí*'?" (*HG* 160)—substituting for it a more pressing question:[25]

> *Who is a Negro?*
> (I am a White in deah ole Norfolk.)
> *Who is a White?*
> (I am a Negro in little old New York.)
> Since my mongrelization is invisible
> and my Negroness a state of mind conjured up
> by Stereotypus, I am a chameleon
> on *that* side of the Mason-Dixon
> *that* a white man's conscience
> is not on.
>
> (*HG* 160)

Himself the product of what he calls "midnight-to-dawn lecheries, / in cabin and big house, / [that] produced these brown hybrids and yellow motleys" (*HG* 163), the Curator bemoans the cause of his mixed heritage even as he deploys his ambiguous and liminal status—in the tradition of that long train of American literary figures from Natty Bumppo to Ishmael to Huck Finn, Sam Spade to Sal Paradise to the Invisible Man—as the source of the authority with which he writes. And thus does the allegorical "good ship *Défineznegro*," on its shakedown cruise "to reach the archipelago / Nigeridentité," sink beneath the waves in "the Strait of Octoroon" (*HG* 164).

Yet however accurate or empathetic may be the Curator's judgment of Hideho's position—or his own—in the politics of race, we would do well to remember that this judgment is solely the Curator's; thus, whatever the politics of his summation, the poem's real political conflict is resolved. As a result, the authority of the Curator becomes quasi-scriptural in the penultimate stanza of "Omega" as

---

[25]Even though he does so in the service of equating the lability of the self with the authority of the self, the Curator's deciding here to reject essentialism for the primacy of the political seems to be an almost postmodern gesture: the Curator, like K. or Tyrone Slothrop, is a "subject" produced by social and ideological forces far stronger than his ability to define himself, and he seems here to acknowledge the fact. For more on the modern/postmodern distinction, see Chapter 4.

the poem closes in the most authoritative, monologic discourse available to poetry, the high vatic mode:

> In the black ghetto
> the white heather
> and the white almond grow,
> but the hyacinth
> and asphodel blow
> in the white metropolis!
> O Cleobulus,
> O Thales, Solon, Periander, Bias, Chilo,
> O Pittacus,
> unriddle the phoenix riddle of this?
>
> (*HG* 173)

Like the oracle at Delphi, the Curator's prophecy is cryptic. Fortunately, however, Tolson explained himself to the uninitiated in a local newspaper: "I say that the flowers representing decay and death are found in the white metropolis, but the flowers of hope grow in the black belt. I speak here of the masses of poor people. They are on the move" (quoted in Bickham 1966, 7).

That the language of the seer in "Omega" should depend for its translation on the language of the interviewee in the *Sunday Oklahoman* is a particularly postmodern irony; that Tolson made such a confident declaration after the long hot summer of 1964, and before the still more cataclysmic eruption of America's inner cities in 1967–68, is a particularly tragic irony. But this is not all that seems somehow askew about the poem's ending, for in a way, all of "Psi" with its discussion of "race" is extremely problematic. Perhaps, as I have argued, the section follows structurally from "Chi," caulking the leaks of narrative translation and cauterizing Hideho's poetics, but it is hard to see how else it can be said to "follow" from the Curator's discovery of Heights's closet modernism.

For in what sense has Hideho Heights been caught in a "white and non-white dichotomy"? What, in the end, *is* "the dialectic of to be or not to be a Negro" (*HG* 146)? If the Curator suggests, as he intends to, that Hideho shrinks from the task of transforming his audiences, succumbing instead to the polarized audience demands of two different literary worlds, then the Curator is also suggesting that modernist poetry is the realm of white folks, and that "the Great White World / and the Black Bourgeoisie" demand African-American poets who are sufficiently "primitive" and technically incompetent—in a word, folk poets only. The dichotomy here, recall, is based on "the racial ballad in the public domain / and the private poem in the modern vein" (*HG* 145): the Curator's pejorative key-words are not merely *ballad* and *public* but also *racial*, and they are as closely associated and as heavily ideologically weighted as are their counterparts *poem, private,* and *modern*. This much is clear. But then the Curator's characterization of this conflict as the dilemma of "to be or not to be a Negro" must intend "Negro" in the most bitter, cynical tone imaginable—a tone implying that poets who choose to be "Negroes first" are simply conforming to a stereotypical "racial" role, precisely the role expected of them by their worst audiences. This, then, is what I mean by claiming that the poem's real political conflict is resolved: that conflict, between the cultural forms of life of the Curator and Heights, eventually reveals itself as a conflict over whether one chooses to become, as Allen Tate wrote about Tolson in the preface to *Libretto,* "a Negro poet [who] has assimilated com-pletely the full poetic language of his time" (1953, 11) or whether one chooses to become a version of the sea-turtle in the shark. And the example of Heights's "bifacial nature" means to tell us that the conflict is decidable, that the latter choice is finally impossible.

The choice with which the poem leaves us is thus a deliberately false one: in *Harlem Gallery,* the "Afroamerican dilemma" is not over whether to be a Negro; it is not even over whether to be a black separatist; even a good separatist-balladeer like Hideho Heights, when he gets into the privacy of his apartment, becomes a modern-ist despite himself. The Curator's strategy of casting Heights's di-lemma in racial terms, therefore, serves the purpose of converting a difference *between* into a difference *within*—by masking the ideologi-cal struggle between himself and Heights and portraying the conflict instead as all Heights's own, as a conflict over whether the artist can break out of racial stereotypes. This is why, in reading over "E. & O.E.," the Curator juxtaposes the diffidence of Heights's private poem with the militant confidence of his public stand, as he recalls one of Heights's triumphant returns to the Zulu Club—this one after serving a jail sentence for an obscure but apparently Malcolm X–like assault on the "Uncle Tom" leader[26] of the "Ethiopian Taber-nacle":

[26]The leader's name is "Bishop" Gladstone Coffin (*HG* 148). What Tolson meant by echoing in an Uncle Tom minister's name the figures of Henry Sloane Coffin and William Gladstone is, honestly, beyond me.

> "A man's conscience is home-bred.
> To see an artist or a leader do
> Uncle Tom's asinine splits
> is an ask-your-mama shame!"
> The Jamaican bartender had staked off his claim:
> "The drinks are on the house, Poet Defender!"
> A sportsman with ruffed grouse
> on the wing over dogs, the poet had continued:
> "Integrity is an underpin—
> the marble lions that support
> the alabaster fountain in
> the Alhambra."
>
> (*HG* 148)

In construing Heights's modernist poem as somehow a contradiction of his celebration of racial "integrity," then, the Curator holds
out not only Heights's poetry but his entire form of cultural life as
politically and personally self-abnegating—and somehow "illegitimate," in the sense that poets who copulate with the wrong kind of
muses may father illegitimate progeny. An artist whose helm is truly
in line with his keel, the Curator seems to say, will not fail to read
and assimilate modernist poetry, to master the Master, T. S. Eliot.
Black separatism in the form of resistance to the modernist avant-
garde, like the recitation of oral ballads in jazz clubs, will never
make it into the anthologies: lacking central, academic, institutional
means of reproduction, it becomes not only marginal but ephemeral.

I have said that the poem leaves us with a false dilemma; but I
want also to recall here that it contains within it a *real* dilemma, one
which, as I argued in the context of the poem's narrative and historical "time," it remains unwilling or unable to acknowledge. This
"real" dilemma is, unsurprisingly, a function of the poem's real conflict: whether the African-American artist should attempt to create
his or her own audience, or play to the audiences that are already in
existence. This is the conflict "resolved" by *Harlem Gallery*, both
through Heights's fall and (equally) through the poem's refusal to
contemplate the question consequent upon its adoption of the politics of assimilation—the question of the avant-garde's position when
it is no longer (for whatever reason) *avant* of the *garde*. We may see
this refusal, in the Curator's epilogue, in the fact that Heights's unmasking in "Chi" is followed not by a discussion of what it means
for a member of a *truly* marginal group (such as African-American
poets) to adopt the aesthetics and aesthetic ideologies of an already
institutionalized modernist "avant-garde" but instead by a discus-

sion of "race" which declares "race" to be a fiction. The Curator's answer, in "Psi," may be a good answer—but only because he has deliberately asked the wrong question.[27]

In other words, *Harlem Gallery*, in order to uphold the ideal of cultural amalgamation (the homogenized milk of multiculture) embodied in the very person of the Curator, needs not only to avoid confronting explicitly its own contemporary cultural position, and its own possible present-or-future audience, but needs also to delegitimize, to deauthorize, the self-representations of Hideho Heights. Modernist technique thus becomes the *sign* of assimilation, and assimilation of modernist technique, we find in the Tale of Hideho Heights, is inevitable: those who do not assimilate the poetry of their time will divide themselves between two masters, *vox populi* and *vox Dei*, to their destruction. But beyond its will-to-assimilation, into a postmodern conception either of the irreducibility of "marginality" or of the available antiassimilationist critiques of pluralism,[28] the poem cannot and will not go, trusting instead, in the terms of John Ciardi at his vaguest, that its ideal projection of itself will become a shape that impresses itself upon time.

One central question remains. If the poem is so ambiguous about its own cultural position, partially because it is so certain of the position of modernism and the resistance with which it will be met among African-Americans, what then is the Curator's role as Curator? Let us return to the challenge with which Hideho Heights first entered the poem, the suggestion that the Curator serves elite art to an indifferent middle class and the uneducated poor—that in effect the Curator has no audience. How, given the imperative to peddle "in dead ends and on boulevards" the homogenized milk of African-American modernism, does the poem's mediating figure mediate between contemporary art and the markets of contemporary culture?

On this count, the poem is unambiguous: to do anything less than attempt to disseminate modernism to the masses is to give in to

[27]Melvin Tolson, Jr., and Robert Farnsworth report that Tolson had trouble trying to decide how to end the poem after Heights's exposure in "Chi" (Farnsworth 1984, 225; Tolson 1990, 400). The fissure, therefore, is textually "there," just as the two-year gap between stanzas four and five of Wordsworth's "Intimations" Ode lies somewhere between his question ("Whither is fled the visionary gleam? / Where is it now, the glory and the dream?") and his problematic answer ("Our birth is but a sleep and a forgetting").

[28]Pluralism is apparently not the same thing for Tolson as multiculturalism: as one of his journal notes puts it, "Pluralism is an edifice with many doors through which one may escape responsibility as a citizen" (TM).

forces that would patronize and condescend to "the people" by giving them the kind of art which, in Clement Greenberg's words,
"predigests art for the spectator and spares him effort, provides him
with a short cut to the pleasure of art that detours what is necessarily difficult in genuine art" (1939, 44). The Curator writes in
strikingly similar terms in "Omega":

> Should he
> skim the milk of culture for the elite
> and give the "lesser breeds"
> a popular latex brand?
> Should he
> (to increase digestibility)
> break up
> the fat globules and vitamins and casein shreds?
>
> (HG 167)

The answer, of course, is no; and though the Curator's response
characteristically fudges the details of reception—"the binnacle of
imagination / steers the work of art aright" (HG 167)—still, his part
in the drama Art has already been written.

> Those in the upper drawer give a child
> the open sesame to the unknown
> What and How and Why;
> that's *that* which curators, as Pelagians, try
> to do
> in exhibitions,
> when a genius gets through
> with a nonpareil of art whose exegesis
> exacts patience.
>
> (HG 165)

The Curator refers to the Pelagian heresy of the fifth century, which
denied original sin and held that an individual has the free will to
choose not to sin—and therefore the natural ability to seek God
without the help of a church. Thus the Curator, as Pelagian, asserts
his power to refuse to adulterate his Gallery by caving in to the
pressures of the Regents, the Black Bourgeoisie, and the idols of the
tribe; the work of art, with the midwifely aid of a supremely disinterested critic unbound by earthly institutions, gets the exposure it
needs to steer our imaginations aright. In this noble scheme, the
critic emerges not as a "weeping monkey" but as the guardian of the
cross-cultural canon, the cream skimmer of the elite of genius in the

milk of multiculture: "As for the critic, / he is the fid / that bolsters the topmost mast / of Art—an argosy of plunder / from the kingdoms of race and class and caste" (*HG* 169). The Curator gets the last words on the matter, and despite the overtones of "plunder"—which recall Walter Benjamin's claim that barbarism is inseparable from the transmission of the "cultural treasures" of "civilization" (1969, 256)—those last words turn out to sound a good deal like Matthew Arnold's.

As we have seen, however, the Curator's Arnoldian commitment to the best that has been known and thought in the world carries with it also a Greenbergian defense of the avant-garde whom, in Harlem, "no Haroun-al-Rashid greets" (*HG* 172). And the Greenbergian defense is itself the product of specifically modernist conflicts: Greenberg's dichotomy between avant-garde and *kitsch* can be seen, in the text of *Harlem Gallery* as elsewhere, as a version of the dichotomy between art and ideology of which Sacvan Bercovitch writes. And both schemes, that of Greenberg and that of "the old consensus," demand a valorization of the avant-garde (or art) precisely for the fact that it is the polar opposite of *kitsch* (or ideology).[29] In the Harlem Gallery proper, the Curator's pride in the North, East, and West wings demands the castigation of the South Wing's enshrinement of the idols of the tribe; likewise, in *Harlem Gallery* proper, the sustenance of the Curator's aesthetics and author function demands that Hideho Heights be excoriated for feeding the masses "a popular latex brand" of poetry.

But the Curator and Greenberg, for all their mutual antagonism to the forces of *kitsch*, eventually part ways, and the location of their parting is diagnostic of the ideology of *Harlem Gallery* as a whole. In Greenberg's formulation, *kitsch* feeds off "a fully matured cultural tradition, whose discoveries, acquisitions and perfected self-consciousness kitsch can take advantage of for its own ends. . . . when enough time has elapsed the new is looted for new 'twists,' which are then watered down and served up as kitsch" (1939, 40). Though Jauss would add here that the "cultural tradition" itself gets "wa-

---

[29]In Greenberg's argument, although there are what he calls "puzzling border-line cases" that threaten the polarity and comprehensiveness of his dichotomy, still, these apparently do not prevent the dichotomy from being an extraordinarily powerful and totalizing one, especially later in the essay: "If the avant-garde imitates the processes of art, kitsch, we now see, imitates its effects. The neatness of this antithesis is more than contrived; it corresponds to and defines the tremendous interval that separates from each other two such simultaneous cultural phenomena as the avant-garde and kitsch" (1939, 41, 44).

tered down" in its very transmission, Greenberg's is nevertheless a decent (if undialectical) Marxist translation of Pound's "make it new," of the modernist's need to "set going" a "countercurrent" in opposition to "Amygism" and "Lee Masterism." But in Greenberg's conception of the avant-garde's audience, we find neither the Poundian genius for publicity nor the Tolsonian faith in the "vertical" audience; thus, we find neither Pound's nor Tolson's self-contradictions. To Greenberg, the modernist avant-garde is constituted and defined by the fact that it has been abandoned by the only audience high culture ever had.[30] Tolson, on the other hand, combines the logic of a Greenberg or a Pound—that modernism is historically inevitable and carries with it an internal imperative of constant innovation—with the liberal idealism of Ciardi, for whom those innovations will not outrun popular taste forever. And in a 1961 letter to former student Benjamin Bell, Tolson sets out both positions in his *discordia concors* fashion of asserting them simultaneously:

> My work is certainly difficult in metaphors, symbols and juxtaposed ideas. There the similarity between me and Eliot separates. That is only technique, and any artist must use the technique of his time. Otherwise we'd have the death of Art. . . .
>   Now, about the little people. Remember "ideas come from above." If you went into the street and said to a ditchdigger in Chi, "Who is Shakespeare?" he'd say, "The greatest writer that ever lived." Now, he wouldn't know a damned thing about *Hamlet* but he might quote some of THE Bard's sayings that he picked up from the boys in the ditch. Ideas sift down. (TM)

This should give us serious pause. Technique is only technique; but without technique we have the death of Art. Ideas, like Scriptures, come from above; from above, in a kind of supply-side meritocracy, they sift down. And the radical juxtaposition here, like that

---

[30]"Today such culture is being abandoned by those to whom it actually belongs— our ruling class. For it is to the latter that the avant-garde belongs. . . . And now this elite is rapidly shrinking. Since the avant-garde forms the only living culture we now have, the survival in the near future of culture in general is thus threatened" (Greenburg 1939, 38). As some revisionists have noted, however, the academy is precisely the "aristocracy," the "social basis" sought by the modernist avant-garde. Cf. Klein on the relation of modernism to cultural capital: insofar as Anglo-American modernism "enjoined a tremendous amount of scholarship, or, more exactly, a taste for the supposed authority of traditional literary-historical scholarship," it entailed "the virtual definition of literature as the enterprise of an intellectual aristocracy," for "literature was to require special academic training, and of course not everyone went to the university" (1981, 7–8).

in Ciardi's claim for the vertical audience as both outnumbered and outnumbering, carries with it the implication of causal connection: the vertical audience is diachronically larger *because* synchronically smaller; ideas sift down *because* they use the technique of their time. We might even see Tolson's Bard-quoting ditchdigger as a well-meaning version of the Eliotic "ordinary man" who reads Spinoza[31] —except that Tolson's formulation serves the strategy of making modernism a populist imperative. On such grounds as this, it is an indefensible abandonment of the "little people" in the unborn vertical audience if the poet is *not* as difficult as the avant-garde of the age demands. Paradoxically enough, technique itself turns out not to be mere technique after all; in *Harlem Gallery*, it becomes a cultural and political position all by itself, a position through which a work of art can be "a peak in Anthropos . . . / Without a limitation as to height" (*HG* 99) even as it talks to the "little people" distant in space and time. Its difficulty ensures popular resistance, and popular resistance in turn ensures eventual popular acclaim, even if the work so violates its contemporary horizon of expectations that it goes almost wholly unread.[32] The great god Biosis. Of modernist cultural myths, nothing could be more naive—or more reassuring, or more attractive.

And yet it is not enough to call this myth "naive"; it is not enough simply to call it a "myth." To do so is to imply that it is something unworthy of our belief, something that has always been unworthy of our belief. But nothing about Melvin Tolson is as simple as that, and this is no exception—for two reasons. The first is that Tolson, for all that he and *Harlem Gallery* imply to the contrary, did not entirely believe in the myth himself; thoroughgoing modernist that he is, his work is at once dependent on and antagonistic to the institutionalization of literary study, and that he was himself aware of this can be seen most dramatically (in the following chapter) in his correspondence with Allen Tate and J. Saunders Redding. The second

[31]Eliot 1921, 64. A more extreme version can be found in *Poetry*'s notes to "E. & O.E.," in which Tolson writes that the poem's epigraph from Lorca—"Ya mi talle se ha quebrado / como caña de maíz"—"will obviously call to mind Lorca's two ballads on Antoñito the Camborio" (1951, 369). Obviously.

[32]This is a quintessentially Romantic view of literary history, a view unrevised by modernism's various repudiations of Romanticism. Many of Tolson's "modernist" conflicts are inescapably Romantic, in the sense that he places himself in a position akin to Wordsworth's, in the latter's claim to write not for the *masses* but for the *public*, or Keats's, when he claimed to write not for *men* but for *Man*. For illuminating discussions of this conflict as part of the Romantics' anxieties over literary professionalism and their possibilities for audience relation, see Klancher 1987 and Rowland 1988.

reason has to do with the myth itself, not only because it *has* been worthy of our belief for most of this century but because its "worthiness" of "our belief" is no longer the primary issue. We need not look at whether such a myth is true, in this case, so much as look at its results: criticism, promulgated even (and especially) by institutional critics, which holds that objects of institutional inquiry somehow exist independently of their institutional creation. Hugh Kenner, for one, would have us believe that the modernist canon was made "chiefly . . . by the canonized themselves" (1983b, 374); Helen Vendler, seconding Kenner some years later, opines that "canons are not made by governments, anthologists, publishers, editors, or professors, but by writers" (1988, 37), writers who doubtless form an ideal Eliotic order among themselves. And though Kenner and Vendler are not in the front lines of academic debates over canons, they remain far more recognizable to the general literate public— readers of the *New Yorker* and *New York Times Book Review*, watchers of PBS specials on Stevens or Whitman—than are most of their more clear-sighted counterparts such as Barbara Herrnstein Smith or John Guillory; and their fantasy of a self-generating literary history remains well in public view. The great god Biosis, venerated now by distinguished chairs in twentieth-century literature at Harvard and Johns Hopkins.

The paradoxes here are many, but I close by noting just one: that the institutionalization of the myth makes one part of it true. Even if academic critics insist, as many still do, on masking their agency in the historical process of reception, it is quite possible, as Tolson hoped it was, for the modernist to use the technique of his time and yet reach some of the "little people"—perhaps not so wide an audience as to include ditchdiggers, but a considerable audience nonetheless, even of college students, thousands of whom master T. S. Eliot every semester. Of course, since Tolson has not yet reached even so much as a considerable academic audience, his poem appears trapped for now in a cul-de-sac of its making and ours, and this will be the point on which we turn to the problem that *Harlem Gallery* refused to acknowledge, the problem with which it has left us to grapple: its relation to academic canons and critics, including ourselves, including myself.

CHAPTER 3

Tolson's Neglect:
African-American Modernism
and Its Representations

W RITING A reception history poses problems of its own, but writing a history of neglect seems nearly impossible. The very word "neglect" is so little understood, so rarely theorized, that it raises a set of questions unto itself; we may have asked ourselves whether there is a text in this or that class, but we hardly know how to begin asking how it is that most texts never wind up in our classrooms at all. What do we mean by "neglect"? Is there a pure form of neglect? What would it look like? An unsolicited manuscript that was never published or, worse, "neglected" in the strict Latin sense of "not read" at all?[1] Possibly, but here the Latin sense seems to contradict the commonsense notion that a "neglected" object must be somehow available for attention or neglect, hovering someplace on the edge of consciousness—where it remains, being systematically "overlooked." We can thus usually be said to be "neglecting" some of our duties, or our appearance, or our friends and relatives; but we are not normally accused of "neglecting" things of which we are completely unaware.

Contemporary critics may well ask how it is that Tolson's modernist work, both in the 1950s and the 1960s, was immediately celebrated and given awards upon its first appearance and then allowed to fall into obscurity. The less reflective of contemporary critics may conclude that Tolson had his chance, was weighed in time's scales, and found wanting. "E. & O.E." won *Poetry*'s Bess Hokin Prize in

---

[1] For this suggestion I owe thanks to Juan Sola-Montserrat.

1951; with *Libretto* came the title of Poet Laureate of Liberia; and Tolson was awarded, in 1965, one of the year's prizes in literature by the National Institute of Arts and Letters (the same body which, eight years later, would bestow on *Gravity's Rainbow* an award its author would not accept). In 1951, Tolson shared *Poetry's* honors with five other prizewinners: Theodore Roethke, Randall Jarrell, Robinson Jeffers, James Merrill, and Horace Gregory. In 1965 he accepted his national honors alongside such writers as John Barth, James Dickey, and Gary Snyder. More than this, Tolson reached at least two major critical outlets with both *Libretto* and *Harlem Gallery*, receiving generally favorable reviews in early 1954 from the *Nation* and the *Times Book Review*, in 1955 from *Poetry*, and again in 1965 from the *Saturday Review* and *Times* (London) *Literary Supplement*. Still, *Libretto* went out of print in 1980, *Harlem Gallery* in 1987; and MLA bibliographies from 1965 through 1990 list fewer than twenty published responses to his work.

We are not, however, prevented from speaking of Tolson's "neglect" when we acknowledge the kinds of acclaim he once received; on the contrary, the fact that academic critics were once dimly aware of Melvin Tolson is the basis upon which I may now write of his current neglect. For neglect is all the more demonstrable when we find a writer, like Tolson, whose career evinces modest, varying, or tenuous access to the various and shifting centers of cultural reproduction. This point is basic, but its implications are enormous. For one thing, we do not have to prove that a "neglected" writer was never read, or never read well; most important, critics cannot rebut charges of neglect by showing that an author was read and printed somewhere in his or her life, for such a rebuttal fails to acknowledge the role of authorization in reading, just as it fails to acknowledge that an author celebrated in one arena may conceivably be neglected in another. Neglect, too, has its politics; in regard to Tolson, neglect by Houston Baker or Henry Louis Gates, say, is not the same thing as neglect by Hugh Kenner or Frank Kermode, and species of academic neglect differ in turn from neglect by literate nonspecialist journals.

Still, I do not mean to hypostatize neglect. It is not a state of affairs readily susceptible to observation, since there are no such things as "neglecters," people actively and willfully neglecting Tolson as they go about their business doing something else. But by the same token, as I noted briefly in my introduction, neglect is always somehow motivated; consequently, we cannot in good conscience simply adopt Jauss's term "overdue concretization" (1982a,

285), as if neglect were nothing more than a shelter in which writers wait for a tardy canonical bus. My opening point, then, is that neglect is always partial (in both senses), and because even canonical representation is a form of misrepresentation, we might say that canonicity is partial too. The difference, however, is that the partiality of neglect yields the kind of misrepresentation that authorizes nonrepresentation: it tells students, literary professionals, and the general literate public that they don't have to read Tolson, that they don't have to account for Tolson, that there is no cultural imperative (or professional incentive) to know about Tolson. In the case of the neglected writer, therefore, "authorization" is inseparable from the question of how cultural capital is distributed and accumulated generally, for *any* writer can be safely neglected—as long as there is sufficient professional and cultural consensus that "educated people" are not required to be familiar with that writer's name and work.

Thus it is that some facets of Tolson's neglect *are* observable; we can identify reception conditions which, either through their operation or through their failure to operate, practically ensure systematic oversight. Under this heading we might point to the fact that neither the *Times Book Review* nor the *New York Review of Books* assigned a reviewer to *Harlem Gallery*, or that most anthologies of American literature did not until recently feel any obligation to include more than a token sampling of nonwhite writers. Alongside such general "conditions," however, there is another observable feature of neglect, the more elusive and generally unremarked phenomenon which I call misreadings that authorize nonreadings: especially forceful misreadings, including but not limited to devastatingly poor reviews, which implicitly or explicitly discourage further engagement with a text.[2]

Both features of neglect are empirical: hence our ability to observe them. The notion of "misreading" and "misrepresentation" set out

[2]Cary Nelson does not employ "misreading" in this sense, but he cites a splendid example of it from David Perkins's purportedly comprehensive history of modern poetry: "For Muriel Rukeyser (1913–1980) writing a poem was a process of collecting 'surfacings' from the unconscious. When 'collected' these were criticized and revised, but these activities did not essentially modify her product. Her poems are difficult if one seeks intelligibility, but not at all for readers satisfied with vague, intense, idealistic emotion. Her themes were frequently political—the Depression, the Second World War, the war in Vietnam, feminism. She combined an imprecise idiom with committed emotions. A Chinese proverb warns against whipping an ox that is already running, but this is what Rukeyser does. Her poems move persons who share her emotion before they read the poems" (Perkins 1987, 367; quoted in Nelson 1989, 262 n.41).

above, though, requires some elaboration, since of course I myself am not exempt from misreading: the previous chapter on *Harlem Gallery* is neither innocent nor transparent, and I can be fairly sure that I have not put the poem back in quite the order I found it, just as I could not possibly have found "the poem itself" in the first place. The difficulty here, to name just one, is to distinguish among misreadings without invoking once again Rodden's standard of "justice in literary terms": I must be able to speak of misreadings that are endemic to any critical representation, and then again of misreadings that transgress or fall short of what are normally considered the standards of critical representation. This is the kind of distinction among misreadings we practice every time we sit down with a batch of student papers, but it is not readily susceptible to theoretical formulation. The most I can hope to do, perhaps, is to trace the conversation between cultural products and their historical contexts, setting forth the general conditions for what counted (and now counts) as legitimate and recognized communications, and pointing out along the way where certain critics are simply not holding up their end of the conversation.

Paul Breman's reading of *Harlem Gallery* offers a conspicuous example of such a criticism. Writing in a 1969 survey of African-American literature, Breman tried to cast Tolson as Eliot's parodist by making him out to be "an entertaining darkey using almost comically big words as the best wasp tradition demands of its educated houseniggers" (101). Although Breman's reading is itself a response to a tangled network of other readings which I reconstruct in the course of this chapter, even this snippet should suffice to make the point clear: Breman's is not a Tolson worth reading. And Houston Baker himself has agreed on different grounds: in less than a paragraph of 1980's *The Journey Back*, Baker decides that *Libretto*'s "game is not worth the candle" because "each of the poem's gestures seems to seek the vast stolen stores of the West as a final reference" (1980, 74). To ask what Baker intends by this fuzzy sentence, with its incomprehensible "gestures" and "final reference," is to miss the point: his primary intention is to close off discussion of *Libretto*. A closer reading than this, says Baker, is fruitless.

Breman's and Baker's are exemplary misreadings that authorize nonreadings, misrepresentations that sanction nonrepresentation. They are not only demonstrably "partial" but also, in Baker's case, demonstrably wrong, for the assumption that undergirds Baker's dismissal is that, "final reference" or no final reference, there can be a final *reading*, a reading to end all further reading. But reading is a historical process, and—barring mass book-burnings, accidental and otherwise—the reading process does not end. The purpose of exploring Tolson's reception history, therefore, is not to reify "neglect" and single out its alleged perpetrators; it is to understand the ways in which critical conversations are formed, joined, or allowed to sputter. Within this general purpose I have a number of more immediate goals as well, illuminations of issues difficult to bring into focus except by means of a case study: the place of anthologies and general reviews in the precanonical process; the recent history of "race" in American literature; and the question of how reception history modifies or reconstructs literary history.

In reading Tolson's reception history, though, I am confronting something that has so far remained even more obscure than his poetry; if few critics have engaged *Harlem Gallery*, even fewer have engaged its reception, except to say either that Tolson came just too late for modernism or (flipping the coin) that his modernism is the problem. We saw some notable examples of these positions at the outset of the preceding chapter, and both positions ultimately share the assumption succinctly stated in the opening of Patricia Schroeder's otherwise discerning essay on *Harlem Gallery*: "The reasons for this neglect of a modern masterpiece undoubtedly stem from the difficulties of the poem itself" (1983, 152). The salient exception to these text-immanent versions of Tolson's reception history is Nathan Scott's, whose brief but perspicacious account of Tolson's career suggests that "the general neglect of his work [is] but another instance perhaps of the profound reluctance of the literary-intellectual community to reckon seriously with the Negro writer who asks to be considered as something other than merely a special case of ethnic ferment. And, of course, it is precisely the largeness of Tolson's response to the literary world of his time that has guaranteed his disfavor among those espousing the esthetic doctrines of Black separatism" (1979, 326).

"Considered as," in the finite evasions of "as": Scott's suggestion, from which I have taken my cue, is that since reception is contingent on such things as "aesthetic doctrine" and a kind of Wittgensteinian "seeing-as" (reading-as), we cannot simply ask whether Tolson's canonization or neglect would be "good" or "bad"—any more, for that matter, than we can do so with Pynchon. Instead, we have to ask how Tolson can be seen-as, and read-as, today: if the year 1965 was after all an unpropitious moment for the publication of *Harlem*

Gallery, we must ask *how* (and not merely *whether*) Tolson may be retrieved for us now. Again, it will be insufficient for us to stop at saying that 1965 was a bad year for African-American modernist long poems, for even if Tolson was temporarily trapped between a waning New Criticism and a nascent Black Aesthetic, one of the many ironies in which he remains enfolded is the fact that Amiri Baraka and Haki Madhubuti are now represented in the *Norton Anthology of Modern Poetry* (as are Karl Shapiro and Allen Tate), and Tolson is not.[3] Clearly, the terms of canonization have changed since Tolson's death—and, more recently, so have the terms in which academic critics discuss African-American literature.

The preliminary step in a "history of neglect" is therefore the determination of the locations and terms of neglect. And once we conceive of the university as one of those locations, we are, I hope, effectively prevented from characterizing academic criticism as the conservative antagonist of the avant-garde, the agent of its co-optation into "mainstream culture." For as long as academic criticism is so conceived, then Tolson appears poised between two equally unpleasant fates: either we academic critics serve "to kick an authentic poet upstairs into the oblivion of acceptance" (as Karl Shapiro [1965b, 853] charged Allen Tate with doing in Tate's preface to *Libretto*), or we serve to relegate an "authentic poet," unjustly, to the oblivion of neglect. As *Harlem Gallery* puts it, this is a choice "between / the faggot and the noose," in which Tolson's position becomes that of "a Buridan's ass . . . between no oats and hay" (*HG* 20, 19). I take these lines out of context, and yet it should be clear from the preceding chapter that *Harlem Gallery* is in part, always and everywhere, a poem about its own cultural position and attendant possibilities for dissemination or neglect. In the process of opening the question of Tolson's reception, therefore, I will be reopening Tolson's *Gallery* as well; and along the way, we will have to reex-

---

[3]Baraka and Madhubuti are only two of five poets associated with the Black Aesthetic who are anthologized in the *Norton* (Ellmann and O'Clair 1973); the remaining three are Etheridge Knight, Nikki Giovanni, and (more ambiguously) Dudley Randall. Of the 158 poets represented in the anthology, fourteen are black; only Derek Walcott among these is not American. The other eight are Anne Spencer, Claude McKay, Jean Toomer, Langston Hughes, Countee Cullen, Richard Wright, Robert Hayden, and Gwendolyn Brooks. I choose the *Norton Anthology of Modern Poetry* because Nortons are almost by definition "central" anthologies; because, as central anthologies, they represent the consolidation of movements rather than their announcement (as was the function, for example, of Donald Allen's 1960 *New American Poetry*, or, for that matter, *Des Imagistes*); and because the Norton might have been expected to be among the central anthologies most hospitable to Tolson.

amine not only Tolson's texts but their pre-texts: the introductions to *Libretto* and *Harlem Gallery* by Allen Tate and Karl Shapiro.

First, however, I must return to an ellipsis.

Toward the end of the previous chapter I quoted a 1961 comment of Tolson's on his similarity to Eliot: "Any artist must use the technique of his time. Otherwise we'd have the death of Art. . . ." Suppressed by the points of ellipsis in my extract is the end of Tolson's paragraph: "However, when you look at my ideas and Eliot's, we're as far apart as hell and heaven. I guess Shapiro, a Jew of the Jews, sees that and takes me under his wing. I guess I'm the only Marxist poet Here and Now" (TM). And now the passage should give us pause once more, for different reasons.

The ellipsis allowed me, temporarily, to focus on Tolson's idea of the relation of "technique" to the "little people" of whom he writes in his following paragraph; as I suggested in closing the foregoing chapter, the argument gave Tolson a way of eliding the contradictions latent in the Ciardian conception of high culture. But now, although the question of Tolsonian "technique" is no less problematic, it is greatly more complex: the paragraph as he wrote it opposes a content of "ideas" to a patina of "technique," and claims that underneath the husk, inside the mere packaging and wrapping paper is a kernel, a product, that looks as unlike Eliot as possible. The technique/ideas dichotomy is clearly another form of the naive form/content distinction, but as with the "great god Biosis," complaints that the claim is "naive" are not important here. What *is* important is what the dichotomy says about Tolson's conception of himself, for couched in the suggestion that Karl Shapiro has taken to him for political reasons is the implication that Tolson's "technique" is simply a disguise, a mask, and that Shapiro, on the basis of his own opposition to Eliot, has been astute enough to see through the Eliotic mask to the anti-Eliot beneath.

If this is the case, then Tate's preface, in which he writes that Tolson "assimilated completely the full poetic language of his time, and, by implication, the language of the Anglo-American tradition" (1953, 10), does the poet more of a disservice than anyone at the time dared to think. For Tolson's career is a history not of his assimilation of modernist poetics but of his de-formation and transformation of them in the service of "ideas" poles apart from those of Tate and Eliot. Modernism, in this light, begins to look like Tolson's postwar minstrel mask: and although it is not clear that Tolson himself conceived of his career this way from the start, it is certainly worth

pursuing the possibility that he eventually came to do so. Perhaps
Tolson's disguise, if such it was, was an immediately political gesture, meant simply to help an African-American Marxist weather the
era of McCarthyism; but it is arguable also that it was the self-conscious strategy of a poet attempting to negotiate his present and
future place in literary history.

This is a revisionary reading of Tolson indeed, but it is a revision
he himself initiated, in two extraordinary documents. The first is his
review of *Selected Poems of Claude McKay*, which he wrote in 1954 for
Poetry magazine. He opens the review in the idiom of *Gallery*'s Jamaican bartender:

> During the last world war, Sir Winston Churchill snatched Claude
> McKay's poem, *If We Must Die*, from the closet of the Harlem Renais-
> sance, and paraded in it before the House of Commons, as if it were the
> talismanic uniform of His Majesty's field marshal.
>
> The double signature of the role would not have gone undeciphered
> by the full-blooded African poet . . . (1954, 287)

It is something of a shock, then, when five paragraphs later Tolson
writes that McKay's "poems are without ideological vestiges" even
though "If We Must Die" is "a pillar of fire by night in many lands"
(288, 290). The implication is obvious: Tolson seeks to make McKay
safe for New Criticism, especially at a time when African-American
poetry is rapidly disappearing from anthologies. Thus the gratuitous
line about "ideological vestiges" in the midst of a review that calls
out McKay's own ideological contradictions. To complete the unfin-
ished sentence above:

> . . . the full-blooded African poet who could avouch, in spite of apart-
> heid: "I have never regarded myself as a 'Negro' poet. I have always
> felt that my gift of song was something bigger than the narrow limits of
> any people and its problems."
>
> And yet, in the sestet of *The Negro's Tragedy*, with its passive voice
> becoming an artery for an active idea, McKay declares the poetry "is
> urged out of my blood"; and then his raw, taut finality bristles in the
> monosyllables, "There is no white man who could write my book."
> (287)

Clearing away McKay's "ideological vestiges" turns out to be a
strategy for opening a clearing in which we can sound McKay's affirmative blackness; Tolson's negotiations here are adroit. But more
telling, and more provocative, is Tolson's revisionary account of
how he enticed Allen Tate to write the preface to *Libretto*. He told

the story to Dudley Randall the year before he died; the story was repeated as fact by Tolson's first biographer, Joy Flasch, and subsequently by many others, including Eugene Redmond (1976, 256–57, 262) and Karl Shapiro (1990, 222). It was nearly twenty years before Robert Farnsworth's research proved the tale untrue (1984, 138–51). Here is how it originally appeared, in the January 1966 *Negro Digest*:

> Tolson related that after completing *Libretto for the Republic of Liberia* he asked Allen Tate to write a preface for it, and Tate replied that he wasn't interested in the propaganda of Negro poets. Tolson spent a year studying modern poetic techniques and rewriting the poem so that it said the same things in a different way and then sent it to Tate. Tate wrote a preface in which he said, "For the first time, it seems to me, a Negro poet has assimilated the full poetic language of his time." (Randall 1966, 56)

Some critics have been embarrassed by this anecdote, just as, no doubt, some African-American writers may be incensed by it—and all the more incensed or embarrassed at the thought that it might be true: that Tolson, in Robert Huot's words, did not "hesitate to revise to please the white critic" (1971, 28). For on one reading, this presents Tolson (or presents him presenting himself) as a toady in blackface, trapped by his own minstrel mask, 'yes-massa'ing the Great White Critic. And even though the story is, finally, a tall tale, Farnsworth's research into the Tolson-Tate correspondence is perhaps more damaging yet, for Tolson's letters are unambiguous: he was thrilled that Tate agreed to write the preface and went so far as to prepare a representation of their correspondence for the *Sewanee Review* (Farnsworth 1984, 148–50). He was convinced that he had broken into the marmoreal halls, that he had achieved an unprecedented academic recognition of African-American poetry by means of the approbation of a major critic. He agreed to let *Poetry* publish the preface and one section of *Libretto* "as a sort of advance notice": in March 1950 he writes to Tate, "as I look back along the trail of Negro poetry for 250 years, I see the Preface as our literary Emancipation Proclamation. I also believe that the introduction and the *Libretto* ought to go far in re-inforcing your premise in Art. And I shall be delighted to have it appear in *Poetry*." Later the same month, he writes to his friend and former schoolmate Horace Mann Bond: "At last the great Allen Tate has sent in the Preface. . . . As you know, he is the toughest of the New School of Criticism. . . . At long last, it seems, a black man has broken into the rank of T. S. Eliot and Tate!" (quoted in Farnsworth 1984, 146).

This seems, even in comfortable retrospect, extravagant enthusiasm for a preface so meticulously careful to hedge its praise for
Tolson's work. Although, Tate writes, "there is a great gift for language, a profound historical sense, and a first-rate intelligence at
work in this poem from first to last," still, the poem's conclusion "is
rhetorically effective but not, I think, quite successful as poetry. . . .
the movement breaks down into Whitmanesque prose-paragraphs
into which Mr. Tolson evidently felt that he could toss all the loose
ends of history, objurgation, and prophecy which the set theme
seemed to require of him as official poet" (1953, 10). Tolson is
praised for his "historical sense," but there's too much rhetoric in
some of his poetry: the codes are all in place, and we await only a
denunciation of Romanticism to complete the warp of the fabric.
When it arrives, only one paragraph later, it comes in the form of a
query as to whether there can be such a thing as "Negro" literature
at all: heretofore, writes Tate, those who have attempted such a literature have "supposed that their peculiar genius lay in 'folk' idiom
or in the romantic creation of a 'new' language within the English
language." And because, presumably, there is only one language—
"the 'folk' and 'new' languages are not very different from those
that White poets can write"—the only possible signifying black difference can be a difference in topic.[4]

> The distinguishing Negro quality is not in the language but in the sub-
> ject-matter, which is usually the plight of the Negro segregated in a
> White culture. The plight is real and often tragic; but I cannot think
> that, *from the literary point of view*, the tragic aggressiveness of the mod-
> ern Negro poet offers wider poetic possibilities than the resigned pa-
> thos of Paul Laurence Dunbar, who was only a "White" *poète manqué*. [!]
> Both attitudes have limited the Negro poet to a provincial mediocrity in
> which one's feelings about one's difficulties become more important
> than poetry itself. (11)

Thus the problem lies not merely in the "aggressiveness" or "pathos" of individual Negroes; the problem lies deeper yet, in Negroes' assumption that poetry is self-expression. What has pre-

---

[4]"This is indeed a conundrum," writes Aldon Lynn Nielsen, "for Tate is putting
forward the critical theory that a black poet who masters the Afro-American traditions
and idioms will not be distinguishably black because white poets can accomplish the
same thing as well; the only recourse then is in learning to sound like those same
white poets (who sometimes write 'black') and speak in the Anglo-American idiom"
(1988, 112).

vented African-American writers from attaining membership in the
more exclusive anthologies, Tate suggests, is that they have not yet
learned that poetry is an escape from emotion, an escape from personality. But then what kind of escape must it have involved for
Tolson to write back to Tate, "I like your term 'provincial mediocrity'"? (quoted in Farnsworth 1984, 144). There is no evidence that
Tolson himself agreed with Tate that African-American poets had
heretofore been provincially mediocre; on the contrary, the Tolson
Manuscripts contain a letter to Ervin Tax of the Decker Press, dated
1 April 1950, in which Tolson writes that Tate's preface "consigns 'to
a provincial mediocrity' all Negro poets from 1775 to 1950. So you
can see this is an atom bomb!" (TM). Tolson was, we find, perfectly
capable of speaking about Tate the way William Carlos Williams
spoke of *The Waste Land* in his autobiography (1948, 174)—in anything but flattering terms. Nevertheless, there is no evidence that
Tolson ever directly conveyed to Tate any reservations about the
preface.

The point here, however, is not that Tolson's correspondence
with Tate reveals extraordinary contortions on the part of the poet
who calls patrons "bulls of Bashan" and critics "weeping monkeys";
that much is surely obvious. Rather, the point is that Tolson himself
was entirely aware of these contortions. Marxist though he may pro-
claim himself, Tolson's idea of the literary "margin" is, ultimately, a
liberal reformist's. Joshua Nitze's Zulu Club anecdote of the black
stevedore should remind us that one does not simply open one's
restaurant to previously excluded groups without also rethinking
one's menu; and one does not obtain access to the restaurant without expecting that one's presence alters the restaurant's function in
material ways. As Tolson conceives it, that is, the goal of the margin
is to gain access to the center in the hope of reconstructing the center—and reconstructing, in the process, what "access" will thereafter mean. As we may recognize by now, this is the goal of almost all
contemporary canon revision, whether feminist or ethnicist: to retrieve, as Pynchon might put it, the "preterite" texts of the present
and past, in order not only to challenge the canonical "elect" but to
chip away at the very distinction between preterite and elect.

I have said before that "elect" and "preterite" are historically contingent categories; consequently, it should not appear unusual to us
if the terms of marginality change over fifteen years' time. Still, in
Tolson's case, the difference between 1950 and 1965 seems nothing
less than drastic—both for his reception possibilities and for his per-

ceptions of his own career. For even if his appeal to Tate makes sense—in that Tate was at the time the foremost American epigone and emissary of Eliot and, as such, must have seemed to assure Tolson of eventual canonization—nevertheless, there is something genuinely astonishing about his decision. It seems the product of either hubris or folly, especially for a man of Tolson's political stripe; it seems, in short, an inordinately long way to go in order to gain access to the center. Perhaps access was available in other ways; perhaps access could have been imagined differently. Tolson was long an advocate of W. E. B. Du Bois, and like Du Bois he placed much of his hope for the cultural reproduction of African-American history and literature on the creation of an African-American intelligentsia who could oversee the distribution of cultural capital by taking the apparatus of its distribution into their own hands. Tolson himself wrote in one of his notebooks, "Hitherto, white critics have established the reputations of Negro writers—witness Wheatley, Dunbar, Wright—hereafter Negro critics, who are inside, will have perhaps the last say" (TM). If Tolson wanted eventually to be in the center but not of it, a kind of cyst on the body of English literature and criticism, he might well have envisioned "access" to consist not of "[breaking] into the ranks of T. S. Eliot and Tate" but in the creation of African-American studies departments or in the hiring and promotion, by major research universities, of African-American professors of English—some of whom might eventually assign Harlem Gallery to unsuspecting graduate students.

To make this ex post facto suggestion is not to say that Tolson should have seized the means of production and initiated the long-awaited dictatorship of the proletariat; but it is to note that Tolson's potential recovery would now be very difficult to imagine if the apparatus of academic criticism had not itself been transformed by the influx of African-American scholars in significant numbers as a result of the social transformations of the 1960s. But that is precisely the nature of revisionism, whether mine or Tolson's: just as we could see, in 1990, possible visions and versions of Tolson that might have been nearly incomprehensible twenty-five years earlier, so too may Tolson himself have seen in 1965 facets of his relation to Tate which he was in no position to engage in 1950. That is why it is necessary to return to the story Tolson told Randall and to take Tolson's version on its own terms, as his long-after-the-fact attempt to revise and mythologize himself as a kind of Hideho Heights gone right—a populist bard who refused to flee to Paris, who stayed home, lived in the Southwest, and worked as hard at trying to publish "E. & O.E." in the 1950s as at trying to organize Arkansas share-croppers in the 1930s.[5]

When taken as a revisionary autobiographical document, the story can easily be rather appetizing: a modern (modernist) Brer Rabbit story on its face, and even more canny and pointed as a tall tale. It suggests that Tolson wanted to cast his adoption of modernism—once again, even if only retrospectively—as a guerrilla strategy, a means of letting revolutionary discourse sound in the ears of conservative white Americans by masking that discourse in a no-longer-revolutionary poetics. And it suggests also that Tolson's relation to the Anglo-American modernist canon can be read in the context of a broader cultural problematic: the profound ambivalence, previously repressed but now incendiary in the late 1950s and thereafter, with which black America approached the prospects of integration.[6] In both contexts, Tolson seeks to emerge as neither Tate's dupe nor Eliot's but as an African-American literary version of the maroon, the escaped slave living on the frontier, imperialism's margin, raiding the nearest plantation periodically for supplies and planning the long-term offensive in the meantime. And in the image of Tolson as maroon, we find it somehow altogether appropriate that he has been marooned in turn: unread, or, if read at all, read not as maroon but as another form of "primitive"—a marooned colonial who made a cargo cult out of modernism.

Such are the terms in which we may read Tolson's song of himself, and they are terms to which I return in the conclusion of this chapter. But Tolson's Randall-tale is not the only critical response to Tate's preface. Appropriately, the most tangled answer to Tate—an answer that served only to complicate Tolson's position further—itself took the form of a preface: Karl Shapiro's introduction to *Harlem Gallery*, an introduction that casts Tolson against Tate with none of the self-conscious wryness of Tolson's auto-revision. I now turn to the Tate-Shapiro relation, in the hope that "the question of the preface" will dramatize for us some of the central problems in reconstructing Tolson's reception history.

---

[5]Tolson did in fact take on the highly dangerous job of attempting to organize sharecroppers, both white and black; see Farnsworth 1984, 54. For Tolson's tale of how his mother prevented him from journeying to Paris at the age of twelve, see the King interview (Tolson 1966, 192–93), in which he claims that an artist who stepped off a train noticed a painting at which he was working and insisted that Tolson accompany him to Paris. The story is at least as suspect as his version of the Tate correspondence, and more entertaining: I have not here done justice to Tolson's talent for oddly convincing detail.

[6]See, e.g., Woodward 1974, 189–220.

Authorizing Misrepresentation: Tate, Shapiro, Fabio

Tate's preface does not efface itself, sublating itself neatly into the text of Tolson's *Libretto*; rather, it goes so far as to set the terms for the further dissemination of Tolson's work. First, Tate "fathers" the text—that is, gives it a father or, at least, sets forth the basis for a paternity suit: "Mr. Tolson is in the direct succession from Crane" (1953, 9). Second, Tate carves away the problem of race and writing on the ground that Tolson has authorized such carving: "He seems to me to dismiss the entire problem, so far as poetry is concerned, by putting it in its properly subordinate place" (11–12). Third, and most master-fully, he sketchily maps the poem, delineating and distinguishing points of interest from badlands: "I point out what I consider its defects only because the power and versatility of other parts of the poem offset them, and enjoin the critic to pay the poem the compliment of very severe scrutiny" (10).

Tate's disseminations, one might say, are not Derridean scatterings of the seed that does not return to the father, pre-dications of the Book which enact the book as "text," infinitely repeatable and revisable; on the contrary, Tate seeks to direct Tolson's poem very carefully. If the *Libretto* is to be iterable, he suggests, it must be iterated in very specific terms: through its likeness to Crane, in its transcendence of mere "racial" poetry, and despite its occasional loose ends, objurgation, and prophecy. Tate's preface is decidedly un-Derridean in another sense as well. Derrida points out that it is but a convenient fiction, operative especially when the writer of the preface is also the writer of the text, that the preface is written after the text but must be read before: "Writing as such does not consist in any of these tenses (present, past, or future insofar as they are all modified presents)" (1981, 7). But in Tolson's case there remains the more intractable matter of publication tenses, for thanks to a strange misfortune—an automobile accident killed Ervin Tax of the Decker Press in 1950, and the company folded—Tate's preface preceded its text by three full years. Thus, between Tax's death and the decision to publish Tate's preface before the publication of *Libretto*, we find the preface restored to its pre-dicatory function.

Tate's preface appeared so long before the full text of the *Libretto* that its relatively autonomous existence has had two interesting effects. One is that it established an inverse relation between preface and text whereby Tate's preface becomes neither the poem's pre-text nor part of its critical context but, more oddly, the "real text" of the poem itself—so much so that it was reprinted in *Jet* as well as in

Poetry. In one way, in fact, the content of the preface is beside the point: the important thing is Tate's signature, and whatever else Tate wrote gives way before the simple fact that he wrote anything at all. Surely it was to this signature alone that William Stanley Braithwaite was responding when he wrote to Tolson: "It is, apart from anything else, a great achievement to have converted this critical authority to the single standard by which all artists irrespective of race or color should be judged. With patient industry and concentrated devotion you have achieved an art that adds a glory to contemporary American literature" (TM). This is truly wonderful praise; but as a remarkably deadpan Farnsworth notes, "Braithwaite had not at the time read the *Libretto*" (1984, 306 n.12); as the letter itself makes clear, Braithwaite had that day (24 January 1954) read only Selden Rodman's review of *Libretto* in the *New York Times Book Review*. What Braithwaite means by Tolson's "art that adds a glory to contemporary American literature," therefore, is rather open to question: he might just as well be referring to the art by which Tolson persuaded Tate to endorse the poem; and the poem itself, like the printed text of the preface, may be supererogatory.

The second effect is a related one: Tate's preface was not published by itself; it was accompanied by "Ti," *Libretto*'s penultimate section. "Ti" consists of eleven irregular, typographically centered, *Gallery*-like stanzas, most of them launched in the vocative case—"O Calendar of the Century"; "O Africa, Mother of Science" (*L*, lines 255, 273)—and all ending with the one-word Psalmic call "*Selah!*" The juxtaposition of "Ti" and Tate in Shapiro's *Poetry* finds its appropriate response in the juxtaposition of Tolson and Tate in William Carlos Williams's poetry, as all parties to the *Libretto* are jumbled together in a "Ti"-like salute from the fourth book of *Paterson*:

> —and to Tolson and to his ode
> and to Liberia and to Allen Tate
> (give him credit)
> and to the South generally
> *Selah!*
>
> (1963, 183)

We move here with startling speed from Tolson to "the South generally," whatever Williams may mean by that, and in the rush from specific to "generally," Tolson and Tate are all but equated. Or perhaps inverted: the parenthesis has the odd effect of crediting Tate twice, as if there is any danger he will be lost in the shuffle. As

Aldon Lynn Nielsen has argued, the stanza leaves it to us to imagine whether Tate is to be applauded for "the courage required to help a little-known poet find a wider audience for his work or with the courage to have overcome his own substantial prejudices"—or, for that matter, for both. Moreover, writes Nielsen, "it appears symptomatic that Williams will not allow Tolson to take his credits alone," for he links Tolson and Tate just as, earlier in *Paterson*, he had "subsumed the experience of the middle passage within the larger, whiter experience of immigration" (1988, 80).

We find, thus, either that Tate's preface precludes the text—not to render it infinitely open but to close it off prematurely—or that Tate appears, as in Williams's stanza, as if co-author of the text. When we take up the *Libretto*, we find prefaces and readers to be potentially constricting agents after all, and this has had material consequences for Tolson's career, not only insofar as it affects his ability to stay in print but insofar as it caused Shapiro to try to undo some of the damage in *Harlem Gallery*. For if, as Shapiro writes, Tate wrote for Tolson "an essay which is more famous than the poem" (1965b, 11), then Tate has contributed, even if unintentionally, to a situation in which "a great poet has been living in our midst for decades and is almost totally unknown, even by the literati, even by poets," and thanks to which "poetry as we know it remains the most lily-white of the arts." Crucial to Shapiro's argument is the assertion that the critical establishment has more power over the reception of poetry than over that of the novel or drama, and that the canon of contemporary verse therefore "has many of the characteristics of a closed corporation" in which the power of trustees is determinative: "A novelist and pamphleteer like Baldwin is world famous; Tolson, easily the literary equal of any number of Baldwins, is less honored in his own country than the most obscure poetaster" (11).

Shapiro is nothing here if not well-meaning, and perhaps he thought that a preface in response to Tate would clear away once and for all the notion that Tolson was the white critics' houseboy. But he goes on to celebrate Tolson in such a way as to recapitulate Tate's preempting preface. The publication of Shapiro's piece also preceded Tolson's; it was featured on the front page of *Book Week* (in the *Washington Post* and the *New York Herald Tribune*), and, not surprisingly, it "heavily influenced the reception of *Harlem Gallery* for some time after its publication" (Farnsworth 1984, 272). It was reprinted also in *Negro Digest* in May 1965, after the publication of *Harlem Gallery*.

"Maybe the Tate piece unconsciously guided me," writes Shapiro to Tolson in October 1964 (TM). Maybe—for there are two extremely problematic moments in his introduction which are barely fathomable except as veiled responses to Tate. The first of these attempts to set out Tolson as "the enemy of the dominant culture of our time and place":

> He is, to use the term he prefers, an Afroamerican poet, not an American Negro poet accommodating himself to the Tradition. It is probably for this reason that the *Libretto*, despite its *succès d'estime*, failed to tickle the sensibilities of the literati and professoriat. The *Libretto* pulls the rug out from under the poetry of the Academy; on the stylistic level, outpounding Pound, it shocks the learned into a recognition of their own ignorance. *Harlem Gallery* pulls the house down around their ears. (1965b, 12)

It is more accurate, of course, to say that Tolson sought to bring the academic house down around himself; certainly, it is hard to imagine a way in which erudition and technical difficulty in a poet would serve to subvert the purposes of academic critics. Shapiro's attempt to cover himself on this count is jesuitical and unconvincing: "Instead of purifying the tongue, which is the business of the Academy, he is complicating it, giving it the gift of tongues" (13).

Clearly enough, Shapiro's argument here signifies only when read against Tate's "assimilation" argument. But worse yet is Shapiro's claim that "Tolson writes and thinks in Negro, which is to say, a possible American language" (13), which, as Farnsworth notes, is surely aimed at Tate's "effort to minimize" the importance of Tolson's race to his poetry (1984, 272). But we do not necessarily locate the meaning of Shapiro's claim when we locate its intended addressee; letters, we know, sometimes do not arrive at their appointed destinations, and this one was almost immediately intercepted by Sarah Webster Fabio, who, in rebutting Shapiro, set out the terms in which Tolson is most often discussed—or the terms by which he is considered unworthy of discussion. Fabio's response is complicated by the fact that she is replying not only to the introduction but to Shapiro's expansion of his argument in a later article, "Decolonization of American Literature," which was reprinted in *Negro Digest* in October 1965 (Shapiro had written in his October 1964 letter to Tolson about the introduction, "I think I said all I had to say"; but prefaces tend not to work that way). Still, the tenor of her piece—as well as its title, "Who Speaks Negro?"—should make clear what is at issue here: "Melvin Tolson's language is certainly not 'Negro' to any significant degree. The weight of that vast, bizarre, pseudo-literary diction is to be placed back in the American mainstream where it rightfully and wrongmindedly belongs" (1966, 55).

She then proceeds to attack Shapiro on two fronts, and in both sallies she exposes severe self-contradictions in Shapiro's position. First, she contrasts his rhetoric with his critical practice, to devastating effect: quoting his claim that "a literature is the expression of a nation's soul, and a great literature leaves nothing out—that is its greatness" (Shapiro 1965a, 844), she follows it with a pointed example of Shapiro's "leaving out": "Shapiro assisted [Louis] Untermeyer in editing *The Modern American and Modern British Poetry* in 1955, and by his own above definition of greatness the exclusion of Claude McKay, Paul Laurence Dunbar, James Weldon Johnson, Langston Hughes, Melvin Tolson and Pulitzer prize winner Gwendolyn Brooks, *and all black poets writing in English,* fosters the 'status quo mediocrity' which he deplores" (1966, 56; my emphasis). Given his editorial record, Fabio implies, it is mere posturing for Shapiro to write, "To leave nothing out means to go against the grain; it means to dissent. Our modern literature is a literature of dissent" (1965a, 844)—especially if "dissent" never has any practical consequences for the anthologizing and teaching of literature.

But Shapiro wants very much to seize the "dissident," anti-academic high ground, and it is on this ground that Fabio launches her second attack, juxtaposing Shapiro's celebration of Beat poetry to his sponsorship of Tolson. It is on this ground that she makes Shapiro look foolish—and Tolson, by extension, foolish as well. Shapiro had written, in a moment of self-congratulation, that like a Toussaint L'Ouverture of aesthetics, he was struggling to free poetry from academic imperialism (even the "decolonization" of his title is borrowed from Frantz Fanon): "For many years I have been trying to loosen the hold of the academic or 'colonial' mind over poetry. Not only poetry but the entire literature of reference, the kind that refers back in every case to prior commitments, historical, religious, or philosophical" (1965a, 850–51).

Fabio's response is worth following at some length:

> It is sound advice that he [Shapiro] gives when he says "it would be better to ignore the existence of the literature of reference and to create whatever we think valid than to go on tilting at windmills. This is what the beat writers did; they were successful because they refused to *take part in the academic dialogue*" [851; Fabio's emphasis].

Melvin Tolson was not a beat poet; he was a part of the neo-classical scene who—although as able as any to attempt the Quixotic feat of reviving a dead horse, albeit a Trojan horse—was denied a rightful place in this theatre of the absurd. Like many Negroes of this period, he was told to go back and perfect the art, and, then, in the great democratic tradition, he would be accepted into the society of the neo-classicists.

He accepted and perfected the art of classical reference as a pillar for an American tradition in literature but became victimized by the cultural lag that is common between the white and Negro worlds. . . . Therefore, while Tolson busied himself out-pounding Pound, his fellow poets forgot to send him the message that Pound was out. (Fabio 1966, 57)

Fabio cannot be gainsaid here: Tolson is by no stretch of the imagination a Beat poet, and Fabio has undoubtedly descried a real fissure between Shapiro's appreciation of Beats and his advocacy of Tolson—a fissure that Shapiro papers over poorly in his implicit claim that Tolson is de facto a revolutionary, *aux* Beats, simply because he is an African-American poet.[7]

And in the fissure echoes Fabio's retort. "He was told to go back and perfect the art": by December 1966, the Randall-Tolson conversation, published ten months earlier, has made the rounds and become the rationale for avoiding Tolson altogether.[8] In the maelstroms of the day, when in the Congress of Racial Equality (CORE), the Student Nonviolent Coordinating Committee (SNCC), and the conversations taking place across the pages of *Negro Digest*, the relevant questions center on the acceptability of "collusion" with whites, this distorted Tolson looks a lot like Uncle Tom, and *Harlem Gallery* like "a part of the neo-classical scene."[9] Such is the "seeing-as" of

[7]See Shapiro 1965a, 851: "The importance of the Negro writer in the world today is far out of proportion to the number of books we have to go by. But the significance of Negro writing today is paramount because everywhere, not simply in America, the Negro is in the position to ask the questions." And since such questioning literary revolutionaries always win, African-Americans are luckier than other oppressed peoples because they are "unassimilable" (852) and thus eventually canonical: "For a Negro literature to come into being, it had to start from the bottom, not from the top. All great poetry comes from the bottom: Homer, Dante, Chaucer, Whitman, all went to the language of the street for their great poems" (849).

[8]Farnsworth, too, writes that Tolson's story to Randall, whether or not a deliberate fabrication, demonstrates the difficulty of determining any strategy's historical effects: "Unfortunately, what Tolson probably made up either consciously or unconsciously, as a tale to indicate his folk shrewdness, then became an anecdote that Tolson's severest critics would point to as evidence of his kowtowing to a dead tradition" (1984, 290).

[9]As CORE and SNCC began their turn against integration, "a kind of 'blackening' process—which, in *Digest*, for example, took the form of ceasing to publish or endorse white writers and changing its name to *Black World*—occurred in most of these

late 1966, and under these conditions even Tolson's "Psi," which argues that racial distinctions are fictions perpetrated by whites for the oppression of nonwhites, finds an unfriendly nonwhite audience. "[Tolson] asks, 'Who is a Negro?' His answer that 'The Negro is a dish in the white man's kitchen—a *potpourri* . . .' given in *Harlem Gallery*, is too simple a truth; any notion of Negritude which extols the virtue of being a rotten pot with flowers and petals for scent is lacking a full understanding of this concept" (Fabio 1966, 54–55).

The reasonable reply to this is surely that Fabio has not read Tolson closely, that Tolson is neither extolling the virtues of being defined by whites nor setting out a theory of Negritude. But the reasonable reply once again falls short, because although Tolson had not spoken, after the fashion of Aimé Césaire or Léopold Senghor, about "Negritude," Shapiro *had*—in Tolson's name. And Shapiro's recolonization of the term may actually be more damaging to Tolson than anything Tolson himself ever said about his relation to the academy. Once again tilting at Tate's windmills, Shapiro writes: "The falsification I speak of is that of trying to assimilate Tolson into the tradition when he was doing the opposite. The fact that Tolson's *Libretto* is unknown by white traditionalists gives the lie to the critic's assertion that Tolson has risen above Negro experience to become an 'artist.' The facts are that Tolson is a dedicated revolutionist who revolutionizes modern poetry in a language of American negritude" (1965a, 853).

Shapiro goes on from here to claim that Tolson's poetry is a conscious satire of Eliot's; it is a claim to which we will eventually return, but for now we have a more pressing problem on our hands: Tolson is being championed for his "language of American negritude" by an Anglo-American poet-critic who has written, four pages earlier, that "it seems to me there is more *Negritude*, if I may use the word, in Faulkner than in either Wright or Ellison. Faulkner is better

---

new journals" (Redmond 1978, 562). *Negro Digest* editor Fuller had opened the decade by publishing Arna Bontemps's "The New Black Renaissance"; later, with the help of Addison Gayle, Fuller looked to younger writers for his magazine, "which, as the only national black literary magazine with a paid staff and a reliable publishing history, naturally assumed a position of leadership in the black arts movement. Until well into the seventies, Gayle, one of the most influential black aestheticians, dramatically aided Fuller in charting the journal's vision. He, along with Don Lee (Mad-hubuti) and Baraka (who later renounced *Black World*'s position), developed into a kind of axis force that monitored the evolution of the movement" (564). The *CLA Journal*, by contrast, remained in a more ambiguous position during this period, continuing to devote roughly half to two-thirds of its pages to traditional scholarship on the Western canons (548).

able to present the sensibility of the Negro, albeit the Mississippi Negro, because Faulkner's characters are *not* always at the point of dramatic crisis" (849). Shapiro here finds "Negritude" in the writer who publicly opined that African-Americans were not ready for integration; and, I think, once we read in its entirety the article to which Fabio was responding, our wonder is not that Tolson's poem disappeared in the fray but that Fabio's rebuttal of Shapiro managed to be temperate at all. For even if Fabio was not unconsciously responding to Shapiro's recolonization of the term "negritude," she may well have been struck by his definition of the word: "All three of these great poets [Césaire, Senghor, and Tolson] write in Negro. That is what negritude means in literature. . . . It means insistence on the pride of selfhood without hatred. No oppressed people in history has had less sense of revenge than the Negro. Retribution is not Negro" (852).

We could follow this path longer; we could look next at Shapiro's more recent attempt to confer honor on Tolson, in a lecture of 1981 entitled "The Critic Outside," which was published in *American Scholar*. We could find there a Shapiro who wants to defend Milton from "his newest enemies, the feminists" (1981, 199); who hates contemporary "mass poetry or welfare poetry" (206), Creative Writing programs (208), and "postmoderns" who adopt "the drop-out strategies of the fifties and sixties" (209); who culminates his Hilton Kramerisms with a faith in "the solid and authentic achievement of modern poetry" which, as the classic standard to which we fail to measure up, will sustain us in these trivial times (210). We could find a Shapiro who defends yet again, digging himself ever deeper, his claim that Tolson writes in Negro (205). We could find there, most of all, an embittered Shapiro who fails to understand why African-Americans rejected his approval of Tolson and who believes that "the Black Recoil or whatever it is called" has created an "apartheid," "a separate nation of blacks in this country, this time on their own terms" (206). And having found all these things, we would begin to realize that Shapiro is not Tolson's ideal representative.[10]

But it is time to choose another path. Part of the problem with Shapiro and Tate is precisely that they have deflected discussion

[10]Farnsworth links the Shapiro-Tate dispute to a line from *Libretto*'s "Sol," one of the proverbs of the African griots: "It is the grass that suffers when / two elephants fight" (*L*, lines 206–7; Farnsworth 1984, 172). Shapiro has recently given us one last glimpse of what happened to his advocacy of Tolson, and though he still has not reconsidered his constructions of "black apartheid" and writing "in Negro" (far from it), his sincere esteem for Tolson is quite clear (1990, 221–23).

from Tolson to themselves for so long; and there remains a body of critical response to Tolson's work which has managed to dodge or ignore the formidable questions of these prefaces. Likewise, there remain many re-soundings of these prefaces—veiled allusions to, assumptions about, and rearticulations of Tate, Shapiro, and their specific Tolsons. To borrow an apt phrase from Tony Bennett, such re-soundings echo a Tolson whose reception arrives already "humming with meanings" (1983a, 207); and because those meanings hum in the domain of the intertext, rather than as the constructions of individual readers facing stable textual objects, we may reconceive the terms of their dissemination as Bennett has revised Derrida: texts, for Bennett and for my readings below, are not "'free-floating' travellers, wandering hither and thither in the intertextual of their own volition. What should be stressed is not so much their 'iterability' as their 'inscribability'—their ability to be written into a potentially infinite variety of signifying contexts" (221).

Humming Off Key: Tolson and the White Critical Response

Tolson's first book of poems, *Rendezvous with America*, was published in 1944, and in one way his debut date is paradigmatic of his position throughout his career. As Paul Lauter details in his discussion of race and gender in the shaping of the American canon, the 1940s mark the beginning of ebb tide for American recognition of poetry by African-American men and women, the onset of a period that saw African-American writers increasingly retrenched even in those few anthologies, such as Louis Untermeyer's, to which they had gained access in the 1920s:

> Untermeyer's editing exemplifies the rise and fall of interest in black writers. His first two editions (1919 and 1921) contained poems by Dunbar, joined in the 1925 version by Countee Cullen, James Weldon Johnson, Claude McKay, and Alex Rogers, and then later by Langston Hughes and Jean Toomer. By the 1942 sixth edition, however, only Dunbar, Johnson, Cullen, and Hughes remained; the seventh edition witnessed the elimination of Dunbar. The general and poetry anthologies uniformly omitted all black women with the solitary and rare exception of Phillis Wheatley. (Lauter 1983, 437–38)[11]

[11]Not that Afro-American literature had flooded the mainstream in the 1920s; although "substantial collections of black writings were issued in that decade and dur-

This retrenchment proceeds apace for most of the remainder of Tolson's career, to the point that "by the end of the fifties, one could study American literature and read no work by a black writer" (440).

Just as the "question of the preface" has meanings for Tolson it could not have for Derrida, so too does Tolson's late debut, at the age of forty-six, suggest something about belatedness which Harold Bloom would not think to discuss: namely, the relation of "movements" to the printing and composition of anthologies. Tolson took his inspiration from the writers of the Harlem Renaissance; he wrote his M.A. thesis on the writers of the Harlem Renaissance; he spoke of a "New Negro" and a "New Negro poetry" after the fashion of the Harlem Renaissance—yet he is not *of* the Harlem Renaissance. We may talk about Tolson's relation to the Renaissance either in terms of his *clinamen* and *apophrades* or, more pragmatically, in terms of its influence on the determination of his relevant critical contexts. He arrives too late for any of the compilations of the 1920s and 1930s, and until the appearance of the African-American anthologies of the late 1960s and early 1970s—which, as we shall see, tell a curious tale of their own—he proves difficult to package as a "post–Harlem Renaissance" writer, partly because the "post–Harlem Renaissance" period in American literature is marked by its inattention to African-American writers.

Let me make this point materially clear. Lauter's research points up the scarcity of African-American writers in "general" anthologies, and I can add that the period between the 1930s and 1960s was a very dry one for the production of new African-American anthologies as well. After Brown, Davis, and Lee's *Negro Caravan* in 1941, only one major anthology was published in the United States for the next twenty years, Hughes and Bontemps's *Poetry of the Negro* in 1949. The years between 1965 and 1975, by comparison, saw the publication of over eighty anthologies devoted exclusively or substantially to African-American authors, thirty of them by major publishers.[12] Thus, as one of the Harlem Renaissance's unacknowledged

---

ing the thirties, and at least some black writers managed to make a living from their trade," still, "these facts were in no way reflected in the teaching of American literature, in general anthologies, or in most critical discussions by whites of the literature of the United States" (Lauter 1983, 437).

[12]See French, Fabre, and Singh 1979, 30–51. My total excludes anthologies of students' and children's poetry (nearly twenty in 1965–75) and prison anthologies (five from 1970 to 75), in which Tolson could not possibly have been included; however, their abundance is as important an index of the period as is the publication boom in

progeny set adrift at a time when the American literary world was purging even Claude McKay and Jean Toomer from its cultural record, Tolson fits into no ready-made pedagogical categories, categories of the kind that shape anthology sections and reading lists.

Even when, after the 1960s, the tide turns again in American letters, that tide does not bring Tolson with it: the recent Chelsea House Library of Literary Criticism, which includes critical reviews of and excerpts from 373 twentieth-century American writers, includes no Tolson; the remarkably catholic *Heath Anthology of American Literature*, edited by Paul Lauter, retrieves no Tolson. For that matter, Tolson continues to be excluded from revisions of the Harlem Renaissance, and there appears to be no compelling reason to rewrite literary history so as to place Tolson with his contemporaries in a movement to which he did not properly belong. Yet in being "post-Renaissance" he has fallen into an odd cul-de-sac wherein, for instance, Houston Baker's 1971 anthology classes Tolson in a section devoted to writers of the 1930s and 1940s. Even in more recent African-American anthologies, the institutional effects of his "belatedness" have not diminished; the 1985 revised edition of Long and Collier's 1972 *Afro-American Writing* declares that "generally speaking, the novel was by far a more innovative genre during the fifties than was poetry" (1985, 445), despite the production of *Libretto* and Hughes's *Montage of a Dream Deferred* (1951) in the midst of the decades of bebop, hard bop, and the birth of the cool.

I will return to questions raised by Tolson's debut date in the process of examining his anthologization history, but first I offer some explanation for the questions excluded or marginalized by the following study. In reconstructing Tolson's reception I dwell only briefly on the critical reaction to *Rendezvous with America*, for two reasons. First, *Rendezvous* looks nothing like his later work and pre-

---

general anthologies, and one could say much about the historical and institutional conditions of their production. My total from "major publishers" counts general anthologies (excluding reprints, of which there were many) as follows: three each from Houghton Mifflin, Macmillan, Bantam, and Dodd, Mead; two each from Morrow and Random House; one each from Harper & Row, McGraw-Hill, Penguin, Harcourt, Doubleday, Fawcett, Hill & Wang, and Holt, Rinehart; and those from such near-majors as New American Library (three), Arno (one), Free Press (which published *Dark Symphony*), and New York University Press (the first edition of Long and Collier's *Afro-American Writing*). This "majors" count is hardly a definitive statistic: it leaves out the six anthologies printed by Randall's important Broadside Press—and the very proliferation of small, independent presses is an index of the period as well. However, I intend my figure simply as a significant measure of the willingness of large and midsized houses to publish collections of African-American literature.

sents us with none of the problems of the later work's reception; in fact, the disparity has moved Arthur Davis to remark that "between his early works and his later ones, there is . . . a greater growth in outlook and sophistication than is found in any other American poet. . . . one gets the impression that he is reading two different authors" (1974, 167). Here Davis sensibly contests our faith in organicist metaphors of individual poetic "development," preferring instead to speak of Tolson's "phenomenal poetic transformation" between 1944 and 1951, a transformation that transforms his conditions of reception significantly. Second, Tolson's current and future reputation cannot rest, even slightly, on the achievement of *Rendezvous*. An uneven volume, *Rendezvous* does contain a number of valuable poems, but if we are to meet the challenge of Tolson's work today and retrieve it for further discussion, we will have to do so by grappling with his most formidable efforts. A major reason for Tolson's near-anonymity is precisely that his readers and anthologizers have shied away from his work after *Rendezvous*, with the result that there is no definitive reading, as yet, of either *Libretto* or *Harlem Gallery*—and word of mouth, whether in space or in time, does not travel in a vacuum.

To the exclusion of most newspaper and some journal reviews of Tolson's work, I focus first on Tolson's reception in the most influential American (and British) nonacademic journals and magazines—that is, the kinds of venues that were most likely to have made Tolson available for further critical attention.[13] These reviews give us a good idea of Tolson's appropriation by white audiences of the 1950s and 1960s, and the terms in which he was offered for discussion (and nondiscussion) in the years immediately following *Harlem Gallery*'s publication. The critical organs of white American and British literati do not present a complete picture of Tolson's place in postwar African-American letters, but Shapiro's claim about the "lily-white" status of Poetry, Inc., is surely underwritten and borne

---

[13]I take this method of charting "precanonicity" through exposure in major journals, as well as the idea of "precanonical" texts, from Ohmann 1983. My use (following Ohmann) of Hover and Kadushin 1972 and Kadushin, Hover, and Tichy 1971 is confined to their listings of the most influential journals selected by their control group: *New York Review of Books, New Republic, Commentary, New York Times Book Review, New Yorker, Saturday Review, Partisan Review,* and *Harper's* constitute the top eight, after which there is a significant dropoff to *The Nation* and *Atlantic Monthly*. In order to err on the side of caution, however, I have included in my own survey *The Nation*, which was rated highly among English professors (Kadushin, Hover, and Tichy 1971, 15), and the *Times Literary Supplement*, which, as a British publication, was not included in the study.

out, institutionally, by the relative narrowness of the channels through which poetry (as opposed to fiction and nonfiction) is diffused in the postwar period.

For one thing, reviews of Tolson in influential white or black journals are few and far between: *Phylon* alone reviewed both *Libretto* and *Harlem Gallery*. Moreover, Tolson received sustained attention from journals (influential or otherwise) only twice in his career—from *Poetry* in the early 1950s (during Shapiro's tenure as editor) and from *Negro Digest* in the mid-1960s. Rarely did any journal keep Tolson visible for more than a few months after the publication of his work; between *Libretto* and *Harlem Gallery*, he is invoked only once, in a 1958 *Partisan Review* piece by Stanley Edgar Hyman, who spends two paragraphs linking *Libretto* to "the associative organization of the blues" (207). And for another thing, Tolson's reception in the leading African-American journals of his day proved to be, in the 1960s, as important to his representation in African-American anthologies as were his "major" reviews. I therefore examine both reception contexts, predominantly white and predominantly black, and conclude my survey with a discussion of Tolson's representation in African-American anthologies.

The anthologies, for their part, serve two pivotal functions. They are in a sense the culmination of Tolson's nonacademic reception, and they instantiate, in turn, one aspect of his academic reception, because they are (of course) coeval with the creation of college-level courses in African-American literature and cultural studies, at once responding to and creating (with or without the aid of campus demonstrations) a new, institutional reception context for African-American letters. And thanks to their function as miniature archives, circulated primarily in academic, institutional marketplaces, these anthologies are also the most reliable and wide-reaching means by which Tolson is currently involved in the process of cultural reproduction. Not only are they often explicitly canon-forming and canon-revising documents, but their long shelf half-lives constitute them as a continual source of critical representation, unlike all but the most notable and influential (and reprinted, cited, re-cited) reviews. Seven of the twenty-five anthologies in which Tolson appears, in fact, remain in print to this day; as of 1980, twenty were still in print. And since all of Tolson's individual titles except *A Gallery of Harlem Portraits* are out of print, anthologies are now the only vehicles keeping Tolson's postwar poetry "current."[14]

[14]Aside from the sole exception of Robert Boynton and Maynard Mack's *Introduction to the Poem*, a college-level poetry primer whose second and third editions (1973; 1985)

Even if there is no causal gatekeeping link between Tolson's reviews and his representation in anthologies, most of the reviews have a temporal priority. Yet both areas of reception present material instances of the same general ideological construction of African-American literature, and the reviews, especially, resound with echoes of the Shapiro and Tate prefaces in ways that set the general context for Tolson's later representations in anthologies. For like the prefaces, with notable variations, even Tolson's "good" reviews undermine him in the very terms of their endorsement; some do so by reading Tate more thoroughly than Tolson, but then again, even white American critics who did not have a long history of agrarianism and stand-taking praised Tolson for transcending "provincial Negro literature." Not surprisingly, this kind of praise did not endear Tolson to the reading formations of the mid-1960s, under which his favorable reception by Tate, John Ciardi, and Selden Rodman could be transformed into a retroactive damnation.

In 1966, *Negro Digest* editor Hoyt Fuller pointedly called attention to white critics' terms of access in an article entitled "Negro Writers and White Critics," which cited as one of its case-in-point malefactors none other than John Ciardi. Ciardi, in a 1964 piece on James Baldwin, had had the indiscretion to claim that critics "have always tended to be especially generous to Negro writers and for understandable reasons" (Ciardi 1964, 16; quoted in Fuller 1966, 37). This generosity, however, apparently did not extend to Baldwin himself, and the significance of the suggestion was not lost on Fuller:

> In a recent, somewhat belated attack on James Baldwin's *Another Country*, which he clearly misunderstood, poet John Ciardi showed how richly he deserves status among the philistines by writing that, "in the long run, I must insist, there must be no Negro writers, but only men as other men and committed to all man" [Ciardi 1964, 16]. . . . What is so insidious here is not that Ciardi rejects the legitimacy of Baldwin's "protest"—he professes full sympathy—but, more subtly, that he wishes to disavow the necessity that there be "Negro writers" at all, without first assuring the demolition of the barriers which make certain

include "The Sea-Turtle and the Shark," Tolson's poetry is currently available only in anthologies of African-American writing. Information from *Books in Print* for 1970–90 indicates that the average life of an African-American anthology is approximately fifteen years; one lasted no more than three years (1972–74); all others stayed in print for at least eight; and four of those currently in print have lasted twenty years or more (see Appendix A). No publishing house with which I corresponded was willing to release precise sales data on its current titles, but some editors did cite general industry standards for a text's continued reproduction: one quoted an annual sales threshold in the low hundreds; another, annual sales of roughly 1,000 (generally, the bigger the house, the higher the threshold).

that Negro experience is radically different from that of "other men."
(36)

Fuller links Ciardi's comments, in turn, to Louis Simpson's more
fulsomely doctrinal review, in the *New York Herald Tribune*'s *Book
Week*, of Gwendolyn Brooks's *Selected Poems*. Simpson wrote: "I am
not sure it is possible for a Negro to write well without making us
aware that he is a Negro. On the other hand, if being a Negro is the
only subject, the writing is not important" (Simpson 1963, 25;
quoted in Fuller 1966, 36).[15] The problem for Fuller—as it should be
the problem for us, twenty-odd years later—is not merely that Ciardi claims to have lower standards for "Negroes" but that Ciardi
exposes himself, retroactively, as having praised Tolson—à la Allen
Tate or Louis Simpson—for having "transcended" his race, in the
course of asserting that literature is the domain of universal Man.
Indeed, Ciardi had closed his review (1954, 183) by quoting Tate's
line about Tolson's assimilation of the Anglo-American tradition.
Thus, in Ciardi, Tolson had picked up the endorsement of a well-
placed white critic, only to have it revealed a decade later that the
critic had endorsed him because his poetry was not mere Negro poetry—and, accordingly, important for its not-blackness.

So too with Selden Rodman's ostensibly commendatory notice in
the *Times Book Review*, which at the time was cause for celebration by
Tolson's readers (some of whom, like Braithwaite, wrote letters of
congratulation) and, notably, by his publishers: as Jacob Steinberg at
Twayne wrote on 25 January 1954, "I suppose you have now seen
the Sunday *Times* and are riding on a cloud" (TM). But Rodman's
opening paragraph begins in the manner of the later Ciardi, claiming that critics have heretofore handled African-American writers
with kid gloves; moves to the assertion that such critics are covering
for African-Americans' inability to turn the other cheek; and ends
with a sentence of verbatim Tate phrases, only the last of which is
placed in quotation marks:

> It is a reflection on so-called "white" culture that up to now "Negro
> poetry" in English has had to be considered as such and handled with
> special care to avoid giving offense. Praised for its moral intentions and

[15]And just as Fabio (despite the apparent vehemence of "Who Speaks Negro?")
actually seems to have given Shapiro's "Decolonization" an easier time than she
might have, so too does Fuller pull even this punch by declining to quote the penultimate sentence of Simpson's review (1963, 25): "Miss Brooks must have had a devil of
a time trying to write poetry in the United States, where there has been practically no
Negro poetry worth talking about."

excused for its formal shortcomings, it has generally been tolerated as a literary poor relation. The fact of the matter is that most of this poetry has been second-rate, and that critics, partaking of the general responsibility for the Negro's unreadiness to take the "Negro problem" in his stride, have hesitated to say so. The Negro poet's attitude of resigned pathos was followed by one of tragic aggressiveness, and both, as Allen Tate says in his preface to "Libretto for the Republic of Liberia," limited him "to a provincial mediocrity in which feelings about one's difficulties become more important than poetry itself." (Rodman 1954, 10)

Discussion of the preface precedes the text once again—this time so as to include Tate's cartoon "pathos-aggressiveness" periodization of African-American literary history, and then so as to present Tate's words on "provincial mediocrity" as if they are corroborating known facts about that literary history.

And then, once again, there is the question of Tolson's relation to the Anglo-American tradition—this time with a twist. In the final third of the review, Rodman directly compares Tolson with Eliot, pointing out lines in *Libretto* which "Eliot surely would have been proud to have written" (10), but also distinguishing Tolson's taste from Eliot's at the expense of the former. The basis for the distinction is a passage from "Ti," which, in all fairness to Rodman, is one of *Libretto*'s weaker moments:

> The *Höhere* of Gaea's children
> is beyond the *dérèglement de tous les sens*, is beyond
> gold fished from cesspools, the *galerie des rois*,
> the seeking of cows, *apartheid*, Sisyphus' despond,
> the Ilande intire of itselfe with *die Schweine* in mud.
> (*L*, lines 403–7)

But whether one is offended more by this or by, say, the tale of Albert and Lil in "A Game of Chess" may depend on one's intellectual commitments—or, for that matter, one's facility with languages, or one's annual income.

Certainly, Rodman's objection is more bothersome still than the five lines that occasioned it. "This kind of writing," claims Rodman, "becomes at its best academic and at its worst intellectual exhibitionism, throwing at the reader undigested scraps of everything from Bantu to Esperanto in unrelaxed cacophony. Eliot's taste was equal to giving the results of such a method dignity; Tolson's taste is much more uneven" (10). Aside from asking the obvious question this passage provokes—does Eliot's taste really extend to Bantu?—we should note that Rodman's is exactly the kind of review that Hoyt Fuller had in mind when he wrote: "Occasionally, a Negro writer is singled out for praise, but only when he seems to be disdaining 'protest' and 'moving toward the American literary mainstream.' He is then regarded as a near-*evolue*, an almost-man, ready to be accepted because his technique and themes are all but indistinguishable from those of his white peers" (1966, 38). The image of Tolson as an Eliot without "dignity" is not only a handy tool for shielding Eliot from the comparison Tolson invites but also a means of casting Tolson as a near-*evolue*, for Rodman's construction of "dignity" depends solely on the key word "taste." And Tolson's lack of taste, apparently, has ill effects on the whole of his gastrointestinal tract, for it leaves him, as the almost-Eliot intellectual exhibitionist, unable to "digest" the scraps of material he has overheard in the salons.

Harlem Gallery's two major reviews, in the *Times Literary Supplement* ("New Light on the Invisible") and the *Saturday Review*, are not nearly so racially charged; and the latter piece, by Robert Donald Spector, is by any standard among the half-dozen most sympathetic and intelligent commentaries ever written on Tolson. Better yet, Spector's review presents no subtextual or contextual qualifiers whatsoever: the piece is devoted to *Harlem Gallery* and Auden's *About the House*, thus associating Tolson with a solitary, established major figure; and it avoids the Anglo-Tolson issue altogether, concluding simply and forcefully that "whatever his reputation in the present critical climate, Tolson stands firmly as a great American poet" (1965, 29). But Spector's review—like the anonymous one in the *Times Literary Supplement* and Lorenzo Turner's treatment of *Libretto* in *Poetry* (the only review to discuss Tolson's poetry in depth)—has itself defied cultural reproduction; it was neither amplified nor refuted, never cited at all until 1984, by Farnsworth. Even in the reference guide *Contemporary Literary Criticism* (*CLC*), for example, none of these reviews has been judged representative enough to be included; none, apparently, has seemed sufficiently important or persuasive to merit mention. According to Richard Ohmann, *CLC*—which purports to excerpt criticism of "writers of considerable public interest"—"constitutes a sampling of the interests of those who set literary standards, and it monitors the intermediate stage in canon-formation" (1983, 384–85). *CLC* does excerpt three Tolson reviews that originally appeared in major journals (as well as a less "major" review by Laurence Lieberman, which I examine below), but those three tell a story with which we are already familiar: the excerpts are drawn from Tate's preface, Ciardi's review in the *Na-*

tion, and Shapiro's introduction. Somewhere, therefore, between the initial and the intermediate stages of canonization, Tolson's name, as it is used by his most insightful critics and as it appears in most influential journals, has been dropped from consideration.

In place of one kind of use of Tolson's name we find another: one that explicitly makes of him a pawn, played by both black and white Americans, in the game of racial-literary politics. I have already noted that Tolson's name does not appear in major journals for very long after his work is published. Stanley Edgar Hyman's 1958 article is one exception. Jack Richardson's 1968 "The Black Arts" is another; that piece not only marks Tolson's only notice by the *New York Review of Books* but is also one of only two Tolson notices to date to appear in *any* generalist forum, other than *Negro Digest*, after 1965.[16] Yet it invokes Tolson's name only in passing, and only as a means of bludgeoning the seminal anthology of the Black Aesthetic. The immediate impetus of Richardson's argument is Larry Neal's introduction to *Black Fire*, edited by Neal and Amiri Baraka:

> If one is to look for fullness of expression in black literature, one must confront the work done by novelists like Ellison and Wright and poets like Melvin Tolson. . . . To say, as Larry Neal does, that *Native Son* and *Invisible Man* are no longer particularly relevant to the new black attitude is to say that experience itself is not relevant to the black artist. What lies behind this historical dismissal is that these writers are ready to make qualifications as artists that Mr. Neal is not ready to accept, nor can he accept their virtuosity at meeting standards of intelligence and craft that have little to do with his notions of a hermetic folk culture. (Richardson 1968, 10)

Actually, what lies behind the historical dismissal is much the same impulse that lies behind any manifesto's gerrymandering of history—but this is a nice point, and neither Neal's nor Richardson's polemic has room for nice points.[17]

Other placements of Tolson along the white-black spectrum are equally polarized and polarizing. Laurence Lieberman's two-page discussion in the *Hudson Review* begins with puzzlement over Shapiro's claim that Tolson writes in Negro; although he himself is white, writes Lieberman, he teaches on the island of St. Thomas, and his college students "do not understand [Tolson]. He simply

---

[16]The other was Blyden Jackson's "Reconsideration" of *Harlem Gallery* (1976, 31), which I discuss briefly below.

[17]I rely for this characterization of the manifesto's rhetorical tropes on Lyon 1992.

does not speak their language" (1965, 456). Lieberman then protests that he *wants* to like Tolson, sounding, in the process, like a Ciardi-caricature liberal: "I feel that *Harlem Gallery* does have some of the hallmarks of an important work of art, and I share the sort of literary wishful-thinking that makes me want to support Mr. Shapiro's en-thusiastic response. (And then there is the matter of paying the Ne-gro artist in America his due)" (457). But the crux of Lieberman's review—and one of the excerpts that appears in *CLC*—is his argu-ment that although Tolson often

> successfully ridicules the cultural establishment from which he derives so much of his imagery, more often he is too steeped in that tradition to work against it. . . . The tradition that the poem supports *is* basically that of the "Graeco-Judaic-Christian culture," and not a distinctly Negro heritage. I think Tolson defines his own difficulty in breaking away from the dominant culture of America in a few lines of the poem:
>
> > I was a half-white egghead with maggots on the brain.
> > I ate my crow,
> > for the unconscious of the artist
> > cannot say to itself *No*.
>
> (457)

This is a version of Audre Lorde's claim that the Master's tools will never dismantle the Master's house, and it is a version to which Tolson's detractors continue to appeal; recall Houston Baker's dis-missal of *Libretto*'s "gestures" which seek the vast stolen stores of the West as a "final reference." We will return to Lieberman's—and Shapiro's, and Tate's—ideas of the tradition of "Graeco-Judaic-Christian culture" and the individual talent, for they replay and re-inforce the assumption that African-American modernism's relation to Euro-American modernism can be only secondary, whether in re-sistance or in imitation.[18] For that matter, it is possible that Baker is echoing and updating Lieberman's reservations about Tolson's rela-tion to the "tradition" by reminding the keepers of the tradition that their museums contain stolen goods or, in the Curator's words, ar-

---

[18]Farnsworth, however, contests Lieberman by questioning who owns the house: "If one assumes that the Greco-Judeo-Christian culture is a white culture—surely a racist act of the historical imagination—and that a revolution in the name of black people must hence be within a totally different cultural matrix, then clearly Tolson is not a revolutionary poet" (1984, 274).

gosies of plunder. But then we should look again at Lieberman's citation of the Curator in "Phi," which is taken radically out of its context—that is, the Curator's confrontation with Heights prior to the reading of the "sea-turtle and the shark"—and used as Tolson's self-incrimination.

Lieberman's incriminatory recontextualization is not only suspect in itself; it is almost diagnostic of Tolson's hostile critics. The Lieberman piece, for example, finds its critical cousin in David Littlejohn's 1966 survey of African-American literature, in which an ironic moment of Tolson's 1965 interview with M. W. King is read so as to paint Tolson, once again, as the academy's willing slave. "*Harlem Gallery*," writes Littlejohn, comparing it to *Libretto*, "I found similarly tedious, similarly clogged with literary allusions. In a recent interview, Tolson revealed the source of his strange difficulties" (1966, 82). He then goes on to splice together Tolson's avowal that he studied "all the great Moderns" (in order to transform *A Gallery of Harlem Portraits* into *Harlem Gallery*) with Tolson's response to King's question about Hyman's *Partisan Review* article. This is a tangled intertextual web, but I will try to unknot it as efficiently as possible. When King recalled that Hyman had associated *Libretto* with the blues, Tolson's response was this:

> That acute observation surprised me, for, in the *Libretto*, to which it referred, there was no surface sign of the blues; however, I do write jazz ballads, but the *Libretto* is very literary, to say the least. I thought the Establishment, the Academy, would like it. (Tolson 1966, 185)

The wry humor with which Tolson treats his academic aspirations (and, I might add, the disdainful tone of the last sentence, which belongs to the mode of the Randall tale) is wholly lost in Littlejohn's cut-and-paste; and because Littlejohn does not cite the pages from which he takes Tolson's words, there is no indication that the passages on either side of his ellipsis actually appear seven pages apart in King's interview. Here, then, is Littlejohn's edited version:

> I had read and absorbed the techniques of Eliot, Pound, Yeats, Baudelaire, Pasternak, and, I believe, all the great Moderns. God only knows how many "little magazines" I studied, and how much textual analysis of the New Critics. . . . the *Libretto* is very literary, to say the least. I thought the Establishment, the Academy, would like it. (Littlejohn 1966, 82–83)

Where Lieberman's Tolson is trapped, willy-nilly, in academic amber, Littlejohn's Tolson, worse yet, is the academy's parrot who speaks a few words plainly.[19]

We can now return to Shapiro's version of Tolson's relation to the "tradition" and factor it into the Lieberman-Littlejohn intertext: in "Decolonization," Shapiro had written that "the forms of the *Libretto* and of *Harlem Gallery*, far from being 'traditional,' are the Negro satire upon the poetic tradition of the Eliots and Tates" (1965a, 853). Without such a justification, no doubt, Shapiro would have found it hard to serve as Tolson's champion. But these various attempts to jockey Tolson against the Tradition wound up serving a purpose neither Shapiro nor Lieberman nor Littlejohn could have imagined. Paul Breman's grotesque vision of Tolson—the "misreading that authorizes nonreading" with which I opened this chapter—is more or less a moiré of all three critics. Breman's is at once the photographic negative of Littlejohn's Tolson, wherein the poet is not pastiche parrot but *parodic* parrot; a variation on Lieberman's ambiguously successful agent of ridicule; and, most of all, a slippery affirmation-and-negation of Shapiro's satirist, which casts Tolson's distance from the Black Aesthetic in vivid terms.

The passage appears in the context of Breman's distinction between "black" and "Negro" writers—that is, between nationalists and integrationists/accommodationists, or between the pre- and post-Baraka eras—and it construes Tolson, as did Tate in a very different way, as somehow "more intensely Negro" (Tate's phrase) in his charged integrationism: "Karl Shapiro said that he 'writes in Negro,' a true word, of which Shapiro never seems to have fathomed the true meaning: that Tolson postured for a white audience, and with an ill-concealed grin and a wicked sense of humour gave it just what it wanted: an entertaining darkey using almost comically big words as the best wasp tradition demands of its educated house-niggers" (1969, 101).

Outrageous as it is, Breman's Tolson can be seen, as I suggest, simply as an extrapolation of Shapiro's; still, the claim is preposterous on its face. As we now know, Tolson's modernism was not just what the white audience wanted; it has almost never been what *any* white audience wanted. Breman would apparently have us believe, moreover, that Tolson worked through fifteen years, two hundred pages, and, toward the end, a series of battles with cancer sim-

---

[19]I allude to David Hume's denigration of Francis Williams, the Cambridge-educated Jamaican writer of Latin verse (Hume 1964, 252 n.1; quoted in Gates 1986, 10).

ply in order to be puttin' on ol' Massa in style. The problem is not that Breman offers us a Tolson in blackface; the problem is that Breman suggests that Tolson put on his *own* blackface in order to "posture for a white audience." And if Tolson's audience is all white, says Breman, then there are only two alternatives: either Tolson really wanted their approval, or his appearance of wanting their approval was really just Tolson's cynicism and irony at work.

For various reasons, then, most of Tolson's white critics have done him far more harm than good—either by praising him, in the 1950s, for not writing black, or, later, by simplifying his relation to "the tradition" to the point at which he appears either a deluded aspirant or a delusive satirist. This too is a choice between the faggot and the noose, for it is a version of the dominant question white critics have for so long asked of African-American literature: should the African-American writer assimilate, resist, or ignore hegemonic Anglo-American literary forms? As long as the question is posed in this way, it not only guarantees African-American "secondariness," as I noted above, but reinscribes and monumentalizes a unitary, monolithic "tradition" against which a culture's marginal forces must continually define themselves. In Tolson's case especially, the question is the product of an older sense of "ideology" as "false consciousness," for we cannot juxtapose Tolson to "the modernist tradition" without also remarking that "the modernist tradition" is not exclusively Euro-American in the first place. Whether white modernists derived their inspiration from the cultural products of Benin, New Orleans, or Harlem, the "tradition" that spawned "Les Demoiselles D'Avignon," *The Bridge, The Emperor Jones,* and *Porgy and Bess* is a tradition blackest at its roots—especially in the United States, most of whose indigenous art forms were never European in origin.

We will come back to this question below, when, in African-American anthologies, it takes the form of a dichotomy between blackness and universality. In the meantime, only Spector and the *Times Literary Supplement* reviewer stand as wholehearted and unproblematic white endorsers of Tolson. If there is a hidden racism to be found in Tolson's reception history, perhaps it lies in the fact that neither of these endorsements were ever remarked upon, for better or worse, by the central Euro-American and British reviews or academic journals of the time. We do not need to uncover hidden racisms everywhere, though, since various overt racisms can be found in the reviews of Ciardi, Rodman, Tate, Shapiro, and Lieberman, racisms to which Breman's may be the most extreme corrective response. Yet although Breman's judgment cannot stand uncorrected—Tolson, for one, did not consider himself to be writing for solely white audiences, even if he did envision Anglo-American critical approval to be the first step in the distribution of his work—still, as the opening pages of this chapter indicate, I agree with Breman that when he dealt with Anglo-American critics, Tolson had more up his sleeve than many of his readers have chosen to believe.

Not until another fifteen or twenty years after Tolson's death, however, do academic critics such as Henry Louis Gates and Houston Baker come up with a conception of "blackness" in literature which will deliver him from the aspirant/satirist dichotomy sketched out above—and even those critics do not speak of Tolson. Before Gates and Baker arrive on the scene, we need to take up Tolson as Breman would leave him to us, as an African-American poet writing for a white American audience, and on this drawing board we have two more maps to sketch out: a map of his reviews in African-American journals, and a map of his appearances in African-American anthologies. These maps will eventually run into each other, as Tolson's reception milieu moves from reviews to anthologies during the late 1960s boom in production of African-American anthologies, and in the overlap they introduce us to the epochal transformation of the African-American critical landscape between 1950 and 1970.

Blackness, Universality, and the Production of Anthologies

The story in African-American journals of the 1940s and 1950s is fairly clear: African-American reviewers generally liked "Dark Symphony" and *Rendezvous with America*, even if, in the words of Chicago poet Frank Marshall Davis, Tolson "is yet too complex for the masses" (TM). Whereas white reviewers such as William Rose Benét in the *Saturday Review* and Robert Hillyer in the *New York Times Book Review* gave the collection mixed, respectful notices, African-American writers and critics, among them Margaret Walker and Nathaniel Tillman (in *Phylon*), were enthusiastic.

The only notable exception to Tolson's acclaim by African-American critics in the 1940s is a notice by Robert A. Davis, whose critique of "Dark Symphony" in the *Chicago Sunday Bee* of 21 September 1941 apparently affected Tolson greatly. Davis offered strong support for the poem overall (and a schoolmasterly injunction for its further dissemination): "The poem is definitely worth reading. It will be talked about for a long time to come and you should have comments based on your own impressions to contribute to the discussions 'Dark Symphony' will provoke." But alone among the poem's critics, Davis considered the work lamentably uneven. Citing Tolson's "use of well worn allusions . . . coupled with the obvious fault of redundance," he suggested that some sections were "far short of what the author is capable of and intends." Davis particularly contrasted the poem's "perfect" first six lines with its next six, protesting that "it is almost sacrilege to follow such magnificent lines with others as flat and Pollyannaish" as these:

> And from that day to this
>   Men black and strong
> For Justice and Democracy have stood,
> Steeled in the faith that Right
>   Will conquer Wrong,
> And Time will usher in one brotherhood.
>   (TM; quoted in Davis 1941)

Davis's objection is well taken, and apparently Tolson thought so too, for he revised the stanza before it was published in *Rendezvous*. Some anthologists have reprinted only the earlier version, however, so let us look at both versions side by side. Here is the revision:

> Waifs of the auction block,
>   Men black and strong
> The juggernauts of despotism withstood,
> Loin-girt with faith that worms
>   Equate the wrong
> And dust is purged to create brotherhood.
>   (1944, 37)

Because Tolson has so long and so often been accused of revising *Libretto* at Allen Tate's behest, it may be helpful to note that this revision (together with a few minor adjustments to the third stanza) appears to be the only section of the Tolson oeuvre whose different versions were motivated by published professional criticism. Though Allen Tate, like Robert Davis, had deigned to point out Tolson's weaknesses, it appears that Tolson was no more moved by Tate's reservations than he was by *Poetry*'s initial rejection of *Libretto* in 1948—a rejection upon which he signified when he wrote to

James Decker, at the Decker Press, that "maybe [*Poetry*'s editors] think the propaganda sticks through the seams of the verse" (TM).

Whatever the importance of Robert Davis to Tolson, however, it cannot be said that Davis's brief review contains any suggestion that Tolson should eschew Pollyannaism in favor of the formidable idiom of the *Libretto*; Tolson's conversion to high modernism remains largely his own doing, and there are no extant public documents of the moment of that conversion. Whatever his immediate sources and influences, then, with the publication of *Libretto* he lost much of his African-American audience. A year prior to Lorenzo Turner's strong and detailed praise in *Poetry* (1955), both Arthur Davis, in *Midwest Journal*, and Howard Fussiner, in *Phylon*, lodged various complaints against the poem's stylistic overkill. And as with major "white" reviews of *Harlem Gallery*, the number of responses is itself significant, for surely, "it did not help that the book drew only two other reviews in journals particularly concerned with the black experience" (Farnsworth 1984, 168).

One would think that this reaction was to be expected—if not because of *Libretto*'s staggering density and inaccessibility, perhaps because of the double-edged sword of Tate's preface. But the notable thing is that despite the anti-Tate wave of the 1960s, in whose undertow Tolson found himself disastrously caught, there is little evidence that Tate's endorsement of Tolson worked, in the 1950s, anything like an endorsement of a local African-American politician by Strom Thurmond. As a matter of fact, there is an abundance of evidence directly to the contrary: that to black and white readers and writers alike, the praise Tate's preface bestowed upon Tolson was not immediately experienced as patronizing. Now that we have seen Ciardi's and Rodman's ruminations on race and writing, let us look once again at the preface, this time at Tate's closing paragraph, which phrases its ideology as "common sense" in a way that should satisfy any post-Gramscian Marxist:

> It seems to me only common sense to assume that the main thing is the poetry, if one is a poet, whatever one's color may be. I think that Mr. Tolson has assumed this; and the assumption, I gather, has made him not less but more intensely *Negro* in his apprehension of the world than any of his contemporaries, or any that I have read. But by becoming more intensely Negro he seems to me to dismiss the entire problem, so far as poetry is concerned, by putting it in its properly subordinate place. In the end I found that I was reading *Libretto for the Republic of Liberia* not because Mr. Tolson is a Negro but because he is a poet, not because the poem has a "Negro subject" but because it is about the world of all men. (1953, 10–11)

Although "properly subordinate place" is so loaded a term that it almost blinds one to its grammatical antecedents (what should be properly subordinate here, the Negro problem—or the Negro? and whose "problem" is Tolson allegedly dismissing?), the rest of the paragraph, which may strike contemporary readers as so offensive, was actually intended—and read—as an unambiguous congratulation of a writer who had transcended the "provincial mediocrity" of mere "protest" poetry, a writer who had somehow made even blackness readably universal. Far from being the imperious dic-Tates of negrophobic whites, these are terms that even African-American writers and critics of the day embraced: witness W. S. Braithwaite's high praise for the *Libretto* he had not read. More widely, according to Houston Baker, "the dominant critical perspective on Afro-American literature during the late 1950s and early 1960s might be called the poetics of integrationism," in which writers such as Richard Wright and Arthur P. Davis "represent a generation whose philosophy, ideology, and attendant poetics support the vanishing of Afro-American literature qua *Afro-American* literature" (1981, 3–4).

The poetics of integrationism informs also the reading practices in African-American letters in the early 1950s; as C. W. E. Bigsby (1970) points out, *Phylon's* September 1950 issue, which surveys African-American literature in a way that will seem unquestionably dated only fifteen years later, inadvertently shows that an integrationist-assimilationist politics of canonicity makes it as difficult for African-Americans to enter "American literature" in the crucial postwar decade as it was for them to enter the Universities of Alabama and Mississippi. For integration in both cases comes on whites' terms, if not explicitly at whites' instigation, and the limited hope of African-American critics, before 1960, lies in the promulgation of "universal" aesthetic criteria in opposition to the separate and unequal "American" and African-American canons—like the promulgation of universal legal criteria in opposition to separateness and inequality in Montgomery municipal transit, or at Central High School in Little Rock: we will recall that, as Braithwaite put it, Tolson's achievement was the conversion of Allen Tate to "the single standard by which all artists irrespective of race or color should be judged." Remarking on Nick Aaron Ford's assertion that Frank Yerby and Willard Motley have joined Richard Wright among "first-rate American novelists" (1950, 374), Bigsby writes that Ford's piece exemplified *Phylon's* outlook:

> This rather bizarre judgment serves at the same time to highlight the almost universal praise accorded to those who chose to turn away from

the supposed "limitations" of a purely racial theme. One critic [Hugh M. Gloster] even went so far as to declare that the "preponderating use of racial subject matter has handicapped the Negro writer . . . it has retarded his philosophical perspective to the extent that he has made only meagre contributions to national and world ideologies . . . it has usually limited his literary range to the moods and substance of race in the United States . . . it has helped certain critics and publishers lure him into the deadly trap of cultural segregation." If this particular critic's admiration for Frank Yerby were not sufficient evidence of the consequence of such dogmatism, the emergence, during the 50s, of writers like Baldwin, Ellison and Hansberry serve to underline the naivete of this attitude. (1970, 218–19)

But Tolson did not need to read *Phylon* to get wind of a perceived dichotomy between "Negro" and "universal" art; there was, we could say, nowhere he could turn to get away from this dichotomy, and it was not unusual for him to find it even in his mailbox. Back in 1944 he had received a letter from one of his former star debaters at Wiley, a student whose name, R. Henri Heights III, most likely served as the original of Hideho's. Heights closed his letter with an injunction: "I have gone through my copy of 'Rendezvous' many times and my conclusion is this: As a Negro poet you are tops. But you are too big to be a Negro poet. Take up the cause of humanity and become a world poet" (TM). Some ten years later, Tolson would find that for Arthur Davis, the more sympathetic of *Libretto*'s journal reviewers, Tate's preface was "indeed high praise, perhaps the highest that any Negro poet has received from an American critic of Allen Tate's rank" (1954, 75). Davis's phrasing is regrettably somewhat tautological, but the point should be clear: when we historicize Tate's preface, we find that although it raised a good number of critical hackles in 1965 and has heavily contributed to Tolson's neglect or rejection by African-American critics ever since, it was not immediately the barrier to *Libretto*'s reception which it later became.

Libretto's contemporary African-American critics take issue instead with the *Libretto* itself; only Fussiner explicitly took his cue from an Anglo-American critic, Selden Rodman, and even then he did so in order to second Rodman's reservations: "I feel (as does Mr. Rodman) that the work is not helped by his emphasis on esoteric virtuosity" (1954, 97). For his part, Davis conceives of himself as timidly dissenting from Tate's yea-vote: "I hesitate to say what I must in all honesty say, which is simply this: for me *Libretto* is not a completely successful work; in spite of its astonishing word-magic and its undoubted power, it doesn't quite come off as a poem" (75–76). What we have here, it seems, is a replay of the very early reaction to *The*

Waste Land, a debate over whether a "poem" can be composed of a battery of ill-embedded allusions and untranslated snippets of European (or African) languages. Rodman may have articulated a ramshackle means for distinguishing Tolson from Eliot on the basis of "taste," but for Tolson's African-American critics the issue is more basic: has Tolson abandoned his responsibility to communicate—to the point that he fails to communicate to any but the most elite audiences?

It is in this context that Tolson receives his most devastating review—the only review, apparently, to which he ever responds directly (see Farnsworth 1984, 166–68). The reviewer is one of the era's most well-known African-American literati, J. Saunders Redding. His review in the *Afro-American* is launched not only against *Libretto*, for which he has some praise, but, at a wider reach, against "poetry which the author must himself interpret for his readers in an addendum of notes," to which he has "a fundamental objection": "At best, such notes indicate one of two things, and at worst, both things: that the poet found his talents unequal to the full requirements of the particular necessary communication; or that he was deliberately uncommunicative and obscure—in which case his notes are a patronizing gesture to minds the poet assumes to be less recondite or subtle or appreciative than his own" (1954, 2).

"It seems," Tolson had written, with his customary self-awareness, in his first letter to Tate, "that belatedly I have initiated the modern movement among Negro poets" (quoted in Farnsworth 1984, 138). For Tolson, the matter is one of modernism and literary history: I am both belated and unprecedented. For Redding, the matter is one of audience: who do you think you're talking (down) to? And in the gulf between the two we will find, eventually, *Harlem Gallery*, Tolson's most extended and thoughtful response to the obligations and dangers of an African-American modernism. For the nonce, however, Tolson's immediate response is also worthy of attention.

Writing to the president of the *Afro-American*, Carl Murphy, rather than to Redding himself, Tolson begins on safe ground. "Mr. Redding did not review the book: he reviewed his prejudices against modern poetry." From here, however, the argument expands like a mushroom cloud to cover the relation of poetry to prefaces, explications, and the critical apparatus of the post-Romantic era:

> He is against "an addendum of notes." This bias started in 1800, when William Wordsworth published the Preface to "Lyrical Ballads." For two hundred years poets have given prefaces or notes to readers. T. S. Eliot,

the *only* American poet to win the Nobel Prize in Literature, the Master of the super-intellectuals, added notes to his epic, "The Waste Land." David Jones, in that English masterpiece, "The Anabasis" [*sic*], uses notes. Furthermore, these distinguished poets have had their works explained by the best critics in all the little magazines and countless books of criticism. Critics like Empson, the greatest critical reader in the British Empire, and Blackmur, the greatest critical reader in the United States, have not been insulted by the "addendum of notes"; these critics found neither a failure to communicate nor a patronizing gesture—to quote Mr. Redding—in the poets I have cited. . . .

Now, if one wants to be a modern poet, one must study modern poets—and the greatest—Stevens, Rimbaud, Blok, Eliot, Pound, et al. I have done this for twenty years. Whether I have succeeded or failed, you will have to ask contemporary *major* poets and critics.

Mr. Redding's reaction to contemporary poetry is what mine was twenty years ago. We were all brought up on Tennyson and Spenser and Longfellow, et al. . . .

Away with the simple Negro! This is a book to be chewed and digested. If Negro scholars don't get busy on it, white scholars will. (TM)[20]

There is almost too much here for discussion: Tolson's (rightly placed) emphasis on the post-Romantic interdependence of critical text and innovative poetry—from Wordsworth's "Preface" to Eliot's notes to the importance of institutional criticism (figured in the persons of Empson and Blackmur) in the cultural reproduction of the modern text; his insistence, once more, on the inevitability of modernism and the necessity of "study"; and, not least, his confidence about the audience of his modernist work. Confidence—or is it anxiety? Not a backward-looking anxiety of influence but a prospective "anxiety of audience"?[21] Tolson's last sentence suggests both a threat to Redding ("you'd better get it before they do") and a threat to himself ("or else I will find no African-American audience at all"). And in the ambiguity of this threat lie many of the ambiguities of *Harlem Gallery*'s, and Tolson's, cultural position.

I mean no less: this letter is a document central to Tolson's career, both to its development and to our understanding of its development—and we are indebted yet again to Farnsworth for unearthing

[20]The reference to *Anabasis* may be a telling misidentification (I assume Tolson was referring to *The Anathémata*), insofar as it suggests that despite his roll call of poets, Tolson's conception of modernism revolved entirely around Eliot: hence, perhaps, his unwitting substitution of St. John Perse's *Anabase*, as translated by Eliot, for the work of Jones, his contemporary.

[21]I borrow the idea of "anxiety of audience" also from Lyon 1992.

it from the Tolson manuscripts, for like the Tate correspondence, it went unpublished during Tolson's lifetime and for almost twenty years after his death. Certainly, as I suggested briefly in Chapter 2, it informs the unmasking of Hideho Heights in *Harlem Gallery*; its "anxiety of audience," especially, informs *Gallery*'s discussion of the position of the avant-garde African-American artist, as well as *Gallery*'s reluctance to discuss the contemporary position of the modernist avant-garde, or the position of the avant-garde of Tolson's own time.

That is to say, if we wish to read *Harlem Gallery* as both the culmination of Tolson's career and a meditation on Tolson's possible contexts of reception, his response to Saunders Redding provides us with very good focus for such a reading. The letter not only explains why Tolson's Curator so insistently characterizes Hideho's modernist work as a contradiction of his public image—why, as we will recall, the desire to be taught in World Lit is in such irreconcilable conflict with the desire to be the bard of Lenox Avenue–but also sheds light on why Tolson would imagine Heights hiding "E. & O.E." from his African-American public in the first place. In this letter we have the source of the power by which, in *Harlem Gallery*, modernist "technique" becomes a necessary meaning unto itself, and perhaps we have also the source of the cynicism latent in the Curator's lament on the "white and not-white" dichotomy to which Hideho falls victim. For the letter's implication, shadowed dimly yet unmistakably, is not that modern poetry *is* the realm of white folk but that African-American poets and critics will *perceive it to be* the realm of white folk, and will reject Tolson accordingly.

About this possibility Tolson could not have been more prescient, and there is something consoling in the fact that he did not live long enough to read Fabio's article in *Negro Digest*. Yet *Harlem Gallery* itself was not uniformly panned by African-Americans: Gwendolyn Brooks turned in a good review in *Negro Digest*; *Phylon*, after having damned *Libretto* with faint praise eleven years earlier, gave *Gallery* an unqualified rave, calling it "the great American poem . . . epic poetry at its best" (Thompson 1965, 409); and an anonymous reviewer from the Nation of Islam's *Muhammad Speaks* (whose famous founder had been assassinated in Harlem's Audubon Ballroom not long before) was similarly enthusiastic. Likewise, although *Harlem Gallery* reached few more African-American journals than did *Libretto*, there is one major difference in the two poems' reception conditions: *Negro Digest*, revived by Hoyt Fuller in 1961 after a ten-year publishing hiatus, ran six articles on Tolson in 1965–66 alone and kept his name circulating into the 1970s. From the journal that has been called "the most important single periodical" of the decade (Long and Collier 1985, 446), "the best source of cultural news in black magazine history" (Redmond 1978, 552), this is highly significant exposure. In various ways, whether in articles (including Shapiro's preface) and obituaries or in brief mentions, news, and notes, *Negro Digest* served to keep Tolson's name (and face, on its June 1966 cover) in public view after the publication of *Harlem Gallery*, and after its author's death, in a way no journal did in the wake of *Libretto*.

Perhaps this is one reason why, when anthologies of African-American writing began to be compiled or reissued in the 1960s, excerpts from *Libretto* appeared in only three of them.[22] Critical venues for African-American poetry were few in number, *Phylon* and J. Saunders Redding had not been kind, and no new major anthologies were published until 1964: *Libretto* could not have appeared at a less propitious moment. In the meantime, as the anthologies became Tolson's major arena of reception, his journal-jury apparently remained hung for some time. Dudley Randall (of all people) turned thumbs down in 1971, but in 1972 Ronald Walcott, in *Black World* (the renamed *Negro Digest*) dealt *Gallery* a sustained and sympathetic critique.

The split between Randall and Walcott is fairly diagnostic of the battle lines drawn everywhere on Tolson, and it will help us to understand his anthologization. Randall, who spends a paragraph repeating the *Libretto* story Tolson had told him six years earlier, decides that "reading this poem [*Gallery*] is like reading other learned poets, such as Milton and T. S. Eliot," and concludes, in the manner of Fabio, by disavowing Tolson as a representative African-American: "Tolson rewrote the poem according to the tenets of the New Criticism. The irony is that, about this time, the New Criticism was declining, and the Beat poets, with their looser, freer, more emotional language and form, were coming into popularity. In any case, the learned allusive language is not the spontaneous speech of the Negro people" (1971a, 231). We should notice by now the implicit

---

[22]The forum in which *Libretto* was most extensively excerpted, in fact, was not an anthology at all: Jacob Drachler used three sections of the poem ("Do," "Re," and portions of the closing verse paragraphs) in his 1964 study, *African Heritage*—and Tolson, ever alert to advertisements for himself, mentioned the fact (1966, 187) to M. W. King. The only other citation or use of *Libretto* during this time was Hyman's. At present, all three anthologies with *Libretto* excerpts have gone out of print, the latest being Hughes and Bontemps (1970), in 1985.

preface-shuffle here, as Randall leaps from the Tate story to rebut Shapiro's "Tolson writes in Negro"; we should also notice by now that this nondiscussion of *Harlem Gallery* is itself symptomatic of the response that approaches Tolson by way of Shapiro and Tate. For why would anyone think for a moment that *Libretto* or *Harlem Gallery* were failed attempts at spontaneous speech? And who would pause to ask whether *The Waste Land* is truly the spontaneous speech of the "people" of Eliot, or *Gravity's Rainbow* the speech of Pynchon's "people"? Finally, why would anyone—especially Randall, who reprinted "The Sea-Turtle and the Shark" as part of his Broadsides series (number 5)—think that Tolson was somehow hamstrung by a New Critical false consciousness?

Ronald Walcott, on the other hand, instructively reconceives the poem by recasting its "tradition": "Incorporating elements of the very best of contemporary poetry and informed with a truly impressive grasp of learning, *Harlem Gallery* is an unabashed tribute to Black tradition, tradition which has inspired the vigor and human diversity it is the poem's stated purpose to render" (1972, 27). What this conflict suggests is that readings of *Harlem Gallery*, as well as nonreadings, are conditioned by reading formations whereby Tolson is understood either to be an African-American poet writing about African-Americans, or to be a "part of the neo-classical scene" (Fabio) who keeps company, or wants to, with Eliot, or Tate, or Milton. The latter paradigm, as we now know, is one under which Tolson can go wholly unread: neither African-American critics nor their white counterparts have evinced any interest in the idea of an African-American poet who, stocked with allusions, footnotes, and hair relaxers, tried to look like Eliot and failed. But the former paradigm has also proved limiting, both theoretically and institutionally: it has determined readings that sift through Tolson's poems and set aside everything that does not look sufficiently "black"; and, in making Tolson a black poet writing about black America for black Americans, it has both assumed and effected precisely the racial polarization of his audience which *Harlem Gallery* so desperately sought to avoid.

Nowhere is this phenomenon so visible as in the African-American anthologies of the period. I must emphasize strongly the importance of these anthologies, partly because they indicate how Tolson has been textually represented in archives of African-American literary history, and more generally because so little has been said about their composition and proliferation in the late 1960s and early 1970s—or about the dearth of new anthologies between 1975 and

1990. And the period before 1975 marks not only unprecedented African-American access to central media such as Random House and Scholastic Book Services but also the parallel development of new means of production and forms of consumption, ranging from New York's "Panther House" and Watts's "House of Respect" to Dudley Randall's influential Broadside Press and Joe Goncalves's radical *Journal of Black Poetry*. Indeed, I will go so far as to say that for all the outpouring of African-American poetry in the 1960s—or, more precisely, because of this outpouring—the period's major genre simply *is* the anthology. By 1971, for instance, the African-American anthology was so self-conscious a genre that Dudley Randall's *Black Poets* (a text to which I shall return) spends half its introduction positioning itself against other current anthologies, and Nick Aaron Ford's shorter-lived *Black Insights* opens by establishing its editor's impeccable credentials as a teacher of African-American literature since 1936, which, writes Ford, he needs to do because of the "ready market for 'instant' anthologies by specialists in the field, even by 'instant' specialists only mildly interested in the subject" (1971, vii).

First, let us examine the reprints. Tolson had already appeared in the two major anthologies of the 1940s, prior to his conversion to modernism—*Negro Caravan* (Brown, Davis, and Lee 1941; rpt. 1969), and *The Poetry of the Negro* (Hughes and Bontemps, 1949; rev. ed 1970). Both chose "Dark Symphony" to be their solitary Tolson poem. This much is to be expected; although either might reasonably have taken a wider selection from *Rendezvous with America*, "Dark Symphony" was, through 1950, Tolson's greatest hit. But Bontemps's *American Negro Poetry* obeyed the same principle of selection in 1963; and even when Bontemps expanded his collection in 1974—precisely in order to do justice to the volumes of new African-American poetry that appeared just after his original edition had been compiled—he added more poets, but no more poems by his original poets. Both before and after *Harlem Gallery*, that is, Bontemps's collection operates as if "Dark Symphony" remains Tolson's representative work.

In his collaboration with Langston Hughes, on the other hand, Bontemps does Tolson no such disservice: even after Hughes died in 1967, the revised 1970 *Poetry of the Negro* not only adds *Libretto*'s first section, the seven-stanza "Do" (thus becoming the first anthology to excerpt *Libretto*), but throws in for good measure *Gallery*'s "Lambda," in which Hideho first enters the poem. But wait: this 1970 "Lambda" doesn't look like Tolson's. It opens with the same three lines—"From the mouth of the Harlem Gallery / came a voice

like a / ferry horn in a river of fog"—but proceeds, by skipping the
next forty lines, to the ballad of Louis Armstrong, and there is no
indication in the text that Tolson's poem has been abridged. Thus
the excerpt excises all that is not Hideho in "Lambda," even as it
neglects to mention that the ballad is the work of Hideho. Tolson
had attributed "E. & O.E." to Heights; here, in an almost perfect
reversal, the 1970 *Poetry of the Negro* attributes Heights's ballad to
Tolson—and the effect is to make *Harlem Gallery* seem a much
friendlier, much less challenging poem than it really is. It is not exactly criminal to distort *Harlem Gallery* so as to make it appear more
accessible; perhaps Bontemps actually does so in the hope of attract-
ing readers to the poem. And *Harlem Gallery*, for its part, is a poem
so difficult to anthologize that surely any reproduction of it is bound
to be "partial." Nevertheless, even in the forum historically most
congenial to Tolson, the anthology of African-American literature,
we find a composite sketch of *Harlem Gallery* which amounts to a
picture distorted almost beyond recognition.

The Black Poets (Randall 1971b) exemplifies this distortion: the only
snippets of *Harlem Gallery* to be found there are the ballad of Louis
Armstrong (*sans* "Lambda" and titled "Louis Armstrong") and a representation of "John Henry" (titled "John Henry") in which nothing but Hideho's ballad itself appears on the page. Randall's text
operates as if the *Gallery*, after the fashion of the Gallery's South
Wing, is composed entirely of ballads to African-American heroes of
the public domain. Similarly, two other anthologies, *Dark Symphony*
(Emanuel and Gross 1968)—which does not include "Dark Symphony"—and *3000 Years of Black Poetry* (Lomax and Abdul 1970),
although they reprint both the John Henry ballad and its narrative
frame (thus giving some idea of the ballad's context as a Zulu Club
reading), do not open their excerpt from "Xi" where "Xi" itself
opens—with the Curator's rhetorical question about Heights and
Wovoka the Paiute messiah. Instead, the excerpt runs from the
opening of the ballad to the end of Joshua Nitze's story about the
black stevedore trying to order chitterlings in the South, thereby
representing *Harlem Gallery* at its most "oral," at the apex of
Heights's trajectory in the poem, without the frame provided by the
Curator at the outset of the section.

Similar patterns can be found in nearly every anthology of the
period. After Bontemps's, only three collections restrict their Tolson
selection to "Dark Symphony," and two of these are textbooks
aimed at secondary schools. "Dark Symphony" appears more often
than any single excerpt from *Harlem Gallery*, but on the whole, *Gal-*

lery excerpts outnumber the reprints of the earlier poem. *Libretto*, as I have mentioned, appears only three times, and the remainder of Tolson's non-*Gallery* reprints is made up of a smattering of his "premodern" lyrics, especially "African China" (which he rewrote in the late 1940s as a combination of two poems from the then unpublished *Gallery of Harlem Portraits*), as well as two other poems unavailable except in anthologies: "John Henry in Harlem," not Hideho's but a rewrite of an earlier *Portrait*; and "Abraham Lincoln of Rock Spring Farm," date of composition uncertain (early 1940s?).[23] Of the excerpts from *Harlem Gallery*, every one is Hideho's—the sea-turtle and the shark (three appearances), John Henry (three), and Louis Armstrong (four, two of which include "Lambda" in its entirety)— with the exception of "Psi," the Curator's section on race (five). Only Long and Collier (1972; rpt. 1985) break this pattern, choosing instead to excerpt the unveiling of John Laugart's *Black Bourgeoisie* in "Zeta." Otherwise, the general rule is, as Ruth Miller has it in her introduction to "Lambda," "Hideho Heights is the prototype of the modern Harlem poet and he brings the Curator the news of the ultimate in art"—in this case, because "he has just heard Satchmo, Louis Armstrong, play" (1971, 575).

Some of the anthologies simply reproduce works with little or no critical introduction, lining up writers in the order of their birth dates; but especially interesting, for our purposes, are the more comprehensive anthologies that seek to define the field altogether: its major writers, its periods, and its various hierarchies of genre.[24] Most anthologies keep Tolson out of the 1960s, although only Houston Baker (1971) brushes him as far back as the 1930s and 1940s. Ruth Miller's *Blackamerican Literature* (1971) places him in the 1940–63 section; in *On Being Black* (Davis and Walden, 1970), Tolson is an "early modern" alongside Margaret Walker and Owen Dodson; and Randall in *The Black Poets* classes him as "post-Renaissance" with Frank Marshall Davis and Robert Hayden. None of these classi-

---

[23]"African China" was first published in the "Negro Poets Issue" of *Voices* (Winter 1950, pp. 33–35), which was edited by Langston Hughes; it was first anthologized (and was Tolson's only entry) in Cuney, Hughes, and Wright 1954. "African China" appears in anthologies four times, more than any poem not originally published in book form (see Appendix A). Besides "Dark Symphony," three other poems from *Rendezvous* have been reprinted: "A Hamlet Rives Us," "A Legend of Versailles," and "An Ex-Judge at the Bar."

[24]By the standards of the 1990s, however, the writer most clearly and pervasively under- and misrepresented in these anthologies is not Tolson at all but Zora Neale Hurston, whose work (usually one of her short stories) appears infrequently.

fications is wrong, precisely, but Tolson is, after all, something of a periodization problem: though he emerged in the interstitial period between the Harlem Renaissance and the Black Arts movement, his most sustained and important work appears in 1965. By contrast, *Black Writers of America* (Barksdale and Kinnamon, 1972) and *Dark Symphony* (Emanuel and Gross, 1968) include Tolson among writers of the 1960s, the former in a category devoted to "major authors" of "The Present Generation: Since 1945." The point, clearly, is that determination of Tolson's stature depends in part on how his "generation" is construed. Periodization, too, involves a form of reading-as; and Barksdale and Kinnamon, wisely heedless of the American tendency to deal with African-American poets in bulk (poets of the 1920s, poets of the 1960s), close their introduction to Tolson by calling him "one of the major poets of the mid-twentieth century" (669).

Doubtless, some of the features of this composite sketch are the result of anthology-inertia, wherein each new anthology tends to reprint the material made available in previous anthologies. We can be certain, however, of one thing: permissions costs have nothing to do with the rationale for excerpting *Harlem Gallery*, for the Hideho scenes were not made available at lower rates per line than the Curator's sections, or Starks's *Harlem Vignettes*. And though this inertia is itself worthy of discussion, it is not so notable as the deliberate work of a few anthologists to qualify their inclusion of Tolson, for these qualifications themselves amount to misrepresentations that authorize—and even approach—nonrepresentation. The most salient example is Nick Aaron Ford's *Black Insights*, which devotes more space to *Libretto* than does any other anthology but, finally, does so only in order to warn readers away from Tolson's modernism. Placing Tolson in a "Torchbearers" section along with James Weldon Johnson, Countee Cullen, Saunders Redding, and Ford himself, Ford prefaces his excerpt by calling *Libretto* "unsuitable for [its] occasion and incompatible with the unpretentious manifestations of other forms of African art" (100); he closes the excerpt with a list of "recommended reading" which cites only *Rendezvous with America*. Robert Hayden's *Kaleidoscope*, the first post–*Harlem Gallery* anthology to publish Tolson, takes a similar tack, except that after briefly introducing Tolson as a writer whose "poetry often strikes one as being too intricate, erudite, and obscure" (1967, 57; one wants to ask, *for what?*), Hayden reprints, from all of *Harlem Gallery*, only the sea-turtle and shark ballad. The introduction thus seems not only unkind but inappropriate, since Hayden, like other anthologists, declines to represent Tolson's most intricate, erudite, and obscure work.[25]

If, therefore, we read these anthology excerpts in toto, we find that Tolson qualifies as an African-American poet, in *Harlem Gallery*, under one of only two possible rubrics: either when (as in the Hideho excerpts) he employs an oral discourse in the form of the ballad or the parable, or when (as in "Psi" and, more tenuously, "Zeta"), he is explicitly addressing the question of race in art. Thus the anthologized portions of Tolson's longest modernist work display only those moments at which the poet is being least modernist, or those moments when his modernist Curator finally gets around to addressing and writing about Black Boy and White Boy. The other 80 or 90 percent of the poem, which is by no means deracinated, has gone so far unanthologized. By the same token, the Hideho Heights who wrote "E. & O.E." is a Heights the anthologies don't know. As far as these anthologies are concerned, Heights never wrote "E. & O.E." at all; it was most probably planted in his apartment by a crafty rival poet named Melvin Tolson. This, then, is the white and not-white dichotomy of *Harlem Gallery*—a dichotomy to be explored not in the work itself but in the structure of its reception.

I am suggesting that Tolson's representation in African-American anthologies has tended to reproduce a false dichotomy between Tolson's "blackness" and his "universality," even when the anthology in question has set out explicitly to undo, contest, or deny the dichotomy as it has operated in American literature to date. But this suggestion alone is clearly incomplete, because it does not note the institutional conditions under which African-American anthologies, no matter what their specific intentions, have been forced to reproduce this dichotomy. The introduction to Hayden's *Kaleidoscope* closes, appropriately enough, by remarking these very conditions: "Neither the editor nor his publisher should be understood as necessarily endorsing the long-established custom of segregating the work of Negro poets within the covers of a separate anthology. Yet where, except in a collection such as the present one, is the student to gather any impression of the nature and scope of the Negro's contribution to American poetry?" (1967, xxiv).

Where, indeed? Ernece Kelly's 1972 study of American literature

---

[25]The introduction itself may have been motivated, consciously or unconsciously, by the fact that Tolson had dramatically upstaged Hayden at a writers' conference at Fisk University in 1966—upstaged him on, of all things, the issue of "race" in literature; see Llorens 1966.

textbooks, conducted by the National Council of Teachers of English (Task Force on Racism and Bias in the Teaching of English and Textbook Review Committee), found that texts with such titles as *American Poetry* and *American Poets from the Puritans to the Present* included no nonwhite writers whatsoever; and "the American tradition in literature," as construed by the editors of the Norton two-volume compilation of that title, consists entirely of white people—until the anthology's third edition in 1967, which includes two poems by Baraka, prefaced with these words: "Jones [Baraka] is easily the most interesting of the young Negro poets, but race is not often an issue in his poetry and does not restrict its appeal" (Bradley, Beatty, and Long 1967, 1905; quoted in Kelly, 1972, 16).

The dichotomy between blackness and universality, in other words, can be located even within African-American anthologies; but it is more powerfully and more pervasively the institutional condition for the production of these anthologies, whose very titles mark their blackness (black voices, black insights, black poets, black writers of America) while their contemporaneous all-white anthologies are marketed under the univeralist rubric of "American literature." If Tolson's own white and not-white dichotomy is far less visible in "American" anthologies, this is simply because Tolson has so rarely been published in any anthology that was not devoted exclusively to African-American writers.[26] In order to frame adequately our understanding of Tolson's anthologization history, therefore, we should keep always in mind the frame in which Tolson was enclosed in the first place. As Sarah Webster Fabio pointed out, Shapiro's celebration of the "dissident" element in American literature did not affect his editorial policies as an anthologist when it came to including African-American writers; and as Fabio might also have pointed out, Tate's professed admiration in 1950 failed to result in Tolson's appearance in Lord David Cecil's and Tate's 1958 *Modern Verse in English*. Worse yet, in that volume's "Introduction to American Poetry," Tate writes of "the poetic variety and vitality of the twentieth century" in an anthology which includes no African-American poets at all (but does include Vachel Lindsay's "Simon

---

[26]Tolson has appeared in five "general" poetry collections to date, including Boynton and Mack (see note 14). Levine 1977 (5th ed.) included "The Sea-Turtle and the Shark," but dropped the poem from its subsequent editions (1982, 1987). Lowenfels 1969 opened with two dozen strangely truncated lines of "Dark Symphony"; Ray 1981 reprinted three poems from *A Gallery of Harlem Portraits*; and most notably, the fourth edition of *Understanding Poetry* (Brooks and Warren 1976), excerpted "Do" from *Libretto*. Both Lowenfels 1969 and Brooks and Warren 1976 are out of print.

Legree—A Negro Sermon") and for which he chooses nine poems by Yvor Winters on the ground that Winters has been "grossly neglected" (Cecil and Tate 1958, 44)[27]

I have said that the anthologies serve both to culminate Tolson's nonacademic reception and to set the terms for his academic reception; at this point I can be a good deal more specific about these terms. The composite anthologization sketch I have described transformed Tolson, in effect, from Breman's posturer before white audiences to a member of the supporting cast of African-American letters. We may see the immediate effect of this transformation in the most recent treatment of Tolson in a major Anglo-American journal,[28] where Blyden Jackson (writing in the *New Republic*) calls him "an apostle of blackness" and goes on to negotiate between his blackness and his aspirations to "universality": "Tolson accepted the brotherhood of man and the universality of serious art. The title of *Harlem Gallery*, however, is not a misnomer. The brotherhood of man and the universality of serious art do catalyze its perceptions. Nevertheless, *Harlem Gallery* is a black man's poem about black people in a black community" (1976, 31). I might quibble that *Harlem Gallery* is about much else besides, notably the idea of an avantgarde. But I have no real quarrel with Jackson, whose review is eminently fair—and in many ways a remarkable exception to Tolson's reception history in nonacademic journals. Still, it remains likely that the terms of Tolson's anthologization have helped to frustrate his ambition to cross over into the realm of "American" as well as African-American academic recognition, after the manner of the man whom he may have considered his counterpart, another self-proclaimed African-American modernist—Ralph Ellison.[29]

Tolson's "anthologization effect," however, proceeding as it does

[27]As far as one reviewer was concerned, however, "you could hardly lay down better than Professor Tate some of the principles of an 'inclusive' anthology" (Robert Conquest, in *Spectator*, 28 Nov. 1958). Tate does include 14 women in his 63 poets; of these, he singles out for special praise Louise Bogan and Emily Dickinson, "the greatest American poet of the nineteenth century" (Cecil and Tate 1958, 652)—this no doubt accompanied by a significant cough in the direction of Whitman.

[28]My own article in *PMLA* (1990), rather than Jackson's *New Republic* piece, may now be considered Tolson's most recent treatment by the mainstream; still, even that was enabled by the modification of the "mainstream," since my article appeared in *PMLA*'s first "special topics" issue—one devoted to African and African-American literature (edited by Henry Louis Gates).

[29]See Farnsworth 1984, 299–300, for Tolson's final encounter with Ellison—at the award ceremonies at which *Harlem Gallery* was honored by the American Academy of Arts and Letters.

from the ideological conflicts in postwar African-American letters, has worked to legitimate a field of questioning on Tolson's work which delimits and validates a narrow and predictable range of critical responses. That delimitation has proceeded, unchecked and uncritiqued, to the point at which Arnold Rampersad can write, as late as 1983, that "probably the central critical question" of Tolson studies "is whether there is an inherent conflict between the standards and practices of Euro-American modernism and the vivid depiction of Afro-American and African reality" (354). Rampersad's is yet one more static opposition between African-American culture and a monolithic, untransformable (white) modernism, and it is surely regrettable that the opposition has survived so long in American literary history. And though much of Tolson's reception, as we have seen, has depended on such an opposition, still, even by 1975, this was not the only "critical question" raised by his academic critics; Tolson had by then received some quasi-academic treatment in the form of articles by Dan McCall (1966, on *Libretto*) and Roy Basler (1973, on Tolson generally), both of which, it seems, might have changed drastically the nature of the discussion.

McCall sought a way of conceiving Tolson's modernism as neither mere epigonism nor simplistic rebellion—"Tolson is not just turning back on the white culture its own methods; he does it in the name of a new culture" (1966, 541)—and what makes his attempt more persuasive than, say, Shapiro's or Breman's, is his willingness to offer specific arguments about, for example, the allusion to Dryden in *Libretto*'s opening stanza (see McCall 1966, 539–40). Basler, far more ambitious than McCall, sought nothing less than Tolson's canonization as the poet who "best represents, or comes nearest to representing, in his comprehensive humanity, the broadest expanse of the American character, phrased in the richest poetic idiom of our time" (1973, 64). But neither McCall nor Basler—despite Basler's reproduction in *Contemporary Literary Criticism*—wound up contributing to the formation of "central critical questions" on Tolson. It is hard to imagine, in some respects, how Basler's article might have done so, since he unfortunately advances his claims for Tolson's greatness without buttressing them with the kind of close reading and explication that confers and secures poetic value for institutional (academic) criticism; however, since Basler is responsible also for the solicitation of the Tolson papers, he remains one of the more important, if more indirect, gatekeepers in Tolson's reception history. McCall's specific argument, on the other hand, remains important today, and will emerge again at the end of this chapter.

The present cultural context of Tolson's reception is that of the exclusively academic audience. About *Harlem Gallery*'s exclusively academic reception I have relatively little to say, except to reiterate my appreciation for the work of Patricia Schroeder (1983) and Rita Dove (1985);[30] for it is less my intention to play games of one-upmanship with Tolson's academic critics than to reestablish and analyze the conditions under which he first became available for academic discussion. Two final points on this count should suffice, and I have left the most obvious for last.

Insofar as Tolson is taken, has been taken, or will be taken exclusively as a citizen of African-American letters, he falls into a more benign version of the trap from which Jean Toomer never managed to extricate himself—more benign, because Tolson was by no means as conflicted about his racial status as was Toomer, whose ambivalence about race "intensified" after the publication of *Cane* "until he reached a climactic denial that African blood flowed in his veins" (Turner 1975, xxiii). Yet Toomer, like Tolson, sought a negotiation of African-American cultural forms and Anglo-American modernist experimentation; and my argument, like Toomer's and Tolson's, is that African-American literature can neither be ignored nor colonized by traditional scholars of American literature simply because it has won the struggle to be considered a discipline, a "field," in its own right and on its own terms (and here too, the place of anthologies in this struggle can hardly be underestimated). For all too many departments of English in the United States, the creation of courses and syllabi in African-American literature has meant that survey courses in "American" literature can go wholly or substantially unrevised, since, as Gerald Graff would say, English departments can now rest safe in the conviction that the "field" of African-American literature is being covered elsewhere, inside or outside the department. If, therefore, my reading of Tolson has overemphasized his relation to Anglo-American modernism at the expense of charting his position in African-American literature, it has done so in the hope of re-establishing Tolson's cultural claims and cultural purchase on the most comprehensive available description of "American" literature

---

[30]One other article bears mentioning here. William Hansell's perceptive discussion of artists in the poem brings him to the confrontation between Heights and the Curator in "Phi," but once he runs up against it, his article mysteriously ends. About Heights's possible swipe at Hughes (the *"howl-howl-with-the-combo* quacks"), Hansell has this to say: "Langston Hughes is famous for his experiments with jazz accompaniment for public readings throughout his career of over forty years. Tolson had the highest regard for Hughes and for his work" (1984, 127).

in the twentieth century: that is, in the hope that Tolson will be considered not only another major poet in the African-American canon but also an important poet in the African-American canon who requires us to reconceive the history of modernism in American literature, and the relation of canonical to "apocryphal" modernisms in the United States.

My second point is less sweeping, more pedestrian: current readings of *Harlem Gallery* are conditioned both by the institutional matrices of African-American and American literature, *and* by the work of retrieval and recovery within the field of African-American literature which has made the project of recovering "authors" an indispensable item on the agenda of canon and discipline revision. Without some sense of Tolson's career, in other words, we can have no sense of the terms on which he aspires to engage us. The importance of biography and critical annotation in this project should need little further elaboration. Until the publication of Farnsworth's biography in 1984, readers of *Harlem Gallery* were faced with a most difficult set of circumstances: a highly complex poem unadorned by critical annotation, written by a poet about whom little was known. Just as *Libretto*'s reception was impeded in part by its outlandishly self-complicating footnotes, so too was *Harlem Gallery*'s reception impeded by the lack of more garden-variety self-clarifying footnotes.[31] And until Farnsworth's publication of the Redding letter and the Tate correspondence, a vision—never mind a revision—of Tolson was scarcely imaginable.

This much is, as I say, obvious. But recall here the second sense of Foucault's "author function," in which the author is "the ideological figure by which one marks the manner in which we fear the proliferation of meaning" (1984, 118–19). What Tolson's case shows us, however, as I argued in Chapter 1, is that a text without any reliable author function may proliferate no "meaning" at all, insofar as it fails to reproduce itself culturally. Recall also that Foucault's second definition of "author function" leads him to the patently false conclusion in which he surmises that "the author function will disappear" (119), and we can ask with impunity the Barthesian and Beckettian question, "What difference does it make who is speaking?" (120). But in the unauthorized text no one speaks—or we cannot

---

[31]*Harlem Gallery and Other Poems* is due to be reprinted as part of the *Callaloo* Poetry Series (Charles Rowell, general editor) with much-needed footnotes by Raymond Nelson. Robert Huot's annotated *Harlem Gallery* (1971) has so far been very little help—to me or to Nelson.

determine who is speaking, or why. For Tolson's reception, therefore, it matters a good deal who is speaking, and whence; and this is
an issue on which Pynchon—and his critics—will have more to say.

The relevant question now, however, following Farnsworth's
biography, is somewhat more explicitly theoretical: how have
the terms for academic discussion of African-American literature
changed in ways that now make it possible for us to reopen the
Harlem Gallery? Of course, no matter what the nature of the reading
formations in which Tolson's reception has so far taken place, it will
not be possible for us to see our own position in the totality of its
possibilities for reading; no reading formation, however it makes itself part of its legitimated objects of inquiry, can be entirely self-
adjudicating in this way. Yet I would not have embarked on this
study had I not felt that ours was a promising moment both for
understanding the conditions of Tolson's neglect and for envision-
ing his work in such a way as to effect its re-vision.

A Game of Chess on Lenox Avenue: Modernism and Marronage

Among *Harlem Gallery*'s many wonders is its evidence that Tolson
was not blindsided by the emergent Black Aesthetic, as most of his
readers have assumed; his portrayal of Hideho Heights as the author of both "the sea-turtle and the shark" and "E. & O.E." is, as we
have seen in Chapter 2, both an anticipation of and a response to
the questions raised by the proposition of a black separatist poetics.
On the questions of separatism, black essentialism, and a Black Aesthetic, then, Tolson's antiessentialist response is entirely germane,
and the response runs something like this: it is fruitless to inhabit
the right-hand side of a racial dichotomy, whether by coercion or by
choice;[32] to choose sides in the "Afroamerican dilemma in the Arts"
so as to purge all traces of "whiteness" in literature is to take up a
1960s version of Paul Laurence Dunbar's position—a position about
which Dunbar himself said, "I've got to write dialect poetry; it's the

---

[32]According to Gates, the Black Aesthetic was a form of resistance which in its
essentialism unintentionally reproduced the confinement of African-American art:
"As healthy politically as such a gesture was . . . we must also criticize the idealism,
the notion of essence, implicit in even this gesture. . . . Negritude already constituted
such a claim of blackness as a transcendent signified, of a full and sufficient presence;
but to make such a claim, to feel the necessity to make such a claim, is already . . . to
take the terms of one's assertion from a discourse determined by an Other" (1984b,
7).

only way I can get them to listen to me" (quoted in Johnson 1922, 35–36).[33] As Tolson would have it, then, African-American writers who refuse to engage or de-form modernism will reinforce an audience relation and author function whereby they will be confined to a new form of dialect poetry—whether ballads to Louis Armstrong or verse emulations of John Coltrane. Likewise, to Audre Lorde's line about the Master's tools and the Master's house, Tolson would no doubt reply, with pragmatist élan, that tools are only tools—and that, in Lillian Robinson's words, "people have to live in a house, not in a metaphor" (1987, 34).

Powerful dichotomies, however, are not easily disposed of; it is possible, as it was for African-American anthologies, to "retrieve" Tolson by preserving only the discourse of Hideho Heights.[34] And though I am somewhat in sympathy with such a project, I don't think that a reversal of the Curator-Heights opposition *undoes* the Curator-Heights opposition. *Harlem Gallery*'s modernist imperatives privilege the discourse of the Curator; various Black Aesthetic imperatives privilege that of Heights. In either case, we are left with a gallery that is all yin or all yang. What I try to do in this chapter's closing portion, then, is to retrieve Tolson by undoing the Curator-Heights dichotomy altogether—and, strangely enough, I begin by approaching *Harlem Gallery*, once more with feeling, by way of reading *The Waste Land* against the modernist grain.

I do so, however, not to distinguish Tolson from Eliot—as McCall

---

[33]Dunbar's implicit claim is that white Americans will not hear him unless his voice is sufficiently Other; Tolson's position, on the other hand, critiques *nonwhite* American audiences who will not hear a discourse unless it is sufficiently Other than whites'. Redmond, interestingly, likens Tate's praise of Tolson to William Dean Howells's endorsement of Dunbar's dialect poems (1976, 255). But as Nathan Scott suggests in the passage quoted early in this chapter (1979, 325–26), African-American poets who announce themselves as recognizably Other may stand a better chance, today as in Dunbar's day, of achieving Anglo-American critical acclaim: look again at the post-Renaissance African-American poets in the *Norton Anthology of Modern Poetry* (see n. 3 above).

[34]To some extent, even Rita Dove's study saves *Harlem Gallery* by saving Hideho: when she discusses Tolson's "virtuoso use of folk talk and street jive" (1985, 110) or links Tolson to toastin' and testifyin', she focuses on the Zulu Club scenes; when it comes to the Curator, or the poem as a whole, she is less convincing. "Tolson meant for his lines to be read aloud," she writes; "the visual impact of the centered lines contributes to the forward thrust that a lively oral recitation would possess. . . . In fact, the whole of *Harlem Gallery* is very much like the Toasts to Shine and Stag-o-lee, those mythic 'bad-men' heroes in black oral tradition. In Tolson's case, however, his hero is the archetypal Black Artist" (115, 113). These are worthwhile attempts to exonerate Tolson from the charge of having cultivated a bizarre, pseudoliterary diction, but surely some of *Harlem Gallery* is irreducibly *written*, and as unlike toasting as it is unlike rap.

did, on the grounds that Eliot wrote of spiritual decay whereas Tolson writes of spiritual renewal; or as Basler did, on the grounds that Eliot's outlook is retrospective whereas Tolson's is prospective. Instead, I want simply to apply some of *The Waste Land*'s ambiguities to *Harlem Gallery*, both as a means of enabling a discourse that will revise the Curator-Heights relation and as a means of unpacking an ambiguity latent in my own reading in Chapter 2: the question of how Tolson can be a modernist poet who spells out a developed and intricate "argument" in his poetry. For the passage from modernism to New Criticism, from formal experimentation to ossified critical dogma, is a passage that takes us from Pound's determination to write the "poem including history" to the Bollingen Committee's public proclamation that even the most virulently anti-Semitic of the Pisan Cantos are not to be judged by criteria alien to "the validity of that objective perception of value on which any society must rest."[35] It is a passage that ends with the determination that even Pound's work is autonomous, ahistorical, apolitical, "harmless and impotent" (Nelson 1989, 242).[36] Thus, this latter question necessarily leads us back, in turn, to the problem with which this chapter opened: namely, the relation of "ideas" to "technique" in the "hell and heaven" disparity between Tolson and Eliot. And the reconsideration of this problem dovetails, finally, with the consideration of how we can see Tolson's relation to modernism neither as emulation nor as satire but as marronage.

Readers who compare Tolson and Eliot tend to forget that Eliot's major poem is every bit as heteroglot as Tolson's—that where Tolson whisks us from art gallery to nightclub, so too does "A Game of Chess" juxtapose a neo-Cleopatra's burnished throne to Lil's abortion. The confrontation between written and oral, high and low cultures, is played out in both poems; the curious thing about the confrontation in *The Waste Land*, however, is that the outcome is more uncertain than it is in *Harlem Gallery*. In the clash between cultures, avant-garde and *kitsch*, Eliot's poem actually offers us a pair of alternatives. One possibility is that our culture is so attenuated and degraded that we have lost the ability to distinguish between "those are pearls that were his eyes" and "that Shakespeherian Rag," and we find our condition expressible in both the

---

[35]For the text of the Bollingen Committee's public statement as well as a pointed satire and extrapolation of it, see Barrett 1949.

[36]See also Gerald Graff's reading of Archibald MacLeish's defense of the Bollingen Award (1970, 172–79).

most profound and the most trivial terms: both in allusions to Dante ("A crowd flowed over London Bridge, so many, / I had not thought death had undone so many" [Eliot 1971, lines 62–63]) and in a prattle of nursery rhymes ("London Bridge is falling down falling down falling down" [427]). The other possibility, less likely but more interesting, is precisely that Dante and nursery rhymes may, within our present horizon, do similar kinds of cultural work, and that the distinction between them is academic and inapposite.

In other words, *The Waste Land*'s treatment of modernity's cultural literacy tends in two directions. On the one hand, there are clearly moments of the mock epic in the poem, whereby our culture is dwarfed by the magnitude of its own heritage. Take for example the movement from Marvell, via John Day and Sweeney, to an Australian ballad in "The Fire Sermon":

> But at my back from time to time I hear
> The sound of horns and motors, which shall bring
> Sweeney to Mrs. Porter in the spring.
> O the moon shone bright on Mrs. Porter
> And on her daughter
> They wash their feet in soda water.
>
> (196–201)

On the other hand, "A Game of Chess," whatever its intention, suggests that the spiritual dryness of our world, its inability to die and consequent inability to live, to create and procreate—its general inability to do anything but press lidless eyes and wait for a knock upon the door—is a phenomenon heedless of class distinctions; its symptoms can be read both in "Are you alive, or not?" (126) and in "What you get married for if you don't want children?" (164), and, moreover, read therein with equal skill and acuity.

Separate classes are not the same thing as separate cultures, however, and it may be objected that although the waste land's aridity infects both high and low classes, such a spread of infection does not imply conflation of high and low *cultures*. Surely, almost none of the poem's evanescent moments of transcendence have their roots in low culture. *Almost* none: for even amidst the hyacinth garden, full fathom five, the *Confessions*, the *Fire Sermon*, and the *Brihadaran-yaka-Upanishad*, we nonetheless

> can sometimes hear
> Beside a public bar in Lower Thames Street,
> The pleasant whining of a mandoline
> And a clatter and a chatter from within

> Where fishmen lounge at noon: where the walls
> Of Magnus Martyr hold
> Inexplicable splendour of Ionian white and gold.
>   (259–65)

Here, the apprehension of Magnus Martyr's splendor is not to be achieved by the denigration of the fishmen's chatter, nor are these fishmen impotent fisher-kings of the "dull canal" (189), nor does Lower Thames Street echo, yet, with the songs of the Thames-daughters. This once, then, there is a peace which passeth understanding in the immense panorama of futility and anarchy which is contemporary history. Perhaps.

We know, of course, that these are not propositions Eliot would be quick to entertain; however, in order to exclude them from consideration, we would have to invoke again the second sense of Foucault's "author function," this time to claim that we know from Eliot's oeuvre that *The Waste Land* is not the expression of its author's conviction of the equivalence of high and low cultures. My point is simply this: modernist imperatives notwithstanding, *The Waste Land* never fully resolves the tension of the relation between high and low cultures. The same is true of cultures ancient and modern: if we read the typist/young-man-carbuncular scene alongside the rape of Philomel by Tereus, then we may be unsure whether the inability to live and love of which Eliot writes is a phenomenon specific to the twentieth century, or whether it is a despair that has dogged us ever since humans first celebrated the rebirth of the god in spring.[37] And if the latter option seems more likely, then there doesn't appear to be much point in distinguishing between a London Bridge over which flow the undead of the *Inferno*'s canto III, and a London Bridge which is simply falling down.

Likewise, *The Waste Land* is capable of deploying allusion in the service of furthering its central ambiguities in much the same way as is *Harlem Gallery*: as we saw in the previous chapter, Tolson's reference to "Belshazzarian tables" in "Delta" left open the question of the range of allusive context on which his poem's context draws—specifically, the question of the existence or nonexistence of a Daniel in the poem. In precisely similar fashion, "Shall I at least set my lands in order?" (in "What the Thunder Said," 426) draws on Isaiah in a way that leaves the issue wholly up for grabs: either we are

---

[37] I owe the ancient/modern argument here to a series of classes and conversations with Michael Levenson.

about to die and must make some vain attempt to shore our fragments against our ruins, or, like Hezekiah, we will appeal to the
Lord and be granted fifteen more years of life—which itself, to extend the ambiguity to its furthest reach, may or may not be a good
thing in *The Waste Land*'s terms. In both cases, the query is one of
intertextual principle: when Milton's Moloch declares in Book 2 of
Paradise Lost that "the ascent is easy then," we know fairly certainly
that he is undercut by his immediate allusive context, *Aeneid* 6.176–
79; when Eliot and Tolson reach back to Isaiah 38:1 and Daniel 5:1–
4, it is sublimely unclear whether the "immediate allusive context"
extends even one verse more, to Isaiah 38:2 and Daniel 5:5.

Given these salient similarities between the poems, then, it might
strike us as puzzling, first, that Tolson felt the need to resolve a
tension left unresolved by *The Waste Land*, to valorize the Curator's
cultural function by dramatically exposing contradictions in Hideho
Heights's; and second, that Tolson declared his "ideas" to be poles
apart from Eliot's. But surely—to deal with the second oddity first—
when Tolson sought to distance himself from Eliot's "ideas," he did
not necessarily mean the ideas of *The Waste Land*; and part of the
reason that *Harlem Gallery*, despite the New Criticism, offers us
"ideas" and "argument" is precisely that Eliot did not have to do the
same in *The Waste Land*. Though Eliot eschewed argument and ideas
in poetry, he hardly needed to worry about access to the central
literary journals of his time; he *created* one of the central journals of
his time, the *Criterion*, and was not shy about launching arguments
from its platforms.[38] Tolson, on the contrary, saw his poems and
reviews published in *Poetry* only when Karl Shapiro edited the magazine, from 1950 to 1955.[39] It may be attributed to Tolson's growing
insight into the marginality of his cultural position, I think, that he
framed his most thorough response to Saunders Redding not in his
letter to the president of the *Afro-American* but in his next poem.

[38]For a thorough critique of antipropositionalism in modernist critical theory, see
Graff 1970.

[39]Shapiro continued to be listed as editor for the nine issues, January-September
1955, during which Henry Rago served as acting editor before officially assuming the
editorship. During his tenure Shapiro published three poems of Tolson's (*Libretto*'s
"Ti" in July 1950, "E. & O.E." in September 1951, and "The Man from Halicarnassus"
in October 1952); one essay by Tolson ("Claude McKay's Art," February 1954); and
two notices, Tate's and Turner's, of *Libretto*—for a total of six appearances in less than
four years. This is by far the most exposure Tolson ever received in the mainstream
press; indeed, until two of his book reviews appeared in *Book Week* in 1965–66, it was
his *only* multiple exposure in a mainstream periodical. Shapiro also edited *Prairie
Schooner*, in which the opening seven sections of *Harlem Gallery* were first published
(Fall 1961, 243–64).

Early in the Redding letter, there is a mildly disingenuous moment in which Tolson avers that he can do nothing to influence his reception even as he attempts to influence his reception: "As to my standing among the major poets of England and America, one can easily discover my status. I would not hit one key on this typewriter to try to prove myself a poet. The critics of the New York *Times, Poetry, Kenyon Review, Accent,* etc. will have to determine that; and there's nothing—absolutely, nothing—that M. B. Tolson can do about that. The 'Libretto' is in the lap of the gods—as we used to say at Lincoln" (TM). But between 1954 and 1965, apparently, Tolson decided that he would not be able to depend entirely on the kindness of strangers (especially the strangers at "*Kenyon Review, Accent,* etc.," who never reviewed the poem) or the disinterestedness of critics; if his position in the "white and not-white dichotomy" were to be understood, he would have to spell out that position for himself.

And even though I claim to have discovered an apparent anomaly in Tolson's smuggling of paraphrasable "ideas" into his modernist verse—an anomaly roughly akin to his claim that Claude McKay's poetry was free of ideology—we should remember, after all, that the "argument" of *Harlem Gallery* is by no means obvious: it has eluded Tolson's readers for over twenty-five years, and even Nathan Scott's otherwise helpful discussion of him in 1979 concludes that "he had not the kind of systematic intelligence that sustains the long poem" (326). The argument's elusiveness notwithstanding, my point is that *Harlem Gallery* is less ambiguous than *The Waste Land* on the relation of the avant-garde to *kitsch* because, very simply, Tolson could count on only one forum for his work by 1965 and therefore had to freight his last poem not only with all his formidable learning and all the phases of his career from the poetry of Mister Starks to the ruminations of the Curator, but also with its own defense of itself, its own defense of its author's decision to follow Des Imagistes down the Macadam Road. My response to the second "oddity"—the relation of "ideas" to *Harlem Gallery*—therefore enfolds my response to the first: Tolson's poem resolves the polar dichotomy between avant-garde and *kitsch* because resolution of the dichotomy is crucial to the construction of its argument.

But, to repeat the point, the poem purchases its certainty on one issue at the price of refusing to engage other, more postmodern issues. It is not as if *Harlem Gallery* is simply quantifiably "less ambiguous" than *The Waste Land*; its central cultural ambiguities are aimed in another direction entirely. Where Eliot leaves open the question of whether the rain will come—or whether his poem's allusive movement, from Limbo and the gates of Hell (63–64) to Arnaut Daniel's hope for absolution (428), implies our eventual subtextual salvation—Tolson's citation of Frost at Kennedy's inauguration, as I have noted, leaves open the question of whether Frost is being celebrated or co-opted, whether he has been duly acknowledged by a brash young Yankee administration or is merely its ornament. And just as we can go elsewhere than *The Waste Land* for answers to my Eliot questions—to "The Metaphysical Poets," to "Ulysses, Order, and Myth," even so far afield as to Clement Greenberg (1939), who will tell us that only a schizophrenic culture would dream of laying Dante and "London Bridge" side by side (or, in his article's opening example, Edgar Guest and Eliot himself)—so too can we go, for answers to the questions raised by Tolson's reference to Frost, either to another document of Tolson's or to a leading theorist of the postmodern, Andreas Huyssen.

Between Tolson and Huyssen, our answers will be drastically opposed—and that, too, is part of the nature of re-vision. Although *Harlem Gallery* is silent on the relation of Frost to Cézanne and the nineteenth-century *vox populi*, Tolson himself was certain that Frost's role in the inauguration was a sign of hope, a sign of our society's empowerment of its greatest artists. In a speech planned, like Hideho's sea-turtle parable, for the centennial of the Emancipation Proclamation, and published posthumously by Farnsworth in the *Kansas Quarterly* ten years later, Tolson concluded that "today, artists and writers are placed in the showcase of civilization. . . . Robert Frost stood at the right hand of President Kennedy during his inauguration. The world now honors the artist and writer. They no longer starve, unknown in a garret" (1973, 35). The juxtaposition of Cézanne to Frost in "Pi," then, is meant to imply that the conditions of Cézanne's initial neglect no longer apply, that in the twentieth century artists have achieved the cultural and institutional access of which a post-Impressionist could only dream. To Huyssen, however, the use of Frost by a federal symbol, as a national symbol, to explicate the federal symbol of the Great Seal, was evidence that

modernism itself had entered the mainstream via mass reproduction and the culture industry. And, during the Kennedy years, high culture even began to take on functions of political representation with Robert Frost and Pablo Casals, Malraux and Stravinsky at the White House. The irony in all of this is that the first time the U.S. had something resembling an "institution art" in the emphatic European sense, it was modernism itself, the kind of art whose purpose it had always been to resist institutionalization. (1986, 193)

In my first chapter on Tolson, I tried to establish a reading of *Harlem Gallery*; in closing this chapter I try, with the help of Eliot, Huyssen, Henry Louis Gates, and Houston Baker, to set out the prospective terms for some rereadings. *The Waste Land*'s unresolved tension between high and low cultures is our model, and the present condition in which we can reestablish a similar tension in *Harlem Gallery* is that of a postmodernism from which we can understand that a denigration of popular culture is not necessary to a valorization of high culture. From the vantage point of the postmodern, we can read *Harlem Gallery* against its own Curator, and against the principle of mutual canonical exclusivity which provides the foundation for the allegation of Hideho Heights's "split identity," in order to propose that Heights be authorized both by "E. & O.E." and by his extempore ballads.

Again, to liberate Hideho's discourse from the Curator's ideological frame does not mean that we perpetuate the modernist dichotomy by reversing it, either by celebrating the popular uncritically or by underlining the Heightsian emphases of Tolson's anthologists. Rather, it means that we employ postmodernism dialectically in order to explore cultural phenomena left unthought by modernism. As Huyssen writes: "Postmodernism is far from making modernism obsolete. On the contrary, it casts a new light on it and appropriates many of its aesthetic strategies and techniques, inserting them and making them work in new constellations. What has become obsolete, however, are those codifications of modernism in critical discourse which, however subliminally, are based on a teleological view of progress and modernization" (1986, 217–18). One of the things we may now understand about our century's art, in other words, is that it does not necessarily proceed—as do missile delivery systems, postindustrial capitalisms, or the works of James Joyce—developmentally into systems of ever increasing complexity. Tolson's conviction that modernism is here to stay as the technical criterion for poetry is itself a thoroughly modernist notion; but by the same token, his critics' idea that Tolson simply missed the deadline for filing his brief on modernism, and thus came too late to make it new, is another modernist notion—and one that points up the telling similarities between a modernist culture industry and a capitalist consumer industry.[40]

[40] As Huyssen puts it, "Modernism and the avantgarde were always closely related to social and industrial modernization. They were related to it as an adversary culture, yes, but they drew their energies, not unlike Poe's *Man of the Crowd*, from their proximity to the crises brought about by modernization and progress" (1986, 217). See also Robbins 1983, 229–34.

We may therefore set out a postmodern re-vision by remarking a contradiction unthought by *Harlem Gallery*: whereas Tolson-as-modernist is careful to pinpoint the self-contradictions in Hideho Heights, we, as antiessentialists and postmodernists, may reread his octoroonish Curator as the sign not of cultural amalgamation but of cultural contradiction, as an emblem of a kind of racial aporia.[41] And by exchanging one aporia for another, we remark that the poem's "resolution" merely disguises the fact that there can really be no resolution of the problems addressed by the Harlem Gallery. Likewise, just as we can trouble *Harlem Gallery* with questions it is not prepared to answer about the present cultural position of the avant-garde artist, Cézanne or Picasso, who has created the taste by which he is enjoyed and has been transformed by the culture industry in turn, so too can we turn the poem inside out, as it were, and suggest that the tension between the Curator and Heights is more compelling than its "resolution." Here we might recall my suggestion, in Chapter 2, that the substitution of Heights for Laugart as the "central figure" yields us a poem which is not demonstrative but performative, a poem dialogically enacted; and this enactment, with its concomitant dramatic and ideological tensions, proceeds for as long as we can imagine the Curator and Heights inhabiting the same cultural and discursive space—as long as we can have both the Curator and Heights, neither to the exclusion of the other, challenging us to think both thoughts at once. The goal, then, is to create a way of seeing *Harlem Gallery* from both sociolinguistic points of view, in a kind of ideological parallax; and the goal is appropriate to our contemporary relation to the poem, for a variety of reasons.

To insist that *Harlem Gallery* retains the tension between the two cultures, to insist on having both, is to ask of the poem no more than mimesis, for African-American culture in the twentieth century has always given us both: in Jay Wright and Public Enemy's Chuck D.;[42] in the juxtaposition between Coltrane's "My Favorite Things" (in which he revives modal possibilities not heard in Western music since the fourteenth century) and Madhubuti's "Don't Cry, Scream"

[41]I am indebted for this suggestion to Jerome McGann.

[42]Wright, meanwhile, has done what he can to kill one of his poetic fathers: in a 1983 *Callaloo* interview, Wright declines a comparison with Tolson on the grounds that although he feels "pleasure" at being linked to Pound, Zukofsky, and Robert Hayden, "I no longer find Tolson deserving of such a high place," and then suggests to his interviewer, *Callaloo* editor Charles Rowell, that he would like to be noted for his appreciation of Dante (15). In substituting Dante for Tolson, Wright is not merely trying to drive up the price of his stock; he seems also to be waging a competition with Tolson for the title of heir to the modernist throne, wherein the poet who can link himself to Eliot in the greatest number of ways wins.

(in which he celebrates "My Favorite Things" with lines like "we-eeeeeee WE-EEEEEEEEEEEEE-EE-EEEEE"). There are, despite the many cultural uses to which we may put the abstruse and highly technical Coltrane, many ways for artists "to be or not to be a Negro"; for that matter, the tradition that runs from the dozens to hip-hop is alive, well, and more the work of dedicated revolutionists than of the "simple Negro."

Moreover, and this will take us a bit further into the poem, the possibility for reconceiving the Curator-Heights tension is latent in what I take to be the text itself. *Harlem Gallery's* exposure of Heights is fueled by Tolson's fear that his African-American audience will not accept anything resembling a modernist aesthetic; and yet Heights is surely not given so much space in Tolson's Gallery exclusively in order that he might be held up finally as a negative exemplum. That is, if we read the struggle between Heights and the Curator more for the spectacle of its enactment than for the closure of its dénouement, more for the power of the conflict than for the force of its formal resolution, then all we are doing is acknowledging that Hideho does indeed disrupt and seize control of the *Gallery*—and that his discourse is a discourse which, once sounded, cannot be entirely silenced. Just as Samuel Beckett's gainsaying, in the closing pages of *How It Is*, of his narrative's previous 140 pages does not cause those 140 pages to disappear, neither does the revelation of Heights's "private gallery" cancel retroactively Hideho's trans-lation of the poem into the gossip world of the Zulu Club.

Furthermore, if we take Heights's unmasking over against Tolson's account of his correspondence with Tate, we get a new interpretive model for the poem as well. For if that unmasking reveals Heights to be a kind of latter-day Dunbar, who has to declaim racial ballads because it's the only way he'll be heard, then the Curator's reading of "E. & O.E." in "Chi" is a call to African-American poets to throw off Dunbar's mask; but it is possible, in light of Tolson's retrospective claim to have rewritten *Libretto* "so that it said the same things in a different way," to see *Harlem Gallery's* conflict not synchronically but diachronically, as part of an explicitly historical argument. And the point of such a historical argument turns on Tolson's separation of "ideas" from "technique," according to which the conflict's "resolution" suggests less an unmasking than a *re*-masking, an *exchange* of masks—suggests that underneath one mask there is only another, the mask of the modernist maroon.[43]

[43]Cf. Tolson in his interview with King: "A person in his lifetime may wear not one mask, but many, which are revelations of his complex nature and nurture" (1966,

And, as some readers have no doubt noticed by now, Tolson's ironic distancing of himself from Heights and Starks is not a uni-dimensional gesture: it is possible to argue that the establishment of such ironic distance only creates, as in James Joyce's *Portrait*, the parallel phenomenon of diminishing authorial "distance." After the manner of, say, Robert Scholes's argument that Joyce's use of a poem from his own early "Shine and Dark" verse (1900–1) as Stephen's villanelle implies something of a conflation of author and character (Scholes 1964, 484–85, 489),[44] so we might wish to reread *Harlem Gallery* as Tolson's psychomachia, as he imagines and lays out the roads not taken in the course of his career. *Harlem Gallery* can therefore be seen as a narrative both of Tolson's personal history—a record of his development from *Harlem Vignettes* to *Harlem Gallery*, and testimony of his ability to bridge both the ballad and the Pindaric ode—and of African-American literary history, a record of a movement from oral to written discourses which parallels the Gallery's "paintings that chronicle / a people's New World odyssey / from chattel to Esquire!" (*HG* 173). Tolson himself suggested time and again that the two narratives were confluent, that (in the terms of what Huyssen would call his customary "teleological view of progress and modernization") his poetic ontogeny recapitulated the century's phylogeny. Perhaps this is why, although he was born in 1898, he always claimed to have been born in 1900—as if he, like Pynchon's Herbert Stencil, saw himself as the century's child.

What is most intriguing about Tolson's position in these revisions is that he now appears less as a belated modernist than as an un-acknowledged precursor, for in the work of the currently preeminent critics of African-American literature, we find the argument that African-American criticism and theory must grapple with the insights of poststructuralism in order to do justice to the signifying

---

187). An otherwise unremarkable comment, but helpful, I think, to the notion that *Harlem Gallery* re-presents a history of masks—both Tolson's, and African-American poetry's.

[44]Scholes, however, uses the villanelle's origin as a means of combatting the "ironic" reading of *Portrait* proposed by W. Y. Tindall and others, and concludes that "the inspiration and the poem are both intended to be genuine. . . . It is at this point that Stephen ceases to be a esthete and becomes a poet" (1964, 489). It seems to me, though, that if Joyce included in *Portrait* a poem he had written more than ten years before his completion of the novel, then irony is inherent in the method; it is not necessarily an irony such as Tindall's, which implies mockery, but rather an irony attendant upon temporal distance—precisely the kind of irony, I suggest, with which Tolson treats Starks's *Harlem Vignettes*.

difference of the African-American text. For Henry Louis Gates, as for Tolson, it is indefensible to pretend that there is a hermetic, indigenous African-American tradition upon which African-Americans must exclusively draw in order to be authentically African-American, "irresponsible to act as if we are not all fellow citizens of literature for whom developments in other sections of the republic of letters have no bearing or relevance" (1987, 347).

The Tolsonian position, however, brings with it Tolsonian dangers: "Can we, as critics, escape a 'mockingbird' relation to theory, one destined to be derivative, often to the point of parody? . . . Only recently have some scholars attempted to convince critics of black literature that the racism of the Western critical tradition was not a sufficient reason for us to fail to theorize about our own endeavor, or even to make use of contemporary theoretical innovations when this seemed either useful or appropriate" (Gates 1987, 350). But such dangers, in turn, offer the chance for reconceiving both African-American critical theory and Tolson's position in relation to Eliot. In response to Joyce Ann Joyce's charges (1987) that he is unduly influenced by Derrida and Foucault, Gates replies, justifiably enough, that his appropriations of theories are necessarily transformations of theory: "Lest I be misunderstood, I have tried to work through contemporary theories of literature *not* to 'apply' them to black texts, but rather to *transform* by *translating* them into a new rhetorical realm" (351).[45] Thus, concludes Gates, sounding more like Tolson with each paragraph, African-American critics must realize that poststructuralism is here to stay—like, say, modern particle physics: "This is the challenge of the critic of black literature in the 1980s: not to shy away from literary theory; rather, to translate it into the black idiom" (352). Theory is therefore simply a means "to *defamiliarize* the texts of the black tradition, to create a distance between this black reader and our black texts, so that I may more readily *see* the formal workings of those texts" (352). We can almost hear here a re-sounding echo of the Curator's characterization of art in "Gamma," just as we can hear, more clearly, Gates protesting that poststructuralism is only technique; any artist must use the technique of his time; and African-American poets and professors must master Derrida. For

[45]Cf. Gates's "Criticism in the Jungle": "Theory, like words in a poem, does not 'translate' in a one-to-one relationship of reference. Indeed, I have found that, in the 'application' of a mode of reading to black texts, the critic, by definition, transforms the theory and, I might add, transforms received readings of the text into something different, a construct neither exactly 'like' its antecedents nor entirely new" (1984b, 4).

who, asks Gates elsewhere, "would seek to deny us our complexity?" (1984b, 4).[46]

Up to this point the analogy between Tolson and African-American poststructuralism is, I think, mutually beneficial; there is, as Gates claims, no intrinsic reason for the African-American critic to eschew theory *qua* theory, and Tolson, for his part, certainly sought to transform and translate the terms of modernist poetics. But in the other response published in the already infamous *New Literary History* debate on theory and the African-American canon, Houston Baker displays the pitfalls of uncritically taking the Tolsonian positions to their extremes. For Baker, like Tolson, is a somewhat belated convert and consequently as given as was Tolson to hyperbolic renditions of the ideology of the avant-garde; unlike Tolson, however, he does not also consider the symbiotic relation between his avant-garde and its institutional matrix. Instead, he fashions something like Richard Chase's (1957) avant-garde conflation of experimentalism and social protest, claiming that deconstruction constitutes "an avant garde in contemporary world literary study" the "sound" of which "has been, and will continue to be . . . the political and academic heralding note of a new and liberating future" (Baker, 1987a, 366, 369). Where Tolson agonizes over the means by which modernism can eventually be made into an expressive possibility, or a habitus, for the masses, Baker simply asserts that the aspirations of "avant-garde" academicians and victims of apartheid are one and the same: "It seems to me that a reading and appropriation of the efforts in philosophy, political economy, psychology, and popular culture of poststructuralist thinkers such as Derrida, Althusser, Lacan, and Baudrillard could well lead one to hear the sound of poststructuralism as a note in clear harmony with, say, the freedom cries of millions of blacks in South Africa bent on a new and revolutionary existence" (369).

The irony of this exchange lies not merely in the repetition of a Tolsonian problematic in an academic context, where the bugbear is not modernism but contemporary theory and where Joyce Ann

[46]Compare Gates's rhetorical question to Gloria Naylor's response to criticism of her 1985 novel, *Linden Hills*: as Lillian Robinson reports, Naylor "has been criticized for adapting the 'white male Christian myth' of the *Inferno* to her allegory of black bourgeois life. Why not use African or Afro-American symbolic systems, one reviewer asked, instead of that same old high European culture? . . . When I mentioned the 'white-male-Euro-Christian' critique to her in a public discussion at the University of Pennsylvania in March of 1986, she asked, as a former comparative literature graduate student at Yale, who the critics are to say that Dante is *not* part of her 'own' culture!" (1987, 32, 35 n.13).

Joyce unwittingly stands in for J. Saunders Redding; a more pointed irony lies in the fact that the theories of Gates and Baker themselves are at points highly relevant to the work of the man they don't discuss. In fact, in Baker's *Modernism and the Harlem Renaissance*, upon which I have repeatedly drawn in the course of these two chapters, Tolson appears only in the first introductory paragraph, his name invoked by one of Baker's former (nameless) interlocutors and never alluded to again. For Baker wants to enact a wholesale change of terms for the discussion of African-American modernism, and if he succeeds, he effectively pulls the rug out from under what Tolson conceived African-American modernism to be. Of course, it may nonetheless turn out to be possible to read Tolson in Baker's vocabulary; as an African-American "cultural performance" in the language of the "mastery of form" and the "deformation of mastery," Tolson's modernist work might prove a valuable sounding-board, an indispensable singing-book, a cultural performer of "radical marronage" (1987b, 75).[47] For instance, using zoologist H. B. Cott's defintions of "phaneric" and "allaesthetic" characteristics, Baker writes:

> Allaesthetic characteristics, in short, are biological *masks*. . . .
>   The mastery of form conceals, disguises, floats like a trickster butterfly in order to sting like a bee. The deformation of mastery, by contrast . . . is a go(uer)rilla action in the face of acknowledged adversaries.
>   . . . Such displays present the type of allaesthetic mask that Cott calls *phaneric*. Rather than concealing or disguising in the manner of the *cryptic* mask (a colorful mastery of codes), the phaneric mask is meant to advertise. (1987b, 50–51)

Whereas Tolson's Randall tale suggests that Tolson saw his adoption of modernism in retrospect as a rope-a-dope, a version of the "mastery of form" which Baker sees as the skillful negotiation of racist reception (32), Tolson's "deformation of mastery" in *Harlem Gallery* surely advertises as vociferously as possible its response to Gertrude Stein's aphorism "the Negro suffers from nothingness" (*HG* 74), fill-

---

[47]Dan McCall's characterization of *Libretto* as "a kind of master singing-book for the country, a storehouse of education for the Futurafrique" (1966, 538), may be apposite here; then again, McCall's claim that "Tolson restores to the poet his function of singing to the community" (538) is precisely the kind of claim to which Baker takes exception (1980, 73) when he writes that *Libretto* "is a text that turns inward to the private spaces of the self." Both claims, I think, are vague, but McCall, at least, has unwittingly left Tolson with two options, for the "singing-book" and the "storehouse of education" may be two different things, and it may be appropriate for the latter to be difficult and irreducibly textual.

ing the alleged void with a plenitude almost beyond comprehension.[48]

At present, however, it is undeniable that Baker seeks to disengage African-American modernism from precisely the "modernism" with which Tolson was engaged:

> I would suggest that judgments on Afro-American "modernity" and the "Harlem Renaissance" that begin with notions of British, Anglo-American, and Irish "modernism" as "successful" objects, projects, and processes to be emulated by Afro-Americans are misguided. . . . Further, it seems to me that the very *histories* that are assumed in the chronologies of British, Anglo-American, and Irish modernisms are radically opposed to any adequate and accurate account of the history of Afro-American modernism, especially the *discursive* history of such modernism. (1987b, xv–xvi)

Baker's, it appears, is a modernism against Modernism, a modernism that disallows the category of "crossover artists": in his formulation, Anglo-American and African-American modernisms are "radically opposed." If, therefore, Baker's "mastery of form" and "deformation of mastery" prove somehow unavailable for a focused revision of Tolson's career, then I suggest we turn to Baker's deployment of the idea of marronage; and under the sign of Baker's use of the term, I want to reactivate Dan McCall's description of Tolson, a description unremarked for two decades but particularly apposite now: "I am a Negro," McCall imagines Tolson saying, "and have made my meals on what I hooked from your white kitchens and now that I have made my way into your study—see here—I walked off with your library" (1966, 541). McCall does not talk of "marronage," but what he is describing here—I think correctly—is a "go(uer)rilla action," the raid for supplies. I would not go so far as to say that Tolson's act of cultural marronage is "radical" in the manner of Ishmael Reed's *Mumbo Jumbo*, which re-founds the entire history of the West (and Western literature, since in *Mumbo Jumbo*, Greek epic and drama, like Christianity, turn out to be derivative, Atonist versions of the legend of Osiris and Set), or even so radical as Mal-

---

[48]"Unlike almost every other literary tradition," writes Gates, "the Afro-American literary tradition was generated as a response to allegations that its authors did not, and *could not*, create 'literature.' . . . Black literature and its criticism, then, have been put to uses that were not primarily aesthetic" (1987, 347–48). The "rope-a-dope," my free translation of Baker's "mastery of form," was the strategy Muhammad Ali designed specifically for his 1974 title fight with George Foreman in Zaire—the bout for which Ali was pegged as a 3-1 underdog.

colm X's claim that Homer was a colonized African slave blinded and forced to sing the military triumphs of the master (Haley 1965, 185); but "marronage" it nonetheless is; "assimilation" it most assuredly is not.

Toward Tolson, however, Baker does not so much as gesture; and though Baker advertises his text as a radical revision of the Harlem Renaissance which will widen its boundaries to include Booker T. Washington's Atlanta Exposition address and a host of figures in the arts and out, as a matter of fact Baker manages to confine the new "Renaissance" to Booker T. Washington, W. E. B. Du Bois, Paul Laurence Dunbar, Charles Chesnutt, and Alain Locke. And though he claims to reconceive the Harlem Renaissance not as a failure but as a success, his only glance past it, into an African-American literature freed of "the felt necessity to produce only *recognizably* standard forms" (1987b, 92), is his brief look at Sterling Brown.

Gates fashions a similar constriction: though his essay on Ishmael Reed's *Mumbo Jumbo* and signifying/signification invokes both poststructuralism and postmodernism, and though he clearly wants to open a new discursive field for criticism of African-American literature, he also articulates criteria for keeping the new field safely enclosed. Writing that *Their Eyes Were Watching God* "revises key tropes and rhetorical strategies received from such precursory texts as Toomer's *Cane* and W. E. B. Du Bois's *The Quest of the Silver Fleece*," Gates sets out the terms for his great tradition: "Afro-American literary history is characterized by such *tertiary* formal revision, by which I mean its authors seem to revise at least two antecedent texts, often taken from different generations or periods within the tradition. . . . It is clear that black writers read and critique other black texts as an act of rhetorical self-definition. Our literary tradition exists because of these precisely chartable formal literary relationships, relationships of signifying" (1984a, 290).

If we set aside Gates's "precisely chartable" qualifications for entry into the tradition, however, we find that his discussion enables revisions of Tolson which deliver him from the white and not-white dichotomy as effectively as do Baker's. For *Harlem Gallery* offers us both a "speakerly text" that "privilege[s] the representation of the speaking black voice" (Gates 1984a, 296) and a Curator who looks a good deal like Gates's characterization of the Signifying Monkey, who "is not only a 'master of technique' as [Roger D.] Abrahams concludes; he *is* technique, or style, or the *literariness* of literary language" (288). The Curator himself claims not to be "gilded . . . / with the gift of tongues" (*HG* 25), yet it is beyond question that the poem he inhabits is informed by a dialogism Gates might productively explore further. "The Signifying Monkey," writes Gates, "perhaps appropriately, seems to dwell in this space between two linguistic domains" (293)—in the space, I would suggest, made available in different ways by the Malcolm X who could speak with both street hustlers and media hustlers, by the Ishmael Reed who can revise the origins of jazz and of the Eleusinian mysteries, and by the Melvin Tolson who could encompass both Eliot and Bessie Smith, Yeats and King Oliver, Cézanne and Touissant L'Ouverture, Jean-Paul Sartre, Langston Hughes, and Liberia, the "ambivalence of classical blues" (*HG* 43) and the "laughing with needles being stuck in you," the Yiddish *lachen mit yastchekes*.[49] *Harlem Gallery*, then, can be seen in readings enabled by Gates as the work of neither an Eliot *manqué* nor an Eliotic parrot-parodist, but as a Gatesian "double-voiced" text, part of an African-American literary expression in which "the texts of the black canon occupy a rhetorical space in at least two canons, as does black literary theory" (1984b, 3, 6–7). For from the vantage point of signifying and marronage, it hardly matters whether Tolson's relation to Eliot is a matter of parody or pastiche; such a choice does not begin to question Eliot's legal right to control where and how modernism will be reprinted. In American literature, there may be no modernist "slaves" practicing a literally precise equivalent of marronage, but there are certainly modernist masters, whose ownership of the sign "modernism" has long gone uncontested.

These are the questions with which Tolson continues to challenge us—about marginality, modernisms, and the roles and responsibilities of institutional criticism. We do ask ourselves such questions, perhaps ad nauseam, in contemporary academic discourse; but we have not so far asked ourselves to confront them in the way Tolson's case presents them. Tolson's refusal to engage postmodernity must therefore provide for us the ground on which he engages postmodernity; his commitment to modernism must provoke our commitment to revisionism. Certainly, *Harlem Gallery* can no longer be read merely as an example of Tolson's uncritical absorption in modernism's self-representations. I suggest, rather, that we take it as a scrupulous, self-critical defense of Tolson's complex attempt to envision and enable an unprecedented African-American modernist practice. Such a reading does not, and could not, "liberate" the poem from all vestiges of modernism and its ideologies. The point

---

[49]Tolson's linking of "ghetto laughter," the ambivalence of the blues, and *lachen mit yastchekes* was first remarked upon by Stanley Edgar Hyman (1958, 208).

to remember is that no thoroughgoing internal critique of modernism is without its self-limitations, whether these be Tolson's silence on the issue of what Huyssen calls "post-avantgarde culture" (1986, 195) or his emphasis on innovative cultural production at the expense of questions about reception, whereby "the binnacle of imagination / steers the work of art aright" (*HG* 167). But, in a final paradox, I want to argue that it is the very depth of Tolson's commitments, the extent of his immersion in the idea of the avantgarde, that makes available for us the critical and self-critical interventions that constitute productive revisionism. What remains most remarkable about Tolson's trajectory, in this respect, is that he began this process of productive revision himself; it is, in many ways, the task to which he continues to call us.

In the meantime, and in order more fully to address the question of a "post-avantgarde culture," we need to turn to the world *Harlem Gallery* was not yet able to imagine—the world of postmodernism, our world, as it is refracted and re-presented in the work and reception of Thomas Pynchon. But as we move from our forgotten modernist to our iconic postmodernist, from the avant-garde to the preterite, from Aunt Grindle's Elite Chitterling Shop to the launching pads of Peenemünde, we should do so with Tolson always close at hand: we have not sounded him for so long simply in order that he might be silenced.

CHAPTER 4

Against the Avant:
Pynchon's Products,
Pynchon's Pornographies

INTO THE POSTMODERN: it is the morning of Joseph K.'s arrest, the moment of his first interrogation by an "Inspector" who has set up temporary shop in Fräulein Bürstner's room. From K.'s first extended speech to the Inspector, Kafka deletes the following:

> As someone said to me—I can't remember now who it was—it is really remarkable that when you wake up in the morning you nearly always find everything in the exactly same place as the evening before. For when asleep and dreaming you are, apparently at least, in an essentially different state from that of wakefulness; and therefore, as that man truly said, it requires enormous presence of mind or rather quickness of wit, when opening your eyes to seize hold as it were of everything in the room at exactly the same place where you had let it go on the previous evening. That was why, he said, the moment of waking up was the riskiest moment of the day. Once that was well over without deflecting you from your orbit, you could take heart of grace for the rest of the day. (1925, 257–58)[1]

---

[1] In reading this passage and its deletion as an emblem of the relation between the modern and the postmodern, I am not claiming anything about the intentions of either Kafka or Max Brod. The opening of *The Trial* is in my reading a signature of the postmodern, but this signature does not have to be the result of an intention to sign. For all we know, Kafka deleted the passage simply because it was clumsy (which it is), and Brod placed it in an appendix because he considered it to constitute "an enrichment of the work either in form or in content" (Brod 1935, 273).

"That man," of course, is Marcel Proust, and the reference is to what he "truly said" in the "Overture" to his *Recherche*; but in the context of *The Trial*, Kafka's citation of Proust appears to be the product of a blistering irony, for, as we and K. will come to learn, Proust couldn't be more wrong here. Waking up, for K., is anything but the day's riskiest moment: waking up is really no problem at all—unless, that is, one is awakened by warders of the State. Marcel agonizes about the status of his room's material objects, about whether and how one exists in one's most primordial states of self-consciousness, about "gradually piec[ing] together the original components of [one's] ego" (Proust 1913, 6) by re-establishing the integrity and self-identity of one's cognitive processes. But what might all this avail when one is caught up suddenly in the macrostructures of power? What's the point of (re)constructing the ground of your authentic existential Being-one's-self when you've been arrested? or when, like Pynchon's Tyrone Slothrop in the Casino Hermann Goering, you find yourself "alone with the paraphernalia of an order whose presence among the ordinary debris of waking [you have] only lately begun to suspect" (Pynchon 1973, GR 202)?

I want not merely to suggest that K.'s arrest ushers us into the postmodern but to propose as well that the textual relation between the Proust citation and the rest of *The Trial* is itself an emblem of the postmodern—or, more precisely, an emblem of those features of postmodernism that I emphasize below in reading *Gravity's Rainbow*. It is not as if the "postmodern," in my usage, denotes something simply different from the "modern," a breaking point at which we abruptly stop asking about selves and epistemologies and begin asking about power, differentially produced subjects, and social constructionism; rather, I ask that we retrieve both moments of K.'s interrogation, the text and that which was deleted from the text, in order that we might consider that one significant feature of postmodernism both transmits and delimits (marginalizes by marking the social, historical, political limits of) the modern. Again, this does not mean that the postmodern necessarily supersedes the modern, or moves beyond it in some progressive way. The relation between the two is, I hope, more tangled than that. I want to read "postmodernism" with less emphasis on the dismissive connotations of the prefix (after the modern, we have put the modern behind us for good) and more on the presence of the name-within-the-name. As Jauss argues, literary works "that evoke the reader's horizon of expectations, formed by a convention of genre, style, or form, only in order to destroy it step by step" (1982b, 24), such as *Don Quixote*, are especially fascinating for a hermeneutics of reception because they operate precisely to include and delimit previous models of literary production and consumption. *The Trial* and *Gravity's Rainbow* are *post-modern* works in this sense, for they stage postmodernism not as period or theme but as a cultural practice that exists alongside resid-ual practices (modernism among them) and, as well, emergent prac-tices we cannot yet describe.

In other words, we retain today not only the artifacts of "modern-ism" as classic texts but modernist ways of reading as well—as has been argued by a number of Pynchon's critics, including those who go on to deliver what I would consider thoroughly modernist rendi-tions of Pynchon. For instance, my argument that Pynchon lures us into modernist ways of reading only to defeat them is very close to Brian McHale's, all the more so because McHale argues that mod-ernist "pattern-making and pattern-interpreting"—a kind of Iserian gap-filling, in which readers fill in the narrative blanks—is eventu-ally futile in *Gravity's Rainbow* (1979, 88, 106). But McHale's distinc-tion between modernism and postmodernism rests entirely on a rigid division between epistemological (modernist) and ontological (postmodernist) unreliability (90–91). This is, for me, an unconvinc-ing criterion for determining why modernist gap-filling is ineffectual in *Gravity's Rainbow*, for such a distinction seems to construe differ-ences in degree (uncertainty number one and uncertainty number two) as differences in kind, and it leads only to the conclusion that we simply don't know what really happens in *Gravity's Rainbow*.[2]

Another modernist postmodernism can be found in Edward Men-delson's "Gravity's Encyclopedia," which offers a description of power and postmodernism more congenial to mine (1976, 178–83) but places overwhelming emphasis on the status of *Gravity's Rainbow* as a member of an outlaw genre of narratives that Mendelson calls "encyclopedic": "Encyclopedic narratives begin their history from a position *outside* the culture whose literary focus they become; they

[2]McHale's argument here is but the germ of his general thesis, later developed at length, that "postmodernist fiction differs from modernist fiction just as a poetics dominated by ontological issues differs from one dominated by epistemological is-sues" (1987, xii). On a related note, Lance Olsen assumes a homology among the "fantastic," the avant, deconstruction, and the postmodern: Derrida and fantasy, we hear, "interrogate all we take for granted about language and experience, giving these no more than a shifting and provisional status" (Olsen 1986, 76). See also Schaub's attempt (1981a, 3–20) to construe Pynchon's "spatialization of narrative time"—that is, spatial form—as the literary enactment of Einsteinian four-dimensional spacetime.

only gradually find a secure place in a national or critical order. . . .
To an extent unknown among other works that have become cultural monuments, encyclopedic narratives begin their career *ille-
gally*" (172). These are residually (and problematically) modernist notions of culture, reminiscent in striking ways of Karl Shapiro's
conviction, in re Tolson, that "all great poetry comes from the bottom." Mendelson's essay is thus at its weakest when it attempts to
distinguish the real "outside" from fake "outsides" as the basis of
the authority and "special cultural position" of putatively authentic
encyclopedias, as opposed to "near-" and "mock-encyclopedias"
(161–64).

But if modernism and postmodernism are not to be clearly distinguished and counterposed, if they are something more like overlapping "structures of feeling," then we must have not only the possibility of reading postmodern works in modernist ways but also the
possibility of reading in a postmodern fashion artifacts not "in themselves" postmodern. If this is the case, then postmodern reading
may involve both including and erasing (but not fully—working
with a palimpsest) all that is "not postmodern" within a postmodern
critical practice—as when, in Barthes's *S/Z*, Balzac's *Sarrasine* is both
preserved (like Kafka's deletion of Proust, at the back of the book)
and rewritten as the plural text in a random play of codes. McHale
too argues as much, deploying "periodicity" as something more
than a simple matter of chronology: "We can conceive of period-
models in literary history as specific sets or repertoires of pattern-
making and pattern-interpreting operations which readers must
undertake in order to render texts intelligible" (1979, 88). Such "repertoires," of course, do not suddenly die out to clear the way for
new "period-models"; we may nevertheless describe "periods" in
terms of their unprecedented or intellectually dominant conventions
and operations, and suggest, à la Raymond Williams or H. R. Jauss,
that periods can be cross-sectioned to reveal overlapping modes of
textual production and consumption.

To take a celebrated neo-Marxist model as analogy, Fredric Jameson's negotiation of synchrony, diachrony, and mediation yields
dehomologized periods such as "late capitalism, in which all the earlier modes of production in one way or another structurally coexist"
(1981, 100). Such cross-sectioning is not a blurring beyond recognition of period boundaries, for just as late capitalism can be distinguished from earlier capitalisms especially by its multinational structure, its welfare apparatus, and its reconfiguration of information as
commodity, so too is postmodernism distinctively marked by its

feminisms, new historicisms, and some of its poststructuralisms—as well as by late capitalism itself, as Jameson would argue, or by anti-essentialist constructions of identity politics, whether forged by the Birmingham Centre for Cultural Studies or by Queer Nation. Modernism, by contrast, may be remarked by varieties of formalism (Russian or Fryean) which, like Freud and Marx and the modern discursive practices they founded, are still available to postmodern readers—just as modes of modernist-industrial capital and the modernist formation of disciplines and professions are still with us in various locations. Jameson himself, of all people, may be dissatisfied with another critic's ability to make Balzac "stand for unenlightened representationality when you are concerned to bring out everything that is 'textual' and modern in Flaubert" or to "rewrite Balzac as Philippe Sollers, as sheer text and *écriture*" (18); yet his rhetorical sally here, launched against what he takes to be Barthes's irresponsible ahistoricism, serves to obscure the possibility that one and another Balzac may simply be the results of two coexisting and overlapping modes of textual production, premodernist (unenlightened, representational Balzac) and postmodernist (Balzac in the play of codes).

The point for us is that although we postmodern readers may have reading practices that vary significantly from those of "modern" readers, many "modern" reading practices persist, and these in turn condition our various options for construing the ostensibly distinctive edge of postmodernism.[3] Probably the most crucial impetus to construing postmodernism in terms of this dual process of inclusion and revision, however, is postmodernism's confusion or erasure of the very distinction between consumption and production.

[3]For salient examples of postmodern readings of modernist novels, see Bruce Robbins (1983, 229–31) on the opening of Henry Roth's *Call It Sleep*; and Karen Lawrence's quasi-Wittgensteinian reading (1981, 128–38) of Joyce's "Oxen of the Sun." Contrast Lawrence with Edward Mendelson, who juxtaposes Joyce's "Oxen" to Pynchon's New Turkic Alphabet (NTA) in order to demonstrate the difference between modern and postmodern treatments of language: "Unlike the language of Joyce's 'Oxen of the Sun,' the NTA does not develop according to an organic model, but is shaped deliberately by the forces of government, forces which are themselves ultimately directed and initiated by the cartels which organize the book's secular world" (1976, 168). The option of reading Joyce's "Oxen" languages as either organic or contingent corresponds, on my reading, to the option of reading them in modernist or postmodernist frameworks. Likewise, one could rescue *The Trial* from my postmodern appropriation of it by relating it to the most existentialist moments of Heidegger's *Being and Time*, especially the discussion of Being-guilty (§§ 58–60), and claiming that K.'s arrest has nothing to do with "power" (in Pynchon's sense) at all, and everything to do with an individual subject's Being-toward-death.

Andreas Huyssen notes in a brief but engrossing aside that "there seem to be fairly obvious homologies between [the] modernist insistence on purity and autonomy in art . . . and Marx's privileging of production over consumption" (1986, 55); once more taking Huyssen as my cue, I might add that even so-called "consumer capitalism," as a postmodernism, troubles the consumption/production distinction as well, insofar as consumption has become for late capitalism itself a kind of production (and notoriously so in the merger-mad United States of the 1980s). Obviously, the same can be said for recent critical theory, especially reception theory, which, more than any other "movement" save perhaps Cultural Studies, maintains that texts are produced only by means of their continued consumption.

The leading edge of my attempt to distinguish modernism and postmodernism, then, is to claim that postmodernism, in economics as in literary theory, attends primarily to *transmission and replication* rather than to either side of the dyad of production and consumption. Because, in this model, "transmission" is simultaneously production and consumption (Kafka/Proust, Barthes/Balzac), the distinction between the two becomes inapposite, and the status of the originary artifact (the thing-as-such that was originally "produced" prior to any replication) is accordingly deemphasized if not actually unrecoverable.[4] But if "transmission" is my model, as it will be for much of my reading of *Gravity's Rainbow*, then I need also to claim that the apparatus for making such a distinction between modernism and postmodernism is thereby itself open to question, inasmuch as postmodernism must also be able, as I argued above, to transmit and replicate residual forms of modernism as well. Likewise, if we rest our cultural descriptions on a postmodernism that challenges binary opposition, we surely cannot do so in a way that reinscribes a binary opposition between modernism and postmodernism—just as a properly Kuhnian account of postmodern science cannot reinscribe a teleology wherein the postmodern understanding of the history of science is verifiably and incrementally superior to the bad, modern, positivist understanding of the history of science.

It may be, then, that such a "definition" of postmodernism is not a definition at all. Besides, after all, the word "postmodern" has been bruited about for over four decades now—by art critics as by

---

[4]I am, nevertheless, obliged to note that this idea is not original with me; for an account of "transmission" as the "precession of simulacra," see Baudrillard 1983; for "transmission" in terms of grafting and iterability, see Derrida 1988.

Spy magazine and real estate agents—and we have reached the point at which its referent has been so unclear and so unstable for so long that it has become a strange kind of essentially contested term—one that many are tired of contesting.[5] By now, it should be clear, one man's postmodernism is another woman's poison.[6] We seem to be beyond all hope of floating a unified field theory of the postmodern, some happily protean formation that would account with equal grace and perspicacity Joseph Beuys, Laurie Anderson, Philip Johnson, MTV, Public Enemy, electronic mail, junk bond financing, the municipal layout of Houston, Reaganism, Thatcherism, and the career of Thomas Pynchon.

The importance of Public Enemy to my understanding of postmodernism should not go understated, however: *sampling*, especially as practiced by the dexterous pillagers of PE's production team, the "Bomb Squad" (Hank and Keith Shocklee, Eric Sadler, and Chuck D), is itself a pointed contestation of the distinction between consumption and production, as the music industry's copyright lawyers have energetically affirmed—and as PE makes explicit in songs that defend sampling, such as "Caught, Can I Get a Witness?" (a song which itself invokes a familiar African-American rhetorical trope and rephrases, inter alia, the guitar work on Isaac Hayes's "Shaft"). That is, the electronic technology necessary to sampling's transmissions and radical recontextualizations of sound co-exists alongside a much older African oral form, as rappers transmit the residual cultural function of the griot with a postmodern signifying difference. Hip-hop's collocation of postmodern studio technology and premodern oral culture is in this sense, I suggest, one salient example of postmodernism's transmissions of antecedent cultural artifacts in postmechanical context, an example similar to but hardly cited as often as Philip Johnson's Chippendale AT&T building—or

[5]C. Barry Chabot, for instance, argues that we may well be better off without theories of postmodernism altogether, for their very proliferation suggests their value; in fact, Chabot concludes that the word "postmodern" itself is "an empty marker" (1988, 19). I cannot agree with so extended a claim (I am obviously using the term as if it *could* mean something), but I do concede that the volume of our current descriptions of postmodernism makes it look almost as if we were dealing in Weimar currency. More striking still is Ihab Hassan's nonresponse to Chabot, which concludes: "I have already written enough of these matters, and like Professor Chabot, though not for his reasons, I would let postmodernism rest" (1988, 22).

[6]This point hardly needs to be footnoted in 1992, but nine years ago, Craig Owens was one of the first men to argue it at length, and to charge his fellow theorists of postmodernism with systematic masculinist oversight (1983). For a stark opposition between postmodernism and feminism (on the grounds that the former has no theory of agency), see Hutcheon 1989.

Thomas Pynchon's hallucinatory historical novels. Hip-hop's closest literary analogue is perhaps Reed's *Mumbo Jumbo*, which itself provides extraordinarily fertile links with sampling, African-American musical and verbal forms, and hallucinatory historical novels.

But hip-hop and *Mumbo Jumbo* are only Afrocentric aspects of postmodernism—admittedly, aspects that usually go overlooked, just as the Harlem Renaissance usually gets dropped out of histories of American modernism, and just as Anglo-American synopses of "the Jazz Age" tend to be more familiar with *The Great Gatsby* than with the technical innovations of Louis Armstrong or Fletcher Henderson. Still, to remind ourselves of African-American contributions to postmodernism is perhaps to be more pluralist than revisionist, especially since we have begun to suspect that postmodernism *is* its diversity, its resistance to critical description. Certainly, as I argue below in regard to Pynchon's pornographies, it is hard to imagine a description of postmodernism that does not rely on the ideas of profusion, polyglossia, and polymorphous diversity.

Nonetheless, it is one thing to recognize postmodernism's diversity and another thing to accede to all its possible manifestations (including its various descriptions). Although I myself do not want to float a unified field theory of postmodernism, any more than I wanted to point out all the possible characteristics of "modernism" in my discussion of Melvin Tolson, I do want to mark off in advance postmodernisms with which mine will have nothing to do—postmodernisms that themselves derive from the impoverished sense of literary "theory" which Bruce Robbins describes as the result of "the invidious slide from theory to European theory (excluding American roads not taken like C. S. Peirce and Kenneth Burke) to French theory (excluding the "Critical Theory" of the Frankfurt School, among other things) to Derrida, who is then held to represent the politics of the whole" (1987, 6). "Postmodernism" in such formulations usually refers to self-referential, self-enclosed, self-deconstructing texts which—like Derrida—are then taken to represent the politics of the whole, in order that they may be celebrated or deplored. Hence the humanist complaint of a Reginald Gibbons, for whom

> the academic prizing of postmodern fiction, like that fiction itself, is tied, it seems, to a preference for the belief that fiction, like poetry in Auden's famous words, makes nothing happen, can make only itself happen. . . .
> This fashion carries with it the implication that poetry and fiction not

only make very little, if not nothing, happen, but *shouldn't* make anything happen, because to have that power of influence on human feeling and thought violates the current critical shibboleths of the purity
and self-referentiality of art and the futility of language. (1985, 23–24)

It would be easy to complain in return that Gibbons has misunderstood both postmodernism and poststructuralism, that he has reduced them both to cartoon caricatures of deconstruction and has
made far too easy an equation of the two. But this countercharge is
less easily made when we realize that Gibbons's gesture is not exclusively part of the body language of the humanist reactionary; rather,
the problem with this version of "postmodernism" stems from its
supporters as much as from its attackers, both of whom conceive
postmodernism in dangerously homogeneous ways. And because
one of these supporters, Allen Thiher, bases his case as I do mine on
the figure of Kafka (of whose "legacy" Pynchon is a part), I single
him out for discussion:

Language is a system of infinite self-enclosed reference. There is no
transcendental horizon lying beyond this alienated *logos* that mirrors
only itself. Hyper-realism [here, specifically, Peter Handke's *The Goalie's
Anxiety at the Penalty Kick*] is, in fact, a form of despair about the way
even the most ordinary language can reveal nothing. . . .
    [Kafka's] work represents in fact a rupture with modernism at the
very moment Joyce and Proust were achieving their greatest works.
This rupture seems most apparent when we consider how Kafka came
to base his writing on what one might call a new mode of grounding
literary discourse: the self-designating mode that, as we have seen in
Robbe-Grillet, Pynchon, and Handke, puts constantly into question its
own quest for representation, revelation, and meaning. What seems
most immediately important in this respect is that Kafka's fictions turn
back upon themselves as forms of auto-representation, grounding
themselves as mirrors of their own functioning, or, more precisely, designating their own dysfunctional nature. To paraphrase received critical
opinion about Kafka, it is not that his works are not reflections of an
absurd world in which the emptiness left by the death of God has been
filled in by the creation of a proliferating bureaucracy. The power of
Kafka's work, rather, lies in its sabotaging any such clear statement
about it; it lies in the work's undermining any binary system of reference beyond the text itself. These works refuse the grounding one
needs in order to generate sense, as they designate, often in par-
odistically fragmented ways, how the fictions these works contain can
only mirror themselves as they attempt to represent a world. (1980, 546)

Since I agree that Kafka's work represents a rupture with modernism during the high-water mark of modernism, I cannot help responding to Thiher: his Kafka and mine would not so much as recognize each other, and his hermetically sealed "Pynchon" is anathema to my "Pynchon," whose texts insist (in *V.* as well as in *Gravity's Rainbow*) on bringing to light the global ramifications of modernization (economic, imperial) as well as the political unconscious of modernism—as in this interpretation of the Germans' genocidal campaign against the Herero in the Südwestafrika of 1904, which we might read alongside *Heart of Darkness*, especially Marlow's admiration for Kurtz[7] as a man who had had "something to say" (Conrad 1901, 148):

> Colonies are the outhouses of the European soul, where a fellow can let his pants down and relax, enjoy the smell of his own shit. Where he can fall on his slender prey roaring as loud as he feels like, and guzzle her blood with open joy. Eh? Where he can just wallow and rut and let himself go in a softness, a receptive darkness of limbs, of hair as woolly as the hair on his own forbidden genitals . . . with no harm done to the Metropolis, nothing to soil those cathedrals, white marble statues, noble thoughts. (*GR* 317)

One can hardly rebut Thiher by claiming that Pynchon and deconstruction have nothing to do with each other; still, it is one thing to note that *Gravity's Rainbow* deconstructs the hierarchical duality of cause and effect by appealing to the V-2 strikes on London and the related mystery of Slothrop's erections, and another thing entirely to claim that the fictions contained in *Gravity's Rainbow* mirror only themselves. For it is not clear how works can be "grounded" in a mode that refuses the "grounding one needs in order to generate sense"; more than this, I question the efficacy and purpose of reading Kafka—and Pynchon—so as to sabotage "any such clear statement" except the statement that they are infinitely self-enclosed and self-referential. As we will see in the following chapter, Thiher is not

---

[7]Thomas Moore has also called attention to this passage in the context of Pynchon's revisions of modernism, but I would not emphasize, as Moore does, Pynchon's good cheer: "Pynchon's post-colonialist and post-Freudian vantage and more active sense of humor enable him cheerfully to play with Conrad's solemn, guilt-haunted equation between European imperializing and an evil plunge out of rational 'civilized' consciousness" (1987, 22–23). Rather, I would say that Pynchon restores to *Heart of Darkness* the importance of the severed heads that surround Kurtz's house, whereas Conrad's story displaces the evil of genocide onto the evil of lying.

alone in reading Pynchon's work as a mass of mutually undercutting ambiguities, as if *Gravity's Rainbow* were a kind of 760-page cold pastoral; nor is he alone in characterizing "postmodernism" in such a way as to underwrite (not "undermine") his reading of "distinctively postmodern" works. For insofar as his own argument is exempt from the general collapse of "grounds," to that extent is he able to set out a kind of "period-function" by which Pynchon (as uniquely representative American avatar of this self-annihilating postmodernism) can be construed to reveal nothing.

Thiher proceeds, for the most part, by finding the *mise en abyme* which, doubling the text, clinches its self-referentiality. His example, from *The Crying of Lot 49*, is "*The Courier's Tragedy*, a defective version of which reveals Trystero, an alternative communication system that may or may not exist today in America. The play is something of a dysfunctional double for the novel itself, and in this respect Pynchon's novel as a parodistic text designates its own failure to communicate while deconstructing the notion of revelation itself" (545). This is prima facie problematic—the existence of a "double for the novel itself" within the novel does not in itself confirm a "failure to communicate"—but it is important to my present excursus on the postmodern for what it misses: *The Courier's Tragedy* exists in a number of versions (none of which can safely be called "defective"), and much of Oedipa's quest is given over to sorting among the various cultural transmissions of the cryptic closing lines of the fourth act, "No hallowed skein of stars can ward, I trow, / Who's once been set his tryst with Trystero" (Pynchon 1966, *C* 75). The wholesale and guaranteed failure of communication is not at issue here; the dependence of communication on various means of cultural transmission *is*.

The means of transmission are particularly crucial to Oedipa's and Metzger's viewing of *Cashiered* (a movie in which Metzger had starred as child actor), for apparently the TV station showing the movie confuses the sequence of reels. But Metzger's running commentary on *Cashiered* challenges also a sequence of reals, in a way that nicely dramatizes postmodernism's indifference to the originary artifact of production. The film is a bizarre World War I drama involving a father, son, and dog whose submarine surreptitiously attacks the Turkish fleet in the Sea of Marmara, and at one point Metzger explains to Oedipa how the submarine gets through the net the Germans have strung through the Narrows: our heroes' enemies, he says,

"built a gate in [the net], so German U-boats could get through to attack
the British fleet. All our E class subs simply used that gate."
    "How do you know that?"
    "Wasn't I there?" (C 32)

A few pages later, he describes the battle with the Turkish forces: "'I
know this part,' Metzger told her, his eyes squeezed shut, head
away from the set. 'For fifty yards out the sea was red with blood.
They don't show that'" (C 36).

Metzger's eerily Reaganesque confusion of war movies with real
"theaters" of war obviously questions the ontological status of film
as realist representation, precisely by insisting so absurdly on *Cashiered* as *verité* documentary; there is something eerie, too, in
Metzger's appearance in a fictional California in the mid-1960s at the
end of Reagan's first term as governor, for Metzger, like Reagan, is
an ex-actor—worse yet, an ex-actor turned lawyer who now denies
the distinction between lawyers and actors, especially since his
friend Manny DiPresso, an ex-lawyer turned actor, is going to portray Metzger in a TV series "based loosely on my career" (C 33). Was
the sea really red with blood, and did Metzger somehow create Reagan's presidency? As we will see again in *Gravity's Rainbow*'s depiction of the relation between the Schwarzkommando and film, it is
thoroughly unclear here, in the novel and in Reagan's California (or
America), whether there is any locatable distinction between the cultural product "in itself" (as a form of representation) and the product's manifestations ("real" and "fictive"). In *Cashiered* as in *The Crying of Lot 49*, I suggest, the distinction between production and
consumption, artifact and reproduction, is quite thoroughly under-
mined, and this undermining has little to do with Thiher's dysfunctional house of mirrors.

For the section that follows, however, the most important operative terms of my vocabulary of postmodernism will be "preterition"
and "paranoia." Again, these are not keywords in a unified field
theory; they are simply features I want to bring to the fore for now,
just as I wanted earlier to emphasize primarily the hostility of modernism to mass culture and the hierarchical relation of writing to
speech in modernist poetry. All other critical disputes aside, it is
nearly axiomatic by now that postmodernism can be distinguished
from modernism precisely by its reconfiguration of the relation between high and mass cultures; we should have no trouble distinguishing Pynchon from Tolson in this respect, or distinguishing
Gravity's Rainbow from *Harlem Gallery* in the latter's insistence on a

practice of avant-garde production which itself secures its own consumption by "vertical" audiences. Fittingly, Pynchon's reconfiguration of high/low and production/consumption shows up also in his various seriocomic confusions of speech and writing, neither of which is prior to the other in *Gravity's Rainbow*.[8] In one notable example, Mitchell Prettyplace, the author of "the definitive 18-volume study of *King Kong*," bases his authoritative text on the thesis "Yeah, well, you know, he *did* love her, folks" (*GR* 275). And in another "classic study," a biochemical account of the drug Oneirine, we may read a similar peculiarity of tone: "'It is experienced,' writes Shetzline in his classic study, 'in a subjective sense... uh... well. Put it this way. It's like stuffing wedges of silver sponge, *right, into,* your brain!'" (*GR* 389).[9]

But whatever our delineations of postmodernism in Pynchon, the significance of "preterition" and "paranoia" remains crucial, not only as they are concerns and themes of postmodern literature but as they pertain to the cultural positions and practices of professional literary critics. I briefly mentioned the current critical concern with preterition in the preceding chapter (in characterizing canon revision as an exploration of the voices and discourses of the cultural preterite), and I return to it below. First, however, I want to describe "paranoia" so that we may understand better its applicability both to Pynchon and to the functions of criticism at the present time.

Practices of Criticism and Parables of Culture

As every Pynchon critic knows, *Gravity's Rainbow* describes "paranoia" as "the onset, the leading edge, of the discovery that *everything is connected*, everything in the Creation" (*GR* 703); but nearly every Pynchon critic has taken this to mean that "paranoia" designates a state of interpretive certainty that accounts for the relative place of everything within the connection, the status of the connection, and the reliability of the "discovery"—like Pointsman's behaviorist dream of showing "the stone determinacy of everything, of every soul" (*GR* 86). But Pynchonian paranoia carries with it no guarantees about any of these things; one may "discover" connect-

---

[8]McHoul and Wills provide what is by far the best discussion of speech and writing(s) in *Gravity's Rainbow*, together with a compendium of Pynchonian citations, mentions, and uses of the materiality of signs (1990, 33–37, 52–53).

[9]I have reproduced Pynchon's suspension points without spaces (...); my own deletions from Pynchon's text are signified by the usual points of ellipsis.

edness of a kind without having any idea of *how* things are connected, or whether the connectedness one sees simply masks a deeper, more insidious and opaque kind of connectedness. It makes no sense, therefore, to write that "paranoia is preferable to uncertainty" in Pynchon's fiction (Slade 1977, 31), because paranoia *is* uncertainty; as Pynchon elsewhere defines it, it is the "Puritan reflex of seeking other orders behind the visible" (*GR* 188). Thus, to the paranoid, things may be connected in some obscure way; but once that obscure way has itself been made visible, it too is subject to the paranoid suspicion of further orders behind the (newly) visible.

This is the core of Leo Bersani's recent reading of *Gravity's Rainbow*, which appears to be the best discussion of Pynchonian paranoia to date. Taking off from Enzian's suspicion that the Zone's "Real Text" is not the rocket at all, but rather some heretofore incomprehensible "distribution networks we were never taught, routes of power our teachers never imagined, or were encouraged to avoid" (*GR* 521), Bersani writes:

> *Is* the rocket the real Text? This question is an urgent one not only for Pynchon's characters but also for us. What if, as Enzian suggests, the rocket-text seduced us and blinded us to an even more important text, something in the work that it is even more necessary to read correctly than the rocket, something that would be the *real key* to its sense? . . . The rocket and the war for which it was built are just "cover-ups," a "spectacle" or "diversion" from "the true war," which is "a celebration of markets" and whose "real business . . . is buying and selling" [*GR* 105]. But if something like international cartels is the real text that the paranoid imagination should be reading, then we, like Enzian, are being deceived by all the prime time and space being given to the rocket. We can't resolve the issue simply by saying that Pynchon's "real" subject is how his characters are victimized by that deception, and that in order to read *that* text the reader has to be set straight about the true center of historical power. For in fact the presumed real historical text is as obscure to us as it is to Enzian. (1989, 105–6)

When, therefore, we combine Pynchon's two definitions of paranoia (as the edge of the discovery that everything is connected; as the reflex of seeking other orders behind the visible), the result is an oscillation between interpretive certainty and radical doubt over the aims and principles of interpretation, consequent on what Bersani calls the "intuition" of "an *invisible interconnectedness*" (102). Translated into critical practice, this formulation suggests not that one kind or another kind of interpretation is "paranoid" but that *all* in-

terpretation involves the paranoid suspicion that the Text can be repeated on different (hidden) discursive registers, which yields in
turn a perpetual uncertainty as to the locus of the "real" Text. Mere
system building, in and of itself, fails to constitute or exhaust paranoia, regardless of what the reader seeks to discover, whether this
be the irony, paradox, and ambiguity that make up the poetic ut-
terance, the material ground of cultural production, the symbolic
structural resolution of real social contradiction, the inscription of
gender difference, the power that produces the subversion it contains, or what-have-you. Neither are the most "systematic" of these
critical inquiries necessarily the most "paranoid," as if one could escape paranoia by turning against method.

It is quite otherwise: to be a paranoid critic in a postmodern era
(and it is well to remember here that the proliferation of theory is
itself a postmodern phenomenon) is not to subscribe to one mode of
criticism or another but, on the contrary, to be unsure as to the status of what Fredric Jameson (1981) calls an "untranscendable horizon": unsure as to whether that "horizon" is truly untranscendable,
able to under- and rewrite all other possible interpretive possibilities, or whether that horizon leaves other orders obscure or invisible, thereby obscuring or missing the Real Text. Readers who believe they have found the interpretive key, the definitive hidden
structure, the true master *récit*—such readers have ceased to be
paranoids; whereas a New Critic, for example, could be certain that
the Real Text was simply the text before him or her on the page,
truly paranoid critics can never be certain that the real text does not
lie elsewhere—in the structures of race, class, gender, sexual orientation, binary opposition, the de(con)struction of binary opposition, historical thick description, or someplace else. Critical paranoia, in other words, is simply interpretation without transcendental
grounds, without agreed-upon stopping points—which is to say,
the kind of interpretation with which contemporary professional
critics profess to be familiar.

Just as preterition may be as much a concern of critics as of the
writers (elect and preterite) whom critics discuss, so too, then, may
paranoia be as much a condition of criticism and theory as a phenomenon made available for criticism and theory by "postmodern"
texts and their characteristics. But by the same token, "preterition"
is as badly in need of definition as is paranoia. As I am employing
the term in relation to critical practice, our retrieval and reinscription
(in Tony Bennett's sense) of the "preterite" does not stop at making
the marginal central and vice versa—indeed, does not so much as

aim at this, as if literary history could be rewritten from the perspective of the vanquished simply by substituting "The Yellow Wallpaper" or *Black Elk Speaks* for *The Ambassadors* in all survey courses of American literature. Rather, as I suggested in Chapter 3, a revisionist understanding of preterition distinguishes itself from mere repetition-with-a-difference of the Romantic/modernist valorization of the "marginal" (the visionary, the exile) by seeking to hold in abeyance, or to undermine, the various bases for the canonical distinction between preterite and elect. One highly successful revisionist strategy has thus sought to reformulate this critical difference entirely, by supplanting the binaries high/low, literary/nonliterary, canonical/apocryphal with something for which such distinctions are inapposite, as in Jane Tompkins's (1985) or Cary Nelson's (1989) sense of "cultural work."[10]

Such a strategy emphatically does not claim that all texts are created equal, as its more indiscriminate critics have charged. On the contrary, re-vision of preterite texts always acknowledges that some texts are "better" than others—but points out also the vast variety of purposes that texts and critics can conceivably serve. We may easily contrast this position with Northrop Frye's famous universalist definition of the canonical: "Nearly every civilization," writes Frye, "has, in its stock of traditional myths, a particular group which is thought of as more serious, more authoritative, more educational and closer to fact and truth than the rest. . . . This distinction of canonical and apocryphal myth, which can be found even in primitive societies, gives to the former group a particular thematic importance" (1957, 54). As long as one maintains this distinction between the canonical and the apocryphal, maintaining also that this distinction is not simply contingent on the material instances of cultural reproduction, then one can maintain further that "the critic will find soon, and constantly, that Milton is a more rewarding and suggestive poet to work with than Blackmore. But the more obvious this becomes, the less time he will want to waste in belaboring the point" (Frye, 1957, 25). If however one works with a paradigm under which Blackmore is as "rewarding" as Milton—say, an inquiry

[10]The phrase is not confined to Tompkins and Nelson, but their own cultural work in the investigation of "cultural work" has been especially important to mine. Tompkins's sense is that texts "offer powerful examples of the way a culture thinks about itself, articulating and proposing solutions for the problems that shape a particular historical moment" (1985, xi); Nelson uses the term in order to argue that throughout the history of American modernism, "traditional forms continued to do vital cultural work" (1989, 23).

into the sociology of publishing and reception in the late seventeenth century—then the basis for the canon/apocrypha distinction collapses as well.[11]

Critical reinscription of the preterite may thus simply follow from the expansion of criticism's functions; or it may proceed also in the manner of Fredric Jameson, claiming that canon revision is a weapon in the struggle for cultural dialogism: "Since by definition the cultural monuments and masterworks that have survived tend necessarily to perpetuate only a single voice in this class dialogue, the voice of a hegemonic class, they cannot be properly assigned their relational place in a dialogical system without the restoration or artificial reconstruction of the voice to which they were initially opposed, a voice for the most part stifled and reduced to silence, marginalized" (1981, 85).[12] Jameson's formulation reveals quite clearly the challenge posed by the discourse of preterition. Like my description of canon revision in Chapter 1, Jamesonian revision is not a liberal affair of taking the proper affirmative action toward "underrepresented" groups which will guarantee healthy pluralism, for

> the affirmation of such nonhegemonic cultural voices remains ineffective if it is limited to the merely "sociological" perspective of the pluralistic rediscovery of other isolated social groups: only an ultimate rewriting of these utterances in terms of their essentially polemic and subversive strategies restores them to their proper place in the dialogical system of the social classes. . . .
>
> Moreover, the stress on the dialogical then allows us to reread or rewrite the hegemonic forms themselves; they also can be grasped as a process of the reappropriation and neutralization, the cooptation and class transformation, the cultural universalization, of forms which origi-

[11]One might also note, in elaborating a taxonomy of "cultural use," that Frye's citation of serious, authoritative, educational, and truthful myths may actually be an invocation of four different kinds of cultural use, which no myth can serve equally well. The tale of the three little pigs is among Americans' more central educational myths, but it is not very well described as serious, authoritative, or close to fact; *Paradise Lost* is serious and educational, but it is "authoritative" and "closer to fact and truth" only for a very few (Arminist or Subordinationist) Christians; and *Tarzan* is a problem by any standard.

[12]Here Jameson's cagey "restoration *or* artificial reconstruction" ducks some important hermeneutical issues (how do we know which one we're doing?) but offers the benefit of dodging also the problematic category of "truth about the culture" which Lillian Robinson proposes (see 1985, esp. 111–12, and the false dichotomy between "excellence" and "cultural history"). The escape clause of "artificial reconstruction," in other words, allows for the description of "*revisionary* truth[s] about the culture," and I take this to have a significant advantage over Robinson's own problematic hermeneutics, insofar as it allows us to intervene in and recast the "truth" that ours has generally been a monologic, sexist culture.

nally expressed the situation of "popular," subordinate, or dominated groups. (1981, 86)

Gravity's Rainbow exhibits both approaches to preterition, at times reappropriating preterite histories for the purpose of historical "re-dialogization," elsewhere suggesting the irrelevance or self-decon-struction of the dichotomy between preterite and elect. In this it may differ markedly from *The Crying of Lot 49*, in which America's pret-erite seem to be unproblematically valorized as the possible carriers of "a real alternative to the exitlessness, to the absence of surprise to life, that harrows the head of everybody American you know" (C 170) and whose voices Oedipa (and we) learn to hear as those of "Americans speaking their language carefully, scholarly, as if they were in exile from somewhere else invisible yet congruent with the cheered land she lived in" (C 180). By contrast, *Gravity's Rainbow's* "Zone-Hereros" are a preterite race whose status is anything but unproblematic. For one thing, their present preterition consists in part in not having been exterminated by General Lothar von Trotha in 1904–6; as Enzian tells Slothrop, the remaining Hereros, suffering as they are from survivor syndrome, may constitute something like a metapreterite, a subgroup of those "passed over" within a larger group of the lost: "We have a word that we whisper, a mantra for times that threaten to be bad. Mba-kayere. You may find that it will work for you. Mba-kayere. It means 'I am passed over.' To those of us who survived von Trotha, it also means that we have learned to stand outside our history and watch it, without feeling too much. A little schizoid" (GR 362). Moreover, Josef Ombindi's splinter group, the Otukungura or Empty Ones, appear to be a metametapreterite: "Revolutionaries of the Zero, they mean to carry on what began among the old Hereros after the 1904 rebellion failed. They want a negative birth rate. The program is racial suicide. They would finish the extermination the Germans began in 1904" (GR 317).

The Herero, it seems, cannot bear the promise of preterite post-war revelation seemingly held out by *Lot 49*'s alien populations, whose rebellion consists of "a calculated withdrawal, from the life of the Republic, from its machinery" (C 124).[13] However, they do per-

---

[13]Stanley Aronowitz distinguishes Baudrillard from Herbert Marcuse on the charac-ter of "refusal": "The refuseniks here are not the intellectuals who insist on the rele-vance of history, philosophy and art to a contemporary world which disdains high culture. On the contrary, it is those who withdraw their participation from society, who engage in a politics of anti-politics and ask only to be freed from its obligations, obligations that are, in any case, simulacra of citizenship" (1987, 105). *The Crying of Lot*

form Jameson's function of allowing us to rewrite in yet one more way the hegemonic forms of twentieth-century history which are under attack always and everywhere in *Gravity's Rainbow* as "at best a conspiracy, not always among gentlemen, to defraud" (*GR* 164), and opposed to which are Pynchon's various apocryphal histories in which "the Germans-and-Japs story [is] only one, rather surrealistic version of the real War" (*GR* 645). The Herero version, in particular, casts new light on Europe's "reappropriation and neutralization" (Jameson) of Africa:

> They are a people now, Zone-Hereros, in exile for two generations from South-West Africa. . . . But only after 1933 did most of the present-day leadership arrive, as part of a scheme—never openly admitted by the Nazi party—for setting up black juntas, shadow-states for the eventual takeover of British and French colonies in black Africa, on the model of Germany's plan for the Maghreb. Südwest by then was a protectorate administered by the Union of South Africa, but the real power was still with the old German colonial families, and they cooperated. (*GR* 315)

Whether or not Pynchon's Counterforce wins in the end or is absorbed by the forces of control, or whether Pynchon himself "cares about" the preterite and the lost, are not relevant here; what is relevant is that Pynchon's revisionary, postwar paranoid politics fashions preterites within preterites, and in so doing constructs histories within History.

The novel abounds, as we know, with versions of the war we thought we won: for example, should we question whether there is "a real conversion factor between information and lives," a narrative voice responds:

> Well, strange to say, there is. Written down in the Manual, on file at the War Department. Don't forget the real business of the War is buying and selling. The murdering and the violence are self-policing, and can be entrusted to non-professionals. The mass nature of wartime death is useful in many ways. It serves as spectacle, as diversion from the real movements of the War. It provides raw material to be recorded into History, so that children may be taught History as sequences of violence, battle after battle, and be more prepared for the adult world. . . . The true war is a celebration of markets. (*GR* 105)

49's preterite are, in the sense mobilized by Aronowitz and Baudrillard, historical "agents" in their passivity, agents whose tracks can be read in such postmodern phenomena as the permanent crisis of public nonparticipation in American "elections."

This alternate "true war" (taking place elsewhere than in History) is a war in which the real historical agents are "outfit[s] like Shell, with no real country, no side in any war, no specific face or heritage" (*GR* 243). And though Bersani's reading conflates Enzian's reading of the Jamf Ölfabriken Werke with the foregoing passage on "celebration of markets," Enzian's suspicion about the Real Text actually suggests that cartels themselves may distract us from other histories. Perhaps, thinks Enzian, "the real crises were crises of allocation and priority, not among firms—it was only staged to look that way—but among the different Technologies, Plastics, Electronics, Aircraft, and their needs which are understood only by the ruling elite"; but perhaps, again, we do not know how *low* the conspiracy goes: "up here, on the surface, coal-tars, hydrogenation, synthesis were always phony, dummy functions to hide the real, *the planetary mission* yes perhaps centuries in the unrolling" (*GR* 521).

These are nonhegemonic cultural voices, to be sure, and their preterite "histories" are infinitely reinscribable. But more important, for my present purposes, are *Gravity's Rainbow*'s numerous refusals of the elect/preterite distinction. This is a novel, we will recall, which has itself been thoroughly celebrated in the language of the ideology of the avant-garde, often specifically for its violation of literary decorum; yet if *Gravity's Rainbow*, like Tolson's Hideho Heights and Bourdieu's working classes, refuses the refusal that distinguishes aesthetic dispositions from ordinary dispositions (which it surely does), then it would seem that *Gravity's Rainbow* makes irrelevant the canons of taste that guarantee the separation of the *avant* from the *garde*. For that matter, as William Slothrop argued to his fellow Puritans in what must be one of the New World's earliest deconstructions, the concept of Election paradoxically valorizes the Preterite as well:

He wrote a long tract about it presently, called *On Preterition*. It had to be published in England, and is among the first books to've been not only banned but also ceremonially burned in Boston. Nobody wanted to hear about all the Preterite, the many God passes over when he chooses a few for salvation. William argued holiness for these "second Sheep," without whom there'd be no elect. You can bet the Elect in Boston were pissed off about that. And it got worse. William felt that what Jesus was for the elect, Judas Iscariot was for the Preterite. Everything in the Creation has its equal and opposite counterpart. . . .

Could he have been the fork in the road America never took, the singular point she jumped the wrong way from? Suppose the Slothropite heresy had had the time to consolidate and prosper? Might there have been fewer crimes in the name of Jesus, and more mercy in the name of Judas Iscariot? (*GR* 555–56)

For contrast we may turn again to Proust, this time to Proust in his own words, whose miniparable of culture and society tends toward precisely the opposite end of Pynchon's. Whereas Swann once possessed "a sort of taste, of tact, so automatic in its operation that . . . if he read in a newspaper the names of the people who had been at a dinner-party, [he] could tell at once its exact degree of smartness, just as a man of letters, simply by reading a sentence, can estimate exactly the literary merit of its author" (1913, 265), his obsessive love for Odette becomes a cautionary tale on the evils of cultural relativism: "Having allowed the intellectual beliefs of his youth to languish, and his man-of-the-world scepticism having permeated them without his being aware of it, he felt (or at least he had felt for so long that he had fallen into the habit of saying) that the objects we admire have no absolute value in themselves, that the whole thing is a matter of period and class, is no more than a series of fashions, the most vulgar of which are worth just as much as those which are regarded as the most refined" (269).

Pynchon, by contrast, has no such Proustian agenda for preserving the artifact from its (mis)appropriation by the *canaille*, or for universalizing (and dehistoricizing) "taste" so as to marginalize the "vulgar." But neither does Pynchon simply reverse this formula, despite the insistent "vulgarity" of *Gravity's Rainbow* and its assortment of low-cultural artifacts like Plasticman, Marx Brothers movies, and King Kong. If therefore we translate Pynchon's idea of preterition as Proust translates Swann's loss of faculties of discrimination, then the cultural (though not the social) opposition between elect and preterite ceases to be a central concern: the novel becomes, to borrow Pointsman's Pavlovian terminology, "this transmarginal leap" where "ideas of the opposite have come together, and lost their oppositeness" (*GR* 50).

In this case, Gerhardt von Göll's characterization of elect and preterite requires our attention: as he advises Slothrop (he is referring to the displaced masses of postwar Europe—but the immediate context need not detain us here), "Be compassionate. But don't make up fantasies about them. Despise me, exalt them, but remember, we define each other. Elite and preterite, we move though a cosmic design of darkness and light" (*GR* 495). However, von Göll, a director and as patently contradictory a figure as Randolph Driblette, his *Lot 49* counterpart, takes his "cosmic design" of yin and yang to author-

ize the continued celebration of markets: "Consider honestly therefore, young man, which side you would rather be on. While they
suffer in perpetual shadows, it's... always—[breaking into song]—
bright days for the black mar-ket" (*GR* 495). Von Göll's is, if not the
wrong conclusion, at least an unsavory one. But more palatable
theses can be drawn from the refusal to exalt the preterite, such as
Andreas Huyssen's:

> From Madison Avenue's conscious exploitation of avantgardist pictorial
> strategies to postmodernism's uninhibited learning from Las Vegas
> there has been a plethora of strategic moves tending to destabilize the
> high/low opposition from within. Yet this opposition—usually de-
> scribed in terms of modernism vs. mass culture or avantgarde vs. cul-
> ture industry—has proven to be amazingly resilient. Such resilience
> may lead one to conclude that perhaps neither of the two combatants
> can do without the other, that their much heralded mutual exclusive-
> ness is really a sign of their secret interdependence. Seen in this light,
> mass culture indeed seems to be the repressed other of modernism, the
> family ghost rumbling in the cellar. Modernism, on the other hand,
> often chided by the left as the elitist, arrogant and mystifying master-
> code of bourgeois culture while demonized by the right as the Agent
> Orange of natural social cohesion, is the strawman desperately needed
> by the system to provide an aura of popular legitimation for the bless-
> ings of the culture industry. (1986, 16–17)

Alec McHoul and David Wills, in a fascinating series of readings-
within-readings, have argued that *Gravity's Rainbow* deconstructs the
distinction not only between elect and preterite but between "use
and mention, serious and parasitic, normal and citational" as well,
creating in place of these distinctions a "material typonomy" by
which "a material equivalence between the signifiers replaces a rhetorical difference between them" (1990, 53). Whereas Huyssen
would call *Gravity's Rainbow* "post-avantgarde," McHoul and Wills
call it "post-rhetorical," in that it "handles or plays with dualistic
differences such that they are overcome by making any dilemma's
dual aspects appear identical, these then producing, conjointly, a
new 'first' term for a further, and qualitatively distinct, duality" (54).
Unfortunately, the introduction to their chapter's final section,
which articulates the formula on which I will draw, announces their
attempt "to show how empirical readings . . . can be resisted"; for
the duration of this effort, McHoul and Wills write, "the question of
textual verification must cease to arise," and "bits of *Gravity's Rainbow* . . . should be treated as bits of other text rather than as privi-

leged 'quotations' or points of determinate verification of the reading" (49). Nevertheless, despite the ostensible unverifiability of their
suggestions, I am going to quote their schema and proceed to attempt to verify it. The general form of the "post-rhetorical" takes the
new right-hand term as the vantage point from which the "differences" between the two left-hand terms may be found not to signify;
these are some of McHoul's and Wills's examples:

use / mention / / *material typonymy*
parable / parabola / / *rocket trajectory*
rocket / penis / / *Jamf*
penis / polymer / / *Imipolex*
reality / fantasy / / *cinema*
us / Them / / *Slothrop* (54, 60–61)

The last two of these, I think, are the most "useful," in the sense
that they are capable of being reinscribed elsewhere; and to them I
will add two of my own:

elect / preterite / / *cultural artifact*
production / consumption / / *transmission*

For what is important about "fictions" in *Gravity's Rainbow* is not that
they can only mirror themselves as they attempt to represent a
world, nor that they give equal space (and apparently equal gravity)
to the *Duino Elegies* and *King Kong*, Tannhäuser and underground
comix, thus allowing allusion-diggers access to both Wagner and
Wonder Wart-Hog.[14] Rather, what is distinctive about *Gravity's Rainbow*'s postsomething (-modern, -avantgarde, -rhetorical) treatment
of Culture is that its emphasis is not on artifacts but on their transmission and reinscription; not on overturning the hierarchy between
canonical and apocryphal but on examining how the canonical and
apocryphal can do various kinds of cultural work for variously positioned and constituted cultural groups.

The dispute between Gustav Schlabone and Säure Bummer, for
instance, over the relative merits of Beethoven and Rossini, cannot
be settled simply by determining, on Jaussian grounds, which composer more successfully defeated his contemporary audience's hori-

[14]Wagner is everywhere in *Gravity's Rainbow*: see, e.g., Cowart 1980, Tate 1983,
Weisenburger 1988. Gilbert Shelton's Wonder Wart-Hog, a major figure in under-
ground comix (though not as canonical as Robert Crumb's Mr. Natural), is cited by
John C. Calhoun (1976, 49) as a pig-hero analogue to Plechazunga.

zon of expectations; still less is there any reason to align Pynchon against Rossini, as does Linda Westervelt, on the grounds that Pynhon "continually surprises and frustrates his reader" (1980, 71). Nor, for that matter, is it necessarily useful to single out in rebuttal of Westervelt the narrator's own strange endorsement of Rossini as "a high point in music which everybody ignored, preferring Beethoven, who never got further than statements of intention" (*GR* 273). For what the Schlabone-Bummer debate shows is that the operative distinction between Rossini and Beethoven has to do with their use: for Bummer, who stresses affect, "all you feel like listening to Beethoven is going out and invading Poland," whereas "a person feels *good* listening to Rossini" (*GR* 440). Gustav, more interested in a kind of German-succession anxiety of influence wherein each strong composer outdoes his predecessor in expanding the utility of the octave, prizes Beethoven not "qua Beethoven" but "as he represents the German dialectic, the incorporation of more and more notes into the scale, culminating with dodecaphonic democracy, where all notes get an equal hearing" (*GR* 440); he mourns Anton Webern's murder accordingly, since Webern stands "at the far end of what'd been going on since Bach. . . . Where was there to go after Webern? It was the moment of maximum freedom" (*GR* 440–41). Each disputant then turns to attack the other's grounds for judgment: Säure scoffs at Gustav and his "musical mainstreams," denigrating the idea of a central, octave-expanding canon, and Gustav replies with a highly unflattering picture of Rossini's current audiences, "half asleep, nodding and smiling, farting through their dentures, hawking and spitting into paper bags, dreaming up ever more ingenious plots against their children" (*GR* 441). Since we are denied, therefore, both the possibility of judgment on common grounds and metajudgment about the relative position of different grounds, the question becomes, simply, what do you want Beethoven or Rossini for, and how is each transmitted?

This may be a trivial example; but the pattern is equally evident in more "serious" cultural products as well, and its implications are far-reaching. Argentine anarchists may use *Martín Fierro* as an allegory of resistance, of "central government vs. gaucho anarchism" (*GR* 386), and may ignore the sequel, *Return of Martín Fierro*, "in which the Gaucho sells out: assimilates back into Christian society, gives up his freedom for the kind of constitutional Gesellschaft being pushed in those days by Buenos Aires" (*GR* 387)—because their present needs dictate the principles of selection and exclusion. The anarchist appropriation and reinscription of *Martín Fierro* is an example of what Tony Bennett calls "reading effects," which operate within the specific "reading formations" in which they are constituted; according to Bennett, we should speak of the "productive activation" of texts rather than their "interpretation" (or, in my terms, textual transmission rather than production or consumption), because although "texts always effect a certain embedding of meanings within a discursive formation—they consist not just of signifiers but of definite orders of relations between signifiers—those meanings can always be dis-embedded and re-embedded in alternative discursive formations through the ways in which texts are productively activated within different reading formations" (1983b, 14).

Moreover, as I argued above, artifacts cannot clearly be distinguished from their uses, their replications: a "productive activation," therefore, or a "reading effect," is not traceable exclusively to an originary text.[15] Only by attending to the means of cultural transmission, rather than to the points of origin of material, determinate texts-in-themselves, can we hope to make any sense of *Gravity's Rainbow*'s account of the Schwarzkommando as a manifestation of the cultural work of *King Kong*, in a kind of hyperreal return of the repressed. As one narrative voice in the novel puts it, "the legend of the black scapeape we cast down like Lucifer from the tallest erection in the world has come, in the fullness of time, to generate its own children, running around inside Germany even now—the Schwarzkommando, whom Mitchell Prettyplace, even, could not anticipate" (*GR* 275). If *King Kong* is thus transmitted and productively activated both by Prettyplace's "definitive study" and by African rocket troops, then the film's "existence" lies in the intertext; and the intertext is not a function of the specific "meanings" of the film itself but (as we will recall from the Tolson prefaces) the echo chamber of their humming.

But if the product is also its manifestations, then Major Weissman/ Blicero's reading of Rilke's *Duino Elegies* and *Sonnets to Orpheus* is as "legitimate" as the Argentine anarchist appropriation of *Martín Fierro*. We would then have no means of claiming that Blicero had "misread" Rilke's Twelfth Sonnet by interpreting the "Flame" to be

---

[15]Referring not to Pynchon's products but to his "characters," Bersani makes this case explicitly, construing *Gravity's Rainbow* as "a dazzling argument for shared or collective being—or, more precisely, for *the originally replicative nature of being*. Singularity is inconceivable; the 'original' of a personality has to be counted among its simulations" (1989, 113). Cf. Brian McHale on character "mapping" (1979, 104–5), where mapping (see *GR* 218) is rather reductively related to modernist analogical patterns.

the flame of the Reich ("'Want the Change,' Rilke said, 'O be inspired by the Flame'" [GR 97]), nor would we have reliable grounds for delegitimizing Blicero's identification with the "newly-dead youth" of the Tenth Elegy (GR 98). Blicero is meant in this respect to represent that strain of German romanticism ("Wandervögel idiocy" [GR 162]) on which rested the emotional appeal of Nazism; and as Charles Hohmann has written, "Pynchon's account of pre-war Germany, although pushed to extremes, is not unwarranted considering the way Rilke was read during the days of National Socialism" (1986, 334–35). Blicero's Rilke, in other words, is not a personalized Rilke but part of a larger cultural appropriation of Rilke, an appropriation made available as a reading effect by the discursive formations of the Third Reich.

Readers of Frank Kermode's The Sense of an Ending will recall that the term "Third Reich" is itself a twentieth-century reinscription of the work of a twelfth-century monk, Joachim de Flora, and that National Socialism is one of Kermode's prime examples of the distinction between myths and fictions: "Fictions can degenerate into myths whenever they are not consciously held to be fictive. In this sense anti-Semitism is a degenerate fiction, a myth; and Lear is a fiction. . . . If we forget that fictions are fictive we regress to myth (as when the Neo-Platonists forgot the fictiveness of Plato's fictions and Professor Frye forgets the fictiveness of all fictions)" (1966, 13, 39, 41). Apparently it is this myth/fiction distinction that Molly Hite is thinking of when she writes on system building in Gravity's Rainbow:

> Humanity finds itself serving an antihuman Higher Purpose when it is seduced by the clarity and coherence of its own explanations. The implicit model for all such totalizing systems is the myth of the providential plan, which purports to account for all aspects of human life by directing history to a predetermined end. . . .
> The lure of totality is so great, Pynchon suggests, that people will assent to a system in which "everything is connected" even if the system guarantees their destruction. The culminating irony is that to assent to such a system is to internalize its assumptions and thus to help translate it into reality. (1983, 98)

About Pynchonian internalization Hite's reading is judicious; moreover, Kermode's language of "myth" and "fiction" is indeed a viable means of distinguishing late Yeats from late Stevens, or King Lear from the Führer-principle. But I question whether the distinction carries all that much weight in Gravity's Rainbow. For not only does the novel imply that "myth" and "fiction" are merely two nearly indistinguishable kinds of textual transmission (in the Mc-Houl-Wills formula, myth / fiction // *reading effect*?), but it makes this implication by demonstrating that the cultural and political force of fictions is a variable independent of our "belief" in them. Franz Pökler knows that infinitesimal calculus is "fictional"; as he explains to his wife Leni, "The important thing is taking a function to its limit. Δt is just a convenience, so that it can happen" (*GR* 159). But German rockets will rain on London whether we forget or remember the fictionality of the delta-t, whether we believe it to be a convenience or the gift of God.

This, then, is why it is so important to pay attention to the category of "cultural work" in *Gravity's Rainbow*: because the novel shows us time and again that it is a gesture of political impotence, if not futility, to critique macropolitical forces like the Third Reich on the grounds that they have "misread" or "misappropriated" fictions and made them into "myths." If it is actually the case that we have doomed ourselves to annihilation by forgetting that our fictions are fictive, it is not as if we can do anything about our condition by rechecking the criteria for belief and use. For Kermode, "we know that if we want to find out about ourselves, make sense, we must avoid the regress into myth which has deceived poet, historian, and critic" (1966, 43); for Pynchon, on the contrary, if we want to find out about ourselves, we must plunge into these myths and ascertain the status of their manifestations—as Edwin Treacle, in interpreting King Kong, feces, blackness, and the Schwarzkommando, wants to know why his colleagues won't "admit that their repressions *had*, in a sense that Europe in the last weary stages of its perversion of magic has lost, *had* incarnated real and living men" (*GR* 276–77).

And this brings us finally to a crucial feature of Pynchon's cultural politics: *Gravity's Rainbow*'s myriad "deconstructions"—of myth and fiction, use and mention, elect and preterite, original and replication, Us and Them, reality and fantasy, war and peace—are not simply a matter of indeterminacy and free play, for as Pynchon and Derrida know, "deconstructed" dualisms are not made inoperative by their deconstruction. Since this caveat applies more to Pynchon's would-be deconstructionist critics than to *Gravity's Rainbow* itself, I expand on it in Chapter 5 rather than here; for now it should suffice to note that we are not absolved from determining the political work performed by such ideas as "cause," "origin," and "war" just because they do not "really" have the priority attributed to them by characters like Pointsman, Enzian, and Jessica Swanlake, respectively. Rather, we are asked throughout *Gravity's Rainbow* to attend to the uses and transmissions of Pynchon's fictions, whether we take "fictions" here to mean things like the films of Fritz Lang (or, at another fictional remove, Gerhardt von Göll), or things like residues of a metaphysics of presence.

For example, we might imagine Pynchon responding to Hite and Kermode, with Wittgenstein, that even when it comes to myth, "the meaning of a word is its use in the language. . . . The point is that *this* is how we play the game" (1945, §§ 43, 71, 20e, 34e), regardless of our ability to undermine it, rhetorically or otherwise: Pointsman's dogged belief in causality, outflanked though it is on scientific and epistemological grounds, nevertheless operates well enough to manipulate Roger Mexico, Jessica Swanlake, and Brigadier General Pudding (if not Slothrop)—just as the deconstruction of cause and effect itself depends on the idea of causation.[16] And we might imagine Pynchon elaborating on Derrida, via Ferdinand de Saussure, in the most explicitly grammatological treatment of "cultural work" in the book—the formation of the New Turkic Alphabet in the south central Asian steppes, where phonemic *différance* itself is mandated by committees of varying political clout ("all the Weird Letter Assignments have been reserved for ne'er-do-wells" [*GR* 352]), and where debates over specific alphabets—Arabic, Cyrillic, Latin—are necessarily heated debates among cultures, religions, and forms of life (*GR* 353–55). True, Igor Blobadjian, of the prestigious G Committee, has a distinctively Derridean insight when he finds that "print just goes marching on without him" (*GR* 355), but what's important for Pynchon is the way the new written language begins to operate "in a political way": "On sidewalks and walls the very first printed slogans start to show up, the first Central Asian fuck you signs, the first kill-the-police-commissioner signs (and somebody does! this alphabet is really something!)" (*GR* 355–56).[17]

Pynchon's emphasis on the sociopolitical transmission of cultural artifacts leads us, then, to twin imperatives. The first is that we recognize the political limits of deconstruction just as we recognize the political limits of modernism. If Edward Mendelson is right in suggesting that "Slothrop's disintegration . . . summarizes the historical fate of literary modernism" (1976, 166), so too should we recognize

[16]For a succinct statement and explication of this principle, see Culler 1982, 86–88.

[17]I am indebted here to Edward Mendelson's reading of this episode (1976, 168–71), in which he distinguishes Pynchon from Joyce by reading the New Turkic Alphabet against "Oxen of the Sun" (see n. 3 above).

the critical difference between Nietzsche's deconstruction of causality in *The Will to Power* and the A4 rocket's deconstruction of causality as part of Nazi Germany's will to power; so too should we recognize that our (my, Pynchon's) rhetorical dismantling of "cultural
elect" and "cultural preterite" does not so much as touch the socioeconomic status of the world's elect and preterite populations. What
is possible in one discursive register—undoing hierarchies of cause
and effect or elect and preterite—may be wholly inappropriate to
another. And though I want to preserve the sense in which the
novel *is* beyond elect and preterite, I do not take this as license to
forget that in *Gravity's Rainbow* Pynchon depicts a socioeconomic
"System" whose global purpose is "taking and not giving back, demanding that 'productivity' and 'earnings' keep increasing with time
. . . removing from the rest of the World these vast quantities of
energy to keep its own tiny desperate fraction showing a profit: and
not only most of humanity—most of the World, animal, vegetable
and mineral, is laid waste in the process" (*GR* 412).

This is not a political essentialism, and I am not saying that some
specially "grounded" cultural practices are immune from deconstruction. I *am* saying that for some operations of power and discourse, the signpost is in working order if under *any* circumstances
it fulfills its purpose. The (arbitrary) sign outside 2 Kaiserstrasse in
Neubabelsberg, which is temporarily housing Harry Truman for the
Potsdam Conference, reads "THE WHITE HOUSE" (*GR* 381), and it
operates not by *referring* (since the house is neither white nor the
White House) but by invoking a rule of metonymy in a language
game whose operational status is clear (Slothrop "reads" the sign
"correctly"). This is one of the burdens of Enzian's paranoid insight,
to which I return one final time: as his journey through the "ruins"
of the Jamf Ölfabriken Werke A.G. begins to suggest to him that the
rocket is not the real text, he (and we) eventually come to ask the
most appropriate question:

> This ex-refinery . . . is *not a ruin at all. It is in perfect working order.* Only
> waiting for the right connections to be set up, to be switched on... mod-
> ified, precisely, *deliberately* by bombing that was never hostile, but part
> of a plan both sides—*"sides?"*—had always agreed on. . . .
>   If it is in working order, what is it meant to do? (*GR* 520–21)

The option of reading *Gravity's Rainbow* through Wittgenstein
leads us in turn to our second imperative: namely, that we specify as
carefully as possible our own sociopolitical uses of Pynchon. This, of

course, is something I can do only in the course of the discussion as a whole, in this chapter and the next. But I want to sum up the foregoing argument by pointing out again how easy it is to let Pynchon slip noiselessly into our ideologies of the avant-garde, and by asking that we make this slippage less automatic, less conditioned. And since preterition and paranoia, no less than poststructuralism, have become rubrics under which it is claimed that Pynchon writes himself from the margin, the discussion concluding this section takes up all three.

It is not enough, then, to say that "Pynchon champions the preterite" (Westervelt 1980, 75); or that *Gravity's Rainbow* is written as a "sustained piece of preterition" (Mackey 1981, 20); or that Pynchon himself is somehow preterite—"his elusive near-anonymity . . . is a stance alien to our literary culture; and *Gravity's Rainbow*'s drastic violations of what remains of the tattered fabric of literary decorum assert a further distance from officialdom" (Mendelson 1976, 173). As I hope to have shown above, "preterition" may signify different things in different contexts, each of which asks for relational demarcation: what is preterite in relation to what? And as for the relation between the preterite and the ideology of the avant-garde, we should recognize from our acquaintance with Tolson criticism the strategy by which Pynchon's centrality is based upon his marginality, his preterition, his transgression of "norms"; here, in fact, Mendelson's is actually an inverse-square version of the Jaussian equation, whereby a text's importance increases geometrically with its distance from officialdom.

Just as we need to make explicit Pynchon's own relation to poststructuralism and preterition, so too do we need a working definition of paranoia, like Bersani's, that will deliver us from the false dichotomy of paranoia/anarchy as critical alternatives, and thereby deliver us from the obligation to celebrate Pynchon as the voice of anarchy against stultifying paranoias. Again, critical paranoia is not simply a state in which "the reader discovers that everything is connected in the novel" (Márquez 1983, 96), nor does it "set about anxiously to pacify Pynchon's vitality by schemes, structuralist or otherwise" (Poirier 1976, 18). If we take seriously our reflex for seeking other orders behind the visible, then "paranoia" does not denote a final Theory of the Book so much as the leading edge of the suspicion that everything is connected in ways that make it impossible to determine where interpretation stops, ways that therefore consign us to infinite paranoid regresses of theory. As Bersani puts it, "The theoretician distrusts the theorizing activity *of* paranoia—as if the 'truth' of paranoia might turn out to be that theory is always a paranoid symptom. . . . The theoretician's distrust of theory—the sense that what theory seeks to signify is hidden somewhere behind it—repeats the paranoid's distrust of the visible" (1989, 100–101).

Thus, paranoid interpretation (which by now we should call a redundant term) is not reducible to the rage for order, since all orders, as I have been arguing, contain within their disclosures the possibility of concealing the real text. Accordingly, critical paranoia cannot be countered by appeals for disorderly readings or special attention to aporias. No "scheme" whatsoever, structuralist or otherwise, has the power to "pacify," even if *Gravity's Rainbow* is read as a historical novel, as I so read it. For in this postmodernist history, "real history . . . never quite arrives" (McHoul and Wills 1990, 8), because Pynchon's history, like Jameson's, "is *not* a text, not a narrative, master or otherwise, but . . . is inaccessible to us except in textual form" (Jameson 1981, 35), and we do not know which textual form yields us that access. If one theory has it that the German Inflation was the result of financier Hugo Stinnes's "conspiring with Krupp, Thyssen and others to ruin the mark and so get Germany out of paying her war debts" (*GR* 285), alternate schemes abound—like those of apocryphal learned journals: "Paranoid Systems of History (PSH), a short-lived periodical of the 1920s whose plates have all mysteriously vanished, natch, has even suggested, in more than one editorial, that the whole German Inflation was created deliberately, simply to drive young enthusiasts of the Cybernetic Tradition into Control work" (*GR* 238). And from the perspective that death has given to Walter Rathenau—"here it's possible to see the whole shape at once" (*GR* 165)—the real text of the inflation may lie in "the hearts of certain molecules—it is they after all which dictate temperatures, pressures, rates of flow, costs, profits, the shapes of towers" (*GR* 167).

If Pynchonian paranoia is not a synonym for fixity, still less is it reducible to solipsism (Sanders 1976, 157; Slade 1977, 32); and its opposite number, antiparanoia—"where nothing is connected to anything, a condition not many of us can bear for long" (*GR* 434)—is not even an interpretive possibility. Yet this is not to deny that some Pynchon critics have indeed proferred Theories of the Book whereby *Gravity's Rainbow*'s vagaries are found to be due to the fact that Pynchon himself is simply paranoid (Bell 1973; Thorburn 1973; Sanders 1976); that the novel is not a novel (Mendelson 1976; Mac Adam 1978; Fowler 1980); or that it is "really" an enormous movie (Simmon 1974; Schwarzbach 1976; Wolfley 1977; Plater 1978). Most

horrifying of all may be Mark Siegel's claim to have "the only thematic perspective which accounts fully for all the events of *Gravity's
Rainbow*" (1978, 11), or the brand of self-consolidation that allows
David Leverenz to "dismiss the book as a sermon that [is], quite
simply, wrong" (1976, 242).

But totalizations of this magnitude are actually something of a minority report in Pynchon criticism; more important, such totalizations are not, properly speaking, paranoias. If in the end it truly is
"every paranoid's wish . . . to perfect methods of immobility" (*GR*
572), then paranoia seeks ultimately the cessation of its own restless-
ness; interpretation seeks the discovery of organic wholes or fictions
that signify only themselves, after which discovery it can rest. When
it comes to rest, when its search is "successful," when it results in a
criticism I described above as one that has "ceased to be paranoid,"
then it is no longer a paranoia but, in Pynchon's terms, a *pornography*. And because "pornography" in twentieth-century literature is
itself closely bound up with ideologies of the avant-garde, its function in *Gravity's Rainbow* is of paramount importance to our reading
of the novel, as well as to our readings of our readings of the novel.
For, as we shall find, pornography may be not only something read
but a reading effect as well—like Pynchon's other cultural artifacts,
both a kind of production and a form of consumption.

Up to this point, I have been primarily concerned with clarifica-
tions, choosing among Pynchon's possible connections to postmodernism, poststructuralism, preterition, and paranoia. When now we
reach the last of this chapter's p-words, we are in different territory
altogether. For no one, even after nearly twenty years, has written
on Pynchonian "pornography," and those who have mentioned it in
passing have done so in uncritical terms—celebrating, for instance,
the "sensuality" that gives Pynchon's work a "pornographic exuber-
ance unrivaled in American letters since Henry Miller" (Smith 1983,
253). I am not going to argue that Pynchon is unlike Henry Miller, or
that men or women should not or cannot enjoy Pynchon's sexually
explicit representations; but neither am I going to limit the term
"pornography" to sexually explicit representation. There is no short-
age of sexual explicitness in *Gravity's Rainbow*, and, appropriately,
my argument opens with an example I hope everyone will recognize
as pornographic. But I intend to take this argument in directions
that discussions of pornography do not usually pursue; indeed,
"pornography" itself is such a volatile sign that I feel I need to mark
out beforehand its ability, in *Gravity's Rainbow*, to point in strange

directions. For on my reading, Pynchon's pornography is closely related to (does not underwrite, is not critically prior or superior to) Pynchonian paranoia, and both involve crucial issues for the politics of interpretation.

As for Pynchon's readers' tendency to ignore or marginalize the question of *Gravity's Rainbow*'s pornography, this critical lacuna may itself be due to what Susanne Kappeler has called a pornographic "structure of representation" (1986).[18] It may be that readers like Smith have taken up subject positions within pornography's structure and are capable only of enjoying what they take Pynchon's pornography to represent. But this is matter for a new heading.

Gravity's Pornography: Re-membering Dismemberment

Molly Hite is the Pynchon critic whose analysis may be most easily made available for a discussion of Pynchon's pornography, yet Hite herself does not mention the subject. Arguing that Pynchon's characters parodically enact and expose the human rage for order, Hite describes system building in *Gravity's Rainbow* as "a symptom of a primordial nostalgia for the absent, originating Center" (1983, 38)—or, for Pynchon, a game of "Holy-Center-Approaching" (*GR* 508). "But," Hite explains, "no explanatory structure, however comprehensive, can recapture the unity of the broken center, a center that is not just crumbling but simply does not exist. . . . Language is all that is left, and words themselves must be strung together in molecular chains if anything is to make sense" (35). Here we might amend "molecular chains" (by which she refers to *GR* 391) to "metonymic chains," for reasons that will become clear shortly. I want to argue, then, taking up where Hite leaves off, that Pynchon's

---

[18]Kappeler's is an intriguing argument that "pornography is not a special case of sexuality; it is a form of representation" (1986, 2). Her specific elaboration of pornography's "structure of representation," however, is highly questionable, for she bases her description of pornography on an extended analogy to photographs of the torture and murder of Namibian farmworker Thomas Kasire (e.g., 5–10, 15). Her Dworkinesque construction thus enables an analysis wherein pornography is a literally criminal representation of tortured victims. More important, in Kappeler's cultural-feminist approach the "real" gender of represented subjects does not matter: there can be no feminist pornography, because women who "use" pornography by or for women are themselves being constructed by "a third party behind the scenes," an always already "male" party to exploitation, oppression, and objectification. Even when women control the structure of pornographic representation, writes Kappeler, "the model of this subject is the male gender, the objectification it operates is modeled on the objectification of women" (50).

pornography is in fact central to the trope of the absent center, and I start with one of the novel's most explicitly violent and sado-masochistic scenes—one that itself dramatizes pornography *as scene*.

It is the closing scene of Gerhardt von Göll's *Alpdrücken*, which culminates in the torture, gang rape, and dismemberment of its star, Margherita Erdmann. We learn later that only the torture made it to the film's release prints; the scene of rape and dismemberment was cut, but "found its way into Goebbels' private collection" (*GR* 461). Stefania Procalowska, the minor character who passes on this infor-mation to Slothrop and us, leaves it ambiguous as to whether the final moments of the film are *verité* or not: "After the Grand Inquisi-tor gets through, the jackal men come in to ravish and dismember the captive baroness. Von Göll let the cameras run right on" (*GR* 461). The dismemberment, of course, is not "real" and, according to Procalowska, may not even have been in the shooting script.[19] But the rape *is*: Erdmann's daughter Bianca, so the legend goes, was conceived at some point during the scene, and no one knows exactly who the father was. This makes for an "amusing party game" in which Bianca is made to watch her own primal "scene": "They'd run the film and ask Bianca questions, and she had to answer yes or no" (*GR* 461).

Our first encounter with the scene, however, comes through the eyes of Franz Pökler, and it is with him that we can begin our un-derstanding of Pynchonian pornography. The time is the Depres-sion, the place an Ufa theatre on the Friedrichstrasse, and the reac-tion is Pökler's (though the narrative position is, significantly, indeterminate until "thus"):

> ... yes, bitch—yes, little bitch—poor helpless *bitch* you're coming can't stop yourself now I'll whip you again whip you till you *bleed*.... Thus Pökler's whole front surface, eyes to knees: flooded with tonight's im-age of the delicious victim bound on her dungeon rack, filling the movie screen—close-ups of her twisting face, nipples under the silk grown amazingly erect, making lies of her announcements of pain— *bitch!* she loves it ... and Leni no longer solemn wife, embittered source of strength, but Margherita Erdmann underneath him, on the bottom

---

[19]The confusion here as to when the shooting script ends is similar to that in the epilogue of Roberta and Michael Findlay's highly controversial *Snuff* (uncredited, 1976), in which a "script girl" is dismembered and disemboweled in what purports to be *cinema verité*; for a discussion of *Snuff*, "snuff" films, and the problematic subject positions of the female audience of pornographic film, see Linda Williams 1989, 189–95, 226–28.

for a change, as Pökler drives in again, into her again, yes, bitch, yes.... (*GR* 397)

Just as Erdmann conceives Bianca at some point later on in the scene, so too does Franz go home and conceive a child, Ilse, with Leni—as a result of having seen *Alpdrücken* that evening. His reaction is, by and large, the reaction of every other man who saw the film with him; Pökler emerges from the theater "with an erection, thinking like everybody else only about getting home, fucking somebody, fucking her into some submission.... God, Erdmann was beautiful. How many other men, shuffling out again into depression Berlin, carried the same image back from *Alpdrücken* to some drab fat excuse for a bride? How many shadow-children would be fathered on Erdmann that night?" (*GR* 397).

Prominent here are the submission of and violence against women; the familiar assertion, in so many words, that she loves it;[20] and the mass/massive arousal of the male spectators, by which the film is rendered so clear and present a danger to women as to confirm our most behaviorist theories of pornography's effects.[21] And the cinematic gaze here, as everywhere in Pynchon, is quite clearly the male gaze.[22] Notable also, once more, is the ambiguous status of film as a means of cultural transmission; in an especially strange dissemination, the *Alpdrücken* scene engenders children on both

[20]Hence the absurdity of Erdmann's erect nipples: the (male) spectators on both sides of the film screen need physical evidence that makes "lies of her announcements of pain" and serves to project onto the victim the burden of excitement at the same time that it provides the necessary (visual) objective correlative to "her" stimulation. See also Williams on "hard-core pornography's quest to see pleasure displaced onto pain," which relies on the visual representation of bodily injury in order "to offer incontrovertible proof that a woman's body, so resistant to the involuntary show of pleasure, has been touched, 'moved' by some force" (1989, 194).

[21]Namely, Robin Morgan's "pornography is the theory, and rape the practice" (1980, 139).

[22]Mulvey 1975; see also *GR* 92–93 on the Firm's filming of Katje Borgesius—a passage whose very narrative position, in the first paragraph, is that of "the secret cameraman" (*GR* 92). I do not, however, mean to imply that the (non-Pynchonian) cinematic gaze is essentially male, as if all female spectators are immediately handed over thereby to the position of the Other, or as if female spectators who derive pleasure from sadomasochistic depictions of submissive women are duped by the male gaze into "false consciousness." For two salient contestations of Mulvey's gaze essentialism, see Williams (1989, 196–228), who emphasizes the fluidity of identifications and subject positions in sadomasochism and spectatorship; and de Lauretis (1984, 104–57), who complicates Mulvey convincingly by discerning a second set of "identifying relations" in "the double identification with the figure of narrative movement, the mythical subject, and with the figure of narrative closure, the narrative image," wherein identification with the latter "is supported by a prior, narrative identification with the figure of narrative movement" (144).

sides of the screen's interface, just as King Kong engendered the Schwarzkommando. Pynchon readers will recall that von Göll directed the Schwarzkommando film for the SOE's Operation Black Wing as well, considering it to be "his greatest work" (GR 113). Apparently a great believer in Author-ity, however, von Göll decides that his films "have been chosen for incarnation" and that his mission therefore is "to sow in the Zone seeds of reality" (GR 388); it does not occur to him that the cultural reproduction of "real, paracinematic" (GR 388) images may have nothing to do with the potency of the Father. But whether or not the origin of *Alpdrücken's* disseminations can be located in von Göll, we should ask of this "film" and its closing scene the insistent question: leaving aside for the moment its cause-and-effect on Pökler, what is it meant to *do*?

Before I get to what I want to do with the scene, however, I want to sketch out two things I don't want to do with it. The first is a recognizably modernist defense of high-cultural forms and uses of pornography, and the second belongs uneasily to postmodernism's confrontation with the discourses of popular culture. Of the former the *locus classicus* is perhaps Susan Sontag's "The Pornographic Imagination," where, writing on such narratives as *The Story of O* and Bataille's *Story of the Eye*, she claims that

> if within the last century art conceived as an autonomous activity has come to be invested with an unprecedented stature—the nearest thing to a sacramental human activity acknowledged by secular society—it is because one of the tasks art has assumed is making forays into and taking up positions on the frontiers of consciousness (often very dangerous to the artist as a person) and reporting back what's there. . . . [The artist's] principal means of fascinating is to advance one step further in the dialectic of outrage. He seeks to make his work repulsive, obscure, inaccessible; in short, to give what is, or seems to be, *not* wanted. (1967, 212)

Pornography is transgression, and transgression, for post-Romantic ideologies, is knowledge. As Sontag herself concludes: "that discourse one might call the poetry of transgression is also knowledge. He who transgresses not only breaks a rule. He goes somewhere that the others are not; and he knows something the others don't know" (232). Similarly, in Peter Michelson's *The Aesthetics of Pornography*, "pornography, like any literature, is a way of knowing," part of our modern "urgency to pursue the true" (1971, 11, 13). Thus, for example, William Burroughs (1959) shows us the naked lunch on the end of that long newspaper spoon, and Ihab Hassan writes that for

Henry Miller "obscenity is also a mode of purification, a way of cleansing human sensibilities from the sludge of dogma, the dross of hypocrisy"—as if Miller were nothing less than a Viconian poet whose "obscenity seeks to recover the original power of language" in that "it searches for the sexual and sacramental roots of metaphor" (1967, 37).[23] On such terms Pynchon's pornography can be recuperated as part of *Gravity's Rainbow*'s general "offer to transgress, to cross over into that which the dominant culture has silenced" (Olsen 1986, 84). The only catch is that the pornographic imagination must intone the keywords of Romantic ideology if it is not to be thrown out with the trash: in Sontag's words, "what makes a work of pornography part of the history of art rather than of trash . . . is the originality, thoroughness, authenticity, and power of that deranged consciousness itself, as incarnated in a work" (1967, 214). This is not far from Michelson's claim that "artistic pornography" is distinguished from its more debased simulacra "by the degree to which it meets the criteria of all serious art—how honestly and thoroughly it pursues its imaginative vision" (1971, 51); and since Pynchon is original, thorough, authentic, powerful, and honest because he is serious (and vice versa), his pornography establishes him as a genuine poet of transgression.

In a postmodernism of the popular, on the other hand, *Gravity's Rainbow*'s inclusion of the discourse of pornography can be explained as part of the novel's radical heteroglossia—part of the assault on the modernist separation of high art and mass culture, and a re-presentation of contemporary discourses in their full and clangorous polyphony. Thus Susan Gubar has written that the "inextricable entanglement" of art and pornography "suggests that any monolithic idea of what constitutes 'art' or 'the aesthetic experience' must be radically qualified, a point that has been amply demonstrated through numerous analyses of such devalued genres as folktales, slave narratives, gothic romances, and science fiction" (1987, 729).[24] The rehabilitation of the pornographic, then, can be seen as a project analogous to the projects of our contemporary revisionary

[23]No doubt Hassan writes of the "original power" of a language really spoken by men. Cf. Kate Millett's reading of Miller at the close of this chapter.

[24]Gubar is summarizing recent alternative approaches to pornography, not, as it may appear from this excerpt, endorsing the argument that pornography is just one more ideologeme in our heteroglot discourses. In fact, her essay is an engaging, comprehensive review of critical strategies for confronting pornography, and her discussion of René Magritte's *Le Viol* (The rape) from modernist and postmodern-feminist perspectives is especially helpful (1987, 722–23).

theories of canonicity, for all such projects work in the service of dialogism, of cultural heteroglossia.

This strategy, too, has its means for valorizing pornography. For Andrew Ross, in fact, pornography is a valuable instance of the popular precisely because it *resists* aesthetic sublimation:

> Pornography, it could be argued, is the lowest of the low, because it aims below the belt, and most directly at the psycho-sexual substratum of subjective life, for which it provides an actualizing, arousing body of inventive impressions. That all of pornography's conventions of spectacle and narrative are mobilized towards this greater actualization of bodily impulses runs directly counter to the premises of higher cultural forms, committed to a progressive *sublimation* of these same impulses, whether in the provocative routines of erotica, in the exploratory, transgressive world of avant-garde permissions, in the bourgeois drama of passion and responsibility, or in the aesthete's realm of refined sensibility. (1989, 200–201)

Pornography, claims Ross, is a crucial site of contest over popular meanings, crucial in its challenge to and repudiation of reformist intellectuals "who are committed today, as always, to 'improving' the sentimental education of the populace," since "a large part of pornography's popularity lies in its *refusal* to be educated" (201). Ross's argument is compelling, his work as a whole an exemplary instance of an intellectual engagement with the popular that refuses the position of the vanguardist reformer. Yet he manages, however briefly, to transform pornography from Sontag's discourse of transgressive "knowledge" into a discourse that nevertheless paradoxically educates (by checking the cultural arrogance of) intellectuals, teaching them "lessons about the business of contesting popular meanings without speaking from above" (207).

Certainly, Pynchon's pornography may, if we so desire, disturb and instruct us, whether in its politics of educational transgression or in its refusal to be educated, and *Gravity's Rainbow* is assuredly remarkable for its heteroglot discursive worlds. But both strategies of recuperation, as they make of pornography a means by which to trouble or reconceive the category of "aesthetic experience," have also the effect of (an)aestheticizing pornography and thereby naturalizing it, homogenizing it for easier absorption into an aesthetic or an anti-aesthetic. No doubt, any reading of pornography whatsoever will entail its "naturalization," in Culler's sense (1975, 137), and I admit at the outset that my own reading is no exception. But Pynchon's idiosyncratic use of "pornography," as sexual explicitness and as metaphor, is explained only in small part by theories of transgression or heteroglossia; and in order to begin an analysis more specific to Pynchonian pornographies, I want to focus instead on hard-core pornography's dependence on the logic of the fetish, and its notorious violence against women—which, I argue, go hand in hand, and which are crucial to Pynchon's critique of the lost or absent center.

Steven Marcus writes in his conclusion to *The Other Victorians* that "inside of every pornographer there is an infant screaming for the breast from which he has been torn. Pornography represents an endless and infinitely repeated effort to recapture that breast" (1966, 274). *Gravity's Rainbow*, I believe, gives us something like a poststructuralist version of Marcus's account of (male) deprivation and rage. For in Pynchon, hard-core heterosexual pornography (such as *Alpdrücken*) is associated with a complex fantasy and loss of an integral maternal body: not the physical separation of child from mother so much as the recognition-and-denial, for Freud, of the mother's incompleteness or castration, the denial of which results in the fetish (Freud 1966, 152–57); or the recognition, for Lacan, that the mother's desire cannot be completed by the child in a dyadic unit of desire, for her desire lies elsewhere, and in any case the child is prohibited from fulfilling it by the law of the father, signified by the phallus.[25] This prohibition precipitates the child into Lacan's order of the Symbolic, which is simultaneously and by necessity (as well as by definition) the order of the unconscious and the order of language.

Language, then, as the function of desire, is both the result and the expression of the child's unconscious "perception"-and-denial of lack. In Toril Moi's summary of Lacan, the mother's physical body is central: "The loss or lack suffered is the loss of the maternal body, and from now on the desire for the mother or the imaginary unity with her must be repressed. . . . The speaking subject only comes into existence because of the repression of the desire for the lost mother" (1985, 99). Like all poststructuralist subjects, this one is constituted by the language into which she or he has fallen; as Jacqueline Rose puts it: "Symbolization starts . . . when the child gets its first sense that something could be missing; words stand for objects, because they only have to be spoken at the moment when the first object is lost. For Lacan, the subject can only operate within language by constantly repeating that moment of fundamental and irreducible division. The subject is therefore constituted in language

[25]For more detailed discussion, see Rose 1982, 38–44.

as this division or splitting (Freud's *Ichspaltung*, or splitting of the ego)" (1982, 31).

But language—despite its metonymic chain of signifiers, which mirrors the metonymic chain of desire—gives the subject, retroactively, the illusion of lost unities (unities that were never there to begin with), a mis-recognition of his or her own "splitting," and a supreme fiction of the unity of his or her own ego. Hence a Lacanian rather than Freudian account of the fetish is most germane to Pynchon, for the mother wasn't castrated at all; rather, because she did not contain the phallus, her desire was Other—for the phallus. But, as Lacan says, the phallus is a fraud: it is only weakly signified by the penis; and the father, even in the prohibition enjoined by his law, discloses that there is always desire, or lack, in the place of the Other.[26] That is, no one has the phallus; nobody ever had it, and there is therefore no ground or basis on which the fetishist can complete the dyadic unity of mother and child by restoring the phallus to the castrated maternal body. Only in the order of the Imaginary, prior to the child's recognition of lack, can we believe in dyadic unities, unified selves, completed chains of desire. What Molly Hite called "primordial nostalgia," therefore, is inscribed in language by desire, and it is a nostalgia for the return to the Imaginary, for the unities that never were.

Alpdrücken is doubtless an emblem of heterosexual hard-core's ritual dismemberment of the female body (Erdmann's final dismemberment figures simply as a literalization of her torture and rape), and surely some of this dismemberment can be ascribed to the fetish. But what I suggest is that, paradoxically, such pornographic dismemberment works as a means of re-membering: in its rage against the loss of the maternal body, it paradoxically seeks to piece together the maternal body (or the relation to the maternal body) into that fantasied unity-that-never-was.[27] Re-membering thus involves a remembering, in or of the order of the Imaginary: a strategy of an-

---

[26]See Lacan, "The Meaning of the Phallus" (1958, 74–85). Moreover, the psychoanalytic attempt to deny the "gap" created by desire, "that for each partner in the relation, the subject and the Other, it is not enough to be the subjects of need, nor objects of love, but they must stand as the cause of desire"—this too Lacan terms a fraud, "however piously intended" (81).

[27]As *Gravity's Rainbow* remarks twice (*GR* 299, 653), the German word for mother, *Mutter*, is also the German word for light-bulb socket. The story of Byron the Bulb, then, may suggest an electrical link between union with *Mutter* and a kind of primary illumination (cf. paranoia's "secondary illumination," *GR* 703) in which everything is blindingly One: Byron, "screwed into mother (*Mutter*) after mother" (*GR* 653), is thereby condemned to see the Pattern in its awful totality—in this case, the economic interdependence of the world's meat, power, bulb, and tungsten cartels (*GR* 654), disclosed by Byron's successive Oedipal "illuminations."

amnesia, always profoundly regressive, which recreates nostalgically the unity of the maternal body and the unity of the self.[28]

Anamnesia, as nostalgia, thus dismembers in order to reconfigure into Imaginary unity. Let us now look afresh at one of the most famous passages in *Gravity's Rainbow*:

> Three hundred years ago mathematicians were learning to break the cannonball's rise and fall into stairsteps of range and height, Δx and Δy, allowing them to grow smaller and smaller, approaching zero. . . . This analytic legacy has been handed down intact—it brought the technicians at Peenemünde to peer at the Askania films of Rocket flights, frame by frame, Δx by Δy, flightless themselves... film and calculus, both pornographies of flight. (*GR* 567)

For all the commentary these sentences have accumulated, few critics have stopped to question the unusual use of "pornographies" here. Some have simply noted the accuracy of Pynchon's analogy between film and calculus (Holmes 1983, 11; Grace 1983, 656; Friedman 1983, 74); others have taken "pornography" as a synonym for "parody" or "travesty," claiming that film and calculus are falsifications of spontaneity and "experience" (Weisenburger 1979, 59–60; Fowler 1980, 216; Clerc 1983, 110; Hite 1983, 113).[29] Dwight Eddins has even suggested there is an antidote to pornographies of flight, for "when we integrate, we return to integrity, to all that the original, unbroken arc means by way of momentary grace, momentary freedom, and the natural triumph of gravity" (1983, 78). But this "reintegration" is itself an already performed illusion, already part of the structure of film and calculus: both are forms of dismemberment and reconstitution which are then reassembled into illusions of unity —in this case, unified and continuous motion. For as Pynchon writes elsewhere in *Gravity's Rainbow*, the pornography of film and calculus is not that they carve up originary unities, but that they feign such unities: "There has been this strange connection between the Ger-

---

[28]For the idea of "regressive anamnesia," I am indebted to Janet Lyon; thanks also to Pat Gill for refining my use of Lacan.

[29]This reading of "pornography," wherein "the films are pornographies of flight because they are vicarious, artificial" (Clerc 1983, 110), depends on our faith that Pynchon refers only to the transection of "a flowing reality into still frames" (Weisenburger 1979, 60) and not also to the mechanical *recomposition* of "reality." This is possible in the immediate context, insofar as Pynchon links film and calculus with abstraction and analysis, "reminders of impotence" (*GR* 567); but when the passage is taken together with the notion of "pornographies of deduction" (*GR* 155) and the annual visits between Franz Pökler and his daughter Ilse (see the next section) it becomes clear that we cannot simply equate "pornography" with the stasis of still frames. Cf. Weisenburger's conflation of pornography and paranoia (60).

man mind and the rapid flashing of successive stills to counterfeit movement, for at least two centuries—since Leibniz, in the process of inventing calculus, used the same approach to break up the trajectories of cannonballs through the air" (*GR* 407).

In my reconstruction, then, "pornography" in *Gravity's Rainbow* describes a regressive anamnesia that recreates illusory, prelapsarian (or prelinguistic) unities through a complex mechanism of dismemberment and reconfiguration; and since nostalgia itself works by much the same dynamic, Pynchon's "pornography" gives us fresh purchase on the cultural critique of nostalgia as well.[30] His novel offers us a veritable miscellany of macropolitical nostalgia and fantasied national "restoration": in its American version, the myth of the virgin land; its Argentine equivalent, the "Argentine heart" which, "in its perversity and guilt, longs for a return to that first unscribbled serenity... that anarchic oneness of pampas and sky" (*GR* 264); and Enzian's belief that "somewhere, among the wastes of the World, is the key that will bring us back, restore us to our Earth and to our freedom" (*GR* 525).[31] Enzian's Schwarzkommando are, after all, devoting all their energies to piecing together a rocket, like a nation of anamnesiac detectives,[32] and the leader of the Herero meta-

---

[30]For a provocative discussion of nostalgia and pornography in David Lynch's *Blue Velvet*, see Bienen 1987.

[31]In the text of the novel, this sentence is set off as its own paragraph and preceded by Pynchon's ubiquitous suspension points; it is therefore difficult to determine whether the passage is internally focalized through Enzian (as I claim), or whether Enzian's hope is also, somehow, that of "Pynchon"—as critics have argued (Lhamon 1973, 26; Leverenz 1976, 238). If the latter, then we may critique the text's own moments of primordial nostalgia in the very terms the text makes available for such critique. The status of America as "virgin land" is especially problematic here. As Squalidozzi admits, if only to himself, the ideology of the virgin land is predicated, conceptually and materially, on empire westward making its way and eradicating the indigenous populations in its path: he thinks but does not say to Slothrop, "*We wanted to exterminate our Indians, like you*" (*GR* 264). But some fifty pages earlier, we were presented with Slothrop's vision of the sunset after his epic game of wales tails: "This is the kind of sunset you hardly see any more, a 19th-century wilderness sunset, a few of which got set down, approximated, on canvas, landscapes of the American West by artists nobody ever heard of, when the land was still free and the eye innocent, and the presence of the Creator much more direct. . . . of course Empire took its way westward, what other way was there but into those virgin sunsets to penetrate and to foul?" (*GR* 214). Pynchon here seems willing to exempt landscape painters from his general critique of the pioneer as culture hero. Blicero's nostalgic interpretation of America, by contrast, is less problematic, largely because it is Blicero's (*GR* 722–23).

[32]In this search, of course, the Schwarzkommando resemble most of the Allies, the U.S. and U.S.S.R. most of all, who devoted much of their energy and ingenuity to the reassembly of rockets and teams of rocket engineers—with familiar results. The best Pynchonian discussion of the postwar rocket searches may be found in Tölölyan 1983b, esp. 48–52.

metapreterite of racial suicides, the Empty Ones' Josef Ombindi, "at times self-conned as any Christian, praises and prophesies that era of innocence he just missed living in" (*GR* 321).

More fanciful examples abound: melanocytes whose "prevalent notion" is of a "messenger from the Kingdom" calling them to return to their primal home in the central nervous system (*GR* 148), and the sentient pinballs from the planet Katspiel, "kind round beings in eternal exile, with no chance of ever being gathered back home" (*GR* 584). But most important of all—or, at least, most obvious of all—there is our celebrated antihero, Tyrone Slothrop. For Slothrop, the political is also, literally, the personal, because *his* quest to piece together the information on mysterious rocket 00000, if completed, would seem to piece together also the mystery of his infant sexuality, the secret of his conditioning at the hands of Dr. Laszlo Jamf. Whether Slothrop's relation to the rocket is even causally or statistically explicable—as either Pointsman or Mexico, respectively, would have it—may be beside the point, for insofar as his search for the clue to the rocket is coextensive with his search for self-identity, it is amnesiac, pornographic, and better left uncompleted.[33]

If nothing else, Slothrop's unfathomable "scattering" delivers him from the illusion of self-identity (or the project of establishing his self-identity becomes unimportant to us) as his "albatross of self" breaks apart until it is "only feathers... redundant or regenerable organs" (*GR* 623, 712). And though the sense of Slothrop's ending must be the single most hotly debated issue in Pynchon criticism, his "scattering" clearly has its advantages. Sir Marcus Scammony has already informed us that Slothrop was sent into the Zone to destroy the Herero (*GR* 615), and we hear later a "story" that he was sent "to be present at his own assembly" (*GR* 738). These, surely, are fates well avoided. Similarly, a disassembled Slothrop cannot be "normalized" in Foucault's sense—or, as Pynchon puts it, "it's doubtful if he can ever be 'found' again, in the conventional sense of 'positively identified and detained'" (*GR* 712). As a matter of fact, when the Firm last sets out positively to identify and detain Slothrop, the purpose of the search is Slothrop's castration (*GR* 607–9)—which implies that "his own assembly," had the Firm been able to carry it out, would have involved in some way the fetishistic restoration of his castrated body.

I suggest therefore that Slothrop's scattering is Pynchon's attempt

[33]The 00000 itself, for that matter, turns out to be the "womb" to which Captain Blicero's lover, Gottfried, "returns" (*GR* 750).

to imagine a dismemberment that does not configure itself into a vision of retrospective totality: dissolution works here in the by now routine service of deconstructing supreme fictions of the integrity of the self, and in the more difficult and problematic service of de-Oedipalizing desire and narrative. Of course, this dissolution has its critics, even within *Gravity's Rainbow*; as engineer Kurt Mondaugen would have it, Slothrop has lost "personal density," which, according to Mondaugen's Law, is "directly proportional to temporal bandwidth . . . the width of your present, your *now*" (*GR* 509). But then again, as Hite notes, "Mondaugen is a Nazi collaborator, and in exalting temporal bandwidth, which is really the capacity of containing history, he may be upholding Their idea of historical totality" (1983, 166 n.18). Infinite temporal bandwidth thus might look something like a Reich without end; yet Slothropian dissolution is not the mere assertion of anarchy over (personal or narrative) order, for a Slothrop who dissolves into self-difference also dissolves into his manifestations—that is, into diverse cultural uses, diverse reading effects. Just as Yeats "became his admirers" in Auden's elegy, so too does Slothrop in David Marriott's analysis: "In the latter stages of his dissolution he comes across 'Rocketman was here' chalked on a urinal wall [*GR* 624]. Now Rocketman had not been there, but his myth *had*; his myth begins to make his person insignificant" (1985, 79).

If Slothrop's escape from pornographic reassembly makes him marginal, apocryphal, or unrepresentable, then it may also do substantial critical work in the Pynchonian interplay of margin and center, preterite and elect. As Marriott writes: "Pynchon is fascinated by marginal commentaries, for as an amateur of textual history he knows that over a period of time, through successive transcriptions, they tend to be absorbed into the main text. This in turn creates an ambiguity, for either, what was once unofficial becomes a part of the authorized text and thus loses its vitality, or else the absorbed portion may retain its integrity and undermine its host" (71).[34] And since "*Gravity's Rainbow* is itself an expansive marginal commentary on the twentieth century; an alternate, heretical history which cannot be assimilated by orthodox History," Slothrop's scattering is in this sense "almost a function of Pynchon's fictional technique" (72,

[34]Marriott links his concern with Pynchon's official and apocryphal texts to the most obvious pre-text of them all, the myth of Orpheus: "Slothrop is 'dispersed,' dismembered like Orpheus, only to be recalled in fragmentary and apocryphal traditions" (1985, 76).

76): it permits Slothrop to take on an apocryphal "life" in such diverse cultural products as graffiti, learned journals (*GR* 712, 738), album covers (*GR* 742), and Wall Street's daily diary of the American dream (*GR* 738–39). In each of these productive activations, no doubt (especially the last), he can be said to be recuperated; yet in each productive activation he necessarily does different cultural work—just as Charlie Parker's music, earlier in the novel, is not automatically vitiated by its translation into Muzak but, rather, "may either be emasculated or yet have the potential to 'gainsay the Man's lullabies, to subvert the groggy wash of the endlessly, gutlessly overdubbed strings' [*GR* 64]" (74).

Aside from noting that for Pynchon, resistance always dwells within recuperation and vice versa, I want to ally my thesis on "pornography" with Marriott's on apocrypha and Hite's on primordial nostalgia. For I think we are better enabled to read Slothrop, and *Gravity's Rainbow*, if we make it clear that the "falsity" of Pynchonian pornographies lies not in their rituals of dismemberment but in their fetishistic reassemblies, not in their cutting up of organic (w)holes but in their recomposition of inorganic wholes that fetishize the very idea of organic wholes. At the very least, we should be wary of endorsing the book's various depictions of nostalgia, return, "Diaspora running backwards" (*GR* 737); ideally, we should be wary also of approaching *Gravity's Rainbow* as if fragmentation were a problem to be solved by critical intervention, as if Pynchonian entropy dictated a world of chaos in which our role is to preserve pockets of order (Mesher 1981, 166–69). If it is problematic, as I have argued above, to celebrate Pynchon's indeterminacies, ambiguities and anarchies in themselves, it is still more problematic to make of them a "first term" in a field equation that restores all things to unity—*not* because unitary theories "falsify reality" but for reasons I will make clear in a moment.

Pornographic Reading and the Politics of Restoration

What I've proposed, so far, is a way of reading film and calculus, von Göll's *Alpdrücken* and Slothrop's quest, which can sustain the term "pornography" for a number of uses: first, as a means of explicating various textual data (like the *Alpdrücken* scene itself) in terms congruent with Hite's critique of the trope of the absent center; second, as a phenomenon distinct from "paranoia," to which it is related but to which it may also profitably be opposed;[35] third, as a description of the kinds of macrocultural practice of which nostalgia is a subset; and last, as a description of critical practice. It is this last to which I now turn my attention, because my link between "pornography" and critical fetishisms inevitably implicates our strategies for reading any text and, like Bersani's reinterpretation of Pynchonian paranoia, clearly has significant critical consequences for the reassembly lines of Pynchon criticism. Before I go on to examine these consequences, therefore, I want to hone my definition as finely as possible—remembering that the construction of pornography, like the existence of pornography, depends on its users.

First, one more parable of reassembly: Franz Pökler's daughter Ilse is imprisoned in concentration camp Dora and allowed to see her father once a year—although Franz is never sure whether he is seeing the same child twice. What's distinctly pornographic about this arrangement is that "They have used it to create for him the moving image of a daughter, flashing him only these summertime frames of her, leaving it to him to build the illusion of a single child" (GR 422). Pökler himself remarks on Ilse's re-presentations upon recalling the circumstances of her conception: "That's how it happened. A film. How else? Isn't that what they made of my child, a film?" (GR 398). Here, for our convenience, we have something like a study example of the difference between paranoia and "pornography." Pökler may be paranoid as to Their machinations, or as to the status of his "daughter," or as to the connections between his work on ooooo and his permission to see Ilse—and his concern in each case is surely justified; but the structure of Ilse's representation becomes "pornographic" only if "Ilse" really is a different girl each year, and if the dis- and reassembled "Ilse" is intended (as she assuredly is) to pass for a representation of the real thing. Finally, should Franz rest secure in the hope, belief, trust that it is the same girl each time, then he has forsaken paranoia's uncertainty for a stable subject position within the structure of pornographic representation.

---

[35]Paranoia and pornography may be related in that both work to forge illusions of self-identity: alongside my argument that we can have pornographic illusions of "selves," I might place Bersani's suspicion that "the paranoid structure itself [is] a device by which consciousness maintains the polarity of self and nonself, thus preserving the concept of identity" (1989, 109). And yet paranoia and pornography must at the same time be distinguished; otherwise, we wind up believing that all connection findings, paranoid as they are, are de facto totalizations, and that all interpretation is therefore a search for fixity, a falsification of flux. For an example of how the confusion between "paranoia" and "pornography" creates an excluded middle, see McHale (1985, 93), who divides all reading into "paranoid" and "antiparanoid" modes.

"Their" pornographies of Ilse, in other words, require Franz's participation for their realization. This is also to say that pornography works partially through its interpellation of subjects, and that the formation of subject positions (which are also positions to which we are subject) is necessary to pornography as a practice of representation. It is not that reassemblies constitute Pynchonian pornography per se; there is also this condition to be fulfilled, that the completed reassembly perform the crucial work of subject-ification. Weissman/ Blicero reassembles Ilse the better to control Franz; and *Alpdrücken* itself, like its director, so controls Greta Erdmann that she insists Slothrop whip her on the same rack, on the same set, where she had been tortured and "dismembered" before the cameras (*GR* 394–97).[36] And for Erdmann, we find, this restaged whipping involves "Nostalgia. The pain of a return home" (*GR* 396).

Nowhere in *Gravity's Rainbow* are the myriad interests of sexual control so explicit as in Miklos Thanatz's theory of "Sado-anarchism":

> Why will the Structure allow every other kind of sexual behavior but [sadomasochism]? Because submission and dominance are resources it needs for its very survival. They cannot be wasted in private sex. In *any* kind of sex. It needs our submission so that it may remain in power. It needs our lusts after dominance so that it can co-opt us into its own power game. There is no joy in it, only power. I tell you, if S and M could be established universally, at the family level, the State would wither away. (*GR* 737)

This is a plausible formulation, but it can be contested in a number of important ways. Control is not a zero-sum game; more submission-and-dominance on one sociostructural level does not necessarily mandate less of the same elsewhere. Katje Borgesius's "compensatorial" interpretation of Blicero's S/M Oven-games is in fact directly opposed to that of Thanatz: "In a conquered country, one's own occupied country, it's better, she believes, to enter into some formal, rationalized version of what, outside, proceeds without form or decent limit day and night, the summary executions, the roustings, beatings, subterfuge, paranoia, shame" (*GR* 96). Katje's practice of sadomasochism can thus be read as Andrew Ross describes the "liberationist claims for S/M"—as "a safe cultural space in which

---

[36]We learn later on in the novel that Erdmann's desire for violent sexual submission is not confined to her film career: as Stefania Procalowska tells Slothrop, "Margherita's problem was that she always enjoyed it too much, chained up in those torture rooms. She couldn't enjoy it any other way" (*GR* 461).

to explore, under controlled conditions, the powerlessness felt and experienced by women in the public sphere" (1989, 192). According to Ross's reading, if S/M "could be an official ritual of domination, then it could also be an unofficial theater of opposition and subversion" (192).[37] But then again, sado-anarchism may reinscribe as well as explore domination, as in Alan Soble's disturbing heterosexual male-liberationist reading of pornography as the "attempt to recoup in the domain of sexual fantasy what is denied to men in production and politics" (1986, 81).

Thanatz is right, however, to note that the State (whatever its conceptual status) has an interest in normalizing sexuality, even if he is somewhat self-serving in believing that S/M is the specially persecuted form of "deviant" sexual behavior, or that it constitutes a threat to, rather than a replication of, official forms of repression and control. Instead, we might reply to Thanatz that in making explicit the connection between pornography and the state, he implicitly argues that pornography (including S/M) both depicts or enacts strategies of control and interpellates controlled subjects; we might further acknowledge that the reformist intellectual's category of the "pornographic" often depends upon a conceptual normalization of sexuality (as in the distinction between pornography and erotica).[38] The Firm's Pirate Prentice, for instance, who decodes a message in Kryptosam (an ink readable only when mixed with sperm), is stimulated to ejaculation by material "They" have extracted from his dossier: "Like every young man growing up in England, he was condi-

[37]Linda Williams likewise suggests that "sadomasochistic fantasy offers one important way in which groups and individuals whose desires patriarchy has not recognized as legitimate can explore the often mysterious conjunction of power and pleasure in intersubjective sexual relations" (1989, 217–18). Thanatz's idea that S and M is a power drain on the state, however, has its counterpart in Wimpe's argument that "a rational economy cannot depend on psychological quirks" (*GR* 349) such as drug addiction, a demand "having nothing to do with real pain, real economic needs, unrelated to production or labor... we need fewer of these unknowns, not more" (*GR* 348). Both Wimpe's and Thanatz's arguments seem a good deal more naive than those of William Burroughs on the issues of sex 'n' drugs 'n' state control: in *Naked Lunch*, we will recall, drug addiction and violent pornography are metaphors and enactments of political control—not privatized pockets of exemption from it.

[38]Recall Sontag and Michelson, above; see also Ross 1989 for a trenchant critique of "traditional intellectuals" such as Lord Kenneth Clark, Steven Marcus, and George Steiner, who mark pornography as antiliterary by distinguishing the autonomous freedom of art from the various "unfreedoms" (179) of ideology, action, and coercive mass consumer culture (182–83). Ross links these formulations, all of which depend on the separation of art from trash, to the antiporn feminist distinction between pornography and erotica (see Steinem 1986). See also Kappeler on the "liberal cultural elite" distinction between art and pornography, which depends on the cultural "status of the producer" (1986, 83).

tioned to get a hardon in the presence of certain fetishes, and then conditioned to feel shame about his new reflexes" (*GR* 71–72). Pornography, then, must always be a specifically *instrumental* dis- and re-memberment.

Still, not all things "pornographic" in *Gravity's Rainbow* can be covered by a monistic theory of pornography, which would itself be a pornographic reassembly. The scene between Brigadier Pudding and Katje Borgesius (in which Katje plays Pudding's Domina Nocturna), most notably, seems to work primarily as a kind of naked (coprophagic) lunch, wherein feces are revealed to be the "real" referent of the massacres of the Ypres salient: "They have stuffed paper illusions and military euphemisms between him and this truth, this rare decency" (*GR* 234). Surely this scene, if no other, can be understood as a tour de force of modernist disturbance-and-instruction.[39] Similarly, Blicero's Witch-and-Oven-games (with Katje and Gottfried as alternating Hansels and Gretels) seek to expose and retrieve the "real": "Among dying Reich, orders lapsing to paper impotence he needs her so, needs Gottfried, the straps and whips leathern, real in his hands which still feel, her cries, the red welts across the boy's buttocks, their mouths, his penis, fingers and toes—in all the winter these are sure, can be depended on" (*GR* 97). Yet even in the cases of Pudding and Blicero, where the specific mechanics of disassembly and reassembly seem absent, we can discern forms of regressive anamnesia; by no means are these scenes and characters free of nostalgia, nostalgia for originary moments or, as Pudding needs, "something real, something pure" (*GR* 234) prior to paper replications. The most notable exception to my general argument is *How I Came to Love the People*, an anonymous chronicle of "a megalomaniac master plan of sexual love with every individual one of the People in the *World*" (*GR* 547), which sounds more like a *reductio ad absurdum* of Steven Marcus's idea of a pornotopia than like anything having to do with dismemberment and instrumentalist reconstruction.[40] A

[39]See Paul Fussell (in Mendelson 1978, 213–19): "Here for the first time the ritual of military memory is freed from all puritan lexical constraint and allowed to take place with a full appropriate obscenity" (213). For the story of the debacle of Passchendaele, see Fowler 1980, 144; Weisenburger 1988, 53.

[40]At one point Slothrop studies "a pornography of blueprints" (*GR* 224). I can see no sense in which blueprints involve anamnesiac, Imaginary unity, any more than *How I Came to Love the People* does. Perhaps, however, we might compare Slothrop's blueprints to Steven Marcus's strangely apt description of the "pornotopian" scenes of *The Romance of Lust* (ca. 1870s) as "outlines or blueprints, diagrams of directions or vectors," and Marcus's claim that such scenes "must be read diagramatically" (1966, 277). Nonetheless, Pynchon's sentence remains stranger than I can account for: "por-

seemingly endless narrative of sexual acts related almost tonelessly, *How I Came to Love the People* parodically upholds Marcus's distinction between pornography and literature: "Most works of literature have a beginning, a middle, and an end. Most works of pornography do not. A typical piece of pornographic fiction will usually have some kind of crude excuse for a beginning, but, having once begun, it goes on and on and ends nowhere" (1966, 279).

I am not, therefore, claiming that Pynchon's pornographies are always one thing and not another thing, or never capable of yielding readings that have nothing to do with Lacan or feminist film theory. The question so far has been, instead, how we might read the varieties of pornography in *Gravity's Rainbow* without or before subsuming them under some other rubric: the modernist ideology of the avant-garde, or the postmodernist promiscuity of cultural codes. What has emerged from this reading is my description of a form of representation, itself highly reproducible—or, even in Steven Marcus's words, "infinitely repeated" (274)—which reassembles illusory lost (maternal, cultural) unities as a means to control and domination. Now, at last, having "read" pornography, we may ask how reading itself can be pornographic.

For as many commentators have noted (though not in these terms), we ourselves are implicated in the pornographic process of regressive anamnesia, inasmuch as we read *Gravity's Rainbow* in the hope that it will yield to us at last the all-important clue that will piece the text together. Moreover, we assume at first that our reading process, our detective work, is coextensive with Slothrop's quest for rocket 00000—or with other characters' quests for Slothrop, or (similarly) with the quest for conclusive details about the rocket "whose firing is the center of the novel's action" (Muste 1984, 16). Our desire for narrative closure, therefore, becomes another pornographic strategy for re-membering. One of Pynchon's named extras, Vanya, speaks of "the forms of capitalist expression": pornographies of love, of killing, of sunsets, and, most tellingly, "pornographies of deduction—*ahh*, that sigh when we guess the murderer" (*GR* 155). But if Vanya suggests here that there is a quasi-pornographic mode of writing known more widely as the detective novel, then there is as well a pornographic mode of *reading*, a mode of reading that seeks above all else to restore unity and order to an ostensibly fragmented and challenging text; it would be a reading that meets the

nography" seems here to be almost a naturalist's term, as in "a pride of lions" or "an exaltation of larks."

challenge by mastering the text, taking it apart, fighting its radical "incompleteness" by finding the "key" to unlock/lock it—all, finally, with the goal of reconfiguring it into spatial form, say, or a verbal icon.[41] That totalizing, anamnesiac readings may themselves be pornographic is a possibility that escapes pornography's opponents, be they cultural feminists or the New Right; for them the pornographic is always something practiced elsewhere, and pornographers are always other people.[42] But in contrast to antiporn feminists, New Right sex police, modernist apologists, and postmodern populists, Pynchon enables instead a theory of pornography in which we meet the pornographers and they is us.

Dennis Porter has recently elaborated this possibility in his neo-Lacanian reading of "The Purloined Letter." Noting that the restoration of the letter makes "the female 'exalted personage' (Queen/Mother) whole again," Porter describes Poe's Dupin stories almost as pornographies of deduction:

> In all three Dupin stories the crime involved concerns an assault on, mutilation, and/or murder of women, but it is only in the last of the three that the power of Dupin's analysis is such that he not only wins out over his rivals, but also restores the female body to a fantazied wholeness. . . .
>
> Perhaps the most fascinating consequence of such a reading is that it identifies Poe's hero as a fetishist who denies culturally affirmed sexual difference—a possibility that opens up a whole new approach both to the political question of "restoration" and to the mass appeal of the

[41]My debt to Roland Barthes here is extensive. "At the origin of Narrative, desire. To produce narrative, however, desire must *vary*, must enter into a system of equivalents and metonymies" (1974, 88). Barthes's "hermeneutic code," especially, is the locus of the reader's desire for resolution of the "enigma": "Expectation thus becomes the basic condition for truth: truth, these narratives tell us, is what is *at the end* of expectation" (76). Barthes speaks also of the "diadic unity of subject and predicate" on which the hermeneutic narrative is based; yet this unity troubles his very project, for it conscripts the "multivalence" and "reversibility" (19) of the codes, thus requiring us to read the text "as if it had already been read," for "the 'first' version of a reading must be able to be its last, *as though the text were reconstituted in order to achieve its artifice of continuity*" (15; my emphasis). For a radical revision of and resistance to Barthes's dictum "The pleasure of the text is . . . an Oedipal pleasure" (1975, 10), see de Lauretis 1984, 134–57.

[42]Michelson quotes "an observation on censorship in *Rights and Writers* . . . : 'we know of no case where any juror or judge has admitted that *he* found material erotically stimulating or a stimulus to irregular conduct; on the contrary, the expression of concern is always that someone else or some other class of people will be corrupted'" (1971, 3). See also Kappeler's critique of the high-cultural concern to "protect the spectator"—i.e., the masses—(1986, 26–30); and Ross (1989, 180–207).

detective story genre, which the Dupin stories inaugurated in modern times. (1988, 510)

Porter goes on to suggest that the fetishism of pornography is a fetishism that is always also our own: "In our role as commentators are we not all 'brothers' in relation to the game or maternal body that is the text, claiming to restore to it the purloined 'thing'—one remembers the unabashed fetishism of the New Criticism's insistence on organic wholeness—and ready to repay 'the evil turn' of those who previously dispossessed it?" (516). The answer here, I think, is yes and no. We may all be "brothers" in relation to the maternal body of *Gravity's Rainbow*, but then Teresa de Lauretis would point out that we may also be simply reproducing Oedipal narratives about reading Oedipal narratives. "Dominant cinema," writes de Lauretis, "works for Oedipus" (1984, 155), and her work makes clear that dominant narrative theories—such as those of Roland Barthes, Robert Scholes, Jurij Lotman, and Claude Lévi-Strauss—work for Oedipus as well. According to de Lauretis, "if narrative is governed by an Oedipal logic, it is because it is situated within the system of exchange instituted by the incest prohibition, where woman functions as both a sign (representation) and a value (object) for that exchange" (140). Even Dennis Porter is therefore in Oedipus's employ, alongside the rest of his narrative-theorist "brothers." "It may well be, however," de Lauretis concludes, "that the story has to be told differently" (156).

All Pynchon's "central" characters—Herbert Stencil, Oedipa Maas, Slothrop, Enzian, Tchitcherine—are readers, paranoid readers in search of the real text, and some of them may be explicitly pornographic readers as well. The most convincing example comes not from *Gravity's Rainbow* but from *V.*, in the person of Herbert Stencil, that most mechanical of Pynchon's strong misreaders. Yet Stencil's mistake is not precisely that of "grouping the world's random caries into cabals" (Pynchon 1963, *V* 139) of imposing order on decay, as Eigenvalue accuses him of doing; as *V.*'s readers know, the world's "caries" does not line up neatly into "The Big One, the century's master cabal" (*V* 210), but neither is it entirely "random." The Fashoda and Suez crises are not, in or out of *V.*, chance historical events. Instead, what makes Stencil most thoroughly Stencil is his *method* of grouping caries into cabals: even after he reads in the "Confessions of Fausto Maijstral" the scene, itself somewhat pornographic, of *V.*'s dismemberment—in her presumed instantiation as Malta's "Bad Priest" (*V* 320–23), he insists on denying what he has read, and reassembling a dream of V. "now," composed of things like solenoid relays and servo-actuators (*V* 386–87). Stencil's imaginary reassembly of V. is itself but an emblem of his quest for V., his attempt to reassemble what has become for him "a remarkably scattered concept" (*V* 364). And the nature of this reassembly should become all the clearer when we realize that V. herself may not be identical with all of her "manifestations," including that of the dismantled Bad Priest (so that we and Stencil have to assemble a V. in order to compose any story at all); and, moreover, that V. may literally be Stencil's mother, as some critics have declared (Tanner 1976, 58; Cowart 1980, 67). This last possibility, however, although it would establish beyond all doubt the regressive anamnesia of Stencil's reading, is merely hinted at in the novel; in order to establish it "beyond all doubt," therefore, we readers need to restore *V.* to wholeness by supplying it with something *it* lacks—that is, by becoming second-order pornographers ourselves.[43] For as Alice Jardine has written, "V., this mother-fetish, is not meant to be found, but only deconstructed into her component parts, never adding up to a whole. A true body-without-organs, V. is the purely female desiring machine holding *V.* or any narrative together" (1985, 252).

But if this is to be one more reading paradigm for *Gravity's Rainbow*, then we need to ask ourselves two questions. First, is *Gravity's Rainbow* itself anamnesiac? Does the book, for all the celebrated centrifugality of its last hundred pages, finally re-member itself? And second, how do we re-member *our*selves as readers, and how is it useful to call by the name "pornography" these selected species of re-memberings? Why might we agree to redescribe and extend the term "pornography" so widely as to cover such disparate cultural phenomena as nostalgia and certain academic readings of texts?[44]

[43]For how we might read without becoming second-order pornographers, Hite's Wittgensteinian suggestions are helpful: we can read not for formal unities or thematic correspondences in which all terms have essential properties in common but for a version of Wittgenstein's "family resemblances." As Hite writes on *V.*, "Stencil assumes that things are related only if they have a single trait or property in common. . . . For this reason he remains blind to . . . family resemblances: relations based on 'a complicated network of similarities, overlapping and criss-crossed: sometimes overlapping similarities, sometimes similarities of detail' [quoting Wittgenstein 1945, § 66, 32e]. . . . In their inability to recognize family resemblances, the Stencils have a marked family resemblance" (1983, 52). Cf. Wittgenstein, § 67, also cited by Hite: "The strength of the thread does not reside in the fact that some one fibre runs through its whole length, but in the overlapping of many fibres."

[44]See in this respect Susan Stewart, who ingeniously extends the term, in a manner rather different from mine, to the *Final Report* of Attorney General Meese's Commis-

As for the book's own anamnesia: the sound of the V-2 opens the novel, and a rocket is launched from Peenemünde a few pages later (*GR* 6). At novel's end we are all in a Los Angeles theater, and the rocket, presumably tipped with a nuclear warhead, is delta-t above our heads (*GR* 760). This, it appears, would be spatial form with a vengeance—as the novel's beginning and end are coincident with the rise and fall of the rocket. The strategy whereby the novel re-members its opening may indeed be "pornographic" in the sense in which I have been using the word, and Molly Hite herself has noted that by means of the metaphor of the rocket's arc, "*Gravity's Rainbow* dictates the terms on which totalization should be possible, even as it resists totalization" (1983, 97). If this is the case, and I think it is, then the return of the rocket is a particularly powerful example of the resilience of our pornographies of reassembly. Film and calculus may be pornographies of flight, but as Pynchon knows, Leibniz was real; differential calculus, his closure-and-reconfiguration of Zeno's paradox, is real; ballistics, one of the many sciences enabled by the calculus, is real; and the fifty thousand nuclear warheads with which we are so familiar, like their delivery systems (all of which derive ultimately from the V-2)—these are real as well. *Gravity's Rainbow* does get more fragmented as it approaches its conclusion, true; but for Pynchon (or for us) to pretend that fragmentation, or differential Slothropian dissolution, can be the final word would be simply fraudulent in its turn. Although there are positions from which we can critique pornographic reassemblies, still, some imaginary unities have overwhelming political and cultural force, whether they constitute us as the autonomous thinking subjects we think we are, or whether they threaten to annihilate us all. And—more outrageous yet—they tend to reassert themselves even as we demonstrate their instabilities.

Nor is this all. Lurking beneath, behind, or around *Gravity's Rainbow*'s tales of the twentieth century are a number of related parables, each a cautionary tale about the precariousness of "open" systems, their special and extreme liability to pornographic strategies of reassembly. Squalidozzi may insist that "this War—this incredible War—just for the moment has wiped out the proliferation of little states that's prevailed in Germany for a thousand years" (*GR* 265), but, as we knew well before 1973, the war's eradication of "little

---

sion on Pornography (1986): "The Commission's task is the task of all pornography— to invent a realism which will convince us that our fantasies are inevitable and realiz-able" (1988, 172).

states" was not only an action "just for the moment" but also, more alarmingly, the necessary precondition for new pornographies of East and West, both within Germany and without, in the NATO and Warsaw alliances by which entire "worlds" (the First and the Second, and their "other" definition-by-negation corollary, the Third) have since been assembled. Likewise, the current disassembly of East and West involves both as its impetus and effect the reassembly of a united Germany; the extent to which this reassembly, too, will involve the regressive anamnesia of pornographic nostalgia remains, of course, a geopolitical issue of great concern. And as with the political entity "Germany," so too with I.G. Farben, the cartel that made World War II possible.[45] Officially "broken up" after the war, its Hydra-headed component companies have since reconfigured themselves under various corporate veils, and "the wartime confiscation and peacetime recapture of I.G. Farben property has completed its cycle" (Borkin 1978, 222). This in turn is but one of the myriad ways, as Pynchon writes, in which World War II has been "adjourned and *reconstituted* as a peace" (*GR* 75; my emphasis).

One recent pornography, neither narrowly "political" nor violently "pornographic," is notoriously implicated in Pynchon's work: the pornography known more widely as information theory, by which Norbert Wiener and Claude Shannon converted the destabilizing implications of quantum physics into the new determinacy of cybernetics (see Wiener 1954). In taking the "randomness" and "uncertainty" of Niels Bohr, Ludwig Boltzmann, and Werner Heisenberg and redefining them as preconditions for information, Shannon and Wiener made the postwar world safe for the forces of control once more. David Porush writes:

> Cybernetics' tactic here ranks as one of the great philosophical tricks of the century. Acting on a suggestion made by Leo Szilard as early as 1922, Wiener and then Claude Shannon in the 1940s took the formula for thermodynamic randomness (*entropy*) and used it to define the randomness which provides the necessary precursor for information, and

[45]"Without I.G.'s immense productive facilities, its far-reaching research, varied technical experience and overall concentration of economic power, Germany would not have been in a position to start its aggressive war in September 1939" (U.S. Group Control Council, Finance Division, Germany, *Report on Investigation of I.G. Farbenindustrie*, 12 September 1945; classification canceled by authority of the Joint Chiefs of Staff; microfilmed by the Library of Congress; quoted in Borkin 1978, 1, 225 n.1). Of course, for true Pynchonian paranoids, the very declassification of this document indicates that it too deliberately obscures the real text, that it describes "what even the masses believe" (*GR* 165).

then also called it *entropy*. From there, it was one small step to define information as *negentropy*. This little trick had powerful consequences. It appropriated the idea that the human introduced uncertainty into the system . . . and defined it as nothing more or less than a precondition for having a quantifiable amount of information. (1989, 375)

In a much-cited passage, *The Crying of Lot 49* describes the similarity between the equations for thermodynamic and informational entropy as "a coincidence" (*C* 105). But "Shannon's choice," as N. Katherine Hayles calls it, was considerably more motivated than that, and today "is regarded by many commentators within the scientific tradition as a scandal, for it led to the (metaphoric) knotting together of concepts that are partly similar and partly dissimilar" (1990, 50).

It is not, therefore, as a foundational article on Pynchonian entropy (Mangel 1971) would have it, that information gathering (whether ours, Stencil's, Oedipa's, or Slothrop's) increases the gatherer's uncertainty or increases "randomness."[46] On the contrary, as Porush and Hayles show us, Shannon proposed that information gathering is a probability function (as opposed to the accumulation of "meaning," as most of us think about it) and therefore could take place only in the context of randomness. Thus, when a system of information tends toward greater randomness, Shannon's theory holds that the "average information per symbol" increases accordingly—which is one way of saying, basically, that every piece of information helps when we're clueless. Hence, the greater the randomness of the system, the more information conveyed by each known attribute of the system—or, for Pointsmen, the more indeterminacy, the more potential determinacy.[47]

---

[46]Thomas Schaub (1976), by contrast, offers a skeptical reading of the way thermodynamic and informational entropies are presented in *The Crying of Lot 49*. For the equations, see Mangel 1971, 201–2; even a cursory glance will show that "average information/symbol" in the equation for information corresponds to H (entropy) in the thermodynamic version, and that the former therefore increases with the latter; if we cancel out the right sides of both equations, we end up with Shannon's postulate that information increases with entropy. When on the other hand randomness is at a minimum—when we've been told that we will be given a nonrepeating sequence of single letters in the alphabet, and we've already received 25 pieces of information— then the last letter conveys very little "information." For a more thorough explanation, see Hayles 1990, 44–60.

[47]Hayles explains that the status of the equations' "coincidence" depends on whether one follows Leon Brillouin's or Claude Shannon's model of informational "entropy." "For Brillouin," writes Hayles, "information and entropy are opposites and should have opposite signs"; but Shannon, in devising a probability function whose equation was similar to Ludwig Boltzmann's equation for thermodynamic entropy, decided to call his equation a measure of "entropy" as well, thus inverting the

It may nevertheless be a coincidence, in a particularly Pynchonesque sense of the word, that Norbert Wiener founded his new science on both a Pointsmanian hatred of indeterminacy and a "pornographic" fetish for the restoration of organic wholes. In the introduction to *The Human Use of Human Beings,* Wiener writes that "this recognition of an element of incomplete determinism, almost an irrationality in the world, is in a certain way parallel to Freud's admission of a deep irrational component in human conduct and thought," and he proceeds to explain his resistance to "uncertainty" in no uncertain terms: "This random element, this organic incompleteness, is one which without too violent a figure of speech we may consider evil; the negative evil which St. Augustine characterizes as incompleteness" (1954, 11). In Wiener's Pointsmania, and his desire to defeat the randomness and irrationality of nature (which is also, by way of his reference to Freud, a desire to resist the death drive), Pynchon readers can clearly recognize the telltale signs: Wiener himself, if not Shannon as well, is a member of the Firm.

More important, however, scientifically neutral descriptions of "information" obscure the intimate relation between cybernetics and the sciences of rocketry: "As Norbert Wiener documents . . . one of his original motives for developing a mathematics of control and communication was to further refine the guidance systems and trajectory calculations for mortar and rocket technology during World War II" (Porush 1989, 395 n.20). Cybernetics thus amply fulfills the instrumentalist criterion of my description of Pynchonian "pornography"—and does so in a way that could not be more central to the concerns of *Gravity's Rainbow.* Surely, one can only wonder why Pynchoniana lacks a discussion of the politics of information theory; but for now, at any rate, the point of these histories of "openness" should be enough warning. The Zone, I.G. Farben, quantum physics: each has been reassembled into a "Next Higher Assembly" (*GR* 252)—by means of pornographies that operate, like the New Turkic Alphabet, "in a political way."

Such pornographies, we will recall, are imaginary unities: Wiener's horror of "organic incompleteness" may be seen as a form of New Criticism, which may itself be seen as the expression of a fetish. And information theory, New Criticism, the Cold War, calculus, and ballistics have each—like von Göll with his Erdmann,

---

sign completely and defining "information" in terms of message probability rather than meaning (Hayles 1990, 48, 51–54). Clearly, Pynchon critics, and Pynchon himself, have taken up Shannon's model.

Katje Borgesius with her Brigadier, and Weissman with his Pökler—created either disciplinary subjects (cybernetics, close reading, higher mathematics) or disciplined subjects (alleged Communist sympathizers, scientists, and sadomasochists). But then this idea of imaginary unities that somehow do important cultural work brings back again, with the force of the return of the repressed, the difficulties of representing "pornography." My extension of the term, at this reach, reveals that I have ascribed to "pornography" what Lacan and Derrida would say is the condition of all language: papering over and denying lack, automatically replaying chains of desire, or reconstituting *différance* into a metaphysics of presence. Pornography thus becomes a privileged instance of language-in-general, and I have not only naturalized it but valorized it yet again: Pynchon's pornography as the supreme device for laying bare the device, showing the cultural and psychosexual conditions of possibility for our strategies of constructing unities like "gender" and then gendering everything, including ourselves, our languages, our conflicts. "At Brennschluss it is done—the Rocket's purely feminine counterpart, the zero point at the center of its target, has submitted" (*GR* 223); "Beyond simple steel erection, the Rocket was an entire system *won*, away from the feminine darkness, held against the entropies of lovable but scatterbrained Mother Nature" (*GR* 324).

Notably absent, moreover, from my own re-presentation of Pynchonian pornography is the materiality of the female body, a body that seems to have fallen away, like a rocket stage, as the scope of the term "pornography" grows ever wider. In the process of generalizing Greta Erdmann's torture and dismemberment, too, I have courted the danger of forgetting that the scene of her torture and dismemberment is itself a Pynchonian representation, and that "Pynchon's" position in the structure of representation is more or less that of the "director" of any snuff film.[48] I might respond that my "forgetting" of the female body in *Gravity's Rainbow* is but a repetition of the text's, since it is Pynchon who so extends the term "pornography" as to deploy it in the service of multiple analogies, and

---

[48]Not only for the obvious reason that Pynchon and not von Göll "directs" the scene but also because the scene—and the character of Erdmann herself—perpetuates the image of women's pleasure in violent submission, an image from which, for all we know, Pynchon himself may derive pleasure. (See also Bersani 1988, 209–16, for a discussion of the politics of sexual domination and the social construction of maleness.) It may be that Greta Erdmann is a woman "constructed" by male fantasies of woman's sexual pleasure, "constructed" so effectively as to *be* those fantasies. But then it is not clear whether those fantasies are Ours, Theirs, or the Text's (where and when we can draw such distinctions at all).

all analogies do violence to the specificity of the examples upon which they are built. But such a response would merely yield us one more Romanticism, in the form of a Shelleyan Pynchon who remarks for us the "before unapprehended relations of things"; and it would, more insidiously, deny my own agency in this construction of "Pynchon." Likewise but to the opposite effect, a Pynchon who merely empowers critiques of totality yields us but one more postmodernism of dispersion, unless we refuse the temptation to valorize dissolution *tout court*.[49]

Instead, therefore, I conclude with a more polemical, if no less problematic, claim: to read Pynchon's pornography as a pornography that lays bare its own devices and ours—to make it into a special, extreme demonstration of the politics of re-presentation—is, I think, among the less deceptive things we can do with it. We might turn back here for analogy to none other than Henry Miller—this time, however, to the Henry Miller of Kate Millett's reading, which makes of Miller's pornography a similarly privileged discourse: "Miller is a compendium of American sexual neuroses, and his value lies not in freeing us from such afflictions, but in having had the honesty to express and dramatize them. . . . What Miller did articulate was the disgust, the contempt, the hostility, the violence, and the sense of filth with which our culture, or more specifically, its masculine sensibility, surrounds sexuality. And women too; for somehow it is women upon whom this onerous burden of sexuality falls" (1970, 295).

Millett's sexual politics antedates—and initiates—the more variegated discussions on which this chapter has drawn, and it may seem strange that I close with her rather than with Teresa de Lauretis or Linda Williams. But her argument dramatizes nicely the various senses in which we can say that Pynchon "reveals" or "represents" a pornographic imagination. For Pynchon has often been linked to Miller, and perhaps Pynchon's pornography differs from the Miller of Millett's reading only insofar as it already contains and enables its auto-critique; we cannot be sure we are reading "against" *Gravity's Rainbow* in the way we can be sure Millett reads against the grain of Miller. If Pynchon's pornography self-consciously implicates itself,

---

[49]A critique of (pornographic assemblies of) we-systems may be freely translated as Richard Ohmann's "whenever you hear someone say *we* or *society* as if we were a homogeneous and conflict-free unity, get your hand on your wallet" (1987, 11). However, Jameson reminds us pointedly that the critique of totalities may be counterproductive, especially when political resistance depends on alliance politics, which itself depends on the recognition of family resemblances (1981, 54 n.31).

and us, in the problematics of representation and nostalgic reunification, we need to ask it in turn what *it* re-presents, and to read Pynchon's pornography not as the locus of transgression and disturbance, nor as the limit and instance of popular resistance and discursive carnival, but as the enactment and exposure of strategies of power, domination, and control—which are what imaginary, totalizing unities always seek to enable.

Bersani's treatment of Pynchonian paranoia concludes that Pynchon's interest lies in "depathologizing the paranoid structure of thought" (1989, 101); insofar as Pynchon, like Andrew Ross, refuses the reformist intellectual's separation of pornography from art or "normative" sexuality, he manages to depathologize pornography as well, disclosing to us that we live among millions of unremarked pornographies, just as we live and read as paranoids, whether we will or no. And finally, if *Gravity's Rainbow* affords us a devalorization of the "preterite" alongside these dual depathologizations, then we may not only construct a Pynchon who is less romantically preterite himself (as I argue at the end of the next chapter) but may also prevent ourselves from perpetuating our various knee-jerk, high-culture intellectual responses to his work—our preservation of "Pynchon" from the uncomprehending multitudes (manifested as disbelief at the appearance of *Gravity's Rainbow* on the *New York Times* best-seller list); our fears of academic "co-optation" of Pynchon; our compulsion to insist that Pynchon is marginal on all fronts, to all imaginable cultural centers. We may, instead, eventually say of Pynchon's work what Lawrence Grossberg has said about rock-and-roll: that just because it "has 'become' mainstream (in what sense was it ever not—unless critics simply rejected and ignored the largest part of its fans?) does not guarantee that it is delivered over to dominant ideological positions. Neither does production and distribution outside of the dominant economic institutions guarantee political resistance" (1988, 321).

If Pynchon does mandate our radical reconception of such things as pornography, paranoia, preterition, and postmodernism, then these "reconceptions" are useful just insofar as they produce new possibilities for cultural use, possibilities that produce in turn strategies of intervention in whatever we take, for the moment, to be our "real text": canons, supermarkets, cluster bombs, elections. This includes not only *Gravity's Rainbow* but also the texts of its reception—which I will take for my "real text" in the chapter ahead.

CHAPTER 5

"Surely to Pynchon's Horror":
Canonicity as Conspiracy Theory

IN THE preceding chapter I explored some of the uses of *Gravity's Rainbow*'s cultural artifacts—Rilke's poetry, *The Return of Martín Fierro*, the films of Gerhardt von Göll, *King Kong*, the music of Beethoven and Rossini, the New Turkic Alphabet, the legend of Slothrop/Rocketman—in order to argue that the novel is more concerned with these artifacts' cultural transmission than with their position in the dialectic of margin and center. I also attempted to mobilize Pynchon's "pornography," rather than (and in place of) Pynchonian paranoia, as a means for critiquing political totalities. In this chapter, then, I turn to the cultural transmissions of *Gravity's Rainbow* itself.

"Transmission" is not a transcendental category, and I do not intend to argue that the category of "transmission" is the great leveler of cultural products or that all cultural uses are equal in the eyes of the cultural critic. There does exist, as we shall see, a significant strain of Pynchon criticism which has so depoliticized *Gravity's Rainbow* as to have made it an exercise in narrative technique. Since this is a cultural use I do not wish to endorse, the first section of this chapter sets out to describe such depoliticization as a kind of displacement of Pynchon's politics onto the politics of literary form, whereby Pynchon is celebrated as a subversive writer because his work demands an active, pattern-making reader.

More widely, however, and more interestingly, Pynchon has also been celebrated by academic critics because his work resists academic study, because *Gravity's Rainbow*, especially, parodies and indicts the institutional transmission of cultural products. Accordingly, the second and third sections of this chapter discuss the ways Pynchon's readers have assigned him an author function diametrically at odds with their own. This is not a problem that can be addressed by any one reading of Pynchon, precisely because it implicates all institutional reading of Pynchon. Though I cannot claim to stand outside this question, on the fire escape of the prison house of Pynchon criticism, I can try to offer some explanations of why Pynchon criticism has painted itself into so uncomfortable a corner and of how it nevertheless paradoxically creates new cultural functions for itself in so doing.

Polemical Introduction

Before I begin, a word of apology—or warning. The Pynchon I have so far constructed will no doubt appear in many respects strange to many Pynchon critics, and to them especially I admit that the experience of reading *Gravity's Rainbow* is generally weirder than I have made it out to be. A quick flip through Chapter 4 will reveal none of Pynchon's moments of high lyricism or low puns, no Komical Kamikazes, no clowns with braided nose hair, no bareback dwarves with masks in the shape of the infinity symbol, no Sentient Rocks, not a mention of the local midgetry of the Mittelwerke. Nor, as should be clear by now, have I paid much attention to Pynchon's pyrotechnics of narrative discourse, his myriad variations on what we take to be narrators and narratees, his bewildering self-contradictions, his radical uncertainties.

I do not mean to deny the existence of narrative uncertainties in *Gravity's Rainbow*, any more than I mean to deny the existence of the midgets of the Mittelwerke. I do, however, mean to suggest that these textual phenomena have been severely overemphasized in Pynchon criticism, to the point at which Pynchon's value has been equated with his capacity for paradox, ambiguity, and irony—even by critics who ostensibly claim to have nothing to do with New Criticism. For if there is one immediately striking feature of our current reproductions of Pynchon, it is their formalism; and the corollary of this formalism is that Pynchon's more overt, less ambiguous, and variously political moments have become marginalized—usually on "aesthetic" grounds, but occasionally for "moral" reasons as well. Pynchon's critics have tended, so far, either to skirt the political implications of *Gravity's Rainbow* or to acknowledge them only in order to deny them outright.

In the camp of the "skirters" we can find even Leo Bersani, who writes that if Pynchon were "content to certify that all the plots [his characters] imagine are real plots, he would be making merely a political point, a point for which he has frequently been credited" (1989, 101). But Bersani takes this "point" to be no more than that Pynchon is a "defender of such lovable slobs as Slothrop and, in *V.*, Benny Profane the schlemiel against the impersonal efficiency of information systems and international cartels" (101)—and, of course, one wonders how the revelation of systems and cartels can be called "*merely* a political point," unless we take this to mean simply that Bersani's own untranscendable horizon lies elsewhere than on the plane of the political. But the point for which Pynchon has *not* been frequently credited, the point Bersani does not see fit to mention, is that *Gravity's Rainbow* thinks global capital in such a way as to ask us to reconceive our received narratives of World War II (not even the most revisionist of which can entertain the kind of "histories" Pynchon envisions) and, by implication, to reconceive our understanding of postwar configurations of knowledge and power.

Toward the end of the story of Byron the Bulb, for instance, we read the following entry on Phoebus, the international light bulb cartel:

> Phoebus couldn't cut down bulb life too far. Too many tungsten filaments would eat into available stockpiles of the metal—China being the major world source, this also brought in very delicate questions of Eastern policy—and disturb the arrangement between General Electric and Krupp about how much tungsten carbide would be produced, where and when and what the prices would be. The guidelines settled on were $37–$90 a pound in Germany, $200–$400 a pound in the U.S. This directly governed the production of machine tools, and thus all areas of light and heavy industry. When the War came, some people thought it unpatriotic of GE to have given Germany an edge like that. But nobody with any power. Don't worry. (*GR* 654)

Nor need we worry that anyone with any power will take this passage seriously. As it happens, we can turn for illustration to the most expansive American critic of them all, who, in the introduction to the Pynchon volume of his truly imperial 325-title Chelsea House series, regards Byron as "essentially Childe Harold in the Zone" (Bloom 1986, 4), devoting his piece to Byron's story not because of what it offers us in the way of Pynchon's uncanny negotiation of hallucinatory and historical conspiracies but because it can be made to serve "as a gateway both to Pynchon's Kabbalism and to his authentic nihilism, his refusal of the transcendental aspects of his own Gnostic vision" (vii).

It may be objected here that I am dealing a stacked deck; surely, one would sooner turn to Charles Vidor's 1946 movie *Gilda* than to Harold Bloom for insight into the relation between fictional "plots" and the world's distribution of tungsten. But evasions of Pynchon's politics are not exhausted by this example of the Higher Criticism, and the evasions take numerous other forms as well. First, critics charge Pynchon *himself* (or his narrators or his characters) with paranoia, thereby dodging the question of whether the novel's representations of postwar, multinational economic relations need to be taken seriously. Thus, it is claimed that "several among the powerless in the novel are indeed sufficiently paranoid to suspect that the terrible structure lurking within current history is that of an industrial conspiracy" (Sanders 1976, 146), or that "it is part of the paranoid vision of *Gravity's Rainbow* that the machinery of war is simply another function of the overarching industrial complex that runs the world" (Muste 1984, 15)—because, on such readings, "the novel is not *about* the paranoid vision, but *is* one" (Schickel 1973, 44), the product of "one man's paranoid though erudite hysteria" (Bell 1973, 17).

Second, we can claim to experience the political as boring or irrelevant. Scott Sanders complains that "Slothrop, as the novel's virtuoso paranoiac, subjects us to interminable catalogues of liaisons between General Electric, I. G. Farben, Shell, Siemens and a host of other corporations" (1976, 146). Richard Poirier assures us that "no one . . . will want to keep track of the hundreds of alphabetical agencies from World War II and the international cartels that are mentioned in the book, nor is anyone expected to" (1973, 60). For Thomas Smith, "Pynchon's paranoid scenarios are not to be taken literally," for "they do not 'represent' anything, let alone history. . . . Pynchon's imagination may seem paranoid . . . but he is only using paranoia as a device for building up his novel's massive structure. . . . Paranoia," concludes Smith, "is useful for creating fictions, not for engagement with the world" (1983, 248). The logic here seems to run as follows: because paranoia is only a technical device (Smith), or because the novel's politics are alternately paranoid, boring, or beside the point (Sanders and Poirier), Pynchon's value must therefore lie elsewhere—and, as we shall soon see, that value will often be located instead in his dislocations of narrative.

These evasions are formidable. More interesting, though, are the evasions that look like confrontations. Most of these are straightforward mystifications, as when Antonio Márquez writes that in *Gravity's Rainbow*, "Bad Shit is the social and cultural disorientation, personal and collective fragmentation, that make contemporary life a nightmare" (1983, 93). This not only makes Pynchon out to be T. S. Eliot; it does so in terms scandalously more general and vague than Pynchon's critique warrants.[1] At a slightly smaller remove from specificity there is Thomas Moore, for whom Pynchon has a widely applicable message—but, fortunately, a message so tricked up by artistic genius as to be worthy of mention:

> *Gravity's Rainbow* asserts—with a creativity and synthetic power that rescues the assertion from sounding hackneyed—that at this end of a three-hundred-year Western cultural dispensation our understandings of life, our sympathies for and in it, suffer too much from the habitual reification of 'either/or' contraries out of what is really a holistic cultural field (1987, 3).[2]

But if mystification fails or seems insufficient, we can baldly refute the book: recall that for David Leverenz, *Gravity's Rainbow* is "a sermon that [is], quite simply, wrong" (1976, 242). In Warner Berthoff's emphatic yet undefined terms, the novel "lacks a serious fiction's essential fidelity to a reciprocated human norm" and, more grievously, "imaginatively endorses the removal of historical actions from any commonly accessible realm of judgment and responsibility"

[1]Richard and Carol Ohmann narrate in detail similar mystifications of Salinger's *The Catcher in the Rye*, whereby reviewers and critics "displace the political emotion that is an important part of Salinger's novel, finding causes for it that are presumed to be universal" (1976, 32).

[2]Moore elsewhere quotes a passage I cited in Chapter 4, Pynchon's ecological indictment of a "System removing from the rest of the World these vast quantities of energy to keep its own tiny desperate fraction showing a profit" (*GR* 412), and claims that the passage "*atypically* moralizes directly" on "the clichéd concern, post–*Gravity's Rainbow*, with an energy crisis" (1987, 175; my emphasis). Perhaps Reagan's Environmental Protection Agency and Interior Department, too, operated on the belief that concern over our use of the world's energy is clichéd. Moore then goes on to explain that "'energy' here addresses the waste, not just of oil resources or of the famous environment, but of life's whole pool of counterentropic 'information'" (175). Just in case anybody thought Pynchon was making a merely political point, it is reassuring to know that his concerns are so universal as to embrace life's whole pool of something.

(1979, 70, 75). Similarly, for Scott Sanders, "Pynchon's conspiratorial imagination tends to make our social organization appear even more mysterious than it really is, tends to *mystify* the relations of power which in fact govern our society" (1976, 157), where the mere invocation of words like "really" and "in fact" suffices to rebut Pynchon on the points. Denial of the political Pynchon, it seems, almost necessitates denial on a grand scale—as, most notoriously, in the case of John Gardner, for whom missiles don't really exist: "It is a fact that, even to the rainbow of bombs *said to be circling us*, the world is not as Pynchon says it is" (1978, 196; my emphasis).

None of the foregoing denials operates on anything stronger than the grounds of the writer's convictions; these, we might say, are mere gainsayings of *Gravity's Rainbow*. In Robert Alter's 1975 *Commentary* piece, however, we are presented with a highly articulate, sophisticated rebuttal of Pynchon—one that moves briskly from a cunning mischaracterization of the novel's "history" to a new critical high ground from which the novel may be made to seem simplistic. Alter's argument takes its impetus from Pointsman's fear that the postwar world, in its rejection of determinism, will be nothing more than unconnected "events"—a situation he thinks of as "the end of history" (*GR* 56); but Alter craftily Alters the text to his purposes by implying that Pointsman's behaviorist fear is actually something like the novel's moral.

Alter begins by reading Pointsman's fear as if it were Pynchon's thesis: "If history is no longer a realm of concatenation, if there are no necessary connections among discrete events and no possibility of a hierarchy of materials ranged along some scale of significance, any associative chain of fantasies . . . can be pursued by the novelist as legitimately as the movement of supposedly 'significant' actions. The end of history, in other words, is a writer's license for self-indulgence, and Pynchon utilizes that license for page after dreary page of *Gravity's Rainbow*." But Alter does not stop at declaring Pynchon boring, as do Pynchon's lesser detractors. Rather, he moves from the mild assertion that Pynchon's history is chaotic to the more serious charge that Pynchon's "unwillingness to make differential judgments about historical events results in a larger inadequacy of the novel as a whole"—namely, its refusal to make the proper distinction between good and bad nations, white hats and black hats: "One would never guess from this novel, for example, that there were after all significant differences between a totalitarianism unsurpassed in its ruthlessness and political systems that had some institutional guarantees of individual freedoms, or between a state that was dedicated to fulfillment through genocide and one that was not" (1975, 49).

This defensive, missing-the-point flag-waving is in a way appropriate enough for the pages of *Commentary*, none of whose staff ever personally gave smallpox-infested blankets to Sioux children. But Alter's *coup de grâce* is yet to come: Pynchon's inability to recognize political "differences" (which Alter prefers to call "historical distinctions"), "disastrously encouraged" as it is by "post-Freudian cliché," results in a simpleminded novel that communicates nothing of value about the past or present: "History reduced so exclusively to the working out of the Death Instinct is metapsychological myth, no history at all, and what it generates in the novel is a proliferation of variations on one unswerving formula that in the end tells us nothing new about the challengingly ambiguous interplay of people and power in real historical time" (1975, 49–50). This is obfuscation at a sublime pitch: from Alter's high altar, we now see that the real interplay of people and power is "challengingly ambiguous," whereas Pynchon's excursions into history are no more illuminating than Yeats's Great Wheel. Pynchon is hung, in other words, with his own rope; his historical novel is revealed in all its fraudulent ahistoricity.

But I cannot simply gainsay Alter in my turn; it is, after all, possible to read Pynchon for what we can call his "metapsychological myth," and people have indeed done so. Poirier's early review of *Gravity's Rainbow* surmised that Pynchon "would not like being called 'historical,'" because in Pynchon, "history—as Norman O. Brown proposed in *Life Against Death*—is seen as a form of neurosis" (1973, 59). Lawrence Wolfley followed up the suggestion a few years later, in a 1977 issue of *PMLA*, and his article—not on the *presence* of Norman O. Brown in *Gravity's Rainbow* (for who can say that Brown is not "present" in *Gravity's Rainbow*?) but on the *centrality* of Norman O. Brown to Pynchon's fiction—has the regrettable effect of working to prove Alter's (and Poirier's) point, that history in Pynchon is no history at all. Even Wolfley's brief foray into political Pynchon does not historicize Pynchon, for though Wolfley suggests that *Gravity's Rainbow* is "Pynchon's version of *Why Are We in Vietnam?*" (1977, 875), he does not elaborate on what it might mean that Pynchon's "version" is not about Vietnam at all but about the one war within living memory which, for most Americans and for Robert Alter, was "the good war," unambiguous in purpose and outcome. On this count, historicizing Pynchon gives us a post-Vietnam, post-assassinations (*GR* 688 mentions JFK and Malcolm X explicitly)

reading of World War II, wherein the tales of the Schwarzkommando perhaps have more to do with the suppressed history of our
own segregation of troops than with the paracinematic reality of
black SS rocket troops on the Rhine.

Raymond Mazurek's hitherto little-noticed essay of 1985 makes
very much the same point: remarking that "*Gravity's Rainbow* was
written during the most intense years of opposition to American in-
volvement in Vietnam," he reads the traces of the time in the text's
concern with history and hegemony: "The sense of conflict between
a militarized industrial state of unprecedented complexity and
power and an amorphous but widespread counterculture is inscribed on almost every page of Pynchon's major novel. . . . *Gravity's Rainbow* goes beyond the awareness that historical representations selectively distort the past and raises the question of how
historical narratives function hegemonically within contemporary
history" (77). Thus, in lieu of saying that pop-psychological Pynchon
should not be read lest he bear out Robert Alter, I can only respond
in turn that even though post-Vietnam historical Pynchon is at least
as important as post-Freudian clichéd Pynchon, few critics have chosen to make the case for the former, either to Robert Alter or to
anyone else who may be listening.[3] Perhaps that is why, when
Pynchon's fans have wanted to protect their hero from the slings
and arrows of *Commentary*, they have chosen to rebut David Thorburn's 1973 essay (a much easier target, insofar as its strongest objection is that Pynchon's characters are not round enough to be a
"rich paradigm for the human circumstance" [70]) rather than take
on Alter's more elusive critique.

That the denial or avoidance of the political Pynchon should be
dictated by a critic's conscious political commitments is hardly surprising, and Pynchon critics have long been able to situate themselves comfortably on the left simply by noting that Pynchon has
numerous detractors on the right. My point, however, lies elsewhere: not in the hidden rationales for Pynchon's dismissal but in
the explicit rationales for assertions of his importance. It is to this
end that I call attention below to denials or avoidances of the political Pynchon not per se but insofar as they are allied to or dependent
on varieties of formalism. I want to state at the outset, however, that
these formalisms are by no means confined to Pynchon criticism;

---

[3]Tölölyan 1983b, Marriott 1985, and Mazurek 1985 are the salient exceptions. For
more on Mazurek, see below.

nor are they reducible to ahistoricism. On the contrary, the very model for my characterization of these critical displacements of the political is derived from so formidable a historicist as Hans Robert Jauss, whose account of *Madame Bovary*'s reception relies entirely on the horizonal change brought about by Flaubert's use of free indirect discourse. Distinguishing *Madame Bovary* from Ernest Feydeau's *Fanny* (published in the same year but much more popular at the time), Jauss claims that "the audience's horizon of expectations in 1857 . . . explains the different success of the two novels only when the question of the effect of their narrative form is posed" (1982b, 27), since both novels were at first attacked as amoral. The effect of form, we learn, was that Flaubert's technique "shocked" its initial audience, and after the novel was "understood and appreciated as a turning-point in the history of the novel by only a small circle of connoisseurs" did "the audience of novel-readers that was formed by it" come "to sanction the new canon of expectations" (27–28). Lost in this account, however partially (or Eliotically) justifiable an account it may be, are the details of Flaubert's critique of the Second Empire, from Emma's adultery itself to M. Homais's receiving the cross of the Legion of Honor in the novel's last line. Lost too is the fact that Feydeau's "amorality" did not, by the end of the nineteenth century, seem to have the same critical edge. And even if Flaubert's social realism became less important to "connoisseurs" than the *style indirect libre* in which it was conveyed, there are real social reasons why readers began to narrate the turning points in the history of the novel as a history of advances in form.

In Pynchon criticism, the model of such displacements can be found in David Leverenz's "On Trying to Read *Gravity's Rainbow*," for Leverenz narrates a reading process that explicitly operates according to an inverse relation between the appreciation of Pynchonian "form" and the depreciation of Pynchonian "content." It was only after dismissing Pynchon's "sermon," he writes, that he "rediscovered that [his] primary response lay with Pynchon's language" (1976, 244). The value of Leverenz's reading of his own reader response, however, lies in its effort to narrate its political unconscious, even as it finds confronting its own anxieties all too "easy":

> To the Pynchon who throws shit in my white male established American face and then calls it mine, I respond first with confused intimidation, even guilt, and then with annoyed dismissal, both to what he preaches and to the fact that he preaches. That response, once made sense of, is easy. But to the Pynchon who creates the most powerfully

aching language for natural descriptions in our literature, who can make me feel so keenly the moments of loss, separation, impingement, and simple sheltering human gestures, I respond with astonished praise, again and again, for all the singular exactitudes of feeling. (1976, 248)

Perhaps only the American impoverishment of the word "politics"—by which we understand that civil rights and abortion are very "political," whereas some public issues are not "about politics"—can account for Leverenz's distinction between political Pynchon and "powerful" Pynchon. For "political" Pynchon, on Leverenz's reading, reduces to what Pynchon consciously "call[s] for": "Against the twentieth-century complexities of bureaucracy, colonialism, markets, technology, interest groups, nations, Pynchon offers only the nineteenth-century fantasies (and they were fantasies even then) of anarchic individualism, momentary utopian communities, and the cult of Nature." These, writes Leverenz, are "peasant fantasies of a suburban alien," and they are so naive, and so preachifying, that "we put the book down laden with sympathy for *everybody*, and hostility only for human organization (and analysis) of any kind. . . . [Kurt] Vonnegut at least is clearer about the lines of power, abstraction, and manipulation" (242–43).

The idea here seems to be that a text's "politics" has to do with a narrow sense of textual use: whatever the book makes you want to do (love everybody, invade Poland) is its politics. Hence, Pynchon is an anarchist; *Gravity's Rainbow* is certainly anarchic; and anarchism, coming from suburban, alien flower people, tells us nothing new, as Robert Alter says, about the challengingly ambiguous interplay of people and power in real historical time. In a review of two of the first book-length Pynchon studies (Plater 1978, Seigel 1978), Raymond Olderman puzzled over precisely these kind of evasions, especially the critical habit of attributing "paranoia" to characters:

Why does Siegel say that "Tchitcherine blossoms into full paranoia, believing in an international rocket cartel plot"? (p. 110). Anyone who looked at the cartel arrangements of I. G. Farben, Imperial Chemicals, and International Incandescent Electric Lamp (Phoebus and G. E. included) might consider Tchitcherine an astute intuitive analyst. Is there no credibility to the suspicion that these cartels operated through World War II and into the present in some altered form? Isn't anyone shocked, just a little, by the accuracy of what Pynchon uncovers about Western world political power distribution? (1979, 504–5)

Over a decade later the jury is in, and the answer is no, we're not shocked, not a little. If we ever were "shocked" by anything in Pynchon at all—and some readers do register disgust with scenes involving excreta—we have displaced that shock almost entirely onto what we've been calling, for fifteen years or so, Pynchon's subversions of traditional narrative.

Though there can be no doubt that Pynchon's narratives thematize and implicate reading, most of the critical attempts to locate Pynchon's value on this plane start off by asserting differences in kind only to have them collapse into differences of degree, as one critic after another is forced to admit that, after all, *Tom Jones, Emma,* and *The Mayor of Casterbridge* thematize and implicate reading too. But, so goes the escape clause, these texts do so less thoroughly than do Pynchon's: "Unlike those in *Tom Jones,* however, the shifts in *Gravity's Rainbow* are much more rapid and more subtle" (Westervelt 1980, 78). One notes here the syntactical disjunction between "unlike" and "more" in the awkward effort to describe Pynchon's affinity with Fielding as a radical difference from Fielding. This insistence on Pynchon's narrative difference is important, nevertheless, insofar as we demand that our contemporary texts of value be somehow different—from anything—and thus original, unique, unprecedented (cf. Tompkins 1985, xvi). Thomas Schaub, for instance, claims that Pynchon's "artistic intentions are the reverse of [Henry] James's" in that Pynchon avoids closure, but Schaub proceeds only one sentence later to argue that Pynchon's art is the high art of implication and reader dislocation: Pynchon's "presentation of facts must imply without asserting, so that the facts are released from the rational structures of stable (and false) meaning without supplying at the same time another systematic restructuring which is equally pernicious. As a result, readers are confronted with texts whose meanings are never fixed, and they experience the severe loneliness of continuities that are discontinuous (though congruent) with the literal reality of the words which prompted them" (1981a, 112–13).

We may find Pynchon's importance, therefore, in the fact that his texts, unlike other texts, have no fixed meanings. Or, on strongly similar grounds, we may locate Pynchon's value and difference by repeating ritually the modern litany of reader-response readership: that the text throws us into a profound doubt (questions all our assumptions) which is never really ours in the end, for we have somehow overcome it. Thus, in *Gravity's Rainbow* "the reader's reliable Western reason is being subverted" (Pyuen 1982, 45), with the result that "no form of organizing our sense of ourselves, or ordering our texts, or of making sense of the chaotic world around us is safe in Pynchon's narrative" (Tölölyan 1979a, 317), because "Pynchon continually frustrates reader-expectation by jamming one lexical field against another. He suspends traditional laws of lexical and tonal consistency" (Olsen 1986, 81).

These are highly dramatic stories of reading, full of dangers and rewards, terrifying uncertainties, and hardnosed warnings to less sensitive readers to beware the perils of direct statement. As Jonathan Culler has written in discussing Wolfgang Iser and Stanley Fish, such stories "follow an innocent reader, confident in traditional assumptions about structure and meaning, who encounters the deviousness of texts, falls into traps, is frustrated and dismayed, but emerges wiser for the loss of illusions. It is as though what permits one to describe reading as misadventure is the happy ending that transforms a series of reactions into an understanding of the text and of the self that had engaged with the text" (1982, 79). But in an important sense it is genuinely odd that *Gravity's Rainbow*'s narrative texture should be experienced as "rupture." If, as Culler writes, stories of reading "require that something be taken as given so that the reader can respond to it" (76), why, we may reasonably ask, do Pynchon's readers take as their "given" the workings of "traditional" narratives?

As we saw in Chapter 4, critics such as McHale, Mendelson, and I claim more or less plausibly that Pynchon undoes our modernist habits of reading, though we disagree about what constitutes a modernist habit. But another group of critics would have it that Pynchon's narrative is an assault on a realism long dead by 1973. Lance Olsen has argued—in terms not too far removed from Mendelson's definition of the "encyclopedic narrative" against the "novel" (1976, 161)—that *Gravity's Rainbow*'s subversiveness is a function of its disruption of straw-man "monologic" novels: "As opposed to the uniform language employed by texts like *Clarissa*, *Pride and Prejudice*, *Portrait of a Lady*, [and] *The Sun Also Rises*—texts that fashion through their uniformity of language a uniform view of reality while insuring the reader that no adjustment to style and viewpoint will be demanded in the course of reading—*Gravity's Rainbow* employs a mixed language that revels in variety and potentiality" (Olsen 1986, 81). Yet this carnival does not result, for Olsen, in anything more than a Pynchon for whom "language becomes a meaningless and joyous affirmative freeplay in a world without truth" (81). And if this ludic Pynchon disturbs anyone, we are likely to be told even by one of his most astute critics that Pynchon's detractors "resent his novels because they refuse to fulfill a set of expectations nurtured by reading the great novels of the nineteenth century, or the slighter fictions of our time" (Tölölyan 1979a, 314).

What is suspect here, more than the narrow selection of texts to which Pynchon is opposed, is that his permutations of narrative discourse quickly become his primary, if not his only, means of subversion, transgression, and reader frustration. Thus even Neil Schmitz, who knows that Pynchon "is interested not in those who operated the ovens at Dachau but in those who devised them" (1975, 113), and who considers the National Book Award "the smarmy embrace of toleration" (125)—even Schmitz backs into the *reductio ad formam* conclusion that "the novel is extravagant in style, conception, technique," and that "it is through this extravagance that Pynchon insists on his otherness, his anarchic criminality" (124). Peter Cooper, too, has claimed directly that uncertainty is "an ultimate effect that Pynchon achieves through all of his fictional techniques" (1983, 174). These techniques turn out to be strategies of juxtaposition and narrative attribution, the first of which seems to destabilize our emotional response: "The narrator forces the reader to shift suddenly, even violently, between opposing attitudes and tones: complacency, paranoia, derision, chumminess, pontification, perplexity, morbidity, obscenity, and many more. These leave the reader no sure ground from which to respond to the fictional events" (197). But as we saw in the previous chapter, there are many other reasons why we have no sure ground from which to respond to the fictional events, reasons that have nothing to do with narrative and tonal inconsistencies. For we may be either, as in the case of the German inflation, unsure about the true location of History as Jameson's absent cause, or, as in the cases of *The Crying of Lot 49* and *Cashiered*, Schwarzkommando and King Kong, unsure whether "fictional events" are re-presentative or re-productive, *verité* documentary or paracinematic reality.

Let me once more acknowledge the obvious: *Gravity's Rainbow* is undoubtedly among the more technically challenging texts anyone could ask or be asked to read. But—despite our need to tell dramatic stories of reading—who really expects otherwise on picking it up? Can there be, in the 1990s, any innocent readers left, readers who have no idea that this 760-page Pynchon novel will be fairly rough going? For that matter, could there really ever have been, now or in March 1973 or at any time in between, readers of *Gravity's Rainbow* so naive as to have expected *Emma*? What *were* the reading expectations attached to the sign "Pynchon" in 1973? These are not simply belated rhetorical questions: nowhere in the ever expanding corpus of Pynchon criticism is there any account of a critic who approached *Gravity's Rainbow* expecting to be disrupted; nor are there any accounts, except for David Leverenz's dismissive report, of critics who were relieved to find that the novel did *not* question their fundamental assumptions.

I first read *Gravity's Rainbow* in 1982, returned to it often thereafter, and began my critical work on it in 1987, in the midst of the Iran-Contra hearings, the details of which (military-industrial juntas in the National Security Council, secret missions involving Bibles and good-will cakes) seemed only to confirm the existence of lunatic Pynchonian plots and international orders behind the visible. Throughout the 1980s, that is, Pynchon arrived on my desk already humming with meanings literary and social; and I recall likening *Gravity's Rainbow*, on the first reading, to John Hawkes's *The Cannibal* and William Burroughs's *Naked Lunch*. Those, however, are my own personal associations, for by 1982 Pynchon's stakes were quite a bit higher; through the 1960s, to judge by reviews and early dissertation abstracts, he was keeping critical company with Kurt Vonnegut, Joseph Heller, Ken Kesey, and sometimes John Barth.[4] *Gravity's Rainbow*, then, appeared when "Pynchon," as sign, had already been linked to a postwar American leftist absurd; but *Gravity's Rainbow*'s reviews upped the ante to the highest kind of secular authorization of all, likening Pynchon to writers such as Joyce and Melville. In that context he has remained, of course, as critics parse his relation also to Hawthorne, Lawrence, Faulkner, James, Poe, Mann, Kafka, Emerson, and so on. These days, Pynchon belongs "to the literary heritage in the American tradition represented by Hawthorne and Melville" (Schaub 1981a, 146); or, he "most closely resembles" D. H. Lawrence "in essential vision" (Moore 1987, 24); or, best of all, *Gravity's Rainbow* inhabits an international canon of six

---

[4]The first three dissertations on Pynchon discussed him alongside Joseph Heller, Kurt Vonnegut, and John Barth (1971); Flannery O'Connor, John Hawkes, and Jerzy Kosinski (1972, on violence in American fiction); and Heller and Nathanael West (1972). The first scholarly essay on Pynchon (Hausdorff 1966) links him strongly to Heller as well as Ken Kesey and Terry Southern: starting by noting that "with the publication of his first novel, *V.*, Thomas Pynchon was promptly categorized as a member of the 'Black Comedy' school," Hausdorff goes on to write of "Pynchon's consistent application of the possibilities of literary Absurdity" (258). James Young, by contrast, was the first to argue that "Pynchon seems clearly in the tradition of the major novelists of this century and has only superficial likenesses with the novelists of 'black humor'" (1967, 71).

writers spanning the years A.D. 1300–2000, as in Mendelson's delineation of encyclopedic narrative, where "its companions in this most exclusive of literary categories are Dante's *Commedia*, Rabelais's five books of Gargantua and Pantagruel, Cervantes's *Don Quixote*, Goethe's *Faust*, Melville's *Moby-Dick*, and Joyce's *Ulysses*" (1976, 161).

Such, then, are the terms on which Pynchon comes to us now; but they are not significantly different from the terms on which he was put into play in 1973. *Gravity's Rainbow* was advertised in both of the most influential generalist journals, the *New York Times Book Review* (full page, March 18, 1973) and the *New York Review of Books* (one-sixth page, May 3, 1973). Neither ad carried any illustration, preferring instead to sell the book solely on the remarkable strength of its "serious" endorsements, quoting six reviewers and their journals: Melvin Maddocks, *Atlantic Monthly*; Richard Poirier, *Saturday Review*; R. Z. Sheppard, *Time*; Walter Clemons, *Newsweek*; Geoffrey Wolff, *Washington Post Book World*; and Christopher Lehmann-Haupt, *New York Times*. Poirier, notably the only academic reviewer, was cited in the *Times Book Review*: "*Moby Dick* and *Ulysses* . . . come to mind most often as one reads *Gravity's Rainbow* . . . *Gravity's Rainbow* marks an advance beyond either" (1973, 62), a line that had orginally led the *Saturday Review* itself to publish an issue with the front cover headline "Pynchon's Big Novel: Advancing beyond *Ulysses*." It would appear, then, that far from violating anyone's expectations about "traditional narrative," *Gravity's Rainbow* appeared on the scene so freighted with the highest praise available to our literate culture, and so clearly associated with what any literate bourgeois reader would recognize as notoriously "difficult" texts, that it could not possibly have defeated any horizon of expectations by being too intractable, experimental, or narratively "disturbing."

Mendelson's first negotiation of this knotty problem is exemplary and riddled with telling contradictions. In the *Yale Review* of summer 1973, and in a mere two sentences, he invokes the equation of literary value and horizon-violation, admits that *Gravity's Rainbow* has met with immediate and overwhelming acclaim, and yet concludes that the novel disturbs and discomfits us just the same: "When a book is proclaimed a masterpiece within days of its publication it is usually a sign that the book has merely confirmed the reviewers' theories and prejudices. But *Gravity's Rainbow*, which by now has received every conceivable adjective of praise, is far too complex and disturbing, and demands far too extreme an adjustment in its readers' conception of the scope of the novel, to give much comfort to anyone" (1973, 631). And ever since 1973, as we have seen, even the readings that narrate their own process of reading tend not to be startled by, say, Pynchon's suggestion that the mass-conditioned stimulus of men's pornography is a discourse which can be "read" only through masturbation, or his depictions of "long roundabout evasions of political truth—of bringing the State to live in the muscles of your tongue" (GR 384); rather, as in Mendelson's account, what is unsettling about Gravity's Rainbow is that it adjusts our "conception of the scope of the novel."

We have, in sum, a critical heritage of Pynchon readings so insistent on the demands, dislocations, and indeterminacies of narrative that it now seems as if one has said something significant about Pynchon when one has shown him to have more negative narrative capability than anyone has previously attributed to him. In this reading formation, even Brian McHale's pair of articles (1979 and 1985), each of which argues that Gravity's Rainbow is more radically indeterminate than its critics assume, have themselves been one-upped by Alec McHoul and David Wills. Where McHale argued that critics "have ascribed a greater degree of ontological stability to the fictional world than the text actually warrants" (1985, 112), McHoul and Wills respond that even McHale has unwittingly simplified the text unduly: "McHale, it must be said, does recognise the unreliability of Speed and Perdoo, and concludes that 'we are left with elements whose ontological status is unstable, flickering, indeterminable' [citing McHale 1979, 95], but as long as he retains the notion of (presumably sovereign) consciousnesses being represented in the text, then verification of the ontological status of each datum is an assumed possibility. But we cannot be that sure" (1990, 46). In some ways, however, McHoul and Wills have been bracing and vigorous dissenters from the humanist orthodoxies of Pynchon criticism, and one welcomes their willingness to argue that in Pynchoniana, "the ratio of celebratory prose to critical insight is disturbingly unbalanced" (1990, 2). They undertake their emendation of McHale's argument, in fact, precisely because McHale spends so much time distinguishing "real" events in Gravity's Rainbow from various characters' fantasies. On the other hand, even McHoul and Wills sometimes nod, and lapse into something like affirmations of joyous freeplay: "The fact that discourse can always be quoted or cited, put between quotation marks, moved between texts to make new effects from different material, all this shows that any text can always have indeterminate uses and meanings" (1990, 9).

This is not quite the kind of self-enclosed "deconstruction" of Allen Thiher, Lance Olsen, or Reginald Gibbons, for each of whom deconstruction seems synonymous with meaninglessness; on the contrary, McHoul and Wills follow Derrida's critique of John Searle rather carefully throughout. The problem here, instead, has to do with their sense of "indeterminate uses and meanings," since "grafting" (or sampling), as a form of textual transmission, shows that any text can always have variously *determinate* uses and meanings. Such is the import of Culler's oft-cited dictum, itself a transmission of Derrida's response to speech-act theory, that "meaning is context-bound, but context is boundless" (1982, 123); such too is the import of Tony Bennett's distinction between *iterability* and *inscribability* (1983a; noted in Chapter 3).

Still, McHoul and Wills remain exceptions to the rule, as does Joel Black, who links Pynchon and deconstruction not on the issue of determinacy but on their similar critiques of Romantic and capitalist ideology, evidenced by *Gravity's Rainbow* and Derrida's "Economimesis" (1984, 30–31). But because it is almost characteristic of Pynchon's readers, including McHoul and Wills, to complain about Pynchon's readers (as if there were something gravely and fundamentally wrong with all Pynchon reading hitherto), and because my complaint above partakes of the rhetoric of all complaints in the world of Pynchoniana, I want to make clear one final point. My own call for more "political" Pynchon is only a call for one more (transmission of) Pynchon, a Pynchon I claim is underrepresented among the Pynchons of academic criticism. Nor do I mean to imply that political Pynchons will also be kinder, gentler Pynchons, better, smarter Pynchons, more revolutionary and less mystified Pynchons. Instead, I suggest that we interrogate not only our sense of Pynchon but our sense of "the politics of Pynchon" as well. As Bruce Robbins has pointed out: "Any title of the form 'the politics of x' suggests that we already know what politics is and are about to find out how x measures up against it. 'Politics' serves as a yardstick, an undeviating standard. It does all the questioning but does not itself get questioned" (1987, 4). And if we do extend our notion of literary "politics" beyond the demand that a writer tell us what to do about the Political Situation Today, then perhaps we may also extend our notion of "political Pynchon" beyond our approval or disapproval of Pynchon's purported "political program" of anarchism and the return to Nature.

The narrowly instrumental definition of "politics" has led even so political a critic as Raymond Mazurek to be finally dissatisfied with Pynchon's politics, on the grounds that *Gravity's Rainbow* is too diffuse to be properly and usefully counterhegemonic. Though Pynchon's novel, especially "with its central conflict between the Rocket cartel and the Counterforce, seems to have an uncanny political astuteness," still, writes Mazurek, its "political vision" is "unsatisfactory," because

> within *Gravity's Rainbow*, "Counterforce" is not the "whole story"; a resistance remains between Pynchon's anti-hegemonic vision and the complexity and dissonance of the novel as a whole. And this stylistic issue is symptomatic of the weakness of the text's politics, for the obscurity and density of *Gravity's Rainbow* as a novel can be said roughly to correspond to and reinforce the fragmentation and anarchism of its political vision. . . . The voice of the "Counterforce" in *Gravity's Rainbow* is almost muted as a serious historical alternative by the sheer multiplicity of the novel's voices, leaving an overpowering sense that no workable alternative can be more than momentarily successful in a world so fragmented to our perception and yet so controlled by amorphous structures of power. (1985, 82)

But surely it is as much a mistake to counterpose the novel's "politics" and its "style," to claim that the latter creates so much noise that it is impossible to hear the transmissions of the former, as it is to locate the novel's "politics" exclusively in its transgressions of "style." At the risk of sounding repetitious, I stress that representations are themselves political, regardless of whether they further the programs of alternative Counterforces, and that political Pynchons can be found even where Pynchon is not espousing a "politics," even where he is not historicizing Real Texts, even where his alphabets do not begin to work "in a political way" such that they impel us to kill the police commissioner. Pynchon's representations of gender and race, especially, are both critical and available for critique. But few critics have followed Catharine Stimpson's lead in this respect when, in an essay on pre–*Gravity's Rainbow* Pynchon, she described the "sexual conservatism" through which, "like Mailer, Pynchon endorses a sexuality that links itself to reproduction" (1976, 32), and his participation, at once antihegemonic and exoticizing, in "a custom of white American male writers in the 1950s and early 1960s: the transformation of jazzmen and blacks into savants" (42).

Pynchon's readers' senses of the "political" are a salient feature to me partly because I approached the body of Pynchon criticism hoping to find something else, and perhaps they have therefore become narratable insofar as they constitute violations of *my* reader expectations. But to the critic who is unfamiliar with what Tölölyan has felicitously called "canonical position[s] in Pynchon studies" (1983a, 170), to the neophyte who has read only a small sampling of the 400-odd articles, 30-odd books, 100-odd dissertations and 60-odd *CLC* entries on Pynchon, the salient feature of Pynchon readings does not consist in the critical tendencies of these or those readings at all; rather, what is distinctive for nonspecialists in Pynchon criticism is, first, its sheer volume, its status as the newest burgeoning light industry in the critical enterprise zone; and second, its ceaseless and tortured self-consciousness *about* its sheer volume and its status as a light industry, among the manifestations of which are the numerous histories of Pynchon's reception which are already part of the reception of Pynchon's work (Levine and Leverenz 1976; Tölölyan 1979a, 1979b, 1983a; Schaub 1981b; Callens 1983; Clerc 1983; Moore 1987; Duyfhuizen 1989).

Indeed, one of the most remarkable characteristics of the Pynchon industry is that it was deeply self-conflicted about the critical industry before Pynchon studies were fairly off the ground. For the section that follows, therefore, I take as my text not the specifically "good" or "bad" reproductions of Pynchon (as those distinctions are drawn by my desires) but the phenomenon of Pynchon reading in toto, imaged in Pynchon criticism's images of itself, especially as those images appeared at the onset of academic Pynchon studies in the middle to late 1970s. And this level of metareading brings up issues that cannot be resolved by distinctions between good and bad misrepresentations (or strong and weak misreading), for many of the images of Pynchon criticism I critique are, as it happens, images created by critics I consider to be among Pynchon's best close readers.

Professional Despise Thyself

"Critics of Pynchon's work," wrote Khachig Tölölyan in a pivotal moment, poised on the brink of reviewing no less than seven new Pynchon studies, "are not worried about squeezing his Text dry" (1983a, 165). The truth, however, is almost completely otherwise: it is part of the prolegomena to Pynchon criticism that one be sheepish and apologetic about one's status as a Pynchon critic, that one acknowledge oneself as the butt of Pynchon's ridicule, and, most of all, that one be self-conscious about how one's work will co-opt, enervate, diffuse, and defuse Pynchon's infinitely indescribable masterpieces. This aspect of Pynchon criticism, which is directed not at one or another kind of institutional reader but at the very practice of institutional reading and publishing itself, is so widespread as to be almost beyond citation. Even one of the more recent book-length studies genuflects at the altar of ritual self-incrimination, noting that the book we are about to read "will abet the effort of academic co-option, by the novel's own stipulation one of bad faith" (Moore 1987, 2). Nevertheless, I want to deal briefly with a few of the more important moments of such auto-criticism, moments I take to be significant in part because they all date from 1975 to 1979—the period during which Pynchon's primary arena of cultural reproduction ceased to be that of intellectual journals and nonspecialist reviews and began to be that of the professional readers of the academy writing in academic journals or for academic presses.[5]

Levine and Leverenz's *Mindful Pleasures* (1976, but composed largely of articles published in 1975) is the crucial text here, for a number of reasons. It is the first collection of essays on Pynchon and is highly self-conscious about its primacy. It contains the first, ambivalent attempt at a Pynchon biography, in which we learn of Pynchon's refusal of the 1975 William Dean Howells medal: "I know I should behave with more class, but there appears to be only one way to say no, and that's no" [quoted in Winston, 1926, 262]). It marks the discovery by critics that "one of the conditions of [Pynchon's] staying with his present publishers . . . is that they not publish books about his work" (Levine and Leverenz 1976, 3–4). And it contains the first history of Pynchon's reception, a brief account of a struggle between unintelligent or faithless reviewers who had

---

[5]For verification of Pynchon's "appearances" through this period I have relied on the MLA bibliography and the *Book Review Index*. The *BRI* lists 41 reviews and notices of *Gravity's Rainbow* through 1975 (oddly, however, neither the *BRI* nor the *Book Review Digest* reference the two *Commentary* articles on Pynchon), of which 13 (14 with Thorburn's *Commentary* piece) appeared in the ten most influential intellectual journals in the country (see Kadushin, Hover, and Tichy 1971): *New York Review of Books* (22 March 1973), *New Republic* (14 April 1973), *Commentary* (Sept. 1973), *New York Times Book Review* (11 March 1973, 10 June 1973, 2 Dec. 1973, 10 March 1974), *New Yorker* (19 May 1973), *Saturday Review* (10 April 1973), *Partisan Review* (Fall 1973), *Harper's* (June 1973), *Nation* (16 July 1973), *Atlantic* (March 1973). In other words, within six months of its appearance *Gravity's Rainbow* had been reviewed by every one of the top ten American journals. The *BRI* also lists six British journals: *Listener* (15 Nov. 1973), *Times Literary Supplement* (16 Nov. 1973), *New Statesman* (16 Nov. 1973), *Spectator* (17 Nov. 1973), *Books and Bookmen* (March 1974), and *Encounter* (Fall 1974). (I have not included trade reviews—*Publisher's Weekly*, the Kirkus Service.) By 1979 there were 98 scholarly articles on Pynchon (28 devoted solely to *Gravity's Rainbow*), 38 dissertations, 2 collections of essays, and 3 books (Slade 1974, Plater 1978, Siegel 1978); 1979 is also the year in which *Pynchon Notes* was founded.

Pynchon all wrong, and valiant, farsighted, "serious critics" who "did see that Pynchon was a writer likely to matter" (5). The last phrase is more or less the key to the piece's inattention to the agencies of reception, since Pynchon could have been twice the writer he is and still not have "mattered" had not "serious critics" made sure, precisely by paying prolonged attention to him, that he *would* matter.

According to Levine and Leverenz, for instance, in spite of the "curious dearth of serious reviews" of *The Crying of Lot 49* and Remington Rose's "astonishingly unintelligent" review of the novel in the *New Republic*, "the book was becoming one of those convenient short rich texts that might be used in freshman and sophomore classes" (6–7). It "was becoming" canonical, apparently, all by itself—just as, after the publication of *Gravity's Rainbow*, David Thorburn's "A Dissent on Pynchon" in *Commentary* was a sign that "even *Commentary* will have to come around eventually" (8). The story as told here, then, is one wherein reviewers gradually acknowledge Pynchon's greatness, and pockets of resistance are attributed to various perversities. Despite this slant, Levine and Leverenz do relate some material details in Pynchon's reception history: they notice— and rightly describe as "minority" (5)—the persistent right-wing dislike of Pynchon, and they discover a slight falling-off in Pynchon's acclaim after *Lot 49*'s publication.

But I do not intend to attack Levine and Leverenz because their account of reception does not sound enough like Richard Ohmann's or Felix Vodicka's; what I want to take up instead is their assertion that "the very idea of a collection of essays about Pynchon violates the terms on which he presents himself to us" (3), the conclusion of which is their (somewhat tongue-in-cheek) apology to Pynchon, "wherever you are" (4), for having compiled the collection at all. Variations on this apology, and its assumptions, run through the collection—and Pynchon's subsequent reception—as a whole. Richard Poirier, in the volume's first article, cautions us that "unless academic writers and teachers are extremely careful they will do to him the damage already done to Joyce and Eliot" (1976, 19). And we know that this is a fate well avoided, for "who," writes Edward Mendelson, "witnessing the enormous multinational operations of the IG Joyce cartel, would choose to open an office in the Pynchon industry?" (1976, 170–71).

The function of Pynchon critics, in other words, is to be antagonistic to Pynchon if they are to be faithful to him, for "Pynchon wants no part of the critic's enterprise" (Levine and Leverenz 3).

Even in 1976, apparently, in only the first collection of Pynchon essays, it is not too early to begin worrying about the politics of cultural bureaucracy, for "*Gravity's Rainbow* is now more than three years old and is hovering dangerously on the edge of becoming—surely to Pynchon's horror—a classic" (Levine and Leverenz 8). *Surely to Pynchon's horror*: the very phrase distills the Pynchonian version of a deeply antiprofessionalist ethos (which Levine and Leverenz attribute, rightly or wrongly, to Pynchon himself), wherein the function of cultural institutions is construed as sheer recuperation, repressive tolerance, amalgamation, Weberian routinization of charisma.[6] Pynchon is the *avant*, we are the *garde*, and Pynchon's importance is therefore directly proportional to his "marginality," his well-publicized aversion to publicity, his refusals to cooperate in his co-optation by the cultural center. In Poirier's words, "What's happening to Pynchon, as he is moved increasingly into position for a guide-book study, is a cause not for celebration but for misgiving" (1976, 19). Well might we wring our hands, for the bibliography to *Mindful Pleasures* (compiled by Bruce Herzberg) already logs forty-two items in critical journals and influential reviews, even though it is limited to 1972–75 and is "intended only as a supplement to the exhaustive [bibliography] by Joseph Weixlmann (in *Critique* 14 [1972], 34–43)" (265). But then again, even today Melvin Tolson has not yet accumulated forty-two similar items, and one wonders whether Poirier would consider this a cause not for misgiving but for celebration.

As in that of *Harlem Gallery*, so too, then, in Pynchon's critical heritage: Tolsonian positions reappear in Pynchon's reception history—with a difference. The difference is that the poet in this case is not crying out that he is surrounded by bulls of Bashan; rather, in Pynchoniana we academic critics paint ourselves as the bulls of Bashan, the weeping monkeys of the Critics' Circus. And because, as Mendelson writes in 1978, *Gravity's Rainbow* "has already generated institutions that seem entirely innocent of any sense that the book they honor criticizes precisely the kind of honor they offer" (9), our only alternative, as academic critics, is to make a virtue of our

---

[6]The only minority report I can find here is that of Charles Clerc, who writes that the expansion of Pynchon studies is "all to the good," for "the more *Gravity's Rainbow* can be read and discussed and written about, the greater will be the appreciation and dissemination of its remarkable artistry" (1983, 30). This is a welcome argument in Pynchon criticism, but one wishes it had not hinged so explicitly on a poetolatry which decrees that Pynchon research is all to the good because *Gravity's Rainbow* is "a seminal work of genius" (30).

acute self-awareness: "Collective enterprises have built themselves up around Pynchon's work—and this book is one of them. But I hope this book is one which is at least aware of its paradoxical dilemma in offering Pynchon an honor which he implicitly condemns" (Mendelson 1978, 9). Schaub, in turn, closing the feedback loop, ascribes "the apologetic tone one finds in Pynchon criticism" to Pynchon's rhetorical power, for "that Pynchon's writing engenders such hesitation is a sign of its strength" (1981a, 138 n.17). But there is also a twist here: we are not merely the parasites who infest classics and suck their life blood (making them stronger); we are, worse yet, also the *creators* of "classics," and our every published effort to disentangle Pynchon from the morass of MLA sessions and graduate seminars only implicates him further in the morass. Pynchon's power, according to this anti-reading, lies in his creation of dissenting critics whom his work simultaneously produces and contains, and who simultaneously reproduce and contain his work in turn, while testifying to its power.

The spectacle of self-conflict in Pynchon criticism is in many ways an amusing one and, to "outsiders" in the academy and elsewhere, probably an entirely pointless one as well. Surely, for that matter, some of this self-conflict is pro forma posturing, a simulacrum of critical anxiety over the purposes of criticism which serves to obscure more pressing questions about those purposes, such as (to rehearse some of the material I covered in Chapter 1) whether literary intellectuals serve to reproduce antidemocratic social relations outside the academy, whether criticism needs to locate a client class in the literate public, or whether, more locally, criticism should be quite so invested in explication of the works of major authors. I do think there are real reasons for Pynchon critics to be anxious about their roles, and these reasons have to do with the functions of all institutional criticism: an impoverished notion of criticism's purposes can very easily yield the kind of cultural transmissions I have documented in this chapter, in the form of criticism that unthinkingly glorifies (and occasionally condemns) narrative complexities that cannot be put to an immediate ("political") use. I grant, however, that most of the reasons Pynchon criticism has so far provided for its concerns are byproducts of the Romantic ideology according to which critics are the natural enemies of the avant-garde, and that these "reasons" might therefore be more accurately characterized, after Althusser, as imaginary relations to real reasons. But not every subject position available to Pynchon criticism is interpellated by Romantic ideology, and even the positions that remain Romantic are not unique to Pynchon's critics, though they are well illuminated by Pynchon's critics.

The first of these is easiest to describe, since it follows from Pynchon's status as Romantic culture hero; it is nothing other than the flip side of the idea that academic reception constitutes a routinization of textual charisma. For Pynchon to be *fully* a Romantic culture hero, that is, there must be some audience somewhere that is not adequately appreciating his genius; there must be at least a modicum of readers who resist *Gravity's Rainbow*, if only so that an Edward Mendelson can claim that the novel does not give much comfort to "anyone," or so that a Richard Poirier can cordon off the novel from its would-be middlebrow perusers in the belief that "the mass of good amateur readers—the kind who belong to the Book-of-the-Month Club—not only don't but can't much like him" (1976, 16).[7]

Fortunately, Pynchon critics did not have to look far to locate this audience throughout the mid-1970s: *Commentary* was always willing to check in with a nay-vote; the Pulitzer advisory board notoriously panned the book in 1974; and other hostile reviews can be found in *Harper's*, the *Spectator*, *Prairie Schooner*, and the *Hudson Review*.[8] And since reviews and re-reviews of *Gravity's Rainbow* continued to pile up in nonspecialist venues for an exceptionally long time (more than three years), the first managing directors of the young Pynchon industry could keep up a war on two fronts: against themselves as agents of co-optation, but also against select representatives of the uncomprehending masses who were failing once again to do justice to genius in their midst. By the 1980s, on the other hand, institutional criticism had, in the natural cultural course of events, achieved hegemony over Pynchon's transmission (and over his place in American letters), and hostile audiences became harder to find. Undaunted, Pynchon critics now claimed that Pynchon was

[7]As Janice Radway has argued (though not in the context of Pynchon studies), Poirier's cordon between *Gravity's Rainbow* and the Book-of-the-Month Club is a standard literary-classist move: in the view of scholars and professional critics, Radway writes, "the Book-of-the-Month Club offers . . . neither the best works of contemporary literature nor the worst examples of mindless 'trash.' Its books, rather, fall into that large amorphous middle ground of the unremarkable but respectable. It is worth keeping in mind, however, that . . . mid-range books are seen by such commentators not simply as different from those occupying higher positions but as failed attempts to approximate the achievement of the best books" (1988, 518–19).

[8]Respectively, Shorris 1973, Ackroyd 1973, Sabri 1973, de Feo 1974. Some of the more balanced reviews, as well, contain serious qualifications: see Locke 1973, A. Levine 1973, Morris 1973.

(had always been) marginal to a public sphere of general readers and that *Gravity's Rainbow* was therefore "the most unread best seller in America during 1973, ánd perhaps ever" (Olsen 1986, 74), or, more grandiosely, "among the most widely celebrated unread novels of the past thirty years" (Moore 1987, 1).[9]

It would be beside the point to debate these claims on their merits; there is, in the end, no way to assure ourselves that the novel's purchasers did not read it, or did not read it with a requisite amount of sympathetic intelligence. Nor do we need such assurances, for what is at stake is the very construction of Pynchon's "sign value": the important thing is precisely that *Gravity's Rainbow* was put into discourse, by journalists, academics, and advertisers, as one of the greatest books in years if not decades, a book serious readers would be expected to *own*. And if many people bought the novel but did not finish it, this would hardly be cause for surprise, or for claiming Pynchon's uniqueness; nor would it explain why the novel continues to sell. My point, however, is that the academic cultural center has worked assiduously to establish a margin for Pynchon to inhabit, even when the effort has involved considerable strain—as, for example, when Tölölyan has tried to claim that *The Crying of Lot 49* and *Gravity's Rainbow* "have achieved general, usually negative, but widespread recognition by the public" (1983a, 168). For Pynchon to be marginal, he must be in some sense oppositional (and vice versa); we have already seen how he has been made oppositional to something called "traditional narrative," and now we find that he can be made oppositional to what are portrayed as "traditional" audiences—general readers, academic readers—depending on the historical and rhetorical position of the critic at hand.

Because the construction and depiction of these audiences is a function of nothing more tangible than critical projections and ar-

[9]None of Pynchon's publishers will release current sales figures. According to Kihss 1974, 38, however, as of April 1974, Viking reported that *Gravity's Rainbow* had sold 15,000 hard-cover and 85,000 paperback copies since its publication; Bantam printed 220,000 copies of its paperback edition of the novel, having already printed 800,000 copies of *V.*; and *Gravity's Rainbow* was "the first work by a major novelist to be issued simultaneously in hardcover . . . and in quality paperback." Ironically, though Kihss's article is often cited for its report on the Pulitzer advisory board (members of which were anonymously quoted as having called *Gravity's Rainbow* "unreadable," "turgid," "overwritten," and "obscene"), few critics have seen fit to mention the sales figures it included, since these tend to compromise the spurious "marginal" and "criminal" status the Pulitzer board inadvertently conferred on Pynchon. By the end of 1980, to judge by the novels' copyright pages, the Bantam paperback of *Gravity's Rainbow* had gone through nine printings and two more by 1984; *V.* had seen fourteen printings; *The Crying of Lot 49*, eighteen printings.

ticulations of the relation of professional criticism to a variously construed "public sphere," determining Pynchon's author function and
cultural position tends to be a highly unstable enterprise. The clearest case in point is Tölölyan's provocatively titled essay "Criticism as
Symptom: Thomas Pynchon and the Crisis of the Humanities." The
first two paragraphs, which narrate a brief reception history whose
thesis is that "it is no longer possible to be seriously interested in
contemporary American literature and yet to claim jauntily that one
'just can't get through' Thomas Pynchon's books" (1979a, 314), may
lead one to believe that the "crisis" in question has to do with the
"authorization" process by which "serious people" are now required
to read Pynchon, or to try to. It is unclear at first from Tölölyan's
tone, however, whether these developments are to be cause for celebration or for misgiving; do we want a general culture in which people are not coercively required to be familiar with Pynchon (and
therefore presumably read him on their own, for delight and in-
struction), or a general culture in which people cannot get away
with neglecting Pynchon (and therefore can be charged with unjustly neglecting him)?

The third paragraph seems to clarify matters, for it suggests that
the "crisis" is the crisis of co-optation, the burgeoning, bourgeois,
American and postmodern apparatus for cultural absorption which,
as Walter Benjamin said in another context, "can assimilate an astonishing number of revolutionary themes, and can even propagate
them without seriously placing its own existence or the existence of
the class that possesses them into question" (1970, 90). But then
something odd happens between Tölölyan's paragraphs three and
four:

> As usual, the reception accorded a writer says as much about his
> readers as about him. The eagerness with which academic critics have
> begun to write about Pynchon is due to no single cause. He is ac-
> claimed for many reasons, and is being claimed for several causes. I
> should like to interrogate these responses, in the belief that they have
> much to tell us about the weaknesses that beset and the energies that
> vitalize what we euphemistically call the "discipline" of literary criticism
> or even, more grandly, the Humanities.
>
> Much of the hostility that Pynchon's fiction has aroused comes from
> those who have labored hard to narrow the definition of what can be
> considered literary; they have done so in order to constitute criticism as
> a manageable discipline, and are alarmed by the inability of their nar-
> row generic and modal categories to deal with Pynchon's work. (314)

Even though it is true that Pynchon has met both with acclaim and hostility for no single cause, and though I could not agree more that Pynchon's work challenges "disciplines," surely is it worth remarking that Tölölyan has apparently set out to interrogate the reasons for Pynchon's widespread "acclaim," and has by his fourth paragraph switched over to the claim that Pynchon is not being given his due—by, of all people, academic critics.[10]

Pynchon's purported transgressions of the standards of literary criticism give rise in turn to the most easily overlooked, and yet most intriguing, cultural function he has been made to perform: he has allowed academic critics to position themselves, insofar as they take up the role of the defender of genius against the bulls of Bashan, as something other than academic critics. Pynchon's readers are thereby afforded the possibility of highly mobile affective alliances whereby they can position themselves in a variety of relations to the institutional study of literature: as keepers of Pynchon's flame, defenders of the faith against the infidels of journalism; as cultural bureaucrats uneasy about the social functions of bureaucracy; as *avant* academics, in but not of the discipline; and, most prevalently, as *fans*, in the sense that there are fans of mass-cultural phenomena such as rock-and-roll or (more poignantly) the Chicago Cubs, in the sense that there are *not* fans of academic-cultural phenomena such as econometrics or revisionary accounts of Henry Adams.

The permutations of these positions are many; perhaps the most astonishing is that of J. O. Tate, whose *National Review* notice of *Slow Learner* begins, "No longer will these stories . . . be merely the dusty objects of the sublimated lusts of malnourished graduate students and tendentious professors, photocopied obscurities to be pondered by cultists" (1984, 53). Sneering asides at Pynchon's academic readers are not uncommon—Peter Prescott's *Newsweek* review of *Slow Learner* describes "graduate students who even now are hacking out dissertations on Pynchon's use of 19th-century physics"

---

[10]Despite this confusion about audiences and opponents, Tölölyan is one of Pynchon's best critics and was the first to align Pynchon with Foucault in that both write of "real or dreamed-of institutions, like the Raketen-Stadt of Pynchon and the prisons or clinics of Foucault," and both reveal the workings of power in which "individuals are produced out of whole cloth" (1979b, 233). Thus even though Tölölyan is less than clear as to where, and to whom, Pynchon is oppositional, he has rested his case for oppositionality as much on Pynchon's explorations of history, discourse, and power as on Pynchon's various subversions of narrative. His most sustained treatment of historical Pynchon is "War as Background in *Gravity's Rainbow*" (1983b).

(1984, 100–101), as if academia were a kind of New Grub Street—but what is interesting about Tate's swipe is that Tate is himself an academic critic and has published a pair of articles in *Pynchon Notes*. And needless to say, by 1984 Pynchon's reception was entirely in the hands of academic critics—hence the high incidence of sniping at academia by the nonspecialist press. Such sniping is different from that of the mid-1970s, in which Pynchon was derided as a merely academic novelist, for by 1984 this "generalist" anti-academic prejudice feels as if it has been confirmed: a decade of Pynchon's reception has amply borne out Peter Ackroyd's 1973 prophecy in the *Spectator* that Pynchon "has written a novel which would deter and baffle any but the most avid research-student pursuing a thesis. *Gravity's Rainbow* becomes a specimen of Eng. Lit. as soon as it comes off the presses, and this is the heart of my suspicion of it" (1973, 642).

But if Pynchon allows his critics to imagine (or to be grateful) that they are not academic critics, rarely is the rhetoric of antiprofessionalism so strangely deployed as in J. O. Tate's case. More common—to Pynchon criticism and to antiprofessionalism generally—is the rhetoric of Mendelson: "*Gravity's Rainbow* is in part *about* the kinds of institutions which have sprung up in response to its existence. . . . The Modern Language Association has received petitions urging the maintenance of a continuing study seminar on Pynchon; Pynchon Reading and Study Groups meet regularly in New York and elsewhere; indexers, bibliographers, allusion- and lexica-compilers are all hard at work on their bureaucratically defined tasks" (1978, 9). For Mendelson as for many others (including Jonathan Yardley), the institutional study of literature is a self-sustaining *Interessengesellschaft*, a corporate community of interests, an "IG Pynchon" run by "scholar-magicians of the Zone, with somewhere in it a Text, to be picked to pieces, annotated, explicated, and masturbated till it's all squeezed limp of its last drop" (*GR* 520). The Text under this kind of consideration is thus a seminal text, to be deseminated by annotators and explicators, all of whom are endlessly implicated by *Gravity's Rainbow*'s critique of institutions as epiphenomena of Thanatos: for "if there is a life force operating in Nature, still there is nothing so analogous in a bureaucracy" (*GR* 228).

Mendelson's antiprofessionalist rhetoric occurs in his introduction to collected Pynchon essays (1978), which, like Levine and Leverenz's introduction to *Mindful Pleasures*, presents Pynchon's institutionalization as already a *fait accompli*, a phenomenon to be reported, and lamented, in the present tense. We need, therefore, to ask some

questions of Mendelson's introduction today: is the academic reading of Pynchon really all that bureaucratic? if there is such a thing as
IG Pynchon, in what material practices does such a corporation consist? and, most of all, to what extent is antiprofessionalism authorized by Pynchon himself? If we attend to Pynchon's indictments of
scholarly readers, need we believe that texts are really penises to be
squeezed dry and that critics are really the supplements of genius?

Note that Mendelson is not making any *specific* antiprofessionalist
arguments about our "bureaucratically defined tasks"; rather, Mendelson—like Levine and Leverenz, and like Tölölyan—is claiming
that professional reading in itself constitutes de facto institutionalization and that it can be detected and measured by MLA sessions,
"Pynchon Reading and Study Groups," and "indexers, bibliographers, allusion and lexica-compilers"—whatever these last are. One
might counterargue, conceivably, that academic study of this kind
(indexing and allusion-compiling) is usually undertaken only on behalf of writers who have been so widely *authorized* that the profession requires highly detailed materials for their further study: letters,
variora, critical editions, reader's guides. The professional rewards
for taking on the tasks of compiling and organizing these materials
are often negligible, and professionals engaged in the maintenance
of these tasks may have every reason to feel that their work is rou-
tinized, routine, and routinely taken for granted. Perhaps, then,
from the perspective of critics who have no cause or occasion to
sneer at the "bureaucratically defined tasks" of literary study, the
profession of criticism seems less a means of advocating "authors,"
as a class of clients, than a means of maintaining a vast hierarchy of
organizational charts with various department heads and subheads
(major and minor critics), together with their secretaries (research
assistants and "lexica-compilers"), clustered around senior and exec-
utive vice-presidents in charge of production ("authors" and "theorists"), many of whom bemoan their lack of a universally recognized
CEO. And surely this nightmare vision of Authorship would appear
entirely germane to IG Pynchon, which claims to be uniquely aware
of the "damage" that can be done by the conferral of Major Authorship. But Mendelson, notably, does not contest the formation of IG
Pynchon as a major-author industry. On the contrary, it is Mendelson who has invested the most stock in Pynchon's status as major author, opening his adulatory review of *Slow Learner* with a
memorandum to the effect that "the apprentice work of a major novelist makes better reading than the mature productions of a dozen
minor ones" (1984, 36).

Then again, perhaps Mendelson's is precisely the kind of venera-
tion Pynchon has sought to avoid, and certainly, it would be easy
for me to claim that Pynchon's refusal of the Howells Medal, or his
failure to appear at National Book Award ceremonies, demonstrates
his dissent from the notion that his mere signature is worth a dozen
Harlem Galleries. But I cannot make this claim, for to do so would be
to position Pynchon once more against the bulls of Bashan, this time
to say that Pynchon supports my own argument concerning the critical industry's relation to its major authors, and thus that the writer
Mendelson honors criticizes precisely the kind of honor he offers.
Worse yet, to make this claim would also be to ascribe to Pynchon a
kind of Tolsonian "marronage," a marronage consisting of attempts
to escape the slavery of canonization while raiding the academy's
cultural capital every so often; but such a deployment of "marronage" as sign would do such extraordinary symbolic violence to
the actual African-Caribbean experience of slavery that it simply
seems unthinkable to cast Pynchon as maroon. I contest Mendelson's value equation, therefore, because it is idolatrous and self-
contradictory: idolatrous in that I find nothing attractive in reading
Pynchon's short stories for what Mendelson calls "an exhilarating
spectacle of greatness discovering its powers" (36); self-contradictory
in that, if taken seriously, Mendelson's formulation leads us to picture an industry in which no one bothers with "minor" writers
(since the apprentice works of the majors are far better reading) until
these "minor" writers suddenly become "major," at which point, lo,
all their productions increase in value by twelvefold or more. I will
not, however, contest Mendelson's equation by objecting to it in
Pynchon's name, by declaring that the preterite Pynchon is marginal
to Mendelson's IG.

But if Pynchon cannot plausibly be cast as maroon, what then are
we to make of the fact that Pynchon has been read as Invisible
Man—even, quite recently, by Salman Rushdie, whose review of
Vineland in the *New York Times Book Review* registers some signifying
resentment at Pynchon's comparatively unnecessary reclusivity
(1990, 1)? And what are we to make of the strange coincidence that
it was Ralph Ellison who nominated *Gravity's Rainbow* for the National Book Award in 1973? Although Pynchon has been un-
photographed for about forty years (or, roughly, since the publication of *Invisible Man*), and though his disappearance may be as
mysterious as Tod Clifton's, allow me to suggest that he is in some
respects less like Ellison's invisible man than like Toni Morrison's
"men without skin," as the phrase goes in *Beloved* (1987, 210). For

chief among the things about which Pynchon criticism does not speak, when it wants to speak about co-optation and repressive tolerance, is Pynchon's race—because, apparently, Pynchon has no skin, and no race, to reviewers and critics who see themselves as having no race either. As I noted at the end of Chapter 1, no one to date has asked whether or not Pynchon is a legitimate voice of his people; and I can add here that no one has so far suggested that Pynchon's canonization is the work of guilty liberal academics who are bending over backward to accommodate the writing of white male novelists, or the work of repressively tolerant white critics seeking to incorporate and deracinate *Gravity's Rainbow* as they once did *Invisible Man*. If we look for issues about which fears concerning Pynchon's co-optation have not so far coalesced, and could not imaginably coalesce, then we might do well to start with Pynchon's whiteness, which has—until now, at any rate—remained remarkably invisible.[11]

It will be objected that Pynchon has his very own journal, *Pynchon Notes*, and that an author's "journalification" is a reliable measure of his or her institutionalization.[12] The argument runs something like this: the forty-one-year lag time between *Ulysses* and the founding of the *James Joyce Quarterly* has been telescoped, as it were, into a mere six years between *Gravity's Rainbow* and the first appearance of *Pynchon Notes* in 1979, and the existence of such a journal guarantees a modicum of Pynchon articles every year, even if Pynchon himself never produces any more work after *Vineland*. This then (the argument continues) is one of IG Pynchon's material practices, and it is the very locus of routinization. Moreover, since the profession of criticism has undergone such lamentable hypertrophy, Pynchoniana proceeds apace at ever increasing speed: merely for their own promotion, tenure, and self-advancement, people now churn out Pynchon criticism so quickly that papers on *Vineland* appeared at Oklahoma's Cultural Studies conference in October 1990 and the MLA convention in December 1990 before the ink on Pynchon's latest novel was dry.

To this argument I respond again that all we are seeing in

[11]For the suggestions that eventually produced the foregoing two paragraphs, I thank Harryette Mullen.

[12]*Pynchon Notes* lists its circulation as 250. By comparison, the *James Joyce Quarterly* has a circulation of 1,300. *Callaloo* lists a readership of 500, *BALF* 1,100, *CLA Journal* 1,400, *Diacritics* 1,750, *New Literary History* and *New German Critique* 2,500 each, *Critical Inquiry* 4,500, *Signs* 7,500, *PMLA* 33,500, and *New York Review of Books* 120,000.

Pynchon's reception, even in *Vineland* criticism, is competition among various centers of cultural reproduction; and though academic critics undoubtedly undertake their work partially in the hope of professional reward, they do not differ in this respect from journalists. Surely the profession's willingness to discuss *Vineland* so quickly is a sign of vitality rather than bureaucracy, if one contemplates the alternative. For if academic criticism were suddenly to forswear its interest in living writers, declaring that no paper on any author could be published in a refereed journal or delivered at an academic conference until the author's copyright had expired and his or her work was released into the public domain, who would benefit from this arrangement—except nonspecialist reviewers?

Finally, even though Pynchoniana has its own journal, Pynchon studies are actually proceeding with fewer institutional trappings than most other major-author industries: IG Pynchon consists almost entirely of people simply reading and writing about Pynchon; there isn't yet an annual Pynchonian Award given out for the best published Pynchon essay, a Pynchon Fellowship for study at the Pynchon House in Oyster Bay (or the Lake District of upstate New York), a special Pynchon Conference at Cornell every May to commemorate the anniversary of his birth, or even so much as an American Pynchon Society renting out a hotel ballroom every year just after Christmas for its official dinner. There have been, since November 1987, annual mass public readings of *Gravity's Rainbow* at Princeton, readings that can only invite comparison with the annual readings of *Ulysses* on Bloomsday.[13] But readings by themselves, published or unpublished, do not an industry make, unless one wants to condemn *all* formal study of literature and theory. What, then, can be the referent of the Pynchon critic's distrust of academic Pynchon?

Academic feminists have for a decade worried that their "acceptance," when, how, and to what extent it has occurred, is a form of repressive tolerance, a pretense on the part of departments of English that their enterprise could be smothered and subsumed under an expanded definition of "institutional criticism." And though the

---

[13]"A Marathon on Pynchon Stirs Readers" (1987, 61) makes explicit the public-reading parallel between *Gravity's Rainbow* and *Ulysses* or *Finnegans Wake*, and reports that Michael Kowalski, who began the readings, said that he "chose the novel for the reading marathon because it has achieved a cult status since its publication and because it interests people in a wide spectrum of disciplines, from literature majors to physicists," and that he "conceived of the project as a way to revive the neglected art of reading out loud and to create an audience for avant-garde writers [!] like Mr. Pynchon."

rhetoric of Pynchon studies takes much the same line of argument, I suggest that the primary reasons for Pynchonians' anxieties have less to do with repressive tolerance than with, for one thing, the idea of the academy as mausoleum and, for another, the nostalgia consequent upon the death of the author—a nostalgia complicated in Pynchon's case by the nagging suspicion that it is we who have killed him. These "reasons" are closely related. For if Pynchon critics are themselves the curators of the exhibitions in which Pynchon has been hung, then their museums, as in Theodor Adorno's "Valéry Proust Museum," are "like the family sepulchres of works of art" (1967, 175).

Adorno's "museum" is connected to the mausoleum "by more than phonetic association" (175); in Pynchon criticism, W. T. Lhamon, Jr., was the first to made this connection, when he opened the coda to his *New Republic* review of *Gravity's Rainbow* with the following plea: "Like Joyce's *Ulysses*, this novel will surely go into the seminars all over the land. May it not be buried there" (1973, 28). Even though Lhamon is himself an academic critic, he too evokes an image of the university as a necropolis of decaying cultural artifacts (Michele Wallace's mummies) which have long since given over their erstwhile role in the living culture of any community. In this sense of "living culture," which we usually invoke only by qualifying it with "mass" or "popular," we might say of culture what Norman O. Brown says of meaning, that "if it is not evanescent it is not alive" (1966, 247).

Appropriately enough, it is this sense of "culture" that Pynchon critics like to deploy whenever they consider Pynchon's non-academic reception: "Within a year of the 1966 publication of Thomas Pynchon's short novel, *The Crying of Lot 49*, muted post horns began to appear across the country, scribbled on notebooks, lipsticked onto bathroom tiles, painted on subway walls, cut into wooden desks. The intent? To communicate. The message? Possibility" (Kolodny and Peters 1973, 79). Pynchon's reception in graffiti is a fitting antimonument, a kind of enactment of his work's concerns with graffiti's sustenance of historical and cultural apocrypha, from the "Bird Lives" in *V.* (*V* 49) to the "hieroglyphics" of the post horn's many uses (*C* 52) to the "Rocketman was here" of late Slothropiana (*GR* 624).[14] And such graffiti, in their way, constitute a cul-

---

[14] I am not, of course, implying that Charlie Parker remains apocryphal. On the contrary, bebop is by now so diffusely transmitted that one can walk into a club almost anywhere in the United States and hear it, and Parker himself is both canonical and legendary. But the point is precisely that some marginal graffiti do eventually

tural transmission of Pynchon no less legitimate, though less legitimated (for that is one of the pleasures of engaging in it), than scholarly studies.

But as I said of "control" in the foregoing chapter, so too, here, of
reception: it is not a zero-sum affair; it is not as if academic study of
Pynchon somehow forestalls or forecloses the proliferation of muted
post horns. Instead, the post horns seem to appear afresh every
year, as new legions of undergraduates and other readers are introduced to the novel. Or, to take up Lhamon again, it is not as if
Pynchon's work could be "routed into a 'no return' solitary confinement among the tastes of academe" (1973, 28), as though universities were elaborated versions of roach motels, never letting out
what they let in. Quite the contrary: as long as Pynchon's academic
reception continues, and as long as that reception involves the as-
signment of Pynchon texts in academic courses, then we can be sure
that Pynchon's apocryphal audience will coexist alongside his canonical audience all the longer.

But even if we could prove beyond doubt that the academy is not
always and everywhere museal, and that academic reception is not
necessarily a contravention of less formal cultural uses, there would
remain one intractable source of concern for Pynchon critics: the radical plurality of his work, especially *Gravity's Rainbow*. We have already seen, in this chapter and in Chapter 4, that Pynchon critics are
at pains to establish and maintain the plurality, the indeterminacy,
of Pynchon's novels. What I intend to show here is not that our
defenses of Pynchon's plurality follow from a misunderstanding of
terms such as "paranoia" and "certitude" but, in addition and by
contrast, that the emphasis on Pynchon's plurality can be understood as an epiphenomenon of Pynchon's death. Since Pynchon is
still alive—and still publishing, as *Vineland* attests—this last point
merits a subdivision of its own.[15]

Disposing of the Body of the Dead Author's Work

Tony Tanner was the first to link Pynchon with Barthes's essay
"The Death of the Author," to literalize Barthes's claim that "the
birth of the reader must be at the cost of the death of the author"

---

wind up in cultural centers, even when this process is not so literal as in the case
of Jean-Michel Basquiat or Keith Haring. See Marriott 1985, 73–80, for the best
discussion of Pynchon and Parker to date.

[15]Curiously, the consensus among early reviewers of *Vineland* seems to be that it is
not the novel Pynchon has been working on for seventeen years, and that we are due
to see a behemoth, *Gravity's Rainbow*–like work in the near future.

(Barthes 1977, 149; quoted in Tanner 1982, 11), to contrast the invisible Pynchon with the always already visible Norman Mailer, and to ask, finally, "is there any other modern author of whom there is only one known photograph?" (1982, 14).[16] Perhaps the Pynchon industry will boom only after its author dies, whereupon we will have at last the annual dinners and Pynchon House tours I lampoon above; but what's more interesting is that for now it is, as Tanner suggests, as if Pynchon is already dead. He does not talk back to his critics, he does not lay out for them in interviews tracks to follow and areas to research, he does not so much as take the podium to tell us whether he believes we will prevail or merely endure.[17] Instead, he has allowed us to do the talking for him, to echo and reecho his name among ourselves, whether in worship or in vain.[18]

We find ourselves, then, as many Pynchon critics have acknowledged, in a quintessentially Pynchonian plot: we have been left a Will, a textual legacy of some kind, whose import is unclear but which seems to reverberate across the disciplines, through the human history of the past few centuries. And we can no more appeal to Pynchon to sort out the bequests than can Oedipa Maas appeal to her dead Author, Pierce Inverarity, to sort out what seems to be real Trystero and what seem to be Trystero's coincidental cultural reinscriptions, such as children's songs or the Inamorati Anonymous

[16]Since the publication of Clifford Mead's comprehensive bibliography (1989), which includes photographs from Pynchon's high school yearbook, the critical industry now has more than one photo to work with (and reviews of *Vineland* often included one of these yearbook photos, so strong are the conventions by which we expect reviews to "represent" writers-as-people); but there are still no photographs of post-adolescent Pynchon.

[17]It is possible, as we now know, to overstate Pynchon's aversion to the official machineries of acclaim. Although the appearance of Irwin Corey at the National Book Awards is the rough equivalent of Pig Bodine at the Utgarthaloki dinner party (at which Bodine's presence helps save Roger Mexico from being eaten), and though Pynchon's rejection of the Howells Medal is rightfully the stuff of minor legend, still, he has accepted the MacArthur Fellowship—gracefully.

[18]To the standard argument that Pynchon has become the manipulative They to the reader's We, I am adding and adapting here John Carlos Rowe's discussion of *The Turn of the Screw* (1984, 120–46). Arguing that the governess's employer secures his authority precisely by displacing his power onto his servants, Rowe writes: "Invisible and silent in the course of the dramatic action, with the exception of his one appeal *for* silence, the Uncle prompts a psychodramatic struggle between masters and servants at Bly that he has already inscribed and continues to control in and by his absence" (128). The reception of *The Turn of the Screw* replays this scenario as well, according to Rowe, as "the law of Henry James persists in the reassertion of his mastery, his genius, in the most triumphant interpretations of his readers" (144). I was made aware of Rowe's chapter by Paul Armstrong, who reads accounts of James's reception history up to and including Rowe and Shoshana Felman, arguing in this metametareading that "configuring the text and emplotting its heritage are correlative acts" (1988, 705).

insignia.[19] Doubtless our position is a liberation: to return one last time to Foucault, we may say that if the Father is dead or missing, then we no longer have an ideological figure through whom we can mark our fear of the proliferation of meaning, and we may let a thousand meanings bloom.[20] For if the Author is dead, it is because he has had so many children, born readers, who have since banded together to kill the father, forming a new order, an *interessengesellschaft*, and a new god in the process.

But then, as in Freud's account, comes the reassertion of primeval ambivalence, of primordial guilt: the critic of Pynchon turns out to be not at all as unambivalently free as Barthes and Foucault suggest she or he should be. Faced with a (dead) Pynchon and his staggeringly plural texts, the critics have, generally and to their credit, *not* chosen to reduce the texts' plurality in order to claim that the intent of the Father's Will is clear. Rather, the critics have tended to complain that *other critics* have done so and tended therefore to warn the Author's other sons and daughters against the desecration of the body of his work. The salient exception here is Mark Siegel, who denies that the Father can be carved up at all and asserts that the would-be carvers are responsible for critical discord: "The ambiguity and relativity of the various perspectives which the narrator [of *Gravity's Rainbow*] advances suggest an obvious reason for the controversy over the novel's interpretation: each critical view has tended to isolate one of the relative points of view in the novel as an objective conception of Pynchon's point of view, while actually each point of view is really a part of an entire spectrum which is the 'rainbow' of possibilities encompassed by Pynchon's vision" (1977, 51).

Does Pynchon contradict himself? Very well then, he contradicts himself; he is large, he contains multitudes; he is both a synoptic father and a whole, integral maternal body. But then such a

---

[19]I am assuming that *The Crying of Lot 49* ends with its famous binaries precisely because Oedipa's theory of meaning does not allow for "coincidental cultural reinscriptions" or, indeed, "reinscriptions" of any kind. Oedipa's mistake, as a reader of the texts of Trystero, would thus seem to be that she falls into the trap of thinking either that all Trystero's manifestations are motivated by a single source and intention or that, in the absence of such a single source, the texts are all random and meaningless. See also McHoul and Wills 1990, 74–75.

[20]See Barthes, *S/Z*, for the classical statement of the relation between plurality and paternity anxiety: "A multivalent text can carry out its basic duplicity only if it subverts the opposition between true and false, if it fails to attribute quotations (even when seeking to discredit them) to explicit authorities, if it flouts all respect for origin, paternity, propriety, if it destroys the voice which could give the text its ('organic') unity. . . . For multivalence . . . is a transgression of ownership" (1974, 44–45).

Pynchon would license a voracious pluralism, a pluralism impossible to sustain in any specific political, institutional, or critical context. Most of Pynchon's readers have wanted nothing to do with such a Pynchon; wary as they are of the arbitrariness with which desire perpetuates (is) the metonymic play of signifiers, they have recognized also that all reading is desire, and that the challenge is to stop the metonymic chain so as to be more productive than reductive.

Hence the injunction against resurrecting the body of the Author, against reestablishing a dyadic unit of writer and reader, parent and child. As Tölölyan puts it: "The critics' response, so preoccupied with discovering the real Pynchon or with assigning him a voice within his texts, betrays the impulses long concealed by pious gestures towards 'objectivity.' Much of contemporary literary or cultural criticism is in fact an effort to converse with a living author, either by-passing his works or, as in the case of Bellow and Mailer, acclaiming the books for what the author 'is saying' in them, in his own voice" (1979a, 315). Tölölyan could not have been borne out more clearly than by Thomas Schaub, who, writing not long afterward, based a book-length study on "Pynchon's development from a writer of narrative prose to a speaker of oratory and singer of song, as he puts aside the guise of disinterested author and speaks directly to his audience in the great song of *Gravity's Rainbow*" (1981a, 4).

Apparently, one does not kill off the author, the voice, or the possibility of a conversation, and then proceed as if nothing has happened; as McHoul and Wills have written, "This obsession with the person or its absence is often posed as a threat: as though the possible absence of an empirical author's life and character might spell the end of the critical project" (1990, 2). The "end"—or, on my reading, the terrifying *boundlessness* of the critical project: as I suggested in Chapter 1, a dead and plural Pynchon threatens not merely our narrative conception of "representation" but a canonical or cultural one as well. That is, even if Pynchon is represented on a syllabus of American, twentieth-century, or postmodern literature, it is not clear what *he* represents—and we can make him represent practically anything we want, for "as readers we have only the novels," and "the novels are not always consistent in their perspective" (Duyfhuizen 1984, 5),[21] This means that neither the author's life and

[21]Duyfhuizen's worry over Pynchon's representability is heightened by the fact that he is, as he writes, introducing the special deconstructionist issue of *Pynchon Notes*

character nor even an idea of his corpus-as-a-whole restrains critical free play: "When a decision as to the real is based only on a comparison of text with more-text—and we have demonstrated that traditional hierarchisations of textual material, such as those which place a narrative or authorial voice at the top, clearly collapse in *Gravity's Rainbow*—there can be no intratextual justification. . . . and yet we know of no critical reading which can do without one or the other (present company included)" (McHoul and Wills 1990, 46).

It is not, then, a question of squeezing dry the seminal text, of de-seminating it, but, rather, a question of how to meet the challenge of disseminating the text—and not in the name of the father, for either the father has abandoned the household, or we have killed the father and are repressing the memory. Stephen Schuber has described our condition in terms very close to mine:

> While the text is in orbit, the question of its point of launch is subject to debate, and in the absence of a ruling authority, the name-of-the-father cannot be enunciated. The text again is suspended, for there exists no authority for its issue. . . .
>
> Beyond these considerations, there is a collateral and cultural habit asserting that an individual logic and talent produces a property that is consumed as text. Again according to this tradition or critical orbit, the progenitor of a text is at liberty to legitimize certain approaches to the text. That is, in certain circles, the *logos* of the progenitor permeates and sustains the text, and since progenitors typically are taken for males, a certain phallogocentrism governs many of the orbits around *Gravity's Rainbow*.
>
> But again, the text mocks or elides such phallogocentrism. The "penis of official commendation" (*GR* 516) is absent, and it is a mistake to assume that one can double-integrate, stop the action, determine a legitimizing source. (1984, 71–72)

(February 1984), as luck would have it (but can it be luck?), at just the moment Pynchon has published his introduction to *Slow Learner* (1984b). Writing that Pynchon's introduction is "far from invalidating the essays that follow," Duyfhuizen nevertheless feels backed into a corner, because Pynchon's latest installment "makes some statements about the function of literature with relation to life that seemingly contravene many of the assumptions regularly made about his texts" and which lead one to the point at which "one almost has to conclude he must be putting us on again" (1984, 5–6). The irony here is pointed. After several years of complaining that criticism has approached Pynchon's protodeconstructive narratives too traditionally, IG Pynchon finally publishes a series of deconstructions of Pynchon, only to have Pynchon launch a preemptive strike in which he says that one's characters should live on the page, that "undeniably authentic" writers live their personal lives in their fiction, and that it is wrong to begin a story with an abstract concept.

One thinks here, especially in the second quoted paragraph, of Terry Eagleton's critique of E. D. Hirsch's intentionalism as a theoretical form of the defense of private property, the property of the Author who has the sovereign copyright over his meaning (1983, 68–69). But though we can certainly say, with Schuber, that Pynchon "mocks" such capitalist phallogocentrism, we can also plausibly say that Pynchon partakes of or endorses such phallogocentrism every time he mocks criticism as a subsidiary, secondary, parasitic, or supplementary exercise—as he seems to do in the figures of Mitchell Prettyplace or Natasha Raum, author of "'Regions of Indeterminacy in Albatross Anatomy,' *Proceedings of the International Society of Confessors to an Enthusiasm for Albatross Nosology,* Winter 1936" (*GR* 712), an article that attempts to explain and analyze Slothrop's scattering.

The problem for the father's children, then, is this: although the king is dead and we have thrown off his law (only to reassert it in enjoining other critics from dis-membering the father), we are left, as critics, playing a game of cultural representation presided over by no one but ourselves. This is not to repeat the standard anti-Barthesian argument to the effect that the infinitely plural text becomes the infinitely trivial text, because the issue here is not Pynchon's importance or triviality but the rationales for his importance (no one suggests that Pynchon is unimportant because elusive). Rather, it is to suggest that the death of the author is experienced partially as exhilaration and partially as terror—because playing games without established rules is alternately fun and appalling, and culture abhors the vacuum consequent upon the author's disappearance. Beneath the Pynchon critic's admonitions to other Pynchon critics, in other words, we may sense a kind of regressive nostalgia for the Author: an author, as Tölölyan says, to talk to—as in the movie queue in Woody Allen's *Annie Hall,* where Allen produces Marshall McLuhan from offscreen in order to silence the pompous critic behind him, to have McLuhan himself inform the offender that he knows nothing about McLuhan's work. This need to justify readings by authorizing their meanings (to silence other critics), I suggest, is why "it is very rare to encounter a reading of Pynchon's work which does not at some stage revert to a precritical notion of the author as not only integral consciousness but also identifiable historical person, and that in spite of the fact that the person is recognised as an enigma, and the 'author,' in at least one of the novels, dissolves into an array of conflicting voices" (McHoul and Wills 1990, 6). For Pynchon criticism has tended to naturalize even this "array of conflicting voices" under the sign of *presence*. Thus Thomas Schaub writes both that "Pynchon's voice retains the advantages of the intrusive, visible guide, but undermines the stability commonly associated with it, for his knowledge of the world of *Gravity's Rainbow* is fragmentary" and, two pages later, that this narrator's fragmentary knowledge is part of "Pynchon's ever-present voice" (1981a, 131, 133).

We have, then, a number of constructions of Pynchon's reception, which I summarize as follows. On one reading, the Pynchon critic's fear is that academic reception will dissipate and trivialize the force of the novels; and though I attribute this fear to a Romantic ideology that is registered here as a nostalgia for the avant-garde and its resistance to reception, I want to note also that the fear is not completely ungrounded simply because it is "ideological." Any theory of oppositionality will hold that recuperation of "margins" is one of the more effective means by which the cultural center maintains its hold over its most unruly citizens; and though the relevant question on this count has to do with whether Pynchon is truly "marginal," still, as I myself argued at the outset of this chapter, there exists a significant strain in Pynchon criticism which has done some of the work of recuperation, in deflecting onto narrative technique Pynchon's potentially oppositional functions.

At the same time, because the rhetoric of Pynchon criticism is not devoted wholly to self-indictment, Pynchon's critics have been able to position themselves against various areas of production in American letters—from professional reviewers to "amateur" readers to the Modern Language Association—and, in so doing, to imagine margins on which Pynchon can be said to exist. Finally, on yet another reading, this mobility of critical affinities appears as a deeply paradoxical freedom, not only because of the similarities between the function of the academy and the function of the museum (which suggest to the critics that they are not merely disseminating Pynchon but killing him) but, more specifically, because Pynchon's absence and near-silence throw into high relief the cultural center's power of representation, whereby academic critics are explicitly confronted with their power to re-present a contemporary writer and thereby to make him somehow representative insofar as he is made canonical.

I close my summary, then, by isolating two phenomena: that announcements of the author's death should take the form of warnings, and that the prospect of the author's canonicity should be characterized, to quote Poirier again, as "a cause not for celebration

but for misgiving" (1976, 19). Having suggested above some explanations for these phenomena, I want now to juxtapose them to my
discussion of Tolson's reception—partly to recall that this conception of canonical authorization, and of the institutional critic's cultural position, can be construed otherwise, and partly to reconceive
Pynchon's implications of reading in order to produce a criticism
that is a generative rather than supplementary endeavor.

Here we return to a side issue of Chapter 4, one that I discussed
in the course of redefining "paranoia" so that it is not a synonym for
"fixity": namely, the notion that interpretation involves the imposition of form upon chaos, that reading is Stencil-ing, that "a critic of
Pynchon needs to consider whether he isn't Ned Pointsman to
Pynchon's Roger Mexico" (Levine and Leverenz 1976, 3). Because,
as Barthes has reminded us, "(in the West) meaning (system), we
are told, is antipathetic to nature and reality" (1974, 23), we tend to
back into the false dichotomy between "patterns" and "reality" that
is basic to much of Pynchon criticism, as when Lawrence Daw
writes that Pynchon describes and licenses a world in which "order
is only a fabricated imposition placed on inherently random events
by human desire" (1986, 175). But if we jettison this construction of
the construction of meaning, developing instead a model of interpretation that sees reading as an enterprise of transmission—the
consumption/production of more text alongside the text—then
perhaps we can be less dour about our roles as Pynchon readers.

The fear, as I have described it, has long been that we can produce whatever Pynchon we need to produce, at whatever cost to
Pynchon; but as a moment's reflection will suffice to show, our
needs are not entirely capricious things. If, for example, we say with
Wittgenstein that "the axis of reference of our examination must be
rotated, but about the fixed point of our real need" (1945, § 108,
46e), we are not authorizing ordered, arrogantly fabricated uses of
Pynchon's randomness but demanding an awareness that both we
and Pynchon might continue to do cultural work and that we have
the obligation and opportunity to determine retrospectively what
corrective work we can do. For "is there not also the case," Wittgenstein has written, "where we play and—make up the rules as we
go along? And there is even one where we alter them—as we go
along" (§ 83, 39e).

This conception of cultural transmission as a "generative" criticism, like my definition of "authorization," underwrites nothing; it
is not a method for guaranteeing good readings, progressive readings, or any specific kinds of readings at all. It is, however, a means

by which we might characterize the academy, the professional journal, and the classroom not as places where Pynchon and Tolson will
be taken to die but as places for keeping them "alive," preserving
their work for further replication. This characterization depends in
turn on "preservation" and "replication" as the continuous creation
of new and perhaps eventually unrecognizable Tolsons and
Pynchons, not on the static preservation of a "heritage" transmitted
by means of the cultural taxidermy of the New Right. In other
words, critics do not have to be Ned Pointsman to Pynchon's Roger
Mexico; they can be Argentine anarchists to his *The Return of Martín
Fierro*, Bummers to his Rossini, Schwarzkommando or Edwin Trea-
cles (rather than Mitchell Prettyplaces) to his *King Kong*.

Likewise, canonicity—whether Pynchon's, Derrida's, Kate Chopin's, or anyone else's—does not have to be theorized as dissolution, damage, or the doings of conspiracy theory. By saying this I
mean to suggest two complementary injunctions: first, that the contemporary de- or a-scription of "margins" be taken not as one more
instance of the rhetoric of the avant-garde (even or especially where
it is so intended) but as a means for locating and empowering
writers to do various kinds of cultural work; not as the faithful representation of a cultural dynamic of struggle between a monolithic
center and variously constituted margins but as a sign of relational
and signifying difference, difference *from*, in the sense that Tolson is
different from the modernists to whom he is marginal, or in the
sense that Pynchon is different from the tradition of the American
novel, in which he is central. Thus, and this brings me to my second
injunction, the relational indices of difference *from* always need to be
specified—which in itself should move us beyond the sterile and
often misleading binary opposition between center and margin,
canon and apocrypha, into a micropolitics of cultural production,
reception, and transmission.

If nonetheless we need to locate margins, either in the service of a
more democratic practice of cultural representation or in the service
of resolute opposition to hegemonic cultural practices, a micropolitics of reception asks at minimum that margins be located and produced in relation to their respective "centers" and with the greatest
sociohistorical specificity possible. In Pynchon's case, such a process
of location and production yields a Venn diagram of margins and
centers that complicates the picture instructively. A generation of
theorists of American literature, to take one by now well-worn example, claimed marginal status for Hawthorne, Melville, Thoreau,
Poe, and Whitman, in the sense that none was a commercial success
in his lifetime, in the sense that they were all marginal to Haw-

thorne's "damned mob of scribbling women" (quoted in Baym 1985, 64). And Pynchon fits very well into this marginal mainstream, as Poirier recognized almost immediately: his is "a distinctly American vision, and Pynchon is the epitome of an American writer out of the great classics of the nineteenth century—Hawthorne, Emerson, and Melville especially" (1976, 29). But if one follows Nina Baym or Russell Reising in characterizing the great classics of the American Renaissance as the work of an exclusively male, Anglo-American "margin" that obscures the existence and importance of writers marginal to the American Novel and its Tradition (say, Harriet Beecher Stowe or Frederick Douglass), then Pynchon appears a thoroughly well-pedigreed and well-centered figure after all—one more white man from the Northeast, writing big books about the Puritan origins of the American self.

Reising, like many recent critics, notes that "the 'representative' or 'major' American authors tend to be a fairly predictable and very small group of white, male writers, for the most part those canonized by Matthiessen in *American Renaissance*"; and Reising points out as well that the major postwar theorists of American literature, from Matthiessen to Poirier, based their canons on "a vision of American literature as an isolated body of texts, estranged from, or only vaguely related to, American social or material reality" (1986, 17). Baym, concerned with the "material reality" transmitted by such a literary history, attends to the way in which these "estranged" texts were construed to be voices from the margin: of Lionel Trilling's canonical writers, Baym writes: "They all turn out—and not by accident—to be white, middle-class, male, of Anglo-Saxon derivation or at least from an ancestry which had settled in this country before the big waves of immigration which began around the middle of the nineteenth century. In every case, however, the decision made by these men to become professional authors pushed them slightly to one side of the group to which they belonged. This slight alienation permitted them to belong, and yet not to belong, to the so-called 'mainstream' (1985, 69).

Baym's description of this markedly central "margin" calls its literary tradition a "consensus criticism of the consensus" (69), and the phrase condenses nicely the reasons why margins and mainstreams can be produced only relationally. As we will recall from Chapter 3, for instance, Karl Shapiro has long considered himself a dissident, a decolonizer, a "critic outside"; and on the basis of his Bollingen vote against Pound in 1948, he has reason to do so. From Tolson's perspective, however, Shapiro was himself a member of the closed corporation that was *Poetry*—an insider still oppositional enough to be congenial to "E. & O.E." but a consensus critic of the consensus just the same, as the 1950 essay "What Is Anti-Criticism?" served to demonstrate.

Such are the different relations of Tolson and Pynchon to the American canon of democratic dissenters and liberal critics, and we may say much the same about the critical heritage that has given us a modernist canon composed of self-imposed exiles. In this canon of central outcasts Pynchon appears, and has been taken, as a post-modern perfection of the Joycean ideal: the God paring his finger-nails, "an anonymous figure who occasionally delivers manuscripts that are received and interpreted without the writer's cooperation" (Tölölyan 1979a, 315), who survives on nothing but his extraordinary talent and the blessed trinity of the young Dedalus: silence, exile, and cunning. Indeed, one Pynchon critic has even spoken of "that species of 'silence, exile, and cunning' that his work consistently recommends as a valid response to the world" (Moore 1987, 4). And just as the modernist canon (like the American canon constructed by postwar theorists) was composed of pretenders to margins who claimed no relation to their countries' cultural centers, so too can Pynchon be safely and securely placed in the tradition of Henry James, Henry Adams, T. S. Eliot, Ezra Pound, Ernest Hemingway, and F. Scott Fitzgerald, as an American Adam dispossessed of the legacy of the land. In fact, in 1978 essayist Charles Hollander deduced from Pynchon's family history that "Pynchon does feel somewhat disinherited" (quoted in Tanner 1982, 16), on the grounds that generations of Pynchons—from the heretic William Pynchon (the original of William Slothrop), to the Tory Joseph Pynchon who would have been governor of Connecticut had he not been loyal to England at the wrong time, to the stockbrokers Pynchon and Company who were one of the country's largest brokerage firms until their fall in the Great Depression—have been on the wrong side of American history's formative struggles.[22]

Again, however, if the cultural position of the modernist exile is the basis for claims of Pynchon's preterition, his marginality, we should recall that such "exile" is a highly privileged position, a position in and not against the twentieth-century American grain, a consensus criticism of the consensus. As Marcus Klein has pointed out:

The American makers of the modern movement were with remarkable uniformity of a certain class, one which might well think of itself as a

[22]For a discussion of Pynchon's minibiographies, including Hollander's, see Tanner 1982, 14–18.

dispossessed *social* aristocracy. . . . The American Eliots, as T. S. Eliot well knew, dated back to the year 1670. Ezra Pound, as Pound well knew, went back somewhat further, on the Pound side to the 1630s and on his mother's side to circa 1623. Moreover, the various makers almost without exception came from families which either were wealthy or had been wealthy. These inventors constituted, whether by actual fact of birth or not, a beleaguered gentry, forced quite abruptly, by real history, to assert a glamorous antiquity. It was another function of the "tradition," then, that it provided a homeland for upper-class aliens. (1981, 11–12)

Just as Klein is careful to mark out the contexts in which our canonical modernists were anything but marginal, so too, then, do I want to recall that Pynchon cannot plausibly be construed as marginal either to American literature in general or to American literature in the modern or postmodern era. I do not mean to convict Pynchon of guilt by association, as if he can be made to look like a cultural conservative—if not an outright fascist—simply by being an American exile whose family dates to the *Arbella*, as far back as Pound and further back than Eliot; among the scions of these well-established American families he remains, as I have said above, relationally different *from*. But the point is that if we want to celebrate Pynchon's exile from the means of cultural reproduction, then we need to specify that he truly is marginal to the marketing of his novels, exiled by choice from the *New York Times Magazine*, dispossessed of the right to represent himself in the high courts of culture; to our theories of American, modern, and postmodern literature, on the other hand, Pynchon is as central a writer as we can imagine. From a Tolsonian perspective, by contrast, Pynchon's aversion to publicity and biography appears almost a royal prerogative. For it is all very well to shun the writing of one's personal history when one's family history can be traced back to the Norman Conquest (Winston 1976, 253); when, however, one cannot, as Tolson could not, reliably trace one's family so far back as two generations (Farnsworth 1984, 3–6), biography and autobiography become almost a categorical cultural imperative. Edward Mendelson is not wrong to describe Pynchon's anonymity as "a stance alien to our literary culture" (1976, 173), but since Pynchon's race has not generally been considered as a factor in his reception, no one has bothered to point out also that Pynchon's nonparticipation in his cultural transmission is a cultural position utterly inaccessible to minority writers, alien to *their* literary culture.

Let us turn, then, for a final contrast to the problematics of Pynchoniana, to two contemporary examples of an opposing or al-

ternative approach to authorization, institutionalization, and canonicity. The first is that of Sandra Gilbert, who speaks in a 1985
interview of

> a crucial dissonance between male and female intellectual history.
> Where male critics may well feel themselves both belated and dimin-
> ished, where they may fear, indeed, that they have fallen from a lost
> and glamorous wholeness into the grimy holes of academic bureau-
> cracy, their female peers see themselves as just beginning to enter intel-
> lectual culture and, more specifically, academic society. Thus . . .
> though we feminist critics may be industrious, we don't feel ourselves
> to be part of an industry, at least not in the pejorative sense of, let's
> say, a robot-like assembly line for turning out deconstructive readings
> of Conrad or structuralist analyses of King Lear. (1985a, 112)

To the question with which Gerald Graff closes the interview, a
worry that "once feminism has been safely institutionalized as a
'field,' the rest of us don't need to bother listening any more" (122),
Gilbert's reply is again instructive, not only for its mild rebuke of
Graff but for its attention to the historical contingency of the relation
of margins to centers: "Women's studies directors and participants
still wonder if we're experiencing tokenism—or is it co-optation? We
wonder if we'll be 'mainstreamed' out of existence. We wonder if, as
you say, nobody will bother listening anymore. (But then, Jerry,
how many of our male colleagues *ever* bothered to listen? I find your
use of the phrase 'any more' charming and consoling, but misleading)" (123).

Gilbert's sense that the time is not yet ripe for feminist self-accusa-
tion and recrimination is not, by any means, a definitive position in
feminist theory. For that matter, Gilbert may herself seem at times
too glib during the interview, as when she notes that "we do no
doubt indulge in a good deal of back-patting—or 'networking,' as
the fashionable phrase would have it—but that, too, is for us an
exciting, even unprecedented phenomenon" (112). For Pynchon
critics, however, even this occasional glibness, I think, would be salutory; even if their critical enterprise cannot be called "unprecedented" (and this is itself a sign of Pynchon's centrality), it still retains the potential to work for the reconfiguration of the discipline.
If "Pynchon" can no longer do very much to disturb or reshuffle the
postmodern American canon, his work can still impel us toward in-
terdisciplinary study and the reshuffling and dialogue among academic "fields" which the American importation of British Cultural
Studies has begun.

For counterillustration I draw my second example from the writer who *has* reshuffled the postmodern American canon, Toni Morrison—or, rather, from Nellie McKay's introduction to the first published collection of Morrison essays. One notes that McKay's piece is the structural analogue to Levine and Leverenz's 1976 essay in *Mindless Pleasures*, and one also notes that McKay narrates much the same reception history: good and bad reviews in influential journals, a Book-of-the-Month Club alternate selection (*Sula*, which, like *Gravity's Rainbow*, appeared in 1973), a nomination for the National Book Award, an American Academy of Arts and Letters Award (1978, for *Song of Solomon*), an appearance on the *Times* best-seller list (*Tar Baby*, 1981), and growing acclaim throughout the 1970s and 1980s.[23] The astonishing aspect of McKay's essay, however—that is, astonishing from the perspective of Pynchon criticism—is that Morrison's story is narrated as *triumph*, as cause not for misgiving but for celebration; and the culmination of the success story, sure enough, is the volume of essays itself:

> This volume is the first of its kind to appear on this author and the first in this series on a black woman writer. Now a major figure for the teaching, writing, and research on contemporary American literature, Morrison's place here is richly deserved. Her novels are widely read and discussed in classrooms across the country in courses in Afro-American Studies, American literature, and Women's Studies. Enormous changes in the critical perceptions of her writings and of her importance to American and Women's literature have occurred since 1970, most notably demonstrated by the inclusion of the complete text of *The Bluest Eye* in the Norton Anthology of Women's Literature. Unquestionably, Toni Morrison has entered the canon.
> Another proof of Morrison's status in the academy is in the rapidly growing body of critical attention that her work is enjoying. (1988, 6–7)

Here, finally, we are dealing not with mummies, effluvia, burial seminars, and a decaying corpus of work but with a healthy, "rapidly growing body," happy to be alive and humming with meaning.

I admit that this kind of reception can never quite be Pynchon's; clearly, Pynchon's arrival in the academy does not represent our long-overdue acknowledgment of the Puritan legacy in Anglo-American literature of the United States in the way that Morrison is taken

---

[23]McKay's introduction appeared before *Beloved* (1987) was published—and, therefore, before the furor that erupted when the novel was not given the National Book Award, for which Morrison had been considered the clear front-runner.

by McKay "as one of the vanguard whose work announced the new era in black women's writings in America in the 1970s" (1988, 7). Pynchon critics simply do not have a "new era" whose advent could cause them to be so unambivalently thrilled at their author's cultural reproduction as is McKay about Morrison's. But the contrast *is* the point: cultural representation is a very different matter for Toni Morrisons and Melvin Tolsons than it is for writers such as Thomas Pynchon, because where Pynchon critics can fear that canonical Pynchon may be enervated or misrepresented, critics of "women's" and "minority" literatures have, instead, feared that their authors and their works will go unrepresented altogether. As Sandra Gilbert might have said, the time is not yet right for Nellie McKay to ponder in print the insidious side effects of IG Morrison.

I wrote in my opening chapter that insofar as American critics ask writers of different ethnicities to assume different burdens of representation, canonization is a different affair for different writers. Am I saying now that canons don't kill people, people kill people? that canonicity is neutral, like technology, and that only its human uses are good or bad? Let me not be misunderstood. Pynchon studies cannot look to nascent Tolson studies for a model of comportment, for an illustration of how to stop worrying and love the academic boom. I am not suggesting that Pynchon critics should pretend that their subject is African-American, female, unread or out of print, marginal to everything he is not in fact marginal to; one would not want IG Pynchon to carry out its enterprise in such egregious bad faith. My closing point is simply a further specification of my opening chapter's closing point: the perspective on criticism and author function of a Sandra Gilbert or a Nellie McKay reminds us that canonicity is not the result of conspiracy theory, just as "neglect," even when it is motivated misrepresentation, is not to be confused with repression—or suppression. Canonicity *can* be a means of recuperation, but it is always by definition a continually reproduced means of transmission, a highly visible and highly charged mode of the cultural activation and reinscription of texts.

Institutional criticism thus involves not only Weberian bureaucracy but also, for all of us in post-Weberian capitalism, the power to keep texts in circulation, to keep them *current* in an economic sense, even if only by teaching them, distributing them, assigning them in courses. Though we cannot (and should not) describe our cultural functions solely in terms of pedagogy, perhaps it is diagnostic that there is no discussion, in all of IG Pynchon, of the classroom as a context for reception—no discussion, for that matter, of a social context for reading in any form. It is diagnostic too that there is so little awareness in IG Pynchon, and so pervasive an awareness for "excluded" writers, that access to the cultural center provides also the opportunity to reconstruct the cultural center. And here I presume to prescribe: if Pynchon's academic readers are serious about Pynchon's implications of reading—his critiques of totalities, his parodies of congealed and self-sustaining bureaucracies, his multiple undercuttings of "representation," his explorations into the politics of cultural transmission and the cultural transmission of "politics"— they will do better to change the function of academic microindustries than to bemoan their formation, will do better to make Pynchon's canonicity do cultural work than to describe it as cultural crisis.

I say this only because of where Pynchon studies have come, because mine is one more synoptic view of a microindustry that is notable for its constant, over-the-shoulder, slightly nervous synoptic views of itself. For there is also, as I have wanted to emphasize both in the last two chapters and through juxtaposition with Tolson throughout, a large, lively Pynchon conversation going on, a conversation that is always already my context. Pynchon's readers read Pynchon's readers as well as Pynchon; reviews and revaluations are the order of the day; and the conversation is of a breadth which a Tolson critic can only imagine, to which a Toni Morrison critic can only aspire. Nor is this conversation merely academic babble; it is also, for better and worse, Pynchon's existence. Moreover, as long as the conversants refrain from doing Pynchon such ideological violence as to make him a technical innovator who affirmeth nothing, or a defender and inhabitant of a monologic modern or American Great Tradition, there is also, because of the conversation's existence, always the possibility that one of his books might shake up one of our students—or ourselves. Perhaps, to paraphrase *The Crying of Lot 49* (181), we may even be hounded someday into reading Tolson as well, if he still exists, in his texts, his margins, his waiting to be read above all. For in a nation prone to sanitizing if not forgetting altogether its own history, Tolson and Pynchon retain the potential to do important cultural work, and we retain the opportunity to put them to use as best we can.

APPENDIX A

Tolson in
African-American Anthologies

For this list I have surveyed only those anthologies published after *Libretto for the Republic of Liberia* (that is, from 1963 onward) in order to ascertain how much of Tolson's modernist work has been anthologized, and in what form. The table consists of two parts, anthologies out of print and anthologies now in print. They are given in the chronological order of their publication, along with their respective Tolson poems: *R* denotes a poem first printed in *Rendezvous with America*; *L*, in *Libretto*; and *HG*, in *Harlem Gallery*.

Anthology Editor(s), year (year last published)	Poem(s)
Soon, One Morning Herbert Hill, 1963 (1980)	"Abraham Lincoln of Rock Spring Farm"
Kaleidoscope Robert Hayden, 1967 (1978)	*HG*, "Sea-turtle" "African China"
Dark Symphony James Emanuel, Theodore Gross, 1968 (1989)	*HG*, excerpt from "Xi" (chiefly "John Henry"; miscited as "Nu")
An Introduction to Black Literature in America (in The International Library of Negro Life and History) Lindsay Patterson, 1968 (1976)	*R*, "A Hamlet Rives Us"
Black American Literature: Poetry Darwin Turner, 1969 (1986)	"Dark Symphony"

Afro-American Literature: Poetry William Adams, Peter Conn, Barry Slepian, 1970 (1984)	"Dark Symphony" "John Henry in Harlem"
On Being Black Charles T. Davis and Daniel Walden, 1970 (1977)	HG, excerpt from "Xi" (chiefly "John Henry") "African China"
The Poetry of the Negro Langston Hughes, Arna Bontemps, 1970, rev. from 1949 (1985)	"Dark Symphony" L, "Do" HG, "Louis Armstrong"
Black Identity Francis E. Kearns, 1970 (1978)	"Dark Symphony"
3000 Years of Black Poetry Alan Lomax, Raoul Abdul, 1970 (1989)	HG, excerpt from "Xi" (chiefly "John Henry")
Cavalcade Arthur Davis, Saunders Redding, 1971 (1983)	HG, from "Psi"
Black Insights Nick Aaron Ford, 1971 (1981)	"Dark Symphony" L, "Do"-"Fa"
Blackamerican Literature 1760-Present Ruth Miller, 1971 (1987)	"Dark Symphony" "African China"
Modern and Contemporary Afro-American Poetry Bernard Bell, 1972 (1974)	HG, "Lambda"
Nommo* William H. Robinson, 1972 (1981)	L, "Do," "Re," and a section of "Ti"
Black Culture Gloria Simmons, Helene Hutchinson, 1972 (1979)	"Dark Symphony"
Afro-American Literature Robert Hayden, David Burrows, Frederick Lapides, 1973 (1983)	HG, "Sea-turtle"
Understanding the New Black Poetry Stephen Henderson, 1973 (1982)	HG, "Lambda"

---

*Nommo excerpts African-American writing *about Africa*; hence its exclusive emphasis on *Libretto*, an emphasis shared by no other anthology.

In the currently available anthologies there are no excerpts from *Libretto*. Excerpts from the Curator's sections of *Harlem Gallery* now outnumber those from Hideho Heights's sections: all the poem's Zulu Club scenes are now out of circulation, because the last anthologies to print sections from "Xi" ceased publication in 1989; by contrast, four of the remaining anthologies reprint "Psi" in its entirety, and one reprints "Zeta." "Dark Symphony" continues to outnumber any single *Harlem Gallery* excerpt: it appears in five of the following seven collections. I include each anthology's publisher—as well as editor(s) and date(s)—and note whether it is available in paper or cloth, on the assumption that paperbacks are more generally students' texts and that hard-covers are sold to smaller and more specialized (though stable) markets.

Anthology	Poem(s)
American Negro Poetry Arna Bontemps, 1963, rev. 1974 (Hill & Wang, paper)	"Dark Symphony"
Black Voices Abraham Chapman, 1968 (NAL, paper)	"Dark Symphony" R, "Ex-Judge at the Bar" HG, "Psi"
Black Literature in America Houston Baker, 1971 (McGraw-Hill, cloth)	"Dark Symphony" HG, "Psi"
The Black Poets Dudley Randall, 1971 (Bantam, paper)	R, "Legend of Versailles" HG, "Louis Armstrong"
Black Writers of America Richard Barksdale, Keneth Kinnamon, 1972 (Macmillan)	"Dark Symphony" HG, "Psi"
Afro-American Writing Richard Long, Eugenia Collier, 1972, rev. 1985 (Penn State Univ. Press, cloth)	"Dark Symphony" HG, "Zeta"
The Poetry of Black America Arnold Adoff, 1973 (Harper & Row, cloth)	"African China" HG, "Sea-turtle"; "Psi"

The audience for these anthologies is almost literally a legislative matter: each one is a textbook, and copyright laws rigidly distinguish trade from textbook markets; a publisher who wished to sell an anthology in both markets would be required to pay double reprint permission fees. D. Anthony English, editor-in-chief of Macmillan's College Division, informs me that publishers usually cannot afford both fees; hence, in Macmillan's case, Barksdale and Kinnamon's *Black Writers of America* is handled by the College Division, which exists exclusively to deal with the idiosyncrasies of the academic market. These include a "net pricing policy" according to which the single-copy price of a textbook is, in English's words, "the net price plus the highest mark-up we believe a bookstore would charge" (letter of 10 September 1990).

According to English, Macmillan's threshold figure of annual sales justifying continued reprintings is roughly 500; *Black Writers of America*, by any standard one of the major works in the field, sells safely above this threshold, and, notably, its sales quadrupled over the years 1986–89 (letter of 10 September 1990). Still, only one of the listed anthologies still in print has been revised since 1975 (that is, since the academic boom in African-American letters), largely because, as English reports, reprint permission costs have risen to "three or four times as much" as they were when *Black Writers of America* was first published in 1972 (letter of 29 June 1989). Because market demand for these anthologies is strictly limited to academic contexts (the textbook market), Macmillan calculates that its anthology's annual sales probably could not be raised enough to justify a second edition; their estimated sales ceiling, in turn, is based on an overall projection of "the market in black literature," which, writes English, Macmillan estimates "to enroll fewer than 30,000 students annually" (letter of 29 June 1989).

It is impossible, therefore, to separate the conditions of anthology production (and thus the general status of African-American cultural archives) from the conditions of the reproduction of knowledge in universities. Macmillan's recent increase in anthology sales suggests a renewed strength in the academic market, but it is a strength that must be sustained to be materially effective. Thus, although the announcement of a new African-American anthology from W. W. Norton, for instance, is more than welcome given the current holding pattern described by anthologies still in print, continual and productive revision of the American cultural heritage is not a matter of supply from the publishing industry alone. Absent a sufficient institutional context (and justification) for their revision and reproduction, anthologies of African-American literature remain bound within the current economic limitations of the textbook market; and if student demand is indeed strengthening, as Macmillan's sales would seem to suggest, then we need to ensure that universities and colleges can continue to offer courses commensurate with this demand—courses enough, one hopes, to make economically feasible not merely one or two but a whole generation of new anthologies, comparable in size and scope to the generations of 1925–35 and 1965–75.

APPENDIX B

Critical Industries

MUCH HAS been said about Pynchon's status as our latest Major Author, but no research has examined how much academic work has been published on Pynchon relative to that on other authors, major and minor. For this exploratory attempt I have taken figures from the MLA Online catalogue; they therefore represent not an author's or a work's long-term canonicity but his or her or its relative place in academic discussions of the past decade. In case it should appear that this method measures only the so-called "latest academic fads," I note that the authors best represented here are those who had well-established critical industries long before the 1980s. At any rate, as commentators on the profession have pointed out, for academic publishing there's no time like the present: Jonathan Culler, for instance, marks the growth of the industry by the fact that "bibliographies list fifty-five books and articles on Shakespeare published in 1920 and 448 in 1970; for Milton the number increases from eighteen to 136, for Mark Twain from seven to sixty-five" (1988, 3). Those annual numbers have not increased dramatically since 1970, but they do give some idea of the relative "volume" of various academic conversations (in the acoustic and spatial senses). For 1987, the totals were Shakespeare 554, Milton 113, Twain 72; for 1988, Shakespeare 767, Milton 202, Twain 56. Thus, a measure of academic publishing in the 1980s is a reasonable measure of critical volume, even though many standard critical works published before 1981 are left out of such an account.

This enumeration of bibliography entries, however, is itself a measure only of a certain kind—arguably the profession's most important kind—of canonicity. And it is significant in itself that this appendix, which gauges the amount of scholarly research published and registered annually by the MLA, looks so little like Appendix A: Tolson is not merely "less canonical" than Pynchon, but his work is reproduced *elsewhere* and in vastly different ways. I noted in my introduction that these differences are not referable to a more general heading of reception theory; and I believe the general implication of these two appendixes, outlines though they be, is that canons are not exclusively a matter of Alastair Fowler's six levels, or Wendell Harris's recent *ten* (1991), but a matter of *sites* and modes of production, as well. To put this conjecture another way: Fowler argues that genre is the most important determinant of canonicity (1982, 216), because a writer's continued reproduction is dependent on the relative canonical hierarchy among (say) novels, eclogues, verse satires, and essays. I suggest in return that canons are produced *by means of* a relative hierarchy of genres as well, ranging from literary histories and reader's guides to anthologies and published research; but for now I will leave this only as a suggestion.

My selection of authors is random but not arbitrary. For each one I have included as "major" the work cited most often in the bibliographies (hence *Absalom, Absalom!* and not *The Sound and the Fury*; *Pride and Prejudice* and not *Emma*). I note in advance that the proportion of work citations to author citations is itself indicative of an author's status: less than one-eighth of the Shakespeare items focus on *Hamlet*, and the same proportion holds for Beckett, Kafka, Lawrence, Cather, Dickens, Austen, Woolf, Faulkner, Barth, and Bellow (of those with 100 or more listings)—each a writer with more than one major work to his or her credit. The proportions of Geoffrey Chaucer, Edmund Spenser, John Milton, George Orwell, Kate Chopin, Zora Neale Hurston, and Thomas Pynchon, on the other hand, tell nearly the opposite story: the industry of each of these authors devotes roughly half its energies, if not more, to one major work. Finally, at another level of citation altogether, Derrida, Barthes, and Foucault show up quite frequently but rarely for individual titles. This is partly because they are as often cited for their various articles, essays, and interviews as for their books, and partly because they themselves are, appropriately enough, "founders of discursivity" to some extent, associated less with specific texts than with critical practices.

Here, then, are the totals listed in the MLA Online Bibliography from 1981 through January 1991. The double columns are to be read vertically, not horizontally.

Major Authors	Items	Major Works	Items
Shakespeare	5,761	Canterbury Tales	823
Joyce	1,900	Ulysses	813
Chaucer	1,534	Hamlet	706
Milton	1,422	Paradise Lost	643
Faulkner	1,297	The Faerie Queene	383
Dickens	1,052	1984	265
T. S. Eliot	1,024	The Cantos	243
Melville	953	Moby-Dick	216
Lawrence	897	The Waste Land	218
Pound	897	Gulliver's Travels	192
Kafka	819	Tristram Shandy	191
Hawthorne	782	Heart of Darkness	187
Beckett	741	*Gravity's Rainbow*	*170*
Conrad	740	The Scarlet Letter	164
Woolf	655	One Hundred Years of Solitude	154
G. Eliot	613	Absalom, Absalom!	137
Austen	599	Bleak House	136
Spenser	595	The Great Gatsby	120
Swift	546	Middlemarch	116
Derrida	525	Invisible Man	98
Garcia Márquez	487	To the Lighthouse	95
W. C. Williams	464	Women in Love	92
Orwell	455	The Awakening	86
Nabokov	430	Waiting for Godot	86
Barthes	396	The Trial	83
Bellow	353	Pride and Prejudice	82
Pynchon	*352*	My Antonia	66
Cather	328	Lolita	56
Fitzgerald	293	The French Lieutenant's Woman	56
Sterne	246	Paterson	48
Foucault	237	Song of Solomon	45
John Fowles	188	Their Eyes Were Watching God	42
John Barth	167	Seize the Day	31
Toni Morrison	164	The Sot-Weed Factor	29
Kate Chopin	122	Of Grammatology	24
Ralph Ellison	116	S/Z	24
Norman Mailer	102	Slaughterhouse-Five	22
Zora Neale Hurston	87	Call It Sleep	19
Kurt Vonnegut, Jr.	85	Armies of the Night	13
Henry Miller	51	History of Sexuality	10
Henry Roth	21	Tropic of Cancer	6
Tolson	*13*	*Harlem Gallery*	*6*

These numbers do not necessarily tell a story in and of themselves, but they do indicate that Pynchon is by far the most canonical of postmodern American writers; only Barth and Morrison hover around half Pynchon's entries, though Morrison will no doubt surpass both Barth and John Fowles within a few years. (I am not considering Orwell "postmodern," but I do note that the quantity of his reception here far exceeds Rodden's 1989 estimate of his position in the academy.) For the remaining Pynchon-like postmodernists—that is, authors traditionally cited as Pynchon cognates—the totals are as follows: Hawkes 90, Barthelme 59, Heller 58, Burroughs 56, Gaddis 47, Reed 44, Kosinski 43, Brautigan 29, Gass 28; of postwar writers not regularly associated with Pynchon, I have totaled Doris Lessing 271, Italo Calvino 203, Lawrence Durrell 150, Jack Kerouac 118, John Updike 125, Alice Walker 119, Ursula K. Le Guin 94, Joyce Carol Oates 80, Joan Didion 55, Maxine Hong Kingston 48, Gloria Naylor 10. For the two writers most often cited as Pynchon's heirs, I get 8 entries on Tom Robbins and 17 on Don DeLillo—though DeLillo's position is sure to climb; the number of DeLillo entries has more than doubled in eighteen months (as, for that matter, have entries on *The Awakening*). Among African-American poets contemporary with Tolson, I count 105 entries on Langston Hughes, 56 on Gwendolyn Brooks, 15 on Robert Hayden.

If they accomplish nothing else, the totals here should at least put to rest the belief that *Gravity's Rainbow* "has already been the subject of more books, essays, and apoplexy than any novel since *Ulysses*" (Muste 1984, 5), since both *The Great Gatsby* and *Absalom, Absalom!* have matched or outperformed it even since 1974 (*Gatsby* 220, *Absalom* 208, *GR* 208). Still, we are obviously talking about a very securely represented writer when we measure Pynchon's reception in this way, even if he is not *the* most written-about twentieth-century American writer. These figures are crude—discussions of the novels in book-length studies are particularly ill served by such a quantitative study—but the general point, I hope, is clear. I note, in closing, that in 1988 studies of Toni Morrison surpassed studies of Pynchon for the first but not, I suspect, for the last time.

Works Cited

Abbreviations Used in Footnotes

C   Thomas Pynchon, *The Crying of Lot 49*
GR   Thomas Pynchon, *Gravity's Rainbow*
HG   Melvin Tolson, *Harlem Gallery: Book I, The Curator*
L   Melvin Tolson, *Libretto for the Republic of Liberia*
TM   Tolson Manuscripts
V   Thomas Pynchon, *V.*

Ackroyd, Peter (1973). "Somewhere over the Novel." Review of *Gravity's Rainbow*. *Spectator*, 17 Nov., pp. 641–42.

Adams, William, Peter Conn, and Barry Slepian, eds. (1970). *Afro-American Literature: Poetry*. Boston: Houghton Mifflin.

Adoff, Arnold, ed. (1973). *The Poetry of Black America: Anthology of the 20th Century*. New York: Harper & Row.

Adorno, Theodor (1967). "Valéry Proust Museum." In *Prisms*, trans. Samuel and Shierry Weber, 175–85. Letchworth, Herts.: Garden City Press.

Alter, Robert (1975). "The New American Novel." *Commentary*, Nov., pp. 44–51.

Althusser, Louis (1971). *Lenin and Philosophy and Other Essays*. Trans. Ben Brewster. New York: Monthly Review Press.

Armstrong, Paul B. (1988). "History and Epistemology: The Example of *The Turn of the Screw*." *New Literary History* 19/3: 693–712.

Aronowitz, Stanley (1987). "Postmodernism and Politics." *Social Text* 18:99–115.

Baker, Houston A., Jr., ed. (1971). *Black Literature in America*. New York: McGraw-Hill.

—— (1980). *The Journey Back: Issues in Black Literature and Criticism*. Chicago: University of Chicago Press.

—— (1981). "Generational Shifts and the Recent Criticism of Afro-American Literature." *Black American Literature Forum* 15:3–21.

—— (1987a). "In Dubious Battle." *New Literary History* 18/2: 363–69.

—— (1987b). *Modernism and the Harlem Renaissance*. Chicago: University of Chicago Press.

Bakhtin, Mikhail M. (1981). *The Dialogic Imagination*. Trans. Caryl Emerson and Michael Holquist, ed. Michael Holquist. Austin: University of Texas Press.

Barksdale, Richard, and Keneth Kinnamon, eds. (1972). *Black Writers of America: A Comprehensive Anthology*. New York: Macmillan.

Barrett, William (1949). "Comment: A Prize for Ezra Pound." *Partisan Review* 16:344–47.

Barthes, Roland (1974). *S/Z*. Trans. Richard Miller. New York: Hill & Wang.

—— (1975). *The Pleasure of the Text*. Trans. Richard Miller. New York: Hill & Wang.

—— (1977). *Image-Music-Text*. Trans. Stephen Heath. New York: Hill & Wang.

Basler, Roy P. (1973). "The Heart of Blackness—M. B. Tolson's Poetry." *New Letters* 39:63–76.

Baudrillard, Jean (1983). *Simulations*. Trans. Paul Foss, Paul Patton, and Philip Beitchman. New York: Semiotext(e).

Baym, Nina (1985). "Melodramas of Beset Manhood: How Theories of American Fiction Exclude Women Authors." In Showalter 1985, 63–80.

Beckett, Samuel (1964). *How It Is*. New York: Grove Press.

Bell, Bernard W., ed. (1972). *Modern and Contemporary Afro-American Poetry*. Boston: Allyn & Bacon.

Bell, Pearl (1973). "Pynchon's Road of Excess." Review of *Gravity's Rainbow*. *New Leader*, 2 April, pp. 16–17.

Bell-Villada, Gene H. (1985). "Criticism and the State (Political and Otherwise) of the Americas." In Graff and Gibbons 1985, 124–44.

Benjamin, Walter (1969). "Theses on the Philosophy of History." In *Illuminations: Essays and Reflections*, trans. Harry Zohn, ed. Hannah Arendt, 253–64. New York: Schocken.

—— (1970). "The Author as Producer." Trans. John Heckman. *New Left Review*, July–Aug., pp. 83–96.

Bennett, Tony (1983a). "The Bond Phenomenon: Theorizing a Popular Hero." *Southern Review* 16/2: 195–225.

—— (1983b). "Texts, Readers, Reading Formations." *Journal of the Midwest Modern Language Association* 16/1: 3–17.

Bennett, Tony, and Janet Woollacott (1987). *Bond and Beyond: The Political Career of a Popular Hero*. New York: Methuen.

Bercovitch, Sacvan (1986). "The Problem of Ideology in American Literary History." *Critical Inquiry* 12:631–53.

Berger, Joseph (1988). "U.S. Literature: Canon under Siege." *New York Times*, 6 Jan., p. B6.

Berry, Wendell (1985). "The Loss of the University." In Graff and Gibbons 1985, 207–18.

Bersani, Leo (1988). "Is the Rectum a Grave?" In *AIDS: Cultural Analysis / Cultural Activism*, ed. Douglas Crimp, 197–222. Cambridge, Mass.: MIT Press.

—— (1989). "Pynchon, Paranoia, and Literature." *Representations* 25:99–118.

Berthoff, Warner (1979). *A Literature without Qualities: American Writing since 1945*. Berkeley: University of California Press.

Bérubé, Michael (1990). "Masks, Margins, and African American Modernism: Melvin Tolson's *Harlem Gallery*," *PMLA* 105/1: 57–69.

Bickham, Jack (1966). "Flowers of Hope." *Orbit (Sunday Oklahoman)*, 29 Aug., pp. 6–9.

Bienen, Andrew (1987). "Nostalgia and Pornography: David Lynch's *Blue Velvet*." *Iris* 17:30–35.

Bigsby, C. W. E. (1970). "From Protest to Paradox: The Black Writer at Mid-Century." In *The Fifties: Fiction, Poetry, Drama*, ed. Warren French, 217–40. Deland, Fla.: Everett/Edwards.

Black, Joel (1984). "Pynchon's Eve of De-struction." *Pynchon Notes* 14:23–38.

Bledstein, Burton J. (1976). *The Culture of Professionalism: The Middle Class and the Development of Higher Education in America*. New York: Norton.

Bloom, Harold, ed. (1986). *Thomas Pynchon*. New York: Chelsea House.

Bontemps, Arna, ed. (1974). *American Negro Poetry*. Rev. ed. New York: Hill & Wang.

Borkin, Joseph (1978). *The Crime and Punishment of I. G. Farben*. London: André Deutsch.

Bourdieu, Pierre (1984). *Distinction: A Social Critique of the Judgement of Taste*. Trans. Richard Nice. Cambridge, Mass.: Harvard University Press.

Boynton, Robert, and Maynard Mack, eds. (1973). *Introduction to the Poem*. 2d ed. New York: Hayden.

Bradley, Sculley, Richmond Croom Beatty, and E. Hudson Long, eds. (1967). *The American Tradition in Literature*. 3d ed. New York: Norton.

Breman, Paul (1969). "Poetry into the Sixties." In *The Black American Writer*, ed. C. W. E. Bigsby, 99–109. Deland, Fla.: Everett/Edwards.

Brod, Max (1935). Postscript. In Kafka 1925, 272–73.

Brooks, Cleanth, and Robert Penn Warren, eds. (1976). *Understanding Poetry*. 4th ed. New York: Holt, Rinehart & Winston.

Brooks, Gwendolyn (1965). "Books Noted." Review of *Harlem Gallery*. *Negro Digest*, Sept., pp. 51–52.

Brown, Dee (1970). *Bury My Heart at Wounded Knee: An Indian History of the American West*. New York: Holt, Rinehart & Winston.

Brown, Norman O. (1966). *Love's Body*. New York: Random House.

Brown, Sterling A., Arthur P. Davis, and Ulysses Lee, eds. (1941). *The Negro Caravan: Writings by American Negroes*. New York: Arno, 1969.

Burroughs, William S. (1959). *Naked Lunch*. New York: Grove Press.

Butler, Marilyn (1985). "Against Tradition: The Case for a Particularized Historical Method." In *Historical Studies and Literary Criticism*, ed. Jerome McGann, 25–47. Madison: University of Wisconsin Press.

Cain, William (1988). "Notes toward a History of Anti-Criticism." *New Literary History* 20/1: 33–48.

Calhoun, John C. (1976). "The Concept of Revolution and Its Influence on the Genesis of Art in the Work of Thomas Pynchon." *Perspectives on Contemporary Literature* 2:40–52.

Callens, Johan (1983). "Reading Pynchon into the Eighties." Review of Tanner 1982, Cowart 1980, and Stark 1980. *Dutch Quarterly Review* 13:103–19.

Cecil, David, and Allen Tate, eds. (1958). *Modern Verse in English: 1900–1950*. New York: Macmillan.

Chabot, C. Barry (1988). "The Problem of the Postmodern." *New Literary History* 20/1: 1–20.

Chambers, Ross (1990). "Irony and the Canon." *Profession 90*, 18–24.

Chapman, Abraham, ed. (1968). *Black Voices: An Anthology of Afro-American Literature*. New York: New American Library.

Chase, Richard (1957). "The Fate of the Avant-Garde." *Partisan Review* 24:363–75.

Chase Levenson, Karen (1986). "'Bad' Was My Commentary: Propriety, Madness, and Independence in Nineteenth-Century Women's Literature." Paper delivered to symposium "Women Reading Victorian Literature," University of Virginia, Charlottesville, 3 Oct.

Ciardi, John (1954). "Recent Verse." Review of *Libretto for the Republic of Liberia*. *The Nation*, 27 Feb., p. 183.

—— (1958). "Dialogue with the Audience." *Saturday Review*, 22 Nov., pp. 10–12, 42.

—— (1964). "Manner of Speaking." *Saturday Review*, 11 Jan., p. 16.

Clark, Beverly Lyon, and Caryn Fuoroli (1981). "A Review of Major Pynchon Criticism." In Pearce 1981, 230–54.

Clerc, Charles, ed. (1983). *Approaches to "Gravity's Rainbow."* Columbus: Ohio State University Press.

Conrad, Joseph (1901). *Heart of Darkness, and The Secret Sharer*. New York: Harper, 1910.

Cooper, Peter (1983). *Signs and Symptoms: Thomas Pynchon and the Contemporary World*. Berkeley: University of California Press.

Cowart, David (1980). *Thomas Pynchon: The Art of Allusion*. Carbondale: Southern Illinois University Press.

Culler, Jonathan (1975). *Structuralist Poetics: Structuralism, Linguistics, and the Study of Literature*. Ithaca: Cornell University Press.

—— (1980). "Prolegomena to a Theory of Reading." In Suleiman and Crosman 1980, 46–66.

—— (1982). *On Deconstruction: Theory and Criticism after Structuralism*. Ithaca: Cornell University Press.

—— (1988). *Framing the Sign: Criticism and Its Institutions*. Norman: University of Oklahoma Press.

Cuney, Waring, Langston Hughes, and Bruce McMarion Wright, eds. (1954). *Lincoln University Poets: Centennial Anthology*. Intro. Horace Mann Bond and J. Saunders Redding. New York: Fine Editions Press.

Davis, Arthur P. (1954). "Negro Poetry." Review of *Libretto for the Republic of Liberia*. *Midwest Journal* 6:74–77.

—— (1974). "Melvin B. Tolson." In *From The Dark Tower: Afro-American Writers 1900 to 1960*, 167–74. Washington, D.C.: Howard University Press.

Davis, Arthur P., and Saunders Redding, eds. (1971). *Cavalcade: Negro American Writing from 1760 to the Present*. Boston: Houghton Mifflin.

Davis, Charles T., and Daniel Walden, eds. *On Being Black: Writings by Afro-Americans from Frederick Douglass to the Present*. New York: Fawcett.

Davis, Robert A. (1941). "The Art Notebook." *Chicago Sunday Bee*, 21 Sept.

Daw, Lawrence (1986). "The Limitations of Indeterminacy in Pynchon's Fiction." *CEA Critic* 49:174–79.

De Feo, Ronald (1974). "Fiction Chronicle." Review of *Gravity's Rainbow*. *Hudson Review* 26:773–75.

De Lauretis, Teresa (1984). *Alice Doesn't: Feminism, Semiotics, Cinema*. Bloomington: Indiana University Press.

Derrida, Jacques (1981). "Outwork, Prefacing." In *Dissemination*, trans. Barbara Johnson, 1–59. Chicago: University of Chicago Press.

—— (1988). *Limited Inc*. Evanston, Ill.: Northwestern University Press.

Dickie, Margaret (1986). *On the Modernist Long Poem*. Iowa City: University of Iowa Press.

Dove, Rita (1985). "Telling It like It I-S *IS*: Narrative Strategies in Melvin Tolson's *Harlem Gallery*." *New England Quarterly* 8:109–17.

Drachler, Jacob, ed. (1964). *African Heritage*. London: Collier.

Duyfhuizen, Bernard (1984). "Deconstructing *Gravity's Rainbow*." *Pynchon Notes* 14:3–6.

—— (1989). "Taking Stock: 26 Years Since *V*. (Over 26 Books on Pynchon!)." *Novel* 23/1: 75–88.

Eagleton, Terry (1982). "The Revolt of the Reader." *New Literary History* 13/2: 449–52.

—— (1983). *Literary Theory: An Introduction*. Oxford: Basil Blackwell.

Eddins, Dwight (1983). "Paradigms Reclaimed: The Language of Science in *Gravity's Rainbow*." *Markham Review* 12:72–80.

Eliot, T. S. (1917). "Reflections on *Vers Libre*." *New Statesman*, 3 March. Rpt. in *Selected Prose of T. S. Eliot*, ed. Frank Kermode, 31–36. London: Faber & Faber, 1975.

—— (1921). "The Metaphysical Poets." *Times Literary Supplement*, 20 Oct. Rpt. in *Selected Prose of T. S. Eliot*, ed. Frank Kermode, 59–67. London: Faber & Faber, 1975.

—— (1945). "The Social Function of Poetry." In *On Poetry and Poets*, 3–16. New York: Farrar, Straus & Cudahy, 1957.

—— (1950). Letter. *Poetry* 76:88.

—— (1971). *The Complete Poems and Plays, 1909–1950.* New York: Harcourt, Brace & World.

Ellmann, Richard, and Robert O'Clair, eds. (1973). *The Norton Anthology of Modern Poetry.* New York: Norton.

Emanuel, James A., and Theodore L. Gross, eds. (1968). *Dark Symphony: Negro Literature in America.* New York: Free Press.

English, D. Anthony (1989). Letter to the author, 29 June.

—— (1990). Letter to the author, 10 Sept.

Fabio, Sarah Webster (1966). "Who Speaks Negro?" *Negro Digest,* Dec., pp. 54–58.

Farnsworth, Robert M. (1979). Afterword. In Tolson 1979, 255–72.

—— (1984). *Melvin B. Tolson, 1898–1966: Plain Talk and Poetic Prophecy.* Columbia: University of Missouri Press.

Fish, Stanley (1980). *Is There a Text in This Class? The Authority of Interpretive Communities.* Cambridge, Mass.: Harvard University Press.

—— (1983). "Profession Despise Thyself: Fear and Self-Loathing in Literary Studies." *Critical Inquiry* 10:349–64.

—— (1985). "Anti-Professionalism." *New Literary History* 17/1: 89–108.

—— (1986). "Transmuting the Lump: *Paradise Lost,* 1942–82." In *Literature and History: Theoretical Problems and Russian Case Studies,* ed. Gary Saul Morson, 33–56. Palo Alto, Calif.: Stanford University Press.

Flasch, Joy (1972). *Melvin B. Tolson.* New York: Twayne.

Ford, Nick Aaron (1950). "A Blueprint for Negro Authors." *Phylon* 11:374–77.

——, ed. (1971). *Black Insights: Significant Literature by Black Americans—1760 to the Present.* Waltham, Mass.: Xerox College Publishing.

Foster, Hal, ed. (1983). *The Anti-Aesthetic: Essays on Postmodern Culture.* Port Townsend, Wash.: Bay Press.

Foucault, Michel (1984). "What Is an Author?" Trans. Josué V. Harari. In *The Foucault Reader,* ed. Paul Rabinow, 101–20. New York: Pantheon Books.

Fowler, Alastair (1982). *Kinds of Literature: An Introduction to the Theory of Genres and Modes.* Cambridge, Mass.: Harvard University Press.

Fowler, Douglas (1980). *A Reader's Guide to "Gravity's Rainbow."* Ann Arbor: Ardis.

Frank, Joseph (1948). "Spatial Form in Modern Literature." In *Criticism,* ed. Mark Schorer, Josephine Miles, and Gordon McKenzie, 379–92. New York: Harcourt, Brace.

French, William P., Michael J. Fabre, and Amritjit Singh, comps. (1979). *Afro-American Poetry and Drama, 1760–1975.* Detroit: Gale Research.

Freud, Sigmund (1966). "Fetishism" (1921). In *The Standard Edition of the Psychological Works of Sigmund Freud,* ed. James Strachey, 21: 152–57. London: Hogarth Press and the Institute of Psycho-analysis.

Friedman, Alan J. (1983). "Science and Technology." In Clerc 1983, 69–102.

Frye, Northrop (1957). *Anatomy of Criticism*. Princeton, N.J.: Princeton University Press.

Fuller, Hoyt W. (1966). "Negro Writers and White Critics." *The Progressive*, Oct., pp. 36–39.

Fussell, Paul (1975). *The Great War and Modern Memory*. London: Oxford University Press.

Fussiner, Howard P. (1954). "A Mature Voice Speaks." Review of *Libretto for the Republic of Liberia*. *Phylon* 15:96–97.

Gardner, John (1978). *On Moral Fiction*. New York: Basic Books.

Gates, Henry Louis, Jr. (1984a). "The Blackness of Blackness: A Critique of the Sign and the Signifying Monkey." In *Black Literature and Literary Theory*, ed. Henry Louis Gates, Jr., 285–321. New York: Methuen.

—— (1984b). "Criticism in the Jungle." In *Black Literature and Literary Theory*, ed. Henry Louis Gates, Jr., 1–24. New York: Methuen.

—— (1986). "Writing 'Race' and the Difference It Makes." In *"Race," Writing, and Difference*. ed. Henry Louis Gates, Jr., 1–20. Chicago: University of Chicago Press.

—— (1987). "'What's Love Got To Do with It?': Critical Theory, Integrity, and the Black Idiom." *New Literary History* 18/2: 345–62.

—— (1989). "Whose Canon Is It, Anyway?" *New York Times Book Review*, 26 Feb., pp. 1, 44–45.

Gibbons, Reginald (1985). "Academic Criticism and Contemporary Culture." In Graff and Gibbons 1985, 15–34.

Gibson, Walker (1950). "Authors, Speakers, Readers, and Mock Readers." In Tompkins 1980b, 1–6.

Gilbert, Sandra M. (1985a). "Feminist Criticism in the University: An Interview with Sandra M. Gilbert." With Gerald Graff. In Graff and Gibbons 1985, 111–23.

—— (1985b). "What Do Feminist Critics Want? A Postcard from the Volcano." In Showalter 1985, 29–45.

Grace, Sherrill E. (1983). "Fritz Lang and the 'Paracinematic Lives' of *Gravity's Rainbow*." *Modern Fiction Studies* 29:655–70.

Graff, Gerald (1970). *Poetic Statement and Critical Dogma*. Evanston, Ill.: Northwestern University Press.

—— (1985). "The University and the Prevention of Culture." In Graff and Gibbons 1985, 62–82.

—— (1987). *Professing Literature: An Institutional History*. Chicago: University of Chicago Press.

Graff, Gerald, and Reginald Gibbons, eds. (1985). *Criticism in the University*. TriQuarterly Series on Criticism and Culture, 1. Evanston, Ill.: Northwestern University Press.

Greenberg, Clement (1939). "Avant-Garde and Kitsch." *Partisan Review* 6:34–49.

Grossberg, Lawrence (1988). "'You [Still] Have to Fight for Your Right to Party': Music Television as Billboards of Post-modern Difference." *Popular Music* 7:315–32.

Gubar, Susan (1987). "Representing Pornography: Feminism, Criticism, and Depictions of Female Violation." *Critical Inquiry* 13:712–41.

Guillory, John (1987). "Canonical and Non-Canonical: A Critique of the Current Debate." *ELH* [*English Literary History*] 54:483–526.

Habermas, Jürgen (1989). *The Structural Transformation of the Public Sphere: An Inquiry into a Category of Bourgeois Society.* Trans. Thomas Burger with Frederick Lawrence. Cambridge, Mass.: MIT Press.

Haley, Alex (1965). *The Autobiography of Malcolm X.* New York: Ballantine Books.

Hansell, William H. (1984). "Three Artists in Melvin B. Tolson's *Harlem Gallery.*" *Black American Literature Forum* 18/1: 122–27.

Harris, Wendell Y. (1991). "Canons." *PMLA* 106/1: 110–21.

Hassan, Ihab (1967). *The Literature of Silence: Henry Miller and Samuel Beckett.* New York: Knopf.

—— (1988). "On the Problem of the Postmodern." *New Literary History* 20/1: 21–22.

Hausdorff, Don (1966). "Thomas Pynchon's Multiple Absurdities." *Wisconsin Studies in Contemporary Literature* 7/3: 258–69.

Hayden, Robert, ed. (1967). *Kaleidoscope: Poems by American Negro Poets.* New York: Harcourt, Brace & World.

Hayden, Robert, David Burrows, and Frederick Lapides, eds. (1971). *Afro-American Literature: An Introduction.* New York: Harcourt Brace Jovanovich.

Hayles, N. Katherine (1990). *Chaos Bound: Orderly Disorder in Contemporary Literature and Science.* Ithaca: Cornell University Press.

Heidegger, Martin (1962). *Being and Time.* Trans. John Macquarrie and Edward Robinson. New York: Harper & Row.

Henderson, Stephen, ed. (1973). *Understanding the New Black Poetry: Black Speech and Black Music as Poetic References.* New York: Morrow.

Hendin, Josephine (1975). "What Is Thomas Pynchon Telling Us?" *Harper's Magazine,* March, pp. 82–83, 87–88, 90, 92.

Herrnstein Smith, Barbara (1983). "Contingencies of Value." *Critical Inquiry* 10/1: 1–35.

—— (1989). "Presidential Address 1988. Limelight: Reflections on a Public Year." *PMLA* 104/3:285–93.

Hill, Herbert, ed. (1963). *Soon, One Morning: New Writing by American Negroes, 1940–1962.* New York: Knopf.

Hills, L. Rust (1963). "The Structure of the American Literary Establishment." *Esquire,* July, pp. 41–43.

—— (1987). "Esquire's Guide to the Literary Universe." *Esquire,* Aug., pp. 51–53, 55–58.

Hite, Molly (1983). *Ideas of Order in the Novels of Thomas Pynchon.* Columbus: Ohio State University Press.

Hohendahl, Peter Uwe (1977). "Introduction to Reception Aesthetics." *New German Critique* 10:29–63.

—— (1982). *The Institution of Criticism.* Ithaca: Cornell University Press.

Hohmann, Charles (1986). *Thomas Pynchon's "Gravity's Rainbow": A Study of Its Conceptual Structure and of Rilke's Influence.* New York: Peter Lang.

Holmes, John R. (1983). "'A Hand to Turn the Time': History as Film in *Gravity's Rainbow.*" *Cithara* 23:5–16.

Holub, Robert C. (1982). "Trends in Literary Theory: The American Reception of Reception Theory." *German Quarterly* 55/1: 80–96.

—— (1984). *Reception Theory: A Critical Introduction.* London: Routledge.

Hover, Julie, and Charles Kadushin (1972). "Influential Intellectual Journals: A Very Private Club." *Change* 4:38–47.

Hughes, Langston (1951). *Montage of a Dream Deferred.* New York: Henry Holt.

Hughes, Langston, and Arna Bontemps, eds. (1970). *The Poetry of the Negro, 1746–1970.* Rev. ed. New York: Doubleday.

Hume, David (1854). "Of National Characters." In *The Philosophical Works*, 3:218–36. Boston: Little, Brown.

Huot, Robert J. (1971). "Melvin B. Tolson's *Harlem Gallery*: A Critical Edition with Introduction and Explanatory Notes." Ph.D. diss., University of Utah.

Hutcheon, Linda (1989). *The Politics of Postmodernism.* New York: Routledge, Chapman & Hall.

Huyssen, Andreas (1986). *After the Great Divide: Modernism, Mass Culture, Postmodernism.* Bloomington: Indiana University Press.

Hyman, Stanley Edgar (1958). "The Negro Writer in America: An Exchange. The Folk Tradition." *Partisan Review* 25:197–211.

Iser, Wolfgang (1974). *The Implied Reader: Patterns of Communication in Prose Fiction from Bunyan to Beckett.* Baltimore, Md.: Johns Hopkins University Press.

Jackson, Blyden (1976). "Reconsideration." *New Republic*, 4 Dec., p. 31.

Jacoby, Russell (1987). *The Last Intellectuals: American Culture in the Age of Academe.* New York: Basic Books.

Jameson, Fredric (1981). *The Political Unconscious: Narrative as a Socially Symbolic Act.* Ithaca: Cornell University Press.

Jardine, Alice (1985). *Gynesis: Configurations of Woman and Modernity.* Ithaca: Cornell University Press.

Jauss, Hans Robert (1982a). "Norwid and Baudelaire as Contemporaries: A Notable Case of Overdue Concretization." In *The Structure of the Literary Process: Studies Devoted to the Memory of Felix Vodicka*, ed. Peter Steiner, Miroslav Cervenka, and Ronald Vroon, 285–96. Amsterdam: John Benjamins.

—— (1982b). *Toward an Aesthetic of Reception.* Trans. Timothy Bahti. Theory and History of Literature, 2. Minneapolis: University of Minnesota Press.

Jencks, Christopher, and David Riesman (1968). *The Academic Revolution.* New York: Doubleday.

Johnson, Barbara (1987). *A World of Difference.* Baltimore, Md.: Johns Hopkins University Press.

Johnson, James Weldon, ed. (1922). *The Book of American Negro Poetry.* New York: Harcourt.

Joyce, Joyce A. (1987). "The Black Canon: Reconstructing Black American Literary Criticism." *New Literary History* 18/2: 335–44.

Kadushin, Charles, Julie Hover, and Monique Tichy (1971). "How and Where to Find the Intellectual Elite in the United States." *Public Opinion Quarterly* 35/1: 1–18.

Kafka, Franz (1925). *The Trial.* 2d ed. Trans. Willa and Edwin Muir. New York: Schocken, 1968.

Kappeler, Susanne (1986). *The Pornography of Representation.* Minneapolis: University of Minnesota Press.

Kaufmann, David (1990). "The Profession of Theory." *PMLA* 105/3: 519–30.

Kearns, Francis E., ed. (1970). *Black Identity.* New York: Holt, Rinehart, & Winston.

Kelly, Ernece B., ed. (1972). *Searching for America.* Urbana, Ill.: National Council of Teachers of English.

Kenner, Hugh (1983a). "Faulkner and the Avant-Garde." In *Faulkner: New Perspectives,* ed. Richard C. Brodhead, 62–73. Englewood Cliffs, N.J.: Prentice-Hall.

—— (1983b). "The Making of the Modernist Canon." In von Hallberg 1983, 363–75.

Kermode, Frank (1966). *The Sense of an Ending: Studies in the Theory of Fiction.* London: Oxford University Press.

Kihss, Peter (1974). "Pulitzer Jurors Dismayed on Pynchon." *New York Times,* 20 April, p. 38.

Kimball, Roger (1990). *Tenured Radicals: How Politics Has Corrupted Our Higher Education.* New York: Harper Perennial.

Klancher, Jon (1987). *The Making of English Reading Audiences, 1790–1832.* Madison: University of Wisconsin Press.

Klein, Marcus (1981). *Foreigners: The Making of American Literature, 1900–1940.* Chicago: University of Chicago Press.

Knapp, Steven, and Walter Benn Michaels (1985). "Against Theory." In *Against Theory,* ed. W. J. T. Mitchell, 11–30. Chicago: University of Chicago Press.

Kolodny, Annette, and Daniel J. Peters (1973). "Pynchon's *The Crying of Lot 49*: The Novel as Subversive Experience." *Modern Fiction Studies* 19:79–87.

Kostelanetz, Richard (1973). *The End of Intelligent Writing: Literary Politics in America.* New York: Sheed & Ward.

Krauss, Rosalind (1980). "Poststructuralism and the 'Paraliterary.'" *October* 13:36–40.

Lacan, Jacques (1958). "The Meaning of the Phallus." In *Feminine Sexuality,* ed. Juliet Mitchell and Jacqueline Rose, trans. Jacqueline Rose, 74–85. New York: Norton, 1982.

Lauter, Paul (1983). "Race and Gender in the Shaping of the American Literary Canon: A Case Study from the Twenties." *Feminist Studies* 9:435–63.

—— (1984). "Society and the Profession, 1958–83." *PMLA* 99:414–26.

——, ed. (1990). *The Heath Anthology of American Literature.* Lexington, Mass.: Heath.

Lawrence, Karen (1981). *The Odyssey of Style in "Ulysses."* Princeton, N.J.: Princeton University Press.

Levenson, Michael H. (1984). *A Genealogy of Modernism: A Study of English Literary Doctrine, 1908–1922.* New York: Cambridge University Press.

Leverenz, David (1976). "On Trying to Read *Gravity's Rainbow.*" In Levine and Leverenz 1976, 229–49.

Levine, Al (1973). Review of *Gravity's Rainbow. Commonweal,* 4 May, pp. 217–18.

Levine, George (1973). "V-2." Review of *Gravity's Rainbow. Partisan Review* 40:517–29.

Levine, George, and David Leverenz, eds. (1976). *Mindful Pleasures: Essays on Thomas Pynchon.* Boston: Little, Brown.

[Lewis, Wyndham] (1915). Editorial. *Blast* 2:5–6.

Lhamon, W. T., Jr. (1973). "The Most Irresponsible Bastard." Review of *Gravity's Rainbow. New Republic,* 14 April, pp. 24–28.

Lieberman, Laurence (1965). "Poetry Chronicle." Review of *Harlem Gallery. Hudson Review* 18:455–60.

Littlejohn, David (1966). *Black on White: A Critical Survey of Writing by American Negroes.* New York: Grossman.

Llorens, David (1966). "Seeking a New Image: Writers Converge at Fisk University." *Negro Digest,* June, pp. 54–68.

Locke, Richard (1973). Review of *Gravity's Rainbow. New York Times Book Review,* 11 March, pp. 1–3, 12–13.

Lomax, Alan, and Raoul Abdul, eds. (1970). *3000 Years of Black Poetry.* New York: Dodd, Mead.

Long, Richard A., and Eugenia W. Collier, eds. (1985). *Afro-American Writing: An Anthology of Prose and Poetry.* Rev. ed. 2 vols. University Park: Pennsylvania State University Press.

Lotman, Yury (1982). "The Text and the Structure of Its Audience." *New Literary History* 14/1: 81–87.

Lott, Eric (1988). "Double V, Double Time: Bebop's Politics of Style." *Callaloo* 11/3: 597–605.

Lowenfels, Walter, ed. (1969). *The Writing on the Wall: 108 American Poems of Protest.* New York: Doubleday.

Lyon, Janet (1992). "Feminist Polemics and the Manifesto's 'Hostile Hand.'" Ph.D. diss., University of Virginia.

Mac Adam, Alfred (1978). "Pynchon as Satirist: To Write, To Mean." *Yale Review* 67:555–66.

McCall, Dan (1966). "The Quicksilver Sparrow of M. B. Tolson." *American Quarterly* 18:538–42.

McGann, Jerome (1983). *The Romantic Ideology: A Critical Investigation.* Chicago: University of Chicago Press.

McHale, Brian (1979). "Modernist Reading, Post-Modern Text: The Case of *Gravity's Rainbow.*" *Poetics Today* 1:85–110.

—— (1985). "'You Used to Know What These Words Mean': Misreading *Gravity's Rainbow.*" *Language and Style* 18:93–118.

—— (1987). *Postmodernist Fiction*. New York: Methuen.

McHoul, Alec, and David Wills (1990). *Writing Pynchon: Strategies in Fictional Analysis*. Urbana: University of Illinois Press.

McKay, Nellie Y., ed. (1988). *Critical Essays on Toni Morrison*. Boston: G. K. Hall.

Mackey, Douglas A. (1980). *The Rainbow Quest of Thomas Pynchon*. San Bernardino, Calif.: Borgo Press.

Mackey, Louis (1981). "Paranoia, Pynchon, and Preterition." *Sub-stance* 30:16–30.

Mailloux, Steven (1982). *Interpretive Conventions: The Reader in the Study of American Fiction*. Ithaca: Cornell University Press.

Mangel, Anne (1971). "Maxwell's Demon, Entropy, Information: *The Crying of Lot 49*." *TriQuarterly* 20: 194–208.

"A Marathon on Pynchon Stirs Readers" (1987). *New York Times*, 15 Nov., p. 61.

Marcus, Steven (1966). *The Other Victorians: A Study of Sexuality and Pornography in Mid-Nineteenth-Century England*. New York: Basic Books.

Márquez, Antonio (1983). "Everything Is Connected: Paranoia in *Gravity's Rainbow*." *Perspectives on Contemporary Literature* 9:92–104.

Marriott, David (1985). "*Gravity's Rainbow*: Apocryphal History or Historical Apocrypha?" *Journal of American Studies* 19:69–80.

Mazurek, Raymond (1985). "Ideology and Form in the Postmodernist Historical Novel: *The Sot-Weed Factor* and *Gravity's Rainbow*." *Minnesota Review* 25:69–84.

Mead, Clifford (1989). *Thomas Pynchon: A Bibliography of Primary and Secondary Materials*. Elmwood Park, Ill.: The Dalkey Archive Press.

Mendelson, Edward (1973). "Pynchon's Gravity." Review of *Gravity's Rainbow*. *Yale Review* 62:624–31.

—— (1976). "Gravity's Encyclopedia." In Levine and Leverenz 1976, 161–95.

——, ed. (1978). *Pynchon: A Collection of Critical Essays*. Twentieth Century Views. Englewood Cliffs, N.J.: Prentice-Hall.

—— (1984). "How Gravity Began." Review of *Slow Learner*. *New Republic*, 16–23 July, pp. 36–39.

Merod, Jim (1987). *The Political Responsibility of the Critic*. Ithaca: Cornell University Press.

Mesher, David (1981). "Negative Entropy and the Form of *Gravity's Rainbow*." *Research Studies* 49:162–70.

Michelson, Peter (1971). *The Aesthetics of Pornography*. New York: Herder & Herder.

Miller, J. Hillis (1979). "The Function of Rhetorical Study at the Present Time." *ADE Bulletin* 62 (Sept.–Nov.): 10–18.

—— (1987). "Presidential Address 1986: The Triumph of Theory, the Resistance to Reading, and the Question of the Material Base." *PMLA* 102:281–91.

Miller, Ruth, ed. (1971). *Blackamerican Literature 1760–Present*. Beverly Hills, Calif.: Glencoe Press.

Millett, Kate (1970). *Sexual Politics.* New York: Doubleday.

Moi, Toril (1985). *Sexual/Textual Politics: Feminist Literary Theory.* New York: Methuen.

Moore, Thomas (1987). *The Style of Connectedness: "Gravity's Rainbow" and Thomas Pynchon.* Columbia: University of Missouri Press.

Morgan, Robin (1980). "Theory and Practice: Pornography and Rape." In *Take Back the Night: Women on Pornography,* ed. Laura Lederer, 134–40. New York: Morrow.

Morris, Robert K. (1973). "Jumping Off the Golden Gate Bridge." Review of *Gravity's Rainbow. The Nation,* 16 July, pp. 53–54.

Morrison, Philip (1973). Review of *Gravity's Rainbow. Scientific American* 229:131.

Morrison, Toni (1987). *Beloved.* New York: Plume.

Mukarovsky, Jan (1936). *Aesthetic Function, Norm, and Value as Social Facts.* Ann Arbor: Department of Slavic Languages and Literatures, University of Michigan, 1970.

Mulvey, Laura (1975). "Visual Pleasure and Narrative Cinema." *Screen* 16:6–18.

Muste, John M. (1984). "Singing Back the Silence: *Gravity's Rainbow* and the War Novel." *Modern Fiction Studies* 30:5–23.

Nelson, Cary (1989). *Repression and Recovery: Modern American Poetry and the Politics of Cultural Memory, 1910–1945.* Madison: University of Wisconsin Press.

Nelson, Raymond (1986). "Shadows Cast by His Own Monuments." Review of Farnsworth 1984. *Callaloo* 9/1: 270–72.

"New Light on the Invisible" (1965). Review of *Harlem Gallery. Times Literary Supplement,* 25 Nov., pp. 1046–49.

Newman, Charles (1985). *The Post-Modern Aura: The Act of Fiction in an Age of Inflation.* Evanston, Ill.: Northwestern University Press.

Nielsen, Aldon Lynn (1988). *Reading Race: White American Poets and the Racial Discourse in the Twentieth Century.* Athens: University of Georgia Press.

O'Brien, Eoin (1986). *The Beckett Country.* Dublin: Black Cat Press.

Ohmann, Richard (1983). "The Shaping of a Canon: U.S. Fiction, 1960–75." In von Hallberg 1983, 377–401.

—— (1987). *Politics of Letters.* Middletown, Conn.: Wesleyan University Press.

Ohmann, Richard, and Carol Ohmann (1976). "Reviewers, Critics, and *The Catcher in the Rye.*" *Critical Inquiry* 3:15–37.

Olderman, Raymond M. (1979). "Thomas Pynchon." Review of Siegel 1978 and Plater 1978. *Contemporary Literature* 20:500–507.

Olsen, Lance (1986). "Deconstructing the Enemy of Color: The Fantastic in *Gravity's Rainbow.*" *Studies in the Novel* 18:74–86.

Owens, Craig (1983). "The Discourse of Others: Feminists and Postmodernism." In Foster 1983, 57–82.

Parker, Robert Dale (n.d.). "Material Choices: American Fictions and the Post-Canon." Unpublished essay.

Parrinder, Patrick (1987). *The Failure of Theory: Essays on Criticism and Contemporary Fiction.* Totowa, N.J.: Barnes & Noble.

Patterson, Lindsay, comp. and ed. (1968). *An Introduction to Black Literature in America.* International Library of Negro Life and History. New York: Publishers Co.

Pearce, Richard, ed. (1981). *Critical Essays on Thomas Pynchon.* Boston: G. K. Hall.

Perkins, David (1987). *A History of Modern Poetry: Modernism and After.* Cambridge, Mass.: Harvard University Press.

Perrine, Laurence, ed. (1977). *Sound and Sense: An Introduction to Poetry.* 5th ed. New York: Harcourt Brace Jovanovich.

Pfeil, Fred (1988). "Postmodernism as a 'Structure of Feeling.'" In *Marxism and the Interpretation of Culture*, ed. Cary Nelson and Lawrence Grossberg, 381–403. Urbana: University of Illinois Press.

Plater, William (1978). *The Grim Phoenix: Reconstructing Thomas Pynchon.* Bloomington: Indiana University Press.

Poirier, Richard (1973). "Rocket Power." Review of *Gravity's Rainbow. Saturday Review*, March, pp. 59–64.

—— (1976). "The Importance of Thomas Pynchon." In Levine and Leverenz 1976, 15–29.

—— (1985). "Humans." Review of *Slow Learner. London Review of Books*, 24 Jan., pp. 18–20.

Porter, Dennis (1988). "Of Poets, Politicians, Policemen, and the Power of Analysis." *New Literary History* 19/3: 501–19.

Porush, David (1989). "Cybernetic Fiction and Postmodern Science." *New Literary History* 20/2: 373–96.

Pound, Ezra (1913). "The Approach to Paris." *New Age*, 2 Oct., pp. 662–64.

—— (1914a). "The Audience." *Poetry* 5/1: 29–30.

—— (1914b). "The New Sculpture." *Egoist*, 16 Feb., pp. 67–68.

—— (1915). "Chronicles." *Blast* 2:85–86.

—— (1932). "Harold Monro." *Criterion* 11:581–92.

—— (1950). "To Harriet Monroe," Jan. 1915. Letter 60 in *The Letters of Ezra Pound, 1907–1941*, ed. D. D. Paige, 48–49. New York: Harcourt, Brace.

Pratt, Mary Louise (1982). "Interpretive Strategies / Strategic Interpretations: On Anglo-American Reader-Response Criticism." *Boundary 2* 11/1–2: 201–31.

Prescott, Peter (1984). "The Collegiate Pynchon." Review of *Slow Learner. Newsweek*, 9 April, pp. 100–101.

Prince, Gerald (1973). "Introduction to the Study of the Narratee." In Tompkins 1980b, 7–25.

"Proceedings of the Modern Language Association of America" (1934). *PMLA* 49:1295–1336.

Proust, Marcel (1913). *Swann's Way.* Trans. C. K. Scott-Moncrieff and Terence Kilmartin. New York: Vintage Books, 1982.

Pynchon, Thomas (1963). *V.* New York: Bantam Books.

—— (1966). *The Crying of Lot 49.* New York: Harper & Row.

—— (1973). *Gravity's Rainbow*. New York: Viking Press.

—— (1984a). "Is It O.K. to Be a Luddite?" *New York Times Book Review*, 28 Oct., pp. 1, 40–41.

—— (1984b). *Slow Learner*. New York: Bantam Books.

—— (1990). *Vineland*. Boston: Little, Brown.

Pyuen, Carolyn S. (1982). "The Transmarginal Leap: Meaning and Process in *Gravity's Rainbow*." *Mosaic* 15:33–46.

Qaddafi, Muammar al- (1976). *The Green Book*. London: Martin Brian & O'Keeffe.

Rabinowitz, Peter (1977). "Truth in Fiction: A Reexamination of Audiences." *Critical Inquiry* 4/1:121–41.

Radway, Janice (1984). *Reading the Romance: Women, Patriarchy, and Popular Literature*. Chapel Hill: University of North Carolina Press.

—— (1988). "The Book-of-the-Month Club and the General Reader: On the Uses of 'Serious' Fiction." *Critical Inquiry* 14:516–38.

Rampersad, Arnold (1983). Review of *A Gallery of Harlem Portraits*. *Yearbook of English Studies*, pp. 354–55.

Randall, Dudley (1966). "Portrait of a Poet as Raconteur." *Negro Digest*, Jan., pp. 54–57.

—— (1971a). "The Black Aesthetic in the Thirties, Forties, and Fifties." In *The Black Aesthetic*, ed. Addison Gayle, Jr., 224–34. New York: Doubleday.

——, ed. (1971b). *The Black Poets*. New York: Bantam Books.

Ray, David, ed. (1981). *From A to Z: 200 Contemporary American Poets*. Athens, Ohio: Swallow Press / Ohio University Press.

Redding, J. Saunders (1954). Review of *Libretto for the Republic of Liberia*. *Afro-American* (magazine section), 23 Jan., p. 2.

Redmond, Eugene (1976). *Drumvoices: The Mission of Afro-American Poetry*. New York: Doubleday.

—— (1978). "Stridency and the Sword: Literary and Cultural Emphasis in Afro-American Magazines." In *The Little Magazine in America: A Modern Documentary History*, ed. Elliot Anderson and Mary Kinzie, 538–73. Yonkers, N.Y.: Pushcart Press.

Reising, Russell (1986). *The Unusable Past: Theory and the Study of American Literature*. New York: Methuen.

Richardson, Jack (1968). "The Black Arts." Review of *Rebellion or Revolution?* by Harold Cruse; *Black Fire*, ed. LeRoi Jones [Amiri Baraka] and Larry Neal; *Tell Me How Long the Train's Been Gone*, by James Baldwin; *Soul on Ice*, by Eldridge Cleaver. *New York Review of Books*, 19 Dec., pp. 10–13.

Riffaterre, Michael (1966). "Describing Poetic Structures: Two Approaches to Baudelaire's 'Les Chats.'" In Tompkins 1980b, 26–40.

Robbins, Bruce (1983). "Modernism in History, Modernism in Power." In *Modernism Reconsidered*, ed. Robert Kiely, 229–45. Harvard English Studies, 11. Cambridge, Mass.: Harvard University Press.

—— (1987). "The Politics of Theory." *Social Text* 18:4–18.

——, ed. (1990). *Intellectuals: Aesthetics Politics Academics*. Minneapolis: University of Minnesota Press.

Robinson, Lillian (1983). "Feminist Criticism: How Do We Know When We've Won?" *Tulsa Studies in Women's Literature* 3:143–51.

—— (1985). "Treason Our Text: Feminist Challenges to the Literary Canon." In Showalter 1985, 105–21.

—— (1987). "Canon Fathers and Myth Universe." *New Literary History* 19/1: 23–35.

Robinson, William H., ed. (1972). *Nommo: An Anthology of Black African and Black American Literature*. New York: Macmillan.

Rodden, John (1989). *The Politics of Literary Reputation: The Making and Claiming of 'St. George' Orwell*. New York: Oxford University Press.

Rodman, Selden (1954). "On Vistas Undreamt." Review of *Libretto for the Republic of Liberia*. *New York Times Book Review*, 24 Jan., p. 10.

Rose, Jacqueline (1982). "Introduction—II." In Jacques Lacan, *Feminine Sexuality*, trans. Jacqueline Rose, ed. Juliet Mitchell and Jacqueline Rose, 27–57. New York: Norton.

Rosenbaum, Jonathan (1976). "A Reply to F. S. Schwarzbach." *New Review*, July, p. 64.

Ross, Andrew (1989). *No Respect: Intellectuals and Popular Culture*. New York: Methuen.

Rowe, John Carlos (1984). *The Theoretical Dimensions of Henry James*. Madison: University of Wisconsin Press.

Rowland, William (1988). "Writers against Readers: English and American Romantic Writers and the Nineteenth-Century Reading Public." Ph.D. diss., University of Virginia.

Rushdie, Salman (1990). "Still Crazy after All These Years." Review of *Vineland*. *New York Times Book Review*, 14 Jan., pp. 1, 36–37.

Sabri, M. Arjamand (1973). "Salute to Death." Review of *Gravity's Rainbow*. *Prairie Schooner* 47:269–70.

Sanders, Scott (1976). "Pynchon's Paranoid History." In Levine and Leverenz 1976, 139–59.

Sanguineti, Eduardo (1973). "The Sociology of the Avant-Garde" (1967). In *Sociology of Literature and Drama*, ed. Elizabeth and Tom Burns, 389–97. Harmondsworth: Penguin.

Schaub, Thomas H. (1976). "Open Letter in Response to Edward Mendelson's 'The Sacred, the Profane, and *The Crying of Lot 49*.'" *Boundary 2* 4/1: 93–102.

—— (1981a). *Pynchon: The Voice of Ambiguity*. Urbana: University of Illinois Press.

—— (1981b). "Where Have We Been, Where Are We Headed? A Retrospective Review of Pynchon Criticism." *Pynchon Notes* 7:5–21.

Schickel, Richard (1973). "Paranoia at Full Cry." Review of *Gravity's Rainbow*. *World*, 10 April, pp. 43–44.

Schmitz, Neil (1975). "Describing the Demon: The Appeal of Thomas Pynchon." *Partisan Review* 42:112–25.

Scholes, Robert (1964). "Stephen Dedalus, Poet or Esthete?" *PMLA* 79:484–89.

Schroeder, Patricia R. (1983). "Point and Counterpoint in *Harlem Gallery.*" *CLA Journal* 27:152–68.

Schuber, Stephen P. (1984). "Textual Orbits/Orbiting Criticism: Deconstructing *Gravity's Rainbow.*" *Pynchon Notes* 14:65–74.

Schwarzbach, F. S. (1976). "Pynchon's Gravity." *New Review*, June, pp. 39–43.

Scott, Bonnie Kime, ed. (1990). *The Gender of Modernism: A Critical Anthology.* Bloomington: Indiana University Press.

Scott, Nathan A. (1979). "Black Literature." In *Harvard Guide to Contemporary American Writing*, ed. Daniel Hoffman, 287–341. Cambridge, Mass.: Harvard University Press.

Shapiro, Karl (1950). "What Is Anti-Criticism?" *Poetry* 75:339–51.

—— (1965a). "Decolonization of American Literature." *Wilson Library Bulletin* 39:843–53.

—— (1965b). Introduction. In Tolson 1965, 11–15.

—— (1981). "The Critic Outside." *American Scholar* 50:197–210.

—— (1990). *Reports of My Death.* Chapel Hill, N.C.: Alonquin Books.

Shorris, Earl (1973). "The Worldly Palimpsest of Thomas Pynchon." Review of *Gravity's Rainbow. Harper's Magazine*, June, pp. 78–83.

Showalter, Elaine, ed. (1985). *The New Feminist Criticism: Essays on Women, Literature, and Theory.* New York: Pantheon Books.

Siegel, Mark R. (1977). "Creative Paranoia: Understanding the System of *Gravity's Rainbow.*" *Critique* 18:39–54.

—— (1978). *Pynchon: Creative Paranoia in "Gravity's Rainbow."* Port Washington, N.Y.: Kennikat Press.

Simmon, Scott (1974). "*Gravity's Rainbow* Described." *Critique* 16:54–67.

Simmons, Gloria M., and Helene D. Hutchinson, eds. (1972). *Black Culture: Reading and Writing Black.* New York: Holt, Rinehart & Winston.

Simpson, Louis (1963). "Don't Take a Poem by the Horns." Review of Gwendolyn Brooks, *Selected Poems. New York Herald Tribune Book Week*, 27 Oct., pp. 6, 25.

Slade, Joseph W. (1974). *Thomas Pynchon.* New York: Warner.

—— (1977). "Escaping Rationalization: Options for the Self in *Gravity's Rainbow.*" *Critique* 18:27–38.

Smith, Thomas S. (1983). "Performing in the Zone: The Presentation of Historical Crisis in *Gravity's Rainbow.*" *Clio* 12:245–60.

Soble, Alan (1986). *Pornography: Marxism, Feminism, and the Future of Sexuality.* New Haven, Conn.: Yale University Press.

Sontag, Susan (1967). "The Pornographic Imagination." In *A Susan Sontag Reader*, 205–33. New York: Farrar Straus & Giroux, 1982.

Spector, Robert Donald (1965). "The Poet's Voice in the Crowd." Review of *Harlem Gallery. Saturday Review*, 7 Aug., p. 29.

Stark, John O. (1980). *Pynchon's Fictions: Thomas Pynchon and the Literature of Information.* Athens: Ohio University Press.

Steinem, Gloria (1986). "Erotica vs. Pornography." In *Outrageous Acts and Everyday Rebellions*, 247–60. New York: New American Library.

Stewart, Susan (1988). "The Marquis de Meese." *Critical Inquiry* 15/1: 162–92.

Stimpson, Catharine R. (1976). "Pre-Apocalyptic Atavism: Thomas Pynchon's Early Fiction." In Levine and Leverenz 1976, 31–47.

Striedter, Jurij (1989). *Literary Structure, Evolution, and Value: Russian Formalism and Czech Structuralism Reconsidered.* Cambridge, Mass.: Harvard University Press.

Suleiman, Susan, and Inge Crosman, eds. (1980). *The Reader in the Text: Essays in Audience and Interpretation.* Princeton, N.J.: Princeton University Press.

Tanner, Tony (1974). "V. & V-2." Review of *Gravity's Rainbow. London Magazine* 13 (Feb.–Mar.): 80–88.

—— (1976). "Caries and Cabals." In Levine and Leverenz 1976, 49–67.

—— (1982). *Thomas Pynchon.* Contemporary Writers. London: Methuen.

Tate, Allen (1953). Preface. In Tolson 1953, 9–12.

Tate, J. O. (1983). "*Gravity's Rainbow*: The Original Soundtrack." *Pynchon Notes* 13:3–24.

—— (1984). "Slow Burner." Review of *Slow Learner. National Review,* 16 Nov., pp. 53–55.

Thiher, Allen (1980). "Kafka's Legacy." *Modern Fiction Studies* 26:543–62.

Thompson, Dolphin G. (1965). "Tolson's *Gallery* Brings Poetry Home." Review of *Harlem Gallery. Phylon* 36:408–10.

Thompson, Gordon (1986). "Ambiguity in Tolson's *Harlem Gallery.*" *Callaloo* 9/1: 159–70.

Thorburn, David (1973). "A Dissent on Pynchon." Review of *Gravity's Rainbow. Commentary,* Sept., pp. 68–70.

Tölölyan, Khachig (1979a). "Criticism as Symptom: Thomas Pynchon and the Crisis of the Humanities." *New Orleans Review* 5:314–18.

—— (1979b). "Prodigious Pynchon and His Progeny." Review of Siegel 1978 and Plater 1978. *Studies in the Novel* 11:224–34.

—— (1983a). "Seven on Pynchon: The Novelist as Deconstructionist." Review of Mackey 1980, Cowart 1980, Stark 1980, Fowler 1980, Schaub 1981a, Pearce 1981, and Tanner 1982. *Novel* 16:165–72.

—— (1983b). "War as Background in *Gravity's Rainbow.*" In Clerc 1983, 31–67.

Tolson, Melvin (1944). *Rendezvous with America.* New York: Dodd, Mead.

—— (1951). "E. & O.E." *Poetry* 78:330–42, 369–72.

—— (1953). *Libretto for the Republic of Liberia.* New York: Collier, 1970.

—— (1954). "Claude McKay's Art." *Poetry* 83:287–90.

—— (1955). "Modern Poetry under the Microscope." Review of Jacques and Raissa Maritain, *The Situation of Poetry. Midwest Journal* 7:113–15.

—— (1965). *Harlem Gallery: Book I, The Curator.* New York: Twayne.

—— (1966). "A Poet's Odyssey: Melvin B. Tolson." Interview with M. W. King. In *Anger, and Beyond,* ed. Herbert Hill, 181–95. New York: Harper & Row.

—— (1973). "The Foreground of Negro Poetry." *Kansas Quarterly* 7:30–35.

—— (1979). *A Gallery of Harlem Portraits.* Ed. Robert M. Farnsworth. Columbia: University of Missouri Press.

Tolson, Melvin B., Jr. (1990). "The Poetry of Melvin B. Tolson (1898–1966)." *World Literature Today* 64/3: 395–400.

Tolson Manuscripts. Library of Congress, Washington, D.C.

Tompkins, Jane P. (1980a). "The Reader in History: The Changing Shape of Literary Response." In Tompkins 1980b, 201–32.

——, ed. (1980b). *Reader-Response Criticism: From Formalism to Post-Structuralism.* Baltimore, Md.: Johns Hopkins University Press.

—— (1985). *Sensational Designs: The Cultural Work of American Fiction, 1790–1860.* New York: Oxford University Press.

Trilling, Lionel (1950). *The Liberal Imagination: Essays on Literature and Society.* New York: Doubleday.

Turner, Darwin T., ed. (1969). *Black American Literature: Poetry.* Columbus, Ohio: Charles E. Merrill.

—— (1975). Introduction. In Jean Toomer, *Cane*, ix–xxv. New York: Liveright.

Turner, Lorenzo D. (1955). "Words for a Vast Music." Review of *Libretto for the Republic of Liberia. Poetry* 86:174–76.

Vaughan, Malcolm (1941). *Derain.* New York: Hyperion Press.

Vendler, Helen (1988). *The Music of What Happens: Poems, Poets, Critics.* Cambridge, Mass.: Harvard University Press.

Vodicka, Felix (1941). "The Concretization of the Literary Work." In *The Prague School: Selected Writings, 1929–46*, ed. Peter Steiner; trans. John Burbank, Olga Hasty, Manfred Jacobson, Bruce Kochis, Wendy Steiner, 103–34. Austin: University of Texas Press, 1982.

Von Hallberg, Robert, ed. (1983). *Canons.* Chicago: University of Chicago Press.

Walcott, Ronald (1972). "Ellison, Gordoné, and Tolson: Some Notes on the Blues, Style, and Space." *Black World*, Dec., pp. 4–29.

Wallace, Michele (1988). "Who Dat Say Who Dat When I Say Who Dat?: Zora Neale Hurston Then and Now." *Village Voice Literary Supplement*, April, pp. 18–21.

Weimann, Robert (1975). "'Reception Aesthetics' and the Crisis in Literary History." *Clio* 5/1: 3–35.

—— (1988). "Shakespeare (De)Canonized: Conflicting Uses of 'Authority' and 'Representation.'" *New Literary History* 20/1: 65–81.

Weisenburger, Steven (1979). "The End of History? Thomas Pynchon and the Uses of the Past." *Twentieth Century Literature* 25:54–72.

—— (1988). *A "Gravity's Rainbow" Companion.* Athens: University of Georgia Press.

Westervelt, Linda (1980). "'A Place Dependent on Ourselves': The Reader as System-Builder in *Gravity's Rainbow.*" *Texas Studies in Literature and Language* 22:69–90.

White, Allon (1981). *The Uses of Obscurity: The Fiction of Early Modernism.* London: Routledge & Kegan Paul.

Wiener, Norbert (1954). *The Human Use of Human Beings.* 2d ed. New York: Doubleday.

Williams, Linda (1989). *Hard Core: Power, Pleasure, and the "Frenzy of the Visible."* Berkeley: University of California Press.

Williams, William Carlos (1948). *The Autobiography of William Carlos Williams.* New York: Random House.

—— (1963). *Paterson.* New York: New Directions.

Winston, Mathew (1976). "Appendix: The Quest for Pynchon." In Levine and Leverenz 1976, 251–63.

Wittgenstein, Ludwig (1945). *Philosophical Investigations.* Trans. G. E. M. Anscombe. New York: Macmillan.

Wolfley, Lawrence C. (1977). "Repression's Rainbow: The Presence of Norman O. Brown in Pynchon's Big Novel." *PMLA* 92:873–89.

Woodward, C. Vann (1974). *The Strange Career of Jim Crow.* New York: Oxford University Press.

Wright, Jay (1983). "'The Unraveling of the Egg': An Interview with Jay Wright." With Charles Rowell. *Callaloo* 6/1: 3–15.

Yarborough, Richard (1989). "The First Person in Afro-American Fiction." In *Afro-American Literary Study in the 1990s,* ed. Houston A. Baker, Jr., and Patricia Redmond, 105–121. Chicago: University of Chicago Press.

Yardley, Jonathan (1982). "Old Words in Woolf's Clothing." *Washington Post,* 8 Nov., pp. C1, C6.

—— (1988). "Paradise Tossed: The Fall of Literary Standards." *Washington Post,* 11 Jan., B2.

Yeats, W. B. (1983). *The Poems of W. B. Yeats.* Ed. Richard J. Finneran. New York: Macmillan.

Young, James Dean (1967). "The Enigma Variations of Thomas Pynchon." *Critique* 10/1: 69–77.

Index

Library of Congress Cataloging-in-Publication Data

Bérubé, Michael, 1961–
  Marginal forces/cultural centers : Tolson, Pynchon, and the politics of the canon /
Michael Bérubé.
     p.   cm.
  Includes bibliographical references and index.
  ISBN 0-8014-2620-0 (cloth : alk. paper. — ISBN 0-8014-9921-6 (paper : alk. paper)
  1. American literature—20th century—History and criticism—Theory, etc.   2. Tol-
son, Melvin Beaunorus—Criticism and interpretation.   3. Pynchon, Thomas—Criti-
cism and interpretation.   4. Canon (Literature)   I. Title.
PS221.B44   1992
810.9'005—dc20
                                                                              91-55555